RESTRUCTURING REGULATION AND FINANCIAL INSTITUTIONS

James R. Barth
R. Dan Brumbaugh Jr.
Glenn Yago
Editors

Milken Institute
Santa Monica, California

Milken Institute Press
1250 Fourth Street
Santa Monica, CA 90401

© 2000 Milken Institute

ISBN: 0-9678083-0-8
Library of Congress Catalog Card Number: 99-85810

Cover design: Codesign
Interior design: Edward Kotzen
Publishing Consultant: Neuhaus Publishing

The publisher offers discounts on this book when ordered in quantity for
special sales. For information, contact:
Milken Institute Press
310-998-2600
www.milken-inst.org

Printed in the United States of America
First Edition: March, 2000
10 9 8 7 6 5 4 3 2 1

Table of Contents

Introduction

In the history of financial markets, the period marked by the end of the twentieth century will likely rank among the most dynamic. As with other periods of dramatic transformation of financial markets, the single most important source of change is the rapid development and deployment of new technology. Although technology is affecting every aspect of financial markets, it is notably eliminating technological barriers to global interaction among different countries' financial markets. Other barriers, however, remain. In particular, widely differing financial-market regulatory structures among countries still impede the development of efficient global financial markets.

There is a debate about whether the global development of financial markets is desirable. There are indeed questions that are troubling. Will global financial markets, for example, lead wealthy countries to export their cultures to the detriment of other cultures? Is investment by wealthy countries in less-wealthy countries no more than the former's selfish purchase of the latter's productive assets? Although questions of this sort are important, the economic rationale for the development of global financial markets is compelling.

What global financial markets provide is the ability to transfer the savings of wealthy nations to less-wealthy nations—that is, provide for investment—in order to promote higher economic growth rates and stimulate economic development in the less-wealthy countries. In the United States there is often justified contemporary skepticism of economic growth and development. In the United States economic growth and development can often be associated with unpleasant or worse developments such as the proliferation of clogged freeways adding to frustration and pollution.

Yet, the reality in the rest of the world is quite different. There exists what can only be considered an obscene disparity in wealth among countries that denies billions of people access to fundamentals such as clean water, let alone the prospect of comfort or tranquillity. The 19 countries of the European Union and G-10 group of countries, for example, account for only 14 percent of the world's population (770 million people) but account for 74 percent of the world's GDP.

This leaves 86 percent of the world's population (4.7 billion people) to live off only 26 percent of world GDP.

The result is poverty for billions of people. Because of its enormous wealth and political and economic stability, the rest of the world looks toward the United States for guidance on many fronts. That is certainly true in financial matters. Increasingly, other nations are attempting to develop financial markets that emulate those of the United States. This volume attempts to critique contemporary regulation of U.S. financial markets, and is designed to be read by two groups.

The first is policy makers in the United States, where despite economic good fortune, the goal is still to improve the nation's economic condition—in no little way to improve stubbornly persistent economic disparities. The second group is policy makers around the world. As this group attempts to develop modern financial markets and seeks guidance from the United States, it will benefit from understanding the perceived strengths and weaknesses of U.S. financial-market regulation.

Restructuring Regulation and Financial Institutions in the United States

On November 12, 1999, President Clinton signed into law historic banking legislation that repealed the Glass-Steagall Act. As a result of this new law, banks, insurance companies, and securities firms can now freely enter each other's business functions. The articles in this book anticipate and discuss the importance of these changes and the need for even more restructuring in the U.S. bank and financial services industry.

To address all of these issues, the Milken Institute in March of 1998 sponsored a research roundtable conference on restructuring regulation and financial institutions in the United States. As conference organizers, we approached a group of distinguished economists who were experts in banking and systemic risk, capital markets, mutual funds, pension funds, insurance, derivatives, and government-sponsored enterprises. In each case, the paper presenter was a prominent, and generally long-time participant in his or her respective area. In many cases the presenters had not just been in business, or in academia, or in government, but over time had woven a career in all three fields.

We asked the presenters to address what they considered to be the elements of contemporary regulation that on the one hand most importantly increased efficiency in their area of expertise in financial markets, and on the other hand what elements of contemporary regulation most importantly decreased efficiency in their area of expertise. In response we received thoughtful analyses that can be used by practitioners in the respective areas as well as government officials to contemplate future restructuring of the relevant regulations and financial institutions.

We also assembled an equally distinguished group of discussants, whose comments are also published in this volume. Our goal was to have two or three noted experts respond to the presenter's papers. In this way we thought that we would be able to create a valuable dialog on the pros and cons of the presenter's own assessment of the relative value of the contemporary regulatory environment.

Regulation of Financial Markets: Global Influence of U.S. Regulatory Approaches

The nature and rate of change in laws and regulations affecting financial markets is important because financial markets continue to be among the most highly regulated markets in the world. An important part of the dynamic nature of contemporary financial markets is the interplay between evolving global financial market regulation and the regulation of U.S. financial markets. A major part of that interplay involves widespread adoption of U.S.-style financial regulation, reflecting the preeminent position of U.S. financial markets as both the most stable and dynamic in the world.

In reaction to widespread global banking problems, for example, regulators from the world's twelve largest industrialized countries in 1988 adopted the Basle Accord, a set of international bank regulatory protocols based significantly on U.S. bank capital requirements. As the Mexican and East Asian financial crises emerged in 1994 and 1997 respectively, and as it became clear that excessive bank-credit growth had contributed significantly to the crises, the International

Monetary Fund (IMF) and others urged the affected East Asian countries to adopt these protocols as well.

Between 1980 and 1998, more than 130 of the world's approximately 190 countries have experienced severe banking problems that have led to significant resolution costs. Recently, banking crises have appeared to play a growing role in more general financial crises like those experienced in Mexico and East Asia. As a result, there is ongoing interest globally on the nature of systemic risk—the extent to which banking or wider financial crises can affect the payment and credit mechanisms of a given country, region, or even more widely.

Beyond the effects of these crises, as the world's financial markets are developing more depth and breadth, the world's governments are evaluating U.S. financial-market regulation for guidance on how to structure regulation. As economies develop, for example, relatively smaller equities and bond markets tend to grow relative to bank markets, which previously were dominant. Given that the U.S. equity and bond markets are the most widely developed in the world, one can anticipate growing global interest in the way the United States regulates its capital markets, focusing on the Securities Exchange Commission (SEC) among other agencies.

Areas of Particular Interest within the United States

Although there are seemingly an infinite number of areas of interest in financial markets, certain areas are particularly important in the United States today. Mutual funds, for example, basically did not exist in the United States until 1950 and represented a relatively small percentage of all financial assets held by financial intermediaries until 1990. Since then, mutual funds have exploded in growth. They now represent nearly 20 percent of financial assets in the United States and represent the fastest growing method of financial investment in the United States.

Demographically, one of the most interesting developments in the United States in the first part of the twenty-first century will be the aging of the post-World War II "baby boom" generation. A large percentage of that group has failed to provide adequate financial resources for their imminent retirement. As a result, pension-related issues will loom large at the beginning of the new century.

Part of the technological revolution in finance in the United States has involved the development of derivatives. These financial instruments have provided immense opportunities to improve assessment and implementation of risk-and-return strategies, but simultaneously have led to legal disputes arising in part from their complexity. Technology has also dramatically affected the life insurance industry, which has traditionally invested heavily in information-intensive corporate-finance markets. New technology and other market developments have led to significant changes in the life insurance market.

Both globally and within the United States a growing issue is the appropriate level of direct and indirect government involvement in financial markets. Although most Americans would likely take it for granted that the South Korean government, for example, has been significantly involved in government-directed lending, they would be surprised to discover just how large government-sponsored enterprises are within the United States.

A Sample of Our Presenter's Views

Bank Regulation

With so many banking crises around the globe, it may strike some people as unusual to read University of Chicago economist Dr. Randall S. Kroszner's conclusion that "Banks individually and the banking system as a whole may be less fragile than is generally considered, and much of the modern instability in banking may be attributed to safety-net regulations that purport to mitigate it." Yet, a growing number of economists are increasingly coming to the conclusion that inappropriate government intervention in banking markets is a major source of banking difficulties around the globe.

The primary issue is the appropriate balance between market-driven lending decisions based on assessments of risk and return versus government intervention that affects lending based on nonmarket-based criteria. In the United States, for example, the savings-and-loan debacle of the 1980s and early 1990s was largely the result of government-directed lending. Entering the 1980s, the savings and loans were ravaged by interest-rate risk because by law and regulation they could essentially make only long-term, fixed-rate mortgages. Much of the East Asian banking crisis of the late 1990s has similarly reflected government-directed lending, often to government-favored borrowers.

The paper by Dr. Cara S. Lown and Dr. Stavros J. Peristiani—from the Federal Reserve Bank of New York—and Dr. Kenneth J. Robinson—from the Federal Reserve Bank of Dallas addresses one of the complex examples of government and transnational regulatory interaction with banking markets. They find that the U.S. experience in the late 1980s and early 1990s of adopting capital requirements similar to those of the Basle Accord led to net benefits but not without some difficulties. They conclude that the capital requirements led to a "drastically improved" financial condition in banks, but that the process of improving the banks' financial condition led to perhaps an inappropriate contraction in lending to businesses and consumers.

These deleterious effects in the United States were important, but because of the size of U.S. financial markets, the effects were less severe than they could be in less-developed countries. This suggests that for developing countries that may adopt Basle-type accords, the effect on lending could be far more important and should be a consideration in contemplating the adoption of such accords.

Pension Policy and Mutual Funds

Two papers, one by Dr. Richard Ippolito of George Mason University School of Law, and the other by Dr. Gordon J. Alexander, Dr. Jonathan D. Jones, and Dr. Peter S. Nigro of the University of Minnesota, Office of Thrift Supervision, and the Office of the Comptroller of the Currency respectively, address the expanding union of pension policy and the growth of mutual funds in the United States. As Dr. Ippolito points out there has been a strong trend toward defined contribution plans since the early 1980s, notably in 401(k) plans. By 1995, fully 30 percent of covered private-sector workers had only 401(k) coverage.

As Dr. Ippolito also points out, this trend represents the effect of far-reaching tax-policy changes that have created the growing dominance of 401(k) plans. In particular, these pension plans are privately directed investments that entail a noticeable fusing of the pension and mutual-fund industries. This provides workers with the ability to invest in a wide variety of investment vehicles, all with different risk-and-reward structures.

In some measure due to the effects of pension policy, Drs. Alexander, Jones, and Nigro show that the mutual fund industry, with $4.5 trillion in assets in 1997, is the second-largest and fastest-growing sector of the major financial intermediaries. Drs. Alexander, Jones, and Nigro evaluate mutual-fund investor knowledge of the risk of mutual fund investment, and report on surveys that show that 73 percent of stock-fund investors and 64 percent of bond-fund investors know that it is possible to lose money in such funds.

Of course, what is surprising is that 27 percent and 36 percent of stock and bond mutual-fund investors respectively think incorrectly that it is not possible to lose money in such funds. As the process of disentangling pensions from employers continues—as Dr. Ippolito indicates it will—these individuals will have a greater responsibility for directing their own pensions. Indeed, Dr. Ippolito recommends eliminating all tax-qualification rules and expanding Investment Retirement Accounts to allow up to 25 percent of wages. Thus, it is possible that despite significant apparent limitations on investor knowledge, investors may confront substantially expanded retirement investment opportunities.

Securities Markets

The interrelationship between pension policy and mutual funds extends to the regulation of securities markets more generally. Dr. Susan E. Woodward, formerly Chief Economist at the Securities and Exchange Commission (SEC) and now at the Stanford Law School, provocatively addresses the operation of the three major divisions of the SEC.

She invokes what is widely referred to as the capture theory of regulation to analyze many recent developments in the relationship between the SEC and the securities markets. Stated broadly, the capture theory of regulation analyzes the incentive and behavior of those regulated by a regulatory agency to "capture" the agency in order to produce outcomes favorable to those who are regulated.

Dr. Woodward provides several examples where this kind of behavior has been particularly successful. Research done at the SEC, for example, finds that mutual-fund investors feel they must absolutely have a mutual-fund prospectus, but that they learn very little from them in part because they are impenetrably complex. Dr. Woodward points out that investment firms and their trade associations have an interest in maintaining the complexity in order to maintain investor reliance on investment professionals.

This is an important issue because, as discussed above, more and more individuals will increasingly be in charge of their own investments as they take more control over their pension plans and do so through mutual funds. This is just one of several examples that suggest that changes need to be implemented to promote greater independence at the SEC.

Derivatives Regulation

In a vein similar to that developed by Dr. Woodward, Dr. Christopher L. Culp, Director of Risk Management Services of CP Risk Management and Senior Fellow in Financial Regulation at the Competitive Enterprise Institute, predicts that competing interests among industry participants and regulators will frustrate any major changes in the status quo regarding derivatives regulation. Because no body of law defines the regulation of derivatives contracts and their users, derivatives regulation in the United States is a mixture of fields, including banking, securities, commodities, and bankruptcy law.

As a result, jurisdictional ambiguities create a number of unusual circumstances. Certain types of derivatives products, for example, face stringent regulations while at the same time other products fall outside the jurisdiction of any regulatory agency. In some cases, as Dr. Culp points out, some participants face costly supervision of three or four different regulatory agencies while other participants face no regulation at all.

Dr. Culp argues that the cause of these jurisdictional mismatches is the historical development of a "hybrid" system of regulation in which some regulation focuses on given institutions, hence "institutional" regulation, while other regulation focuses on selected functions, hence, "functional" regulation. As one can easily imagine, the resulting free-for-all in which regulatory agencies protect turf and unregulated competitors fight to keep themselves free of constraints will help to maintain the status quo. Dr. Culp skillfully analyzes the resulting costs and benefits.

Life Insurance Company Investments

The life insurance industry has traditionally specialized in making investments for which there is relatively restricted information. These investments have focused on investment-grade and high-yield corporate bonds, private placements, commercial mortgages, and private equity. Dr. George W. Fenn, formerly Research Associate at the Milken Institute, addresses the dramatic and sustained shift from these private, relatively illiquid, and higher credit-risk investments to more public, highly liquid, and lower credit-risk investments.

This shift began in 1990 when several large insurance companies reported difficulties with their high-yield bond and commercial real estate assets. After decades of financial stability, large insurance companies announced significant write-downs of their bond and commercial-real-estate assets, major life insurance companies were seized by regulators, and major ratings companies downgraded a significant number of companies.

These events, coinciding with the crescendo of the savings-and-loan crisis and recognition of a significant commercial-banking crisis, led to intense evaluation of the life insurance industry investment policies by regulators, the media, ratings agencies, and policyholders. Intense pressure from all quarters led to the dramatic change in life insurance company investment policies. In particular, Dr. Fenn focuses on how policyholders' concerns affected the life insurance companies' investment shifts.

Government Sponsored Enterprises (GSEs)

Farmer Mac, Sallie Mae, Connie Lee, Fannie Mae, and Freddie Mac are not part of a 1950s country western group. These are the monikers of GSEs more formally known as the Federal Agricultural Mortgage Corporation, the Student Loan Marketing Association, the College Construction Loan Insurance Association, the Federal National Mortgage Association, and the Federal Home Loan Mortgage Corporation. They along with the Farm Credit System and the Federal Home Loan Bank System, which have no cute names, provide financial assistance or subsidies in some way to U.S. agriculture, education, or housing.

Although there are constant calls to privatize the GSEs, Dr. John C. Weicher, Senior Research Fellow of the Hudson Institute, points out that the GSEs continue to grow in both numbers and number of programs in their respective areas. Because the federal government charters the GSE's, they are perceived to have an "implicit guarantee" against failure, and indeed, the federal government acted to prevent the collapse of the Farm Credit System in the mid-1980s. Just as with other federally sponsored financial institutions issues regarding safety and soundness, credit risk, and adequate management arise.

Issues also arise about allowable new programs or financial instruments, which may or may not represent additional competition for purely private competitors. Given the current relatively sound economic condition of the GSEs, Dr. Weicher argues that these markets issues are not being addressed. They are not being addressed because GSEs are, with one partial exception, regulated by individual independent regulatory bodies that are easily captured by the regulatees. As a result, the relative costs and benefits of new programs and the effect of these programs on competition are unlikely to be addressed appropriately. What is more, there appears to be no interest in Congress to address these issues, just as there appears to be no interest to address issues of privatization.

Systemic Risk

Finally, Dr. William C. Hunter, Senior Vice President and Director of Research at the Federal Reserve Bank of Chicago, and Dr. David Marshall, Economic Advisor at the Federal Reserve Bank of Chicago, address the issue of systemic risk. That is the risk, as they define it, that a shock to the financial system will crucially impair a central financial function such as asset valuation, credit allocation, and payments and settlements that in turn would significantly affect the real economy.

Drs. Hunter and Marshall particularly investigate whether derivatives securities pose a special risk, as is often stated, because of the high leverage and infrequent payments associated with some derivatives. Their conclusion is that the systemic risk associated with derivatives securities is overstated, in large part because the traditional measure of exposure—the notional value—overstates the amount of capital actually at risk.

After evaluating the many possible sources of systemic risk and providing a thoughtful analysis of past major financial crises, Drs.

Hunter and Marshall suggest that fears of systemic risk may be exaggerated. Nonetheless, they suggest that vigilance in heading off potential system crises is a legitimate role for central banks and their regulatory affiliates. This may explain why the Federal Reserve quickly interjected itself in the hedge-fund difficulties in the United States in 1998, and why many question whether a market solution without the Federal Reserve's intervention may have been more appropriate.

Concluding Remarks

At one point in our conference, a participant noted that one of the most prominent GSEs, which is federally chartered and publicly traded, denied vigorously that it receives any form of federal subsidy, but will fight to the death to protect it. Indeed, one of the most prominent themes that echo throughout the participants' presentations is that a prominent problem with economic regulation is the extent to which it is used to benefit those who are regulated—at the expense of appropriate competition. If one theme emerged, it was that with regard to a wide range of regulatory efforts, there needs to be an assessment of the distribution of benefits and costs of regulation. The clear suggestion was that the benefits are being skewed.

Section One

Restructuring Bank Regulation: Conflicts of Interest, Stability, and Universal Banking

Randall S. Kroszner
Associate Professor of Business Economics
University of Chicago
Graduate School of Business

Thanks to Donald Chew, Benjamin Esty, João Santos and participants in the Milken Institute Research Roundtable on Restructuring Financial Regulation and Institutions, March 16, 1998, for helpful comments. A version of this paper appeared as "Rethinking Bank Regulation: A Review of the Historical Evidence" in the Summer 1998 *Journal of Applied Corporate Finance*, pp. 48-58.

Introduction

Bank regulation has important implications for both the financial system and the proper functioning of the economy. Banks play a key role in encouraging and gathering the savings that finance a country's economic growth. By monitoring the use of the savings that they lend to enterprises, banks are an integral part of the corporate governance system that ultimately affects the productivity of resources throughout the economy. Recent studies such as those by Jayaratne and Strahan and Levine suggest that the development and efficiency of the banking system are important contributors to overall economic growth (see Jayaratne and Strahan 1996 and Levine and Zervos 1998).

While competition is the traditional means of achieving development and efficiency of a sector, in banking, regulation replaces competition. In most countries, regulation rather than competition determines a bank's range of products and services; the types of its assets and liabilities; the legal structure of its organization; the extent of control of nonfinancial companies by banks and of banks by nonfinancial companies; and, until recently in the United States, the number and location of a bank's offices (see Kaufman and Kroszner 1997 for details). Most of the rationales for not permitting unregulated competition in banking and financial services fall into two related categories: controlling potential conflicts of interest (sometimes referred to as investor protection against fraud and abuse), and preventing financial instability that can, in turn, cause upheaval through the economy.[1]

Given the importance of banking to the health of the economy, the special policy attention that banks receive is understandable. The rationales for regulation, however, are open to question and often the regulatory cure can be far worse than the disease. My focus here will be to assess the empirical relevance of concerns about conflicts of interest and stability related to the ongoing congressional debate concerning the repeal of the Banking Act of 1933, known as the Glass-Steagall Act. This act prevents commercial banks from freely expand-

---

1. Interest group politics also plays a large role in determining the type and extent of financial regulation in a country, but my main focus here will be on economics rather than politics. On the political economy of banking regulation and deregulation, see Kane 1988, Kroszner 1997a and forthcoming, Kroszner and Strahan 1996 and 1998, and Kroszner and Stratmann 1998.

ing into a wide range of financial services such as investment banking.

The debate over bank powers has taken on special urgency with the recent flurry of proposed mergers among large financial institutions, such as the Citicorp and Travelers Group combination, that would break down the barriers between commercial and investment banking to create so-called universal banks. After more than a decade of failed attempts to expand the scope of permissible bank activities, the House of Representatives voted on May 13, 1998, in favor of a bill to end these Depression-era limitations. This legislation (H.R. 10) passed by the slimmest of margins, 214-213, but then met a wall of opposition from the president and the Senate. [A revised form of the bill was taken up again in 1999.] As I argued in my testimony before the House Banking Committee a few weeks before the House vote in 1998, the reforms embodied in the legislation could fundamentally alter the role that banks play in the U.S. financial and corporate governance systems.[2]

The next section focuses on the conflicts-of-interest rationale for preventing banks from entering investment banking. In particular, I examine the evidence on whether there was a conflict of interest when commercial banks underwrote securities prior to the passage of the Glass-Steagall Act. While the potential for conflicts existed, financial markets and institutions effectively responded to the potential problems; there is no support for the proposition that purchasing securities underwritten by commercial banks harmed investors. The specific organizational forms and firewalls that evolved through market forces provide important lessons for the current regulatory controversy over what types of firewall, or "Chinese wall," barriers, if any, should be mandated.

The subsequent section focuses on the stability rationale for regulation. I consider whether the banking system is inherently less stable than other sectors and whether the expansion of bank powers into the securities markets would affect stability. A variety of historical and cross-country evidence will suggest that neither commercial banking nor universal banking need to be especially fragile. Much of the regulatory safety net has had the unfortunate impact of undermining,

---

2. "Testimony of Randall S. Kroszner before the Committee on Banking, United States House of Representatives," April 29, 1998.

rather than promoting, financial stability. Explicit cost-benefit analyses of various aspects of the safety net and banking supervision would be valuable to help guide reform efforts in the United States and emerging markets. I conclude with a brief summary and some policy implications.

Conflicts of Interest and Universal Banking

The issue of whether commercial banks should be permitted to be involved in investment banking and act as universal banks has been hotly debated in the United States throughout most of the 20th century. Following World War I, commercial banks became increasingly involved in the securities underwriting business. The Glass-Steagall Act of 1933 halted this evolution by forcing commercial banks to end their corporate securities operations. This separation was further codified in the Bank Holding Company Act of 1956 (see Kroszner 1996). Banks have argued that they have faced increasing competition from other intermediaries (see Table 1), so an expansion of their activities is both important to their long-term viability and valuable to customers who wish to have the option of one-stop financial shopping.

Table 1: Percentage Shares of Assets of Financial Institutions in the United States (1860-1993)

	1860	1880	1900	1912	1922	1929	1939	1948	1960	1970	1980	1993
Commercial banks	71.4	60.6	62.9	64.5	63.3	53.7	51.2	55.9	38.2	37.9	34.8	25.4
Thrift institutions	17.8	22.8	18.2	14.8	13.9	14.0	13.6	12.3	19.7	20.4	21.4	9.4
Insurance companies	10.7	13.9	13.8	16.6	16.7	18.6	27.2	24.3	23.8	18.9	16.1	17.4
Investment companies	--	--	--	--	0.0	2.4	1.9	1.3	2.9	3.5	3.6	14.9
Pension funds	--	--	0.0	0.0	0.0	0.7	2.1	3.1	9.7	13.0	17.4	24.4
Finance companies	--	0.0	0.0	0.0	0.0	2.0	2.2	2.0	4.6	4.8	5.1	4.7
Securities brokers and dealers	0.0	0.0	3.8	3.0	5.3	8.1	1.5	1.0	1.1	1.2	1.1	3.3
Mortgage companies	0.0	2.7	1.3	1.2	0.8	0.6	0.3	0.1	a	a	0.4	0.2

Table 1: Percentage Shares of Assets of Financial Institutions in the United States (1860-1993) *(continued)*

	1860	1880	1900	1912	1922	1929	1939	1948	1960	1970	1980	1993
Real estate investment trusts	--	--	--	--	--	--	--	--	0.0	0.3	0.1	0.1
Total *(percent)*	100.0	100.0	100.0	100.0	100.0	100.0	100.0	100.0	100.0	100.0	100.0	100.0
Total *(trillion dollars)*	.001	.005	.016	.034	.075	.123	.129	.281	.596	1.328	4.025	13.952

a. Data not available.
Sources: Data for 1860-1948 (except 1922) from Goldsmith (1969, Table D-33, pp. 548-9); data for 1922 from Goldsmith (1958, Table 10, pp. 73-4); and data for 1960-1993 from Board of Governors of the Federal Reserve System, "Flow of funds accounts," various years. The table is expanded from Kaufman and Mote (1994).

One of the major motivations for the separation of commercial and investment banking both in the 1930s and today concerns the potential for "conflicts of interest" (Kroszner and Rajan 1994 and 1997). The question is, will the public be harmed by commercial banks engaging in investment banking? The answer some offer is that banks might abuse the trust of their customers and take advantage of them by selling low-quality securities without fully revealing the risks. Such behavior could broadly undermine confidence in the markets and banks themselves (e.g., Greenspan 1987). The potential for taking advantage of investors arises from the fact that the long-term lending relationship between a bank and a client company may make a bank better informed than the public investor about a company's soundness and prospects. This informational advantage can be a double-edged sword.

On the positive side, given the detailed knowledge of the company, the commercial bank might be better positioned than an investment bank to provide information to prospective purchasers of the company's securities. Through the lending relationship, banks might know which companies have particularly good prospects and might be able to help them bring their securities to the public markets earlier than if the young company had to try to start a new relationship with an investment bank. In other words, commercial banks may enjoy a synergy in combining lending with underwriting that could make them more efficient than independent investment banks at monitoring and evaluating companies and securities.

On the negative side, a commercial bank might have an incentive to use its superior information to its own advantage. Unlike investment banks, commercial banks might have a greater incentive and greater ability to take advantage of investors. First, consider the incentives. If the bank is aware of a negative shock to a borrowing company's prospects before the market is, for example, the bank may wish to have its now-risky loan repaid. To raise the money, the bank might underwrite a public offering for this company without adequately disclosing information about the company's troubles to the market. An investment bank without the prior lending relationship would not have the same incentive. Next, consider their access to customers. Commercial banks might be able to exploit their informational advantage more easily than investment banks because depositors might be more easily duped than the more financially sophisticated customers of investment banks.

The positive and negative arguments, however, are not mutually exclusive. Commercial banks could enjoy efficiencies associated with combining lending and underwriting but also be subject to credibility problems due to the potential for conflicts of interest.

Until recently, the commonly held view of the 1920s and 1930s was that not only was there a potential for conflicts of interest, but that the potential was realized and the public was systematically fooled by rogue bankers. This view became the received wisdom even though there had been no systematic study of commercial bank involvement in underwriting during the period. My research with Raghuram Rajan tried to discover what occurred prior to Glass-Steagall (Kroszner and Rajan 1994 and 1997).[3] Investigating this historical episode is crucial because it continues to be a major factor in the policy debates over how reform of the Glass-Steagall Act would affect small investors (see Greenspan 1987) and because it suggests how market forces may address conflict-of-interest issues if Glass-Steagall were repealed.

---

3. Ang and Richardson (1994 and 1998), Benston (1990), and Puri (1994) also have investigated the historical experience and reached similar conclusions to what Rajan and I find.

To determine how investors fared before Glass-Steagall, we compared the performance of securities underwritten by independent investment banks with those underwritten by commercial banks and their affiliates. If the commercial banks did succumb to conflicts of interest, investors would have been lured into purchasing the securities that would have turned out to be poor investments relative to *ex ante* similar securities underwritten by investment banks. We developed a "matched security method" to pair bonds underwritten by commercial banks with otherwise similar bonds underwritten by investment banks. Matching was done on a variety of criteria, including initial ratings from Moody's or Standard & Poor's, or initial yield, maturity, size, date of issue, convertibility provisions, and industry. We matched bonds underwritten by commercial banks in the first quarters of 1921 through 1929. (Little underwriting occurred after the stock market crash.) The matching procedure provided a sample of 121 pairs of bonds. As our measure of *ex post* performance, we used the relative default rates of the bonds through 1940.[4]

Contrary to the conventional wisdom, securities underwritten by the commercial banks performed better than similar securities underwritten by investment banks. By 1940, 28 percent ($127 million) of the value of the bonds underwritten by investment banks had defaulted, whereas only 12 percent ($79 million) of the bonds underwritten by commercial banks had defaulted (see Kroszner 1996, Table 3). In terms of the number of bonds defaulting, not weighted by dollar value, 28 (23 percent) of the 121 bonds underwritten by commercial banks defaulted, whereas 39 (32 percent) of the 121 bonds underwritten by investment banks defaulted (Kroszner and Rajan 1994). The differences are statistically significant. Ang and Richardson (1994) and Puri (1994) subsequently have found similar results. Interestingly, when the relative default frequency is analyzed by whether or not the bond was initially rated investment grade, it is the noninvestment grade bonds that account for the superior performance of the commercial banks. These results clearly are inconsistent with naive investors being duped by the commercial banks.

---

4.   Defaults are used rather than an explicit return measure due to the lack of data for the smaller and lower-rated issues. The final year is 1940 because almost all of the bonds had maturities of 10 years or less.

The relative timing of the defaults also may shed light on whether commercial bankers took advantage of naïve investors. If commercial banks tended to underwrite bonds for companies experiencing a negative shock not yet known to the public markets, then such companies were likely to experience financial distress sooner than other companies issuing debt. The bonds underwritten by the commercial banks, however, tended to default later in their lives than did the bonds underwritten by the investment banks (see Kroszner 1996, Table 4, using the aging analysis of Asquith et al. 1989). By the end of the fourth year after issue, for example, the default rate for the investment banks was twice that for the commercial banks. By the seventh year after issue, only 15 of the 28 bonds (53 percent) underwritten by the commercial banks had defaulted but 30 of the 39 bonds underwritten by investment banks (77 percent) had defaulted. The bonds underwritten by the commercial banks, therefore, did not fall into trouble faster than those underwritten by the investment banks.

Having disposed of the "naïve investor" hypothesis, the next step is to explain the superior performance of the securities underwritten by the commercial banks.

One explanation is that the informational-scope economies allowed commercial banks to bring superior issues to the market. Commercial banks were able to identify "winners" at an earlier stage than investment banks and credibly convey this information to the markets. This explanation implies that commercial banks would have had a competitive advantage in bringing smaller, younger, and perhaps, riskier companies to market.

Alternatively, concerns about the potential for conflicts of interest could have restricted the types of offerings that investors would accept from commercial banks. If this concern were important, investors would discount for this possibility, thereby making it more difficult for commercial banks to underwrite the more information-intensive securities. "Market adaptation" would lead the commercial banks to specialize in underwriting larger, older companies and more senior securities. A reputation for integrity could diminish the effects of the discounting for potential conflicts. Market adaptation thus also implies that the commercial-bank underwriters with the greatest reputational capital would be least subject to these effects.

The data support the market-adaptation explanation. Relative to the investment banks, commercial banks on average tended to underwrite for larger, older, and better-established companies and originated more senior securities, i.e., debt rather than equity (see Kroszner and Rajan 1994). Using either bank capital or median-issue size for the house as a proxy for reputational capital, we found that the activities of the large ("high reputation") commercial banks resembled those of the large investment banks. The underwriting activities of the small ("low reputation") commercial banks, however, were much more "conservative" than the activities of the small investment banks. This evidence is consistent with the implications of market adaptation to the potential for conflicts of interest and with the fact that commercial banks may not specialize in underwriting riskier securities than independent investment banks.

Even before the advent of strict disclosure requirements, the public was not systematically fooled and banks did not "abuse the public trust" by issuing unexpectedly low-quality securities. The historical record suggests that investors would not be harmed by repeal of the Glass-Steagall Act and investors could benefit from the convenience of one-stop shopping in financial services.

Firewall Requirements

As support has grown for relaxing the Glass-Steagall separation between commercial and investment banking, the focus of the current debate in Congress has shifted toward what alternative regulatory structure should replace it (e.g., Greenspan 1997 and Santos 1997). The key issue is what, if any, firewall or "Chinese wall" protections will be required for commercial banks that expand into the securities business.

Firewalls have been proposed both to mitigate the potential conflicts of interest and to prevent the extension of the government's bank safety net beyond protecting depositors. Since 1989, regulators have permitted some commercial bank holding companies, on a case-by-case basis, to engage in a limited amount of securities activities through separately incorporated and capitalized affiliates (see Macey and Miller 1992, Blair 1994, and Kroszner and Rajan 1997). Initially, no more than 5 percent of the revenues of the Section 20 subsidiaries could be from investment banking activities that were otherwise prohibited by Section 20 of the Glass-Steagall Act. Recently, the regulators have raised the revenue cap to 25 percent. In addition, the subsidiaries also face a variety of restrictions on the sharing of personnel and information with the bank.

Again, the historical record can provide some guidance as to how banks would choose to structure themselves if Glass-Steagall barriers were repealed.[5] Prior to the Glass-Steagall Act, banks entered the securities business in one of two ways: internal departments and separate affiliates (see Kroszner and Rajan 1997). The internal securities departments were organized within the bank, parallel with the bank-lending department, much as classic German universal banks have organized themselves. The affiliates were separately incorporated and capitalized companies with their own boards of directors and their own balance sheets, much like Section 20 subsidiaries today.

If informational-scope economies are of paramount importance, banks would keep the lending and underwriting functions together within the bank to best take advantage of them. There would be no benefit and some losses involved in setting up a separate affiliate and, thereby, potentially setting up barriers to information flows.

If, however, concerns about the potential for conflicts of interest dominate, then banks would find it in their own interest to put some distance between lending and underwriting by organizing separate affiliates. Although the affiliates and the bank would still be connected—typically through common board members—the greater transparency and arm's-length structure of the affiliate might improve credibility with investors.

Using data on all types of securities underwritten by commercial banks or their affiliates, we found a strong movement toward the adoption of the affiliate form and away from the use of internal departments during the 1920s (Kroszner and Rajan 1997). Bankers apparently felt that the benefits in terms of increased reputation and credibility with the market outweighed the costs in terms of reducing

5. See Kaufman and Mote (1990) and Kroszner and Rajan (1997) for a discussion of the details of the legal background in the 1920s and 1930s under which banks could choose their organizational forms. Kroszner and Rajan (1997) also consider other motives for the affiliate versus department decision, e.g., branching regulations and liability laws, and do not find that they were important to the choice. For more details on the historical treatment of bank liability, see Esty (forthcoming).

informational-scope economies. Some banks explicitly advertised that they did not have internal securities departments and pointed out that rivals did (see Peach 1941). One of the earliest Harvard Business School case books included an example in which a bank's management debated the trade-off between the public's perceptions of conflicts and savings in overhead in deciding how to structure a securities advisory unit (Biddle and Bates 1931). The bank was also active in securities underwriting. The bank's management chose the separate affiliate structure to avoid "the question of a conflict of interest" and to gain the confidence and trust of the public.

This credibility explanation also has implications for how the market would price securities underwritten by the two types of structures. If internal securities departments did experience credibility problems, for example, such problems would have been reflected in an *ex ante* discount on the securities underwritten internally, relative to similar issues from separate bank affiliates. This discount would have made the separate affiliate form, on average, a more efficient means of organizing a bank's securities operations. If there are scope economies and certification benefits from keeping the underwriting internal to the bank, however, this force would work in the opposite direction, namely, securities of the separate affiliates would tend to be discounted relative to otherwise similar securities underwritten by the internal departments.

After adjusting for *ex ante* factors such as industry, debt-to-asset ratio, size and age, bonds underwritten by internal departments appear to have had lower prices and higher yields than bonds underwritten by bank affiliates (Kroszner and Rajan 1997). The increasing use of the affiliate structure, thus, could be at least in part explained by organizational adaptation by commercial banks to address public concerns about the potential for conflicts of interest.

A key mechanism by which the affiliates gained greater credibility appears to have been through the use of independent directors on the board of the affiliate (Kroszner and Rajan 1997). Independent directors are individuals who are not officers or directors of the parent commercial bank. The public may perceive independent directors, who have their personal reputations at stake, to be less willing than insiders to accede to the pressure of lending officers who might want risky loans repaid through the sale of public securities. Consistent with this, we find that a higher proportion of independent directors on the affiliate's board did lead to higher prices and lower risk premiums on the securities underwritten by the affiliate, holding other quality factors constant. The use of independent directors, therefore, is one device that banks could use to enhance their credibility in the underwriting market; in the past, the markets rewarded banks that had more credible structures with higher prices. Market pressures appear to have played an important role in determining the extent of "independence" of the affiliates' boards and of the extent of firewall separations.

Competitive market forces thus seem to propel banks to adopt the structure that regulators would like to mandate. The legal requirements of a regulation-mandated firewall structure, however, are likely to be insufficiently flexible to allow banks to adapt to ongoing changes in the financial services market. In addition, a specific regulatory mandate does not permit the markets to explore a rich diversity of organizational forms and commitment devices that might provide alternative low-cost means that could effectively address the issue of conflicts.

In summary, the evidence from the recent studies of the pre-Glass-Steagall involvement of commercial banks in investment banking support the repeal of Glass-Steagall. Contrary to the concerns of its defenders, financially unsophisticated investors were not systematically fooled by commercial banks and did not suffer losses. Investor concerns about the credibility of commercial banks as underwriters led the banks to focus on higher-grade and better-known securities. Without regulatory pressure, commercial banks adopted some form of separation between their lending and underwriting operations consistent with addressing investor concerns about their credibility. Unlike in the earlier period, however, deposit insurance and the federal safety net are important factors to consider today. If banks are sufficiently well capitalized and those capital requirements are strictly enforced, then incentives to take advantage of the safety net will be mitigated.

The next section analyzes financial stability and the bank safety net in detail.

Stability and the Safety Net

In addition to conflicts of interest, an important argument made for bank regulation and, in particular, against broadening bank powers, concerns the stability of the banking system.[6] In a system without government guarantees or distortions, private owners of any enterprise have the appropriate incentives to choose the capital structure that permits the (privately) "optimal" amount of stability. The owners and managers of each enterprise decide the degree of risk of loss they will tolerate for a given expected level of return. The optimal amount of stability in any industry including the financial system does not imply zero failures. Any healthy and dynamic competitive sector will have companies entering and leaving the industry. Competition ensures efficiency precisely through a winnowing process that eliminates companies that have poor management or experience bad luck.

In the financial sector, however, stability is widely perceived to be a distinct public concern because of a fear that the owners of individual institutions will not take into account the possibility that a failure of one institution might cause failures elsewhere.[7] Such linkages could lead to a systemwide financial panic or "meltdown," which in turn might cause a broader macroeconomic decline. Bank owners may not take this adverse externality into account in pricing risk and determining the appropriate amount of private capital to invest. The socially optimal capital ratio thus may be greater than the privately optimal one. Since the benefits of systemwide stability accrue to all economic agents, not just the banks, it may not be appropriate to have only the bank shareholders bear its cost. This potential negative externality provides the justification for government intervention to provide a safety net.

Banks are viewed as more fragile than other companies mainly because of two features of a typical bank's financial structure. First, banks and financial institutions tend to be highly leveraged; that is, they have a low capital-to-assets ratio compared with nonfinancial companies. Consequently, their cushion against insolvency is thinner than in nonfinancial companies. Second, banks tend to hold a low ratio of liquid assets relative to their highly liquid liabilities. By pro-

---

6. This section draws on Kaufman and Kroszner (1997).

7. The potential moral-hazard problems of government deposit insurance are discussed later.

viding demand and other short-term deposits on a fractional reserve basis, banks have a much greater liquidity and duration mismatch between assets and liabilities than do nonfinancial companies. This mismatch makes banks particularly sensitive to sudden large withdrawals of funds (bank runs) that cannot be met in full and on time by the banks' cash and liquid asset holdings (see Diamond and Dybvig 1983). Banks thus may be required to sell assets quickly. To the extent that these assets are not traded in highly liquid markets, the banks may suffer fire-sale losses that may exceed their small capital base and drive them into economic insolvency. The duration mismatch also exposes banks to interest-rate risk so that abrupt changes in interest rates can induce (realized and unrealized) losses that can quickly exceed their capital.

Such concerns about bank instability have provided a rationale for restricting the types of assets that a bank might hold in its portfolio. Part of the rationale for maintaining the Glass-Steagall Act is to shield banks from exposure to many types of risks, particularly those of holding equity instruments. Some have gone further to argue for even greater restrictions on bank assets and bank activities. Some "narrow bank" proposals, for example, would require banks to hold 100 percent reserves of liquid, short-term government bonds in order to address and remedy the two main causes of individual bank fragility just discussed (e.g., Litan 1987).

In addition to concerns about the stability of each bank individually, the banking system is seen as particularly fragile as a result of the close interconnectedness of banks through interbank deposits and lending. Losses at any one bank may thus produce losses at other banks, which can cascade throughout the banking system. Moreover, if depositors are unable to differentiate among the financial health of individual banks, troubles at one or a few institutions could spread quickly throughout the system as uninformed depositors withdraw funds indiscriminately from depository institutions regardless of their financial fundamentals. In the absence of offsetting actions by the central bank, such runs from deposits at banks will worsen fire-sale losses, increase the number of bank failures, and cause a multiple contraction of money and credit and macroeconomic instability. In addition, the loss of the banks' information and monitoring services could make it more difficult for companies to reestablish lending relationships, thereby slowing recovery (e.g., Bernanke 1983).

The emphasis on the fragility of banks and the banking system in the absence of a government safety net, however, may be overstated, for these reasons:

1. Bank failures spread throughout the system only if losses exceed a bank's capital by enough to produce losses at creditor banks that exceed their capital and, in turn, force them into insolvency and so on down the chain. If losses associated with individual insolvencies could be minimized, the likelihood of contagion or systemic risk would be greatly reduced. As discussed below, delays that have permitted financial institutions to become deeply insolvent before closure are primarily due to regulatory, not market, failure (e.g., see Benston and Kaufman 1995, Garcia 1996, Kane 1989, Kaufman 1995, and Kroszner and Strahan 1996).[8]

2. Before the introduction of the lender of last resort in the United States, the failure rate of banks was actually lower than that of nonfinancial companies, and losses to depositors and other bank creditors were lower than for creditors of nonfinancial companies (Kaufman 1996a). In addition, U.S. banks held higher capital-to-asset ratios prior to safety-net regulations. Recent international experiences suggest that banks substitute government deposit insurance or public capital for private capital (Peltzman 1970, Garcia 1996, and Kroszner and Strahan 1996). Again, the safety net may have had the consequence of making banks more, not less, fragile.

3. Calomiris and Mason (1998) have examined in detail the bank panic that took place in Chicago in June 1932. Although there did seem to be some temporary confusion about the quality of bank assets and a short-lived general depositor run, they did not find any evidence of failure by banks that were

---

8. A recent study that examined five historical episodes in developing and developed countries found little or no evidence of an adverse macroeconomic impact from imposing losses on depositors at insolvent institutions when it was done as part of a comprehensive government program in which only economically solvent and well-capitalized institutions were permitted to remain in operation (Baer and Klingebiel 1995).

solvent at the beginning of the panic. The runs were directed primarily against the weakest banks and they were the ones that failed. Thus, even during the height of bank panics during the Great Depression, depositor runs do not appear to have generated "contagion" or "systemic" problems that caused otherwise solvent institutions to fail. In addition, Allen and Gale (1998) have provided a formal model of how "panic runs" can be socially efficient.

4. Historically, bankers have developed innovative contracts to attenuate the likelihood of panic runs. One example is the "option clause" that came to be a standard provision in private bank notes circulating in Scotland during its 18th century "free banking" era (see, e.g., Cowen and Kroszner 1989, Kroszner 1997b, and While 1984). The option clause gave the bank directors the right to suspend specie payment for up to six months, but the bank then promised to pay a high rate of interest on the notes during the period of suspension. This clause allowed the banks to stop "panic" runs and to have more time to adjust to negative-liquidity shocks that might occur, thereby avoiding fire-sale losses. Also, banks in Scotland had some form of extended or unlimited liability covering their notes, rather than simple limited liability. These notes were widely and voluntarily accepted, and the Scottish banking system showed much greater stability than the English system during this period.

5. There is little historical evidence that permitting banks to expand their portfolios to include equity reduces stability. White (1986) shows that in the United States during the 1920s and 1930s, commercial banks actively engaged in the securities markets were less likely to fail than other commercial banks.[9] In addition, banks with securities operations tended to have higher capital ratios and lower variance of their cash flows than other banks. Involvement in the securities business, thus, appears to have helped banks diversify and thereby enhance their stability during the 1920s and 1930s. In

---

9.   This result holds even adjusting for the size of the bank. Larger banks, both then and today, are more likely to be involved in the securities markets, but larger banks *ceteris paribus* tend to be better diversified and less likely to fail.

the modern cross-country data, there does not appear to be any correlation between the breadth of bank powers and the likelihood or extent of losses of a banking and financial crisis (Caprio and Klingebiel 1996, Lindgren, Garcia, and Saal 1996, and Rojas-Suarez and Weisbrod 1996). Therefore, universal banking does not appear to have harmed bank stability internationally. However, Boyd et al., (1993) simulated the volatility and probability of failure of combinations of commercial bank and other financial activities and found that some combinations of activities could reduce bank stability. Boyd (1998) also expresses concern that universal banks may be more likely to try to take advantage of the government safety-net system, which is more of a problem of the safety net than universal banking itself. Table 2 provides a brief summary of the relationship between narrow and broad (or universal) powers for banks and a number of characteristics of the financial system.

Table 2: Relationship of Banking Structure and Financial-Sector Characteristics

Financial-Sector Characteristics	Banking Structure	
	Narrow	**Broad**
Stability Without Effective Intervention and Closure Rule	Fewer bank failures and lower losses to bank depositors due to restricted bank portfolio, but may not provide greater overall financial stability.	Larger losses possible as permissible activities widen and assets become more volatile, but diversification can promote stability.
Stability With Effective Intervention and Closure Rule, when Net Worth > 0	Few failures and low losses overall, but the effect of structure depends on ability to monitor: If rules are credible and monitoring is largely independent of riskiness of assets, no relationship between structure and stability. If risky assets more difficult to monitor, greater losses for broader banks. Broader banks may require more-sophisticated supervisors.	
Conflicts of Interest	Less potential if bank is stand-alone and not part of a conglomerate.	Firewalls, privately chosen or mandated, can alleviate potential.
Economies of Scale and Scope	Less likely, particularly scope economies.	More likely to be realized.
Corporate Control	Weak role for banks.	Important role for banks, particularly in managing financial distress.
Note: Adapted from Kaufman and Kroszner (1997).		

Safety Nets and Market Discipline

Given that the concerns about the inherent fragility of banks and the banking system may be overstated, the next step is to evaluate the role of the regulatory safety net that governments, either implicitly or explicitly, have placed under their banking systems. While in principle, safety-net measures could increase the stability of the system, in practice it has proven difficult to design a safety net that does not undermine both efficiency and stability. Improperly designed safety nets may encourage behavior by both the insured banks and their regulators that through time is likely to prove far costlier than the benefits they may generate. As has been clearly demonstrated in almost all countries in recent years, poorly designed and implemented deposit insurance, for example, has greatly reduced depositor discipline of banks and thereby encouraged them to engage in moral-hazard behavior. This has occurred both through assuming greater credit and interest-rate risk exposure in their asset and liability portfolios and through maintaining lower capital ratios.

Insured depositors have little incentive to punish risky or even insolvent institutions with withdrawals and to reward safe and sound institutions with deposits. Rojas-Suarez and Weisbrod (1996), for example, found that risky banks in Mexico expanded much faster during the crisis years (1991-1994) than did the safer banks. This is the same situation found in other countries, including the United States in the 1980s.

By short-circuiting the market discipline, deposit insurance also allows bank regulators to engage in regulatory forbearance, delaying the imposition of sanctions on troubled banks and permitting even economically insolvent institutions to continue to operate. The costs of forbearance can be and have been very large (e.g., Barth and Brumbaugh 1994, Kane and Yu 1994, Kaufman 1995, and Kroszner and Strahan 1996).

Without government guarantees of deposits, insolvent banks could not stay in business for long. Banks receiving low ratings from depositors as well as independent private rating agencies would either have to compensate depositors with higher interest rates or see funds flow out of the bank. Withdrawals by informed depositors might force troubled banks to sell assets quickly and perhaps experience fire-sale losses. If the bank could no longer satisfy the depositors' demands in full and on time, it would close (suspend operations) either voluntarily or at the order of its regulators. In addition, without the strong "heads I win, tails you lose" character of the safety net, the bank owners might have chosen a different initial risk profile for the bank. As noted above, prior to the introduction of the lender of last resort in the United States, bank failure and loss rates were lower than those for nonfinancial companies.

The moral-hazard problems of the safety net are not unique but also exist in many market contexts, so it is valuable to understand how the market deals with such problems. Equity holders and debt holders, for example, have different incentives and this difference is clearest when a company experiences financial distress. Under limited liability, equity holders participate in the upside of risky gambles that pay off and do not have to pay all of the losses of gambles that go bad. In contrast, debt holders do not participate in the upside beyond the prespecified interest and principal payments and may receive nothing if the gamble does not pay off. When negative shocks reduce the market value of the equity holders' investment in a company, the equity holders have greater incentives to increase the company's riskiness since they now have less to lose. Debt holders have precisely the opposite desire because they simply want to protect the value of the debt. The equity holders wish to play "heads I win, tails you lose" with the debt holders' money, paralleling the moral-hazard problem of insured banks gambling with taxpayers' money.

Private markets address this problem through debt covenants that tend to prevent rather than provide forbearance for excessive risk-taking (Kroszner and Strahan 1996). Debt covenants are explicit provisions in the debt contracts that restrict the company's behavior and ability to take risks. Banks often include such provisions in their own loan agreements with companies. Covenants are triggered as soon as earnings or capital fall below prespecified levels or leverage rises above such levels. In some cases, covenants allow the debt holders to seize control of the company as the company experiences financial distress. Covenants thus prevent a distressed company from continuing to operate as it had before and attempt to prevent it from increasing its risk exposure.

When government deposit insurance is implicit or explicit, regulatory discipline should be structured to mimic the way in which the

33

market deals with the moral-hazard problem (Benston and Kaufman 1988 and Kroszner and Strahan 1996). Rather than permit regulatory forbearance, the government should require that the regulators: a) follow clearly defined practices to restrict the risk-taking activities of banks experiencing financial distress, and b) resolve banks before they are permitted to become deeply insolvent. In parallel to private-debt covenants, intervention by the regulators could be related to capital ratios or other performance and solvency measures.[10] Such regulatory discipline would prevent depositor (and taxpayer) losses at individual institutions from growing and possibly causing systemwide problems. The Federal Deposit Corporation Improvement Act of 1991 has taken a first step toward introducing explicit intervention and closure rules in the United States (see Benston and Kaufman 1988, Kaufman 1995 and 1996b, and Kroszner and Strahan 1996).

Conclusions

The focus here has been to assess the importance of two key rationales for banking regulation: conflicts of interest and stability. The evidence discussed earlier indicates that market forces, rather than regulation, can deal with key conflict-of-interest concerns that might arise when commercial banks are engaged in securities underwriting. Contrary to the conventional wisdom, investors appear to have been better off when they purchased securities from commercial banks rather than investment banks during the pre-Glass-Steagall era. Commercial banks tended to underwrite for the larger and more-established companies, not the younger and riskier companies.

Commercial banks also found it in their private self-interest during this period to put some distance between their lending and securities operations to enhance their credibility in the market. Market forces, rather than regulation, can determine the extent of firewalls between lending and underwriting and address potential conflicts of interest. With the repeal of Glass-Steagall and other regulatory reforms, banks might be able to play a more active corporate-gover-

---

10. While estimating the appropriate level of capital at which intervention should occur is difficult, indirect estimates may be obtained from observing the capital ratios maintained by companies that compete with the banks in the same country, but that are not explicitly or implicitly insured, e.g., finance companies, etc.

nance role and help manage the costs of financial distress (Kroszner and Strahan 1998).

Banks individually and the banking system as a whole may be less fragile than is generally considered, and much of the modern instability in banking may be attributed to safety-net regulations that purport to mitigate it. More detailed cost-benefit analysis is required in order to determine which parts of the safety net can promote stability (Kroszner 1997c). Part of the legacy of Glass-Steagall in the United States may be a financial system that has adapted by creating a rich variety of sound alternative financial organizations that compete in both the financial markets and the market for financial regulation. The time for broadening bank powers is upon us.

References

Allen, Franklin, and Douglas Gale. "Optimal Financial Crises." *Journal of Finance* 53 (August 1998): 1245-84.

Barth, James R., and R. Dan Brumbaugh, Jr. "Moral-Hazard and Agency Problems: Understanding Depository Institution Failure Costs." Pp. 61-102 in *Research in Financial Services*, Volume 6, edited by George G. Kaufman. Greenwich: JAI Press, 1994.

Baer, Herbert, and Daniela Klingebiel. "Systemic Risk When Depositors Bear Losses." Pp. 195-302 in *Research in Financial Services*, Volume 7, edited by George G. Kaufman. Greenwich: JAI Press, 1995.

Benston, George. *The Separation of Commercial and Investment Banking*. New York: Oxford University Press, 1990.

Benston, George J., R. Dan Brumbaugh, Jr., Jack M. Guttentag, Richard J. Herring, George G. Kaufman, Robert E. Litan, and Kenneth E. Scott. *Blueprint for Restructuring America's Financial Institutions*. Washington, DC: Brookings Institution, 1989.

Benston, George, and George Kaufman. *Risk and Solvency Regulation of Depositor Institutions: Past Policies and Current Options*. New York: Salomon Brothers Center, Graduate School of Business, New York University, 1988.

Benston, George, and George Kaufman. "Is the Banking and Payments System Fragile?" *Journal of Financial Services Research* 9 (1995a): 209-240.

Benston, George, and George Kaufman. *Commercial Banking and Securities Activities: A Survey or Risks and Returns.* Washington, DC: American Bankers Association, 1995(b).

Bernanke, Ben. "Nonmonetary Effects of the Financial Crisis in the Propagation of the Great Depression." *American Economic Review* 73 (June 1983): 257-76.

Biddle, C., and G. Bates. *Investment Banking: A Casebook.* New York: McGraw Hill, 1931.

Bisignano, Joseph R. "The Ownership and Control Linkages Between Banking and Industry." Pp. 1-60 in *Research in Financial Services,* Volume 6, edited by George G. Kaufman. Greenwich: JAI Press, 1994.

Boyd, John H., Stanley Graham, and R. Shawn Hewitt. "Bank Holding Company Mergers with Nonbank Firms." *Journal of Banking and Finance* (1993): 43-63.

Boyd, John H. "Expansion of Commercial Banking Powers: Or, Universal Banking is the Cart, Not the Horse," unpublished ms., 1998.

Calomiris, Charles, and Joseph Mason. "Contagion and Bank Failures during the Great Depression: The June 1932 Chicago Banking Panic," *American Economic Review* (December 1997): 863-83.

Caprio, Gerard Jr., and Daniela Klingebiel. "Bank Insolvencies: Cross Country Experience." Policy Research Working Paper, World Bank, April 1996.

Cowen, Tyler, and Randall Kroszner. "Scottish Banking before 1845: A Model for Laissez-Faire?" Journal of Money, Credit, and Banking 21 (May 1989): 221-31.

Cowen, Tyler, and Randall Kroszner. "Mutual Fund Banking: A Market Approach." *Cato Journal* (1990).

Diamond, Douglas. "Financial Intermediation and Delegated Monitoring." *Review of Economic Studies* 51 (1984): 393-414.

Diamond, Douglas. "Bank Runs, Deposit Insurance, and Liquidity." *Journal of Political Economy* 91 (June 1983): 401-19.

Esty, Benjamin. "The Impact of Contingent Liability on Commercial Bank Risk Taking," *Journal of Financial Economics*, forthcoming.

Garcia, Gillian. "Comparing and Confronting Recent Banking Problems in Foreign Countries." Working Paper, International Monetary Fund, 1996.

Holderness, Clifford, Randall Kroszner, and Dennis Sheehan. "Were the Good Old Days that Good? Changes in Managerial Stock Ownership Since the Great Depression." *Journal of Finance*, forthcoming.

Hoshi, Takeo, Anil Kashyap, and David Scharfstein. "The Role of Banks in Reducing the Costs of Financial Distress." *Journal of Financial Economics* (1990).

Jayaratne, Jith and Philip Strahan. "The Finance-Growth Nexus: Evidence from Bank Branch Deregulation." *Quarterly Journal of Economics* (August 1996).

Jensen, Michael, and William Meckling. "The Theory of the Firm: Managerial Behavior, Agency Costs, and Ownership Structures." *Journal of Financial Economics* 3 (1976): 305-60.

Kane, Edward. "How Market Forces Influence the Structure of Financial Regulation," Chapter 9 in Kushmeider, ed., *Restructuring Banking and Financial Services*, Washington, DC: American Enterprise Institute, 1988.

Kane, Edward. *The S&L Insurance Mess: How Did It Happen?* Washington, DC: Urban Institute, 1989.

Kane, Edward, and Min-Teh Yu, 1994, "How much did capital forbearance add to the tab for the FSLIC mess?" *Conference on Bank Structure and Competition* (Federal Reserve Bank of Chicago).

Kaufman, George. "Bank Contagion: A Review of the Theory and Evidence." *Journal of Financial Services Research* 8 (1994): 123-150.

Kaufman, George. "The U.S. Banking Debacle of the 1980s: An Overview and Lessons." Financier 2 (1995): 9-26.

Kaufman, George. "Bank Fragility: Perception and Historical Evidence." Chicago: Federal Reserve Bank of Chicago, 1996a.

Kaufman, George. "Designing an Efficient and Incentive Compatible Government-Provided Deposit Insurance Program for Developing and Transitional Economies." *Review of Pacific Basin Financial Markets and Policies* (1996b), forthcoming.

Kaufman, George. "Lessons for Traditional and Developing Economies from U.S. Deposit Insurance Reform." In G.M. von Furstenberg (ed.), *Standards and Politics: Banking and Finance Regulations in the NAFTA Countries*. Boston: Kluwer Academic Publishers, 1997 (forthcoming).

Keeley, Michael. "Deposit Insurance, Risk, and Market Power in Banking." *American Economic Review* 80 (December 1990): 1183-1200.

King, Robert and Ross Levine. "Finance and Growth: Schumpeter Might Be Right." *Quarterly Journal of Economics* (August 1993): 717-37.

Kroszner, Randall S. "The Evolution of Universal Banking and Its Regulation in Twentieth Century America." Pp. 70-99 in *Universal Banking: Financial System Design Reconsidered*, edited by Anthony Saunders and Ingo Walter. New York: Irwin Professional Publishers, 1996.

Kroszner, Randall S. "The Political Economy of Banking and Financial Regulation in the United States." Chapter 8 in *Integrating Economies: Banking and Finance in the NAFTA Countries and Chile*, edited by George M. von Furstenberg. Boston: Kluwer Academic Publishers, 1997a.

Kroszner, Randall S. "Free Banking: The Scottish Experience as a Model for Emerging Market Economies," Pp. 41-64 in Gerard Caprio and Dimitri Vittas, eds., *Reforming Financial Systems: Historical Implications for Policy*, New York: Cambridge University Press, 1997b.

Kroszner, Randall S. "Commentary on Institutions and Policies for Maintaining Financial Stability." Pp. 299-306 in *Maintaining Financial Stability in a Global Economy*, Kansas City: Federal Reserve Bank of Kansas City, 1997c.

Kroszner, Randall S. "On the Political Economy of Banking and Financial Regulatory Reform in Emerging Markets," *Research in Financial Services*, forthcoming.

Kroszner, Randall S., and Raghuram G. Rajan. "Is the Glass-Steagall Act Justified? A Study of the U.S. Experience with Universal Banking before 1933." *American Economic Review* 84 (September 1994): 810-32.

Kroszner, Randall S., and Raghuram G. Rajan. "Organization Structure and Credibility: Evidence from Bank Securities Activities before the Glass-Steagall Act." *Journal of Monetary Economics* 39 (August 1997): 475-516

Kroszner, Randall S. and Philip E. Strahan. "Regulatory Incentives and the Thrift Crisis: Dividends, Mutual-to-Stock Conversions, and Financial Distress." *Journal of Finance* 51 (September 1996): 1285-1320.

Kroszner, Randall S., and Philip E. Strahan. "Bankers on Boards: Monitoring, Financing, and Lender Liability," unpublished ms., University of Chicago, Graduate School of Business, 1998.

Kroszner, Randall S., and Thomas Stratmann. "Interest Group Competition and the Organization of Congress: Theory and Evidence from Financial Services Political Action Committees." *American Economic Review* 88 (December 1998), forthcoming.

Levine, Ross and Sara Zervos. "Stock Markets, Banks, and Economic Growth," *American Economic Review* (June 1998): 537-58.

Lindgren, Carl-Johan, Gillian Garcia, and Matthew Saal. *Bank Soundness and Macroeconomic Policy.* Washington, DC: International Monetary Fund, 1996 (forthcoming).

Litan, Robert. *What Should Banks Do?* Washington, DC: Brookings, 1987.

O.E.C.D., Financial Conglomerates. Paris, 1993.

Peach, W. N. *The Securities Affiliates of National Banks.* Baltimore: Johns Hopkins Press, 1941.

Peltzman, Sam. "Capital Investment in Commercial Banking and Its Relationship to Portfolio Regulation," *Journal of Political Economy* 78 (1970): 1-26.

Prowse, Stephen D. "Corporate Finance in International Perspective: Legal and Regulatory Influences on Financial System Development." *Economic Review* (Federal Reserve Bank of Dallas, Third Quarter 1996): 2-15.

Pulley, Lawrence, and David Humphrey. "The Role of Fixed Costs and Cost Complementaries in Determining Scope Economies and the Cost of Narrow Banking Proposals." *Journal of Business* (1993): 437-462.

Rojas-Suarez, Liliana, and Steven R. Weisbrod. "Central Bank Provision of Liquidity: Its Impact on Bank Asset Quality." Washington, DC: Inter-American Development Bank, 1996.

Santos, João. "Commercial Banks in the Securities Business: A Review," Bank for International Settlements, Basle, Switzerland, December 1997.

Santos, João. "Securities Units of Banking Conglomerates: Should their Location be Regulated?" *Cato Journal*, forthcoming.

Saunders, Anthony, and Ingo Walter. *Universal Banking in the United States*. New York: Oxford University Press, 1994.

Saunders, Anthony, and Ingo Walter, editors. *Universal Banking*. New York: Irwin Professional Publishing, 1996.

Sheard, Paul. "Main Banks and the Governance of Financial Distress." Pp. 188-230 in Masahiko Aoki and Hugh Patrick, eds., *The Japanese Main Bank System*. New York: Oxford University Press, 1994.

Steinherr, Alfred. "Performance of Universal Banks." Pp. 2-30 of *Universal Banking*, edited by Anthony Saunders and Ingo Walter. Chicago: Irwin Professional Publishing, 1996.

White, Eugene. "Before the Glass-Steagall Act: An Analysis of the Investment Banking Activities of National Banks," *Explorations in Economic History* 23 (1986): 33-55.

White, Lawrence H. *Free Banking in Britain, 1800-1845*. Cambridge: Cambridge University Press, 1984.

World Bank. *World Development Report [WDR] 1989: Financial Systems and Development*. New York: Oxford University Press, 1989.

Capital Regulation
and Depository Institutions

Cara S. Lown
Officer and Senior Economist
Research and Market Analysis Group
Federal Reserve Bank of New York

Stavros Peristiani
Senior Economist
Research and Market Analysis Group
Federal Reserve Bank of New York

Kenneth J. Robinson
Senior Economist and Policy Advisor
Financial Industry Studies Department
Federal Reserve Bank of Dallas

The opinions expressed in this paper are those of the authors and do not necessarily represent those of the Federal Reserve Bank of Dallas, the Federal Reserve Bank of New York or the Federal Reserve Board. The authors thank Dibora Amamuel and Justin McCrary for very useful research assistance.

Introduction

Since early 1995, Congress has been debating legislation to reform and modernize the regulation of U.S. depository institutions. These legislative efforts are largely directed at removing Glass-Steagall restrictions on the securities activities of banking organizations. This latest attempt to reform the banking system stems from the cumulated effects of the unintended consequences of prior regulations on banks. Restrictions on banks' securities activities were put in place during the Great Depression in response to allegations of fraud and abuse. While intending to improve financial safety and soundness, these restrictions limited diversification opportunities and made it more difficult for banking organizations to compete in both domestic and international financial markets.

Over the past two decades, regulatory focus has increasingly shifted to the capital adequacy of insured depository institutions. Twelve industrial countries participating in the Basle Committee on Banking Regulations and Supervisory Practices in 1988 signed the landmark Basle Accord, which established for the first time risk-based minimum capital requirements for depository institutions. Institutions with greater perceived credit risk are now required to hold greater amounts of capital. In 1989, Congress enacted the Financial Institutions Reform, Recovery and Enforcement Act (FIRREA). The act significantly increased the capital requirements on thrift institutions, both in the definition of what may be counted as capital and in the amount of capital they are required to hold. The international capital standards initiated by the Basle agreement were further expanded by the Federal Deposit Insurance Corporation Improvement Act of 1991 (FDICIA), which was passed to improve the safety and soundness of U.S. banks and thrift institutions in the aftermath of the financial difficulties of the 1980s. FDICIA, with its prompt corrective-action provisions, now makes capital levels the centerpiece of regulatory oversight, with mandated closure if a bank's leverage ratio falls below 2 percent of assets.

In this paper, we explore the effects on both credit availability and monetary policy of the increasing regulatory focus on insured financial institutions' capital levels. Although U.S. banks and thrift institutions are currently enjoying record profits and most of the industry can be classified as well capitalized, as with previous reform efforts, some unintended consequences resulted from these legislative reforms. Specifically, we argue that lending activity at commercial banks and thrift institutions was adversely affected by the capital requirements, and that the resulting lending slowdown adversely affected economic activity. We also provide evidence that recent weakness in the monetary aggregates, particularly M2, and the associated difficulties in predicting money growth, were related to capital positions at banks and thrift institutions.

While we provide evidence of the unintended negative consequences of a regulatory focus on capital, we also point out the need for some amount of regulation at institutions that enjoy the benefits of the federal safety net. A reliance on market-based incentives alone is likely to be insufficient because market discipline is undermined by the existence of the safety net. A federal guarantee of deposits, access to the discount window, and participation in the payments system in which settlement is guaranteed, point to the need for a degree of regulation and oversight to limit excessive risk-taking and taxpayer exposure in the event of financial failures. The challenge facing policymakers and regulators is to balance the benefits and costs of regulation with the goal of ensuring financial safety and soundness. The debate over the optimal mix of regulatory versus market-based incentives continues to evolve and has given rise to several new approaches to bank regulation.

We proceed as follows. In the next section, we offer a brief history and rationale of capital requirements. In the third section we examine some unintended consequences of capital regulation by focusing on credit availability and monetary policy issues. We show that during the late 1980s and early 1990s, the behavior of the stock of outstanding bank loans, the interest rates charged on loans and the M2 monetary aggregate were all altered by the increased attention paid to bank capital. The fourth section discusses the need for regulation and how regulators are attempting to refine their policies to meet the challenges of an increasingly complex, integrated financial marketplace. The fifth section concludes the paper.

History of Capital Requirements

Regulators have always been concerned with the adequacy of capital ratios at depository institutions, although the degree of concern has varied over the years. Capital requirements have been thought of as the best way to safeguard the financial integrity of the banking system. Not surprisingly, over the years federal and state regulatory authorities in the United States have made several attempts to link perceived risks at banks with a minimum capital requirement. In this section, we provide a brief historical review of capital requirements in the United States.

Early Requirements

In the first half of the 19th century bank capital levels were fairly high, reflecting the considerable solvency risk of U.S. banks (Figure 1). Capital ratios, however, began to drop gradually in the latter half of the century as several financial innovations (e.g., clearinghouses) and government initiatives reduced the solvency risk of banks. In 1864, Congress enacted the National Bank Act, establishing for the first time national banking in the United States. The main goal of this legislation was to create a national currency. However, at the same time, the Office of the Comptroller of the Currency (OCC) imposed minimum capital requirements for banks seeking to obtain a national charter. These capital requirements were based on the population size served by the institution. The National Bank Act also introduced formal capital guidelines for banks issuing national banks notes. National banks were required to maintain their capital-to-national note ratio at 90 percent. As a result of these capital rules, market perceptions about the safety and soundness of the banking system improved, allowing banks to gradually lower their capital ratios.

With the creation of the Federal Reserve System in 1914, member banks continued to become more liquid as they were required to hold higher reserves and were also given access to the discount window. Around the same time, the OCC floated for the first time the idea of capital ratios as we know it today. In particular, the OCC recommended that banks should hold a ratio of capital-to-deposit liabilities of 10 percent. However, this OCC standard was not formally adopted.

Figure 1: Ratio of Bank Capital-to-Asset, 1865-1997

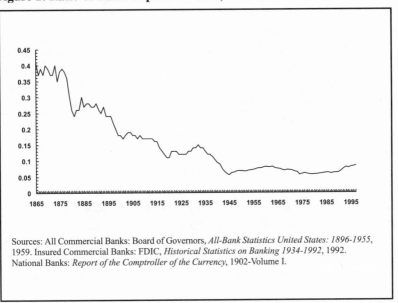

Sources: All Commercial Banks: Board of Governors, *All-Bank Statistics United States: 1896-1955*, 1959. Insured Commercial Banks: FDIC, *Historical Statistics on Banking 1934-1992*, 1992. National Banks: *Report of the Comptroller of the Currency*, 1902-Volume I.

The Depression and its Aftermath

Following the collapse of the banking system in 1933, federal and state governments began to closely regulate the activities of commercial banks. On the one hand, the creation of the Federal Deposit Insurance Corporation (FDIC) provided deposit insurance to member banks, further increasing the safety net for depositors. However, the FDIC also introduced periodic examinations and legislation introduced in the late 1920s and early 1930s mandated geographic and product restrictions on banks. Although the FDIC did not mandate any formal capital guidelines, in 1934 it advocated that its members maintain the OCC's 10 percent capital-to-deposit ratio. Subsequently, in 1939, the FDIC modified the informal capital target to be measured as 10 percent of total assets.

In the 1940s, the focus on capital waned as the federal government was more concerned with funding the war. To encourage banks to participate in the war effort, regulators evaluated capital adequacy relative to risky assets, which excluded cash and government securities from total assets. This approach was essentially a forerunner of the risk-based capital requirements. In the early 1950s, the Federal

45

Reserve Bank of New York formalized this concept by assigning risk weights by category of assets and proposed a mechanical formula to compute an overall capital measure.[1]

Despite the development of these new methods of measuring capital adequacies, during the 1950s and 1960s all three regulatory agencies (OCC, FDIC and the Federal Reserve) drifted away from capital rules, choosing instead to use different judgmental criteria for evaluating the financial soundness of banks. After a string of bank failures in the early 1970s, however, the federal supervisory agencies became increasingly concerned with the lack of homogeneous standards. In 1978, the agencies agreed to assess the overall quality of a bank's condition according to the CAMEL rating method.[2] With bank and thrift institution difficulties looming on the horizon, the agencies decided in 1981 to establish minimum capital requirements. Although initially these requirements were applied differently depending on the size of the bank, by 1985, all U.S. commercial banks were expected to hold a minimum ratio of primary capital to adjusted total assets equal to 5.5 percent.[3]

1988 Basle Accord and Beyond

With the globalization of financial activities in the mid-1980s, United States banks began to lobby for uniform bank standards. They argued that the existing capital requirements left them at a disadvantage with international competitors that were less regulated. To support their plea, they pointed out that during this period the number of foreign banks operating in the United States grew at a particularly fast pace. Concerned by the growing presence of foreign banks, U.S. regu-

---

1.   This risk-based formula was later modified by the Board of Governors. The Board's version (named the Analyzing Bank Capital [ABC] ratio) weighed both assets and liabilities (Orgler and Wolkowitz 1977; Hahn 1966).

2.   The CAMEL rating is based on Capital adequacy, Asset quality, Management, Earnings, and Liquidity. Each of these five areas of performance is rated on a scale of 1 to 5 with 1 indicating strong performance and 5 signaling unsatisfactory performance. A composite rating is then derived from each of the five areas of performance.

3.   Primary capital is mainly made up of common stock, perpetual preferred stock, surplus, undivided profits, and loan loss reserves. Adjusted assets is defined as total assets minus intangible assets, classified loans and a fraction of doubtful loans. In addition to the 5.5 percent primary capital requirement, banks were also required to meet a target of 6 percent of total capital ratio. Total capital included primary capital and remaining preferred stock (secondary capital).

lators determined that they had to level the playing field. At the same time, the rising number of bank and thrift-institution failures reinforced the idea that the existing minimum capital requirements could not adequately deter moral-hazard risks. In 1988, regulatory agencies and central bankers from the Group of 10 reached the landmark Basle Accord.[4]

The Basle guidelines, which were phased in by 1992, represent a fundamental shift from simple capital standards. In short, under the Basle agreement depository institutions have to meet three capital criteria:

- Institutions are required to have a ratio of Tier 1 capital to risk-weighted assets greater than 4 percent.
- Banks have to maintain a minimum ratio of Tier 1 plus Tier 2 (total capital) capital to risk-weight assets greater than 8 percent.
- Depending on their CAMEL rating, banks are expected to keep a minimum unweighted capital ratio (the leverage requirement) between 3 to 5 percent.

The risk weights are assigned to a broad classification of balance-sheet assets and off-balance activities. Since loans are considered riskier investments, commercial and industrial loans and personal unsecured loans are given a weight of 100 percent; securitized home mortgages are considered less risky and are assigned a 50 percent risk weighting; U.S. Treasuries, other obligations of the governments of the Organization for Economic Development, and cash get a zero-risk weight.

Shortly after the Basle Accord was signed, U.S. legislators enacted the Federal Deposit Insurance Corporation Improvement Act (FDICIA) of 1991. The act has given regulators powers of prompt corrective action to classify depository institutions according to their capital strength.

---

4.   The participating countries in the Basle Accord include: Belgium, Britain, Canada, France, Germany, Italy, Japan, Luxembourg, the Netherlands, Sweden, Switzerland and the United States.

Essentially, depository institutions can be classified as "well capitalized," "adequately capitalized," "undercapitalized," "significantly undercapitalized" and "critically undercapitalized."[5] Banks that do not fall into the first two categories face increased regulatory scrutiny and are restricted from certain banking activities. Moreover, a critically undercapitalized bank may be taken over by the appropriate regulatory agency.

The Basle capital rules established risk-weighted capital standards that focus solely on credit risk. One criticism of the risk-based requirements is that they fail to control for other fundamental risks in banking such as liquidity risk, interest-rate risk and general market risk (for more details, see Houpt and Embersit 1991). More importantly, the Basle agreement shifted the incentives in favor of Treasury debt and government-sponsored agency securities (e.g., mortgage-backed securities), which ostensibly have no credit risk. But while these government-guaranteed assets have no credit risk, they expose investors to a significant amount of interest-rate risk. Another shortcoming of the Basle agreement is that it does not weigh the overall risk of the bank's portfolio by computing the cross-correlations of the different positions.

In light of these unresolved problems, participants in the Basle Committee have made several attempts to adjust the existing risk-based capital rules. A number of proposals explored ways of extending the accord to include other risks in the calculation of capital requirements. Some of these efforts took shape in the 1996 Basle Committee market-risk rules. This proposal will allow banks to use their own "internal models" to determine their capital requirement. The Basle revision does not propose a particular internal model; rather banks are expected to apply a value-at-risk approach based on some uniform assumptions on the parameters of the model.

---

5. A depository institution is classified as "well capitalized" if it maintains, at a minimum, a 6 percent Tier 1 ratio, a 10 percent Tier 1 plus Tier 2 ratio and a 5 percent leverage capital ratio. To be considered "adequately capitalized," the bank must hold a Tier 1 ratio of 8 percent, a total capital ratio of 4 percent and a leverage ratio of 4 percent. Banks that fail to meet these requirements are placed in one of the three undercapitalized categories. If a bank is "critically undercapitalized," which occurs when the (tangible) leverage capital ratio is less than 2 percent, the institution is placed in conservatorship.

Capital requirements have evolved over time from an informal set of measures that varied by bank size and location to a formal, uniform set of rules based on the credit risk of each institution. The increased focus on capital reflects regulatory attempts to maintain financial safety and soundness and to avoid a replay of banking difficulties. While regulators have been successful in this regard, there were some adverse side effects to the imposition of the capital regulations. We believe that it is important to understand these consequences so that, when possible, they can be taken into account when future regulatory changes are considered.

Increased Focus on Capital: Some Unintended Consequences

As is well known, bank lending in the United States was unusually slow in the late 1980s and early 1990s, precisely the time that the Basle Accord was discussed and passed. Several studies written in the early 1990s maintained that the Basle Accord was mainly responsible for this lending slowdown (see for example, Syron 1991; Furlong 1992; Peek and Rosengren 1993; Baer and McElravey 1993; and Berger and Udell 1994). Alternatively, some work attributed the decline in bank lending to more stringent bank examination standards. This explanation is not entirely separate from the first, of course, as the discussion surrounding the Basle Accord could have produced a change in the regulatory environment. Yet a third interpretation is that banks were merely responding to previous problem loans that weakened their balance sheets (Johnson 1991). According to this view, independent of any new capital regulations or stricter regulatory enforcement, banks might have chosen to reduce their lending in order to rebuild their capital positions.

Distinguishing between these three explanations for the credit slowdown of the early 1990s—new capital rules, increased regulatory pressure, and weakened bank balance sheets—is difficult. Each implies a need for banks to increase capital relative to their assets. Although some studies have attempted to make such distinctions, more of the focus has been on obtaining some sense of the importance of bank capital for lending. Our focus in this section is in this latter vein.

In this section, we report our results from empirically examining the relationship between bank capital and lending during the late 1980s and early 1990s. Results from examining both the quantity of loans and the price (interest rates) charged are presented, although more time is spent on the former since these results are not discussed elsewhere. Subsequently, we discuss how the increased focus on bank capital affected the behavior of the monetary aggregates.

The motivation for our examination is based on the hypothesis that the link between credit and capital depends on the actual capitalization level of a bank. Low-capitalized banks can expand their assets only when their capital rises and must contract assets when their capital falls. This link is much looser for well-capitalized banks. Moreover, because the largest financial institutions had the weakest balance sheets during the years in question, our examination focuses on banks by asset size. Such a grouping allows us to see clearly how these large institutions, which account for a significant portion of bank lending, behaved and therefore should uncover whether or not there was in fact a capital-induced lending slowdown.

Loan Growth

To analyze loan growth by asset size, we divide banks into six asset-size classes: banks with assets of less than $50 million; $50 million to $250 million; $250 million to $500 million; $500 million to $1 billion; $1 billion to $10 billion; and more than $10 billion. This breakdown, used previously by Boyd and Gertler (1993) in their examination of the U.S. banking system in the 1980s, allows us to test the hypothesis that the largest banks were in the worst financial shape and hence contributed disproportionately to the lending slowdown.

Table 1 helps us to obtain a sense of the relative importance of each of the six categories of banks. The table reports each category's share of total loans, its growth rates and its leverage ratio for the years 1987-92. Two important facts stand out. First, the largest size class (roughly 47 banks) accounted for about 40 percent of all bank loans, while the second-largest size class (roughly 356 banks) accounted for about 30 percent. In contrast, the smallest-size class (more than 4,000 banks) accounted for only 3.5 percent of all loans. Secondly, the average leverage ratio is largest for the smallest size class and smallest for the largest size class. The gap in capitalization reflects the fact that small banks have limited funding sources, so they must maintain extra capital to cushion any outflow of funds.[6]

Table 1: Bank Lending by Asset Size

Asset Size	Year	Level	Share	Growth Rate	Leverage Ratio
Less than $50 million	1987	78.76	4.00		9.54
	1988	79.25	3.78	0.62	9.41
	1989	79.13	3.57	0.08	9.43
	1990	78.81	3.48	−0.63	9.29
	1991	78.08	3.56	−0.93	9.61
	1992	76.15	3.51	−2.47	9.78
$50 – $250 million	1987	226.10	11.49		8.50
	1988	240.28	11.48	6.27	8.58
	1989	251.61	11.32	4.71	8.52
	1990	266.32	11.76	5.84	8.88
	1991	273.11	12.45	2.54	8.90
	1992	285.29	13.17	4.46	8.98
$250 – $500 million	1987	102.93	5.23		7.98
	1988	112.10	5.35	8.90	7.89
	1989	122.10	5.49	8.91	7.80
	1990	129.84	5.73	6.33	7.66
	1991	133.29	6.07	2.66	8.16
	1992	138.86	6.41	4.17	8.04
$500 million – 1 billion	1987	107.15	5.44		7.70
	1988	119.31	5.70	11.34	7.32
	1989	126.78	5.70	6.26	7.22
	1990	131.89	5.82	4.02	6.99
	1991	124.10	5.65	−5.91	7.78
	1992	123.28	5.69	−0.65	7.58

6.   Prior to 1985, the various regulatory agencies imposed capital requirements that discriminated according to bank size. Large liability-managed banks were allowed to operate with capital-to-asset ratios of 4 percent, while midsize and small banks were expected to maintain capital-to-asset ratios between 7 and 8 percent. Since 1985, responding to rising credit-risk problems in the banking sector, the regulatory agencies instituted uniform standards for all sized banks.

Table 1: Bank Lending by Asset Size *(continued)*

Asset Size	Year	Level	Share	Growth Rate	Leverage Ratio
$1 – $10 billion	1987	607.80	30.89		6.83
	1988	691.24	33.03	13.72	6.84
	1989	745.12	33.54	7.79	6.74
	1990	736.21	32.51	–1.19	6.51
	1991	717.88	32.73	–2.49	7.65
	1992	692.85	31.99	–3.48	7.53
Over $10 billion	1987	844.38	42.92		5.02
	1988	850.33	40.63	0.70	5.23
	1989	896.16	40.34	5.39	5.01
	1990	920.88	40.67	2.75	5.35
	1991	866.73	39.51	–5.88	6.92
	1992	849.44	39.21	–1.99	6.55

Notes: Aggregate bank lending is measured in $ billions; all other variables are measured as percents. The data are adjusted for mergers.

One other finding the table highlights is that, over the reported time period, only small changes in the leverage ratios occurred in the first four size classes (0.24, 0.48, 0.06 and -0.12, respectively), while much larger changes occurred in the last two size classes (0.70 and 1.53, respectively). This pattern suggests that the larger banks either were under more pressure or chose to increase their capital-asset ratios relative to small banks.

Our regression analysis of the link between bank capital and lending by size class is based on a simple specification that includes only the leverage ratio and regional dummies as independent variables. This specification allows us to focus directly on the link between capital and lending. For each year a regression is estimated using data from all banks, and then one for each of the six size classifications. The dependent variable is Q4-to-Q4 loan growth and the leverage ratio is measured from the beginning of the period (Q4). The year-by-year regressions allow us to determine whether the relationship between bank capital and lending changed over the sample period.

To present the regression results in a comprehensible and comparable way, we report the estimated coefficient on the leverage ratio from each regression in Table 2. The first column of the table reports the results when all banks are included in the regression. The subsequent columns report the results by bank size.

Table 2: Total Loan Growth and Leverage Ratio Regressions by Year and Bank Size

$$Model : \quad (\frac{\Delta L_{t+1,i}}{L_{ti}}) = \delta_0 + \delta_1 LEVERAGE_{ti} + \sum_{j=1}^{11} \delta_{2j} REGION_{jti} + \zeta_{ti}.$$

Coefficient on LEVERAGE, δ_1

Year	ALL	<$50M	$50-250M	$250-500M	$500M-1B	$1-10B	>$10B
1988	0.42***	0.38***	0.50***	0.18	0.26	1.07***	1.46
1989	0.34***	0.39***	0.20***	0.21	0.55	0.41*	5.73***
1990	0.35***	0.29***	0.31***	-0.05	1.73***	1.10***	3.09*
1991	0.51***	0.41***	0.40***	0.52**	1.47***	0.73***	2.72*
OBS.	10,611	5,474	3,983	514	267	327	46

Notes: The symbols (*), (**), and (***) indicated statistical significance at the 10, 5, and 1 percent level. Variable Definitions: LEVERAGE = tier 1 leverage ratio (percent); $REGION_{jti}$ = 1 if bank (i) belongs in Federal Reserve Region (j), 0 otherwise.

As the first column in the table shows, when all banks are included in the regression, the coefficient on the leverage ratio is quite small but highly significant. The results for the first two size classes of banks are similar to each other and to the all-bank regression. This latter finding is not surprising because these categories contain the thousands of small banks that dominate the overall regression model. For the middle two categories—$250 to $500 million and $500 million to $1 billion in assets—we observe that the leverage ratio is not significant for the first two years, but becomes significant in the last one or two years. Also, in the fourth size class, and in the largest two size classes, the significant coefficients are typically larger than in the smaller size classes.

In their study, Boyd and Gertler found that for banks in the best shape—roughly medium-size banks with $250 million to $500 million in assets—the leverage ratio appears to have had little if any impact on loan growth during the 1980s. For the smallest and largest banks, however, there was a significant link, and that link was larger for the larger-sized banks.[7] Our findings are consistent with their work. Moreover, we uncover some additional insights into studies that have analyzed the relationship between capital and aggregate lending during this time period. For instance, using state-level data Bernanke and Lown (1991) obtained a coefficient of 2.7 on their capital-asset measure for the period 1990:Q2 to1991:Q1. Our coefficients for the largest size class are close to this estimate, 3.09 and 2.72 in 1990 and 1991, respectively. This comparison highlights the fact that large banks dominate lending, and hence regression estimates, at the state level. In fact, during this time period, large money-center and super-regional banks were operating in 20 states, and almost every state had a group of large regional banks (the $1 billion to $10 billion asset size class).

Our results also illuminate another interesting aspect of the link between capital and loan growth. For large banks, the biggest effect of capital on loan growth (a coefficient of 5.7 on capital) did not occur during the quarters of the 1990-1991 recession, as might have been expected, but in 1989—before the recession began. This was precisely the first year when banks could have begun to prepare for the phase-in of the new Bank for International Settlements capital standards. In fact, Bernanke and Lown (1991) used their capital coefficient of 2.7 to conclude that the weakness in bank capital could explain no more than 20 percent of the slowdown in lending (2.7 percent of a 12 percent lending decline in New England between 1988 and 1990). Analogously then, the larger coefficient obtained from our analysis in 1989 suggests that weakness in bank capital across large banks might explain almost half—5.7 percent of the 12 percent decline—of the slowdown in New England bank lending. This finding suggests that at the beginning of the lending slowdown, bank behavior played a larger role than previously thought in affecting the availability of credit.

Two other findings support the conclusion that the use of the term "credit crunch" is most accurately applied to large banks in 1989. First, Bernanke and Lown note that bank data aggregated to the national level suggested that banks might have been responsible for a

---

7. Boyd and Gertler (1993) note that the balance sheets of the smallest banks were not as strong in the 1980s as those of the medium-size banks. They cite small banks' lack of ability to diversify as a possible explanation.

credit crunch in 1989. In that year, only bank lending was slowing, while other forms of credit continued to grow. In the subsequent two years, growth of all forms of credit slowed. However, these authors were examining the 1990 recession and hence did not explore their 1989 hypothesis in subsequent regression analysis. Second, an examination of loan growth by region (not reported) shows that for regions such as New England and the Middle Atlantic states, bank lending growth slowed substantially in 1989.

Although not reported, we also estimated the loan-growth model by asset size using additional measures of banks' balance sheet health. As expected, these added variables generally reduce the importance of the leverage ratio in the regressions.[8] The leverage ratio remains significant for the small and large banks, albeit in many cases the coefficients become smaller in size. Of these additional independent variables, the nonaccrual and loan-to-asset ratios are the ones whose coefficients are consistently significant. However, in contrast to the coefficients on the leverage ratio, these coefficients do not appear to differ significantly across size class or years. Overall, while the inclusion of additional bank-balance-sheet variables reduces the importance of the leverage ratio in many of the regressions, the difference in the size of the coefficients across bank size generally is not affected, nor is the importance of bank capital for lending by the largest banks in 1989.

In summary, our analysis uncovers two facts about the credit slowdown of the early 1990s. First, we find that the link between bank capital and lending during the credit-crunch period found by Bernanke and Lown, and by others, can be explained almost completely by large banks, especially those with assets of $10 billion or more. Second, in 1989, the capital-asset ratios of the largest category of banks had an even bigger impact on loan growth than it did in 1990 and 1991.

---

8. Banks with riskier investments (high nonaccrual ratios) are forced to take bigger charge-offs that deplete capital. As a result, multicollinearity exists between the leverage ratio and the nonaccrual ratio that is problematic for smaller sample size regressions.

This impact is larger than was uncovered in previous studies and suggests that the most appropriate use of the term "credit crunch" was in reference to large banks in 1989.[9]

Loan Rates

An alternative method for evaluating the determinants of the credit slowdown is to examine the relationship between bank capital and interest rates charged on bank loans. A study of this relationship was presented in detail in Lown and Peristiani (1996). Here we summarize the analysis and main findings.

An examination into the relationship between bank capital and loan rates can be thought of as an exploration into the second reduced-form equation derived from the standard demand-and-supply equilibrium condition in the loan market. In fact, under some scenarios, the pricing behavior of depository institutions might be a better indicator than the stock of outstanding loans. For example, in a deteriorating economic climate, banks might prefer to curtail their lending activity, but are compelled to supply credit to businesses with established lines of credit. Thus, banks might continue to lend, but only at higher interest rates. Such a shift could be uncovered by analyzing interest rates.

In this earlier paper, we analyzed the behavior of interest rates on two types of consumer loans over the 1987-1992 period. Focusing on consumer loans allowed us to abstract from concerns about credit rationing, which is considered most relevant for commercial and industrial lending. Such a focus also allowed us to abstract from concerns about declining trends in the intermediation role of banks, since banks have maintained a constant presence in consumer lending.

The loan rates we examined were installment loans on new automobiles and personal loans. The data were obtained from the Federal Reserve System's quarterly survey of interest rates on selected direct consumer installment loans. About 200 U.S. commercial banks are surveyed, and the sample is selected to represent all Federal Reserve districts and all size categories of banks.

---

9.   We are not arguing that these banks could or should have behaved differently. They had no choice but to respond to the new capital regulations and/or "beef up" their balance sheets following previous losses.

The results show that capital adequacy played a significant role in explaining interest rates on automobile and personal loans over the 1987-1992 period. Poorly capitalized banks increasingly charged an above-average consumer loan rate. Similar to the loan quantity regressions, this capital effect was more significant among the lower-capitalized large lenders.

Figure 2: Deviations from Average Loan Rates by Size and Capitalization (1987 – 1992)

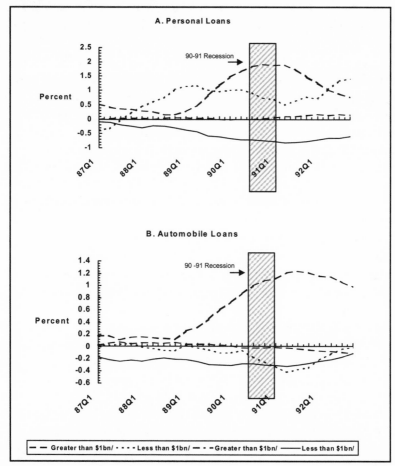

A clear illustration of the relationship between capital and consumer loan rates is presented in Figure 2. The top panel depicts a four-quarter moving average of the personal loan rate, expressed, as in the regressions, as a deviation from its mean. The rates are shown for four categories of banks: undercapitalized banks with assets less than and more than $1 billion, and well-capitalized banks with assets less than and more than $1 billion.[10] Similarly, the bottom panel plots the rate deviation for automobile loans. Both panels show conclusively that large, poorly capitalized banks priced consumer loans higher than well-capitalized banks. In addition, small and midsize undercapitalized banks exhibit similar behavior in pricing personal loans, but not in pricing auto loans. However, the small sample size for this latter category of bank might inhibit uncovering a clear pattern.

An alternative rate premium uses interest rates on time certificates of deposits (CDs) as a measure of banks' funding costs. These data allow us to look at banks' loan rates over costs, to consider if the differential between well-capitalized and poorly capitalized banks remains. The one drawback to this measure is that we are only able to match CD rate information with loan rates from our sample of large banks. By the beginning of 1989, low-capitalized banks began to require a larger premium on auto and personal loans than did well-capitalized banks, even after accounting for funding costs. Thus, at least during this time period, differential-funding costs cannot account for the higher loan rates charged by low-capitalized large banks.

Once again, we see that capitalization levels played a role in bank lending by affecting the interest rates charged on consumer loans. Although the increased attention paid to bank capital in the late 1980s and early 1990s could be characterized as having had only short-term adverse consequences while banks strengthened their balance sheets, the link between bank capital and lending is now permanent. It is not impossible to imagine that a widespread hit to bank capital sometime in the future could result in a capital-induced lending slowdown. For this reason, it is important to understand how the banking system was affected by this transition to more stringent capital requirements.

---

10. A bank is classified as undercapitalized if its average leverage ratio over the period 1987-92 was less than 5 percent. Most banks over the period were well capitalized. Although the sample size varied by quarter, roughly 22 large banks were undercapitalized, and 10 small-to-midsize banks were undercapitalized.

M2 Monetary Aggregate

Perhaps the least well-known adverse consequence of the increased attention paid to bank capital was its impact on the monetary aggregates. Beginning in 1990, and certainly by late 1991, actual M2 growth was well below levels forecast by standard money demand equations (Figure 3). This deterioration in forecast accuracy, along with a breakdown in the relationship between M2 and the ultimate goals of monetary policy, led the Federal Reserve Board in 1993 to formally announce that M2 had been downgraded as an indicator of monetary policy. We believe that the behavior of M2 during this period can be explained in large part by depository institutions' capital difficulties.

Figure 3: Actual and Forecasted* M2 (Quarter-to-Quarter Annualized Growth Rates)

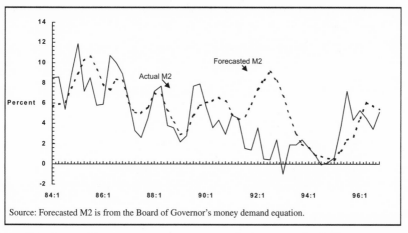

Source: Forecasted M2 is from the Board of Governor's money demand equation.

To show this, we construct two variations on the M2 monetary aggregate: one represents M2 deposits at all banks (excluding thrift institutions), and another represents M2 deposits at all banks that met the minimum capital requirements.[11]

---

11. Although not all thrift institutions were officially capital constrained, many were operating from weaker capital positions than were banks. A bank was classified as capital constrained if it failed to meet the minimum primary capital ratio of 5.5 percent established in 1985. Thrift institutions were considered capital constrained if they failed to meet a minimum leverage ratio of 3 percent and a minimum tangible capital-to-assets ratio of 1.5 percent, as defined in the Financial Institutions Reform, Recovery and Enforcement Act of 1989.

These measures allow us to examine two hypotheses: (1) that it was mostly difficulties at thrift institutions that affected money growth; and (2) that both banks and thrift institutions were capital constrained, and likely faced limits on their ability to lend. Underlying both of these hypotheses is the possibility that these institutions' inability or unwillingness to expand their deposits lowered the growth rate of actual M2 below what was being forecast by conventional money demand models.

Figure 4 adds these two additional series to the previous chart. As the figure shows, constructing M2 growth using only the M2 components at banks, and then calculating M2 growth using only the deposits at nonconstrained financial institutions produces M2 series much more in line with forecast M2. The graph also shows that by 1994, when most institutions resolved their difficulties and were able to meet the regulatory capital requirements, the distinctions among the various series had disappeared.

Figure 4: M2 Comparisons, 1990 – 1996

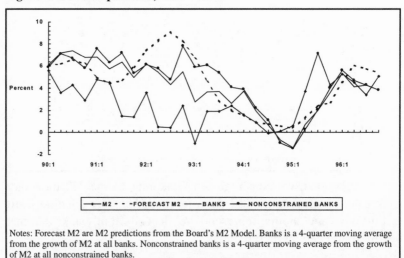

Notes: Forecast M2 are M2 predictions from the Board's M2 Model. Banks is a 4-quarter moving average from the growth of M2 at all banks. Nonconstrained banks is a 4-quarter moving average from the growth of M2 at all nonconstrained banks.

One final way to understand the impact of the capital regulations at a time when many institutions had weakened balance sheets is to consider the behavior of small time deposits at constrained and non-constrained banks. Small time deposits were the category of M2 that appeared to be most affected by the financial difficulties of the late

1980s and early 1990s. In 1989, small time deposits accounted for 36 percent of M2. By 1994, this component of M2 accounted for only 23 percent of the total. As Figures 5A-5B show, small time deposits at constrained banks and thrift institutions fell off beginning in 1990. Even deposits at nonconstrained thrift institutions leveled off and declined, while only deposits at nonconstrained banks continued to expand.

Figure 5A: Nonconstrained Banks and Thrifts Small Time Deposits, 1984 – 1996

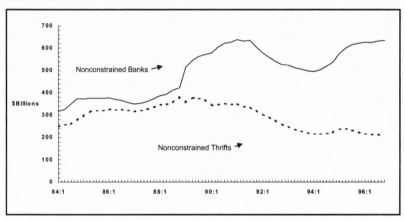

Figure 5B: Constrained Banks and Thrifts Small Time Deposits, 1984 – 1996

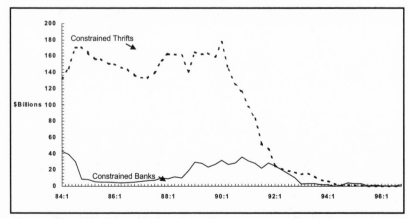

Overall then, the imposition of capital regulations at a time when financial institutions faced weakened balance sheets adversely affected lending and the monetary aggregates and probably contributed to the breakdown in the relationship between the monetary aggregates and the macroeconomy. This evidence suggests that there are consequences of capital regulations that should be recognized and taken into account when these issues are being considered.

Before turning to a discussion of the benefits of regulation, we would like to discuss some longer-term consequences of the current regulations. As we have already mentioned, one could view the slowdown in lending, and in the monetary aggregates during the transition to the new capital regulations, as a short-term consequence of the regulatory changes. Once a bank's capital exceeded the new requirements, consistent with our asymmetric hypothesis, its lending should not have been restrained by its capital. However, the regulations have made the link between bank lending and capital permanent. There will now always be the risk that a widespread hit to bank capital will lead to a capital-induced lending slowdown.

**Figure 6: U.S. Commercial Banks Total Loans/Total Assets
1960:1 – 1997:3**

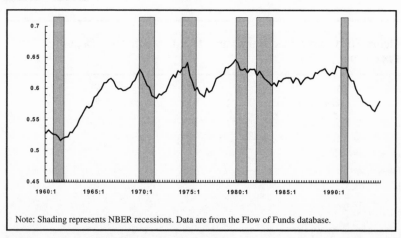

Note: Shading represents NBER recessions. Data are from the Flow of Funds database.

A second long-term consequence of the regulations is that they have encouraged a reallocation of bank assets, away from risky loans (commercial and industrial) toward safe loans (mortgages), and away from loans altogether, toward securities (see Figure 6).[12] With the economy currently so strong, it is hard to make the case that such rebalancing has had an adverse economic effect, but in time this issue could be raised. Furthermore, the shift into securities increases a bank's interest-rate risk, with adverse consequences if rates were to change quickly. Thus, while we might view what happened to bank portfolios in the early 1990s as a one-time event, the new regulations will likely continue to affect financial intermediation in other, more subtle, ways for years to come.

Having discussed at length the adverse consequences of capital regulation, we would like to emphasize that we do not intend our work to imply that we are opposed to the imposition of capital regulation. Given the institutional structure of the U.S. financial system, the benefits of financial regulation also need to be recognized. Balancing the costs of regulatory actions with the benefits that accrue from these actions is an important part of designing a sound regulatory apparatus.

Benefits of Regulation: Where Do We Go From Here?

While a regulatory focus on capital has had some adverse effects, the benefits of regulation should also be considered. Financial safety and soundness is the primary goal of regulatory oversight. In that regard, it is important to point out that, despite the unintended effects that can flow from regulations, U.S. banks and thrift institutions have exhibited record levels of performance recently. As seen in Table 3, about 98 percent of all U.S. banks were classified as well-capitalized at the end of the fourth quarter of 1997, with an almost equivalent amount of the banking industry's assets in well-capitalized institutions. The nation's thrift industry showed a similar high concentration of well-capitalized institutions. Keeping in mind the benefits associated with financial regulation, which ultimately flow from the rationale underlying bank regulation, helps provide a useful framework in the debate about how to structure a regulatory apparatus that minimizes, if not eliminates, the adverse consequences of regulation.

---

12. Admittedly, one factor that might influence the loan-to-asset ratio is securitization, that is, the ability of banks to issue loans and sell them. Bernanke and Lown (1991) found that securitization could not account for the lending slowdown of the early 1990s. More recent data show that this phenomenon does not account for the continued low levels of the loan-asset ratio.

Table 3: Capital Position of U.S. Banks and Thrift Institutions Fourth, Quarter 1997

Capital Category	Banks		Thrift Institutions	
	Number	Assets	Number	Assets
Well Capitalized	9,203	$5,203,826	1,485	$749,169
Adequately Capitalized	183	74,783	33	8,861
Undercapitalized	9	1,486	1	9
Significantly Undercapitalized	4	2,725	0	0
Critically Undercapitalized	4	243	0	0

Notes: Dollar amounts are in millions. Banks include all BIF-member depository institutions. Thrift institutions include all SAIF-member depository institutions. Source: FDIC *Quarterly Banking Profile*, Fourth Quarter 1997, Tables II-D and II-E.

Are Banks Special?

One rationale given in support of bank regulation is the view that banks are different from other financial and nonfinancial companies. The view that banks are unique, or special, stems from the nature of banks' liabilities, the bulk of which are payable on demand. It is also pointed out that banks play a special role in the economy through their role in the monetary policy process and the payments system. Because banks have been viewed as special, they have been subjected to much greater supervision and regulation than other lines of business. Adam Smith, more than 200 years ago, pointed out those features of banks that make them special:

> Over and above the expenses which are common to every branch of trade; such as the expense of house-rent, the wages of servants, clerks, accountants, &c; the expense peculiar to a bank consists chiefly in two articles: First, in the expense of keeping at all times in its coffers, for answering the occasional demands of the holders of its notes, a large sum of money, of which it loses the interest; And, secondly, in the expense of replenishing those coffers as fast as they are emptied by answering such occasional demands. (Smith, 1937, p. 285).

Smith then describes why some regulatory oversight of banking is needed, despite the potential infringements on liberty such regulations entail.

> To restrain private people, it may be said, from receiving in payment the promissory notes of a banker, for any sum whether great or small, when they themselves are willing to receive them; or to restrain a banker from issuing such notes, when all his neighbors are willing to accept them, is a manifest violation of that natural liberty which it is the proper business of law, not to infringe, but to support. Such regulations, may, no doubt, be considered in some respects a violation of natural liberty. But those exertions of the natural liberty of a few individuals, which might endanger the security of the whole society, are, and ought to be, restrained by the laws of all governments; of the most free as well as the most despotic. The obligation of building party walls, in order to prevent the communication of fire, is a violation of natural liberty, exactly of the same kind with the regulations of the banking trade which are here proposed. (Smith, 1937, p. 308).

Besides the special view of banks, another rationale for their regulation stems from their access to the federal safety net. The existence of the federal safety net reflects the unique or special view of banks. The introduction of deposit insurance in the aftermath of widespread bank failures in the early 1930s, along with tighter supervision and regulation of the banking system, was an attempt to restore public confidence in the banking industry. At the same time it was an attempt at restraining incentives insured banks might face to undertake excessive risk (Schwartz 1988). Institutions that enjoy a federal guarantee of a major portion of their liabilities, access to the discount window, and a guarantee of settlement are faced with incentives to engage in excessively risky activities. The erosion of market discipline induced by the existence of the safety net, coupled with taxpayer exposure and the associated macroeconomic consequences of widespread financial difficulties, give rise to the need for oversight of insured financial institutions.[13]

The benefits of limiting risk-taking, however, must be balanced against the cost of excessive regulatory burdens on banks. If regulations are excessive, then insured institutions will find it increasingly difficult to compete in a dynamic financial marketplace.[14] Ideally, market forces and the signals they generate would guide institutions' risk-taking activities. However, the existence of the safety net undermines the disciplining nature of the marketplace.[15] Alan Greenspan summarized the dilemma confronting regulators. "The ideal is an institutional framework that, to the extent possible, induces banks both to hold more capital and to be managed as if there were no safety net, while at the same time shielding unsophisticated depositors and minimizing disruptions to credit and payment flows" (Greenspan 1990).

Regulatory Reform

Chairman Greenspan's "ideal" is hard to achieve in practice. However, regulators have taken steps recently in their approach toward capital regulation that seem to be moving in this direction. Some banking industry analysts are arguing that traditional methods of assessing capital adequacy might not be applicable in today's increasingly complex financial marketplace. Banks are increasingly moving beyond their traditional function of gathering deposits and extending loans. Many banks are now operating beyond the balance sheet and into less traditional areas, with derivatives activities the foremost example.

In response to these developments, several new approaches to capital regulation have been proposed. Prominent among these are what have come to be known as value-at-risk models and the precommitment approach. In the former, banks estimate the largest loss that a portfolio is likely to suffer in all but the most unusual circumstances. With the value-at-risk approach, financial institutions can use their

---

13. For a discussion of this moral-hazard problem, see Merton (1977), Marcus (1984), and Keeley (1990).
14. A 1992 study of the regulatory burdens facing depository institutions cited estimates of the costs of regulatory requirements in 1991 of between $7.5 billion and $17 billion. The American Bankers Association estimated that regulatory costs totaled $10.7 billion in 1991, or 59 percent of the banking industry's profits. See Federal Financial Institutions Examination Council (1992).
15. See White (1989) and the references cited therein.

estimates regarding the maximum losses that can be expected to incur as an important risk-management tool. Under the precommitment approach, banks determine their maximum precommitted trading losses and set aside sufficient capital based on these estimates. If losses exceed the estimated maximums, penalties are imposed. Hence, regulators are required to know only the actual losses, leaving the measurement of the size and riskiness of trading activities to the banks.[16]

Other approaches to regulatory reform have been advocated that also attempt both to protect "unsophisticated" or small depositors and impose more market discipline on bank decisions. Examples include the so-called "narrow bank," which would limit deposit insurance only to those banks that choose to engage in safe activities (such as investing in U.S. Treasury securities); introducing a coinsurance feature of deposit insurance along the lines of private insurance companies; and finally, some even advocate the privatization of deposit insurance altogether (White 1989). While these proposals attempt to provide insurance coverage in a less-regulated environment with greater emphasis on the disciplining role of the marketplace, the current political environment does not seem favorable to their adoption.

Conclusion

In 1988, bank regulators from the 12 large industrialized counties agreed to establish risk-based capital requirements for depository institutions. The Basle Accord represents an important step in financial regulation because for the first time depository institutions in a number of major industrialized countries are required to meet uniform minimum capital standards. The major objective of the Basle capital rules was to improve financial soundness and stability and promote a more fair and competitive environment among banks internationally. There is no doubt that the Basle Accord and the subsequent capital legislation enacted by the Congress have drastically improved the financial strength of U.S. banks. Following the FIRREA and FDICIA, bank profitability rebounded to much healthier levels, reaching record levels by 1993. Today, close to 98 percent of commercial banks and savings and loan institutions are well capitalized. Yet,

---

16. For more on these approaches see Hopper (1996), Kupiec and O'Brien (1995), and Bliss (1995).

despite the stellar performance of banks in the 1990s, capital requirements came at a cost to the economy. This paper has highlighted some of the unanticipated adverse consequences of risk-based capital requirements. We present evidence showing that during the transition to the new capital rules, banks responded by decreasing their lending to businesses and consumers. With banks taking a less aggressive approach to lending, deposits were not expanding as rapidly as was expected. This slow deposit growth was especially apparent during the early years of the current expansion. Although other factors may have played a contributing role, it appears that risk-based capital requirements combined with stricter bank examination standards contributed to a credit crunch and adversely affected the monetary aggregates.

References

Baer, Herbert L., and John N. McElravey (1992), "Capital Adequacy and the Growth of U.S. Banks," Federal Reserve Bank of Chicago Working Paper 92-11.

Berger, Alan, Richard J. Herring, and Giorgio P. Szego (1995), "The Role of Capital in Financial Institutions," *Journal of Banking and Finance*, Vol. 19 June, 393-430.

Berger, Alan N., and Greg F. Udell (1994), "Did Risk-Based Capital Allocate Bank Credit and Cause a 'Credit Crunch' in the U.S." *Journal of Money, Credit and Banking*, Vol. 26 Part 2, 585-628.

Bernanke, Ben S., and Mark Gertler (1987), "Banking and Macroeconomic Equilibrium," in *New Approaches to Monetary Economics*, edited by W. Barnett & K. Singleton, Cambridge University Press.

Bernanke Ben, and Cara S. Lown (1991), "The Credit Crunch," *Brookings Papers on Economic Activity*, No. 2, 205-48.

Bliss, Robert R. (1995), "Risk-Based Capital: Issues and Solutions," Federal Reserve Bank of Atlanta *Economic Review*, September/October, 32-40.

Boyd, John H., and Mark Gertler (1993), "Trends in Commercial Banking," National Bureau of Economic Research *Macroeconomic Annual*.

Estrella, Arturo (1995), "A Prolegomenon to Future Capital Requirements," Federal Reserve Bank of New York *Economic Policy Review*, Vol. 1 July, 1-12.

Federal Financial Institutions Examination Council (1992), *Study on Regulatory Burden.*

Furlong, Frederick T. (1992), "Capital Regulation and Bank Lending," Federal Reserve Bank of San Francisco *Economic Review*, 23-33.

Greenspan, Alan (1990), Congressional testimony before the Subcommittee on Commerce, Consumer, and Monetary Affairs of the Committee on Government Operations, U.S. House of Representatives, October 3.

Hahn, Phillip J. (1966), *The Capital Adequacy of Commercial Banks* (New York: The American Press).

Hopper, Gregory P. (1996), "Value at Risk: A New Methodology for Measuring Portfolio Risk," Federal Reserve Bank of Philadelphia *Business Review*, July/August, 19-31.

Houpt, James V. and James A. Embersit (1991), "A Method for Evaluating Interest Rate Risk in U.S. Commercial Banks," *Federal Reserve Bulletin*, 625-37.

Johnson, Ronald (1991), "The Bank Credit 'Crumble'," Federal Reserve Bank of New York Quarterly Review, Vol. 16, 40-51.

Keeley, Michael C. (1990), "Deposit Insurance, Risk, and Market Power," *American Economic Review* 80, December, 1183-1200.

Kupiec, Paul H., and James O'Brien (1995), "A Pre-Commitment Approach to Capital Requirements for Market Risk," Federal Reserve Board of Governors, Working Paper No. 95-36, July.

Lown, Cara S., and Stavros Peristiani (1996), "The Behavior of Consumer Loan Rates During the 1990 Credit Slowdown," *Journal of Banking and Finance* 20, 1673-94.

Lown, Cara S., and John Wenninger (1994), "The Role of the Banking System in the Credit Slowdown," *Studies on Causes and Consequences of the 1989-92 Credit Slowdown*, Federal Reserve Bank of New York, 69-112.

Marcus, Alan J. (1984) "Deregulation and Bank Financial Policy," *Journal of Banking and Finance* 8, 557-65.

Merton, Robert C. (1977) "An Analytical Derivation of the Cost of Deposit Insurance and Loan Guarantees: An Application of Modern Option Pricing Theory," *Journal of Banking and Finance* 1, 3-11.

Orgler, Yair E., and Benjamin Wolkowitz (1976), *Bank Capital* (New York: Nortrand Reinhold Company).

Peek, Joe, and Eric S. Rosengren (1995), "The Capital Crunch: Neither a Borrower Nor a Lender Be," *Journal of Money, Banking, and Credit* 29, 625-638.

Schwartz, Anna J. (1988), "Financial Stability and the Federal Safety Net," in *Restructuring Banking and Financial Services in America,* edited by W.S. Haraf and R.M. Kushmeider, (Washington, D.C.: American Enterprise Institute.)

Smith, Adam (1937), *An Inquiry into the Nature and Causes of the Wealth of Nations* (New York: The Modern Library).

Syron, Richard (1991), "Are We Experiencing a Credit Crunch," Federal Reserve Bank of Boston *Economic Review* (July/August), 3-10.

White, Lawrence J. (1989), "The Reform of Federal Deposit Insurance," *Journal of Economic Perspectives* 3, Fall, 11-29.

Comments on...

*Restructuring Bank Regulation:
Conflicts of Interest, Stability,
and Universal Banking*

and

*Capital Regulation and
Depository Institutions*

Thomas A. Durkin[1]
Senior Economist
Board of Governors of the Federal Reserve System

When I was asked to discuss some papers on bank regulation at this conference—but before I actually saw the papers—I assumed that my expected role here would be to give some sort of view from Washington. I thought you wanted me to say, "Yes, we know the forest is interesting, but in the capital we have to deal with all these trees."

Then I received the two papers and I would not really characterize either as a forest paper. Each focuses on a specific tree or grove of trees in the rain forest of regulation, albeit a big and important one. After commenting specifically on each of the papers, I will then fulfill expectations and say something briefly about some of the other trees.

I like each of these papers; each provides an interesting perspective on an important problem. Each is readable and accessible. The paper by Cara S. Lown, Stavros Peristiani and Kenneth Robinson examines an issue that has been important in Washington: the impact of risk-based capital requirements on the so-called credit crunch of the early 1990s. The paper by Randall S. Kroszner focuses on the empirical relevance of concerns about conflicts of interest and financial stability in the debate over permitting investment banking powers and equity ownership by commercial banks in this country.

At its outset, Dr. Lown's paper does something I like: it gives a brief historical review of the evolution of the Basle Accord and the risk-based capital rules. Unfortunately, it so often seems that a sense of history is missing in the development of the regulatory apparatus. Naturally, it is not possible to go very far down this road in a short paper, but this treatment gives a glimmer of where the risk-based rules come from, what they are and where they might be going.

Basically, the paper asks the question, "What are the side effects of the capital rules?" Then it explores empirically some effects of

1. Board of Governors of the Federal Reserve System. The views expressed here are those of the author alone and do not reflect those of the Federal Reserve Board of Governors, its members, banks or staff.

changes in the capital requirements on credit availability and monetary policy. The findings in both areas make sense.

Concerning the first question, the authors show empirically that the link of capital to lending and to loan rates depended upon the level of capitalization. Lending and loan rates were affected by the tightened capital requirements at undercapitalized banks, which would be the case if the increased capitalization requirements really affected these institutions.

On the second issue, the authors also find that weakness in M2 growth at institutions during the period in question, as well as difficulty in predicting money growth, is statistically related to capital levels.

One suggestion is that demand factors do not seem to be explored. Although there is discussion of reduced-form equations, there does not seem to be any discussion of demand factors. Since implementation of the new capital rules coincided with the recessionary and slow-growth period in the early 1990s, demand factors affecting different institutions differently clearly could have been important in the measured lending slowdown at some institutions. There was much discussion in Washington concerning this possibility at the time.

In the paper there is also some discussion of the need for regulation to protect the federal safety net, although there is no empirical work on this point. This discussion complements the discussion of problems associated with regulation. However, in the empirical context of the rest of the paper it seems this discussion is a bit extraneous, although it raises the important question, also discussed by others, about whether the federal safety net undermines market incentives. This latter point institutes a direct transition to the second paper.

Like the paper by Dr. Lown, et al., the paper by Dr. Kroszner begins with a useful historical orientation. It reviews a variety of empirical studies (notably including the author's own, with a colleague) on the issue of whether there really were conflicts of interest to the detriment of external securities investors at institutions that combined commercial banking and investment banking before passage of the Glass-Steagall Act. It then moves on to focus on some other aspects of current financial law that might mitigate the positive impacts of universal banking on corporate governance that repeal of

Glass-Steagall might otherwise promise. Finally, the paper discusses the question of whether the banking system is inherently less stable than other sectors and whether expansion of bank powers into securities markets and equity ownership would affect stability.

Unlike the paper by Dr. Lown, et al., this paper does not report tables and equations from new empirical work as it discusses each of the issues of its focus. Rather, it summarizes in an accessible manner a large body of empirical efforts from elsewhere. In the process, the author finds no support for the naive-investor hypothesis that commercial-investment banks took advantage of other investors. Instead, he finds evidence that markets required "adaptation" in the behavior of institutions in which conflicts associated with combining commercial and investment banking might pose a problem, essentially a signalling phenomenon. He also finds support for the view that markets required elements of separation between the commercial-banking and investment-banking components of organizations. He interprets both bodies of evidence as support for repeal of Glass-Steagall.

In a second section of the paper, the author switches gears to focus on how the legal doctrines of "equitable subordination" and "lender liability" may well diminish the benefits of repeal of Glass-Steagall. While I think his points are interesting and are well taken, they necessarily take on the nature of comparisons across countries rather than good, old-fashioned empirical work of a sort that is obviously impossible on a suggestion that is contrary to current legal requirements.

Finally, the author examines the issue of safety nets and market discipline. While other authors have addressed this issue, the question is so important that the effort is not redundant. It is a clear, concise review of a variety of other works, reaching the conclusion that market forces are important and should be utilized whenever possible. He does not have a hard sell with me on those points.

As I have said, both of these papers concentrate on important questions. There is, of course, more to banking regulation than the specific focus of these papers, and it seems that the extent of banking regulation may now be sufficient that it raises questions of economic efficiency. First of all, banks are subject to general business regulations. These include required compliance with laws or rules concerning antitrust, taxes, occupational health and safety, the environment and equal employment opportunity, among others. Banks are also subject to specialized regulations that arise from their nature because they are: 1) central to the payments and economic system (as both Dr. Lown, et al., and Dr. Kroszner note), and 2) institutions whose creditors are neither capitalists nor entrepreneurial risk takers, but customers.

There have been four main thrusts of banking regulation throughout American history, each with specific goals and rationales at various times: 1) market structure and competition, 2) banking safety, 3) monetary and systemic stability, and 4) consumer protection. Each of these is manifest in an extended listing of areas of regulatory concern (see Table 1).

Table 1: Areas of Regulatory Concern

Supervisory Policies	Entry Controls (e.g., Chartering, Change in Control, Branching, Powers)
	Balance Sheet Requirements (e.g., Capital, Lending Limits, Accounting Rules)
	Activity Limits (e.g., Limits on Domestic, Foreign Products)
	Enforcement (e.g., C.&D.s, Rules of Practice and Procedure)
	Insider and Affiliate Transactions (e.g., Employee and Director Requirements)
Consumer Protection Policies	Consumer Disclosure (e.g., Truth in Lending, Electronic Funds Transfers)
	Antidiscrimination (e.g., Equal Credit Opportunity)
	Community Reinvestment (e.g., Home Mortgage Disclosure Act, Community Reinvestment Act)
	Unfair Practices (e.g., Credit Practices, Delayed Funds Availability)

Table 1: Areas of Regulatory Concern *(continued)*

Other Operating Requirements	Operating Procedures (e.g., Payments System, Bank Security, Appraisals)
	Monetary Policy (e.g., Reserve Requirements)
	Deposit Insurance Requirements
	Bank Secrecy Act Requirements (e.g., Cash Transaction Reports)
	Internal Revenue Requirements (e.g., Form 1099 Reporting)
Reporting, Record Keeping, Documentation Requirements	Call Reports
	Other Supervisory Reports
	Other Supervisory Record Keeping Requirements
	Applications
	Reports for Economic Policy Purposes

The specifics of the regulations are so extensive and confining that they prompted the Federal Financial Institutions Examination Council (FFIEC), itself a regulator, to write the following in its 1992 Study on Regulatory Burden (p. II-11): "Although each regulation by itself may not impose an unmanageable cost, the banking regulations taken together create a burden that may be substantial, if not approaching unmanageable, for many institutions."

Sometimes it seems difficult even to illustrate effectively the range of banking regulation. Let me try briefly in a number of ways:

- Federal Reserve regulations, interpretations and other regulatory materials are contained in four telephone-book size binders with pages of tissue-paper thickness and tiny type. There are also three other regulators of depository institutions.
- Currently, the Federal Reserve has 37 docket listings of changes in various stages of the public-comment and implementation process. Seven of these are on risk-based capital alone.
- Truth in Lending, a simple idea, involves more than 300 pages of the tiny type to contain its regulatory materials (including the text of the act).

- The FFIEC estimated that "regulatory costs to the industry in 1991 could be between $7.5 and $17 billion without any adjustment for the costs of reserve requirements." (Study on Regulatory Burden, p. 4).[2] Outweighing costs such as these puts a large responsibility onto the benefits side.

Like the authors of these papers, I do not have all of the answers about all of these issues. None of us even has all of the questions. It seems that capitalism will find a way, however, even if inefficient. Both of these papers contain interesting views of aspects of the problem.

---

2.   An excellent new report by Gregory E. Elliehausen reviews available studies of the costs of banking regulation, puts them on a common footing, and makes methodological suggestions that should be useful for future research. See Gregory E. Elliehausen, "The Cost of Banking Regulation: A Review of the Evidence," Board of Governors of the Federal Reserve System, Staff Study 171, April 1998.

Benjamin C. Esty
Assistant Professor of Business Administration
Harvard Business School

My comments for this session on banking regulation fall into categories: 1) the conference's focus, 2) the paper by Randall S. Kroszner, and 3) the paper by Cara S. Lown, Stavros Peristiani and Kenneth Robinson. I enjoyed reading both papers and think they captured two interesting, and very topical, aspects of banking regulation: Dr. Kroszner examines the impact of regulation on the scope of banking activities while Dr. Lown and her colleagues examine the impact of regulation on the execution of traditional banking activities, namely lending.

Before I get to my comments on the papers, I want to make a few more general comments on our focus here today. The title of this conference, "Restructuring Regulation and Financial Institutions," is very reminiscent of a study commissioned by President Nixon in 1970. The purpose of the President's Commission on Financial Structure and Regulation (known as the Hunt Commission) was: "to review and study the structure, operation and regulation of the private financial institutions in the United States for purposes of formulating recommendations that would improve the functioning of the private financial system." That sounds like it could have been the preamble for this conference.

It is interesting to step back and see what those commission participants concluded at the time and what we have learned in the intervening 25 years. Based on my reading of the report and my observations regarding regulatory change since that time, I come to the conclusion that "the more things change, the more they stay the same."[1]

I am concerned that we, like the Hunt Commission, are adopting an institutional focus. The sessions here today have titles such as banking, mutual funds, pension funds, insurance, and government-

---

1. The Hunt Commission's focus was on consumer finance, particularly mortgage finance. It recognized the importance of technology and inflation as change agents, and recommended leveling the playing field between different types of financial institutions (those that perform similar functions) by removing discriminatory regulation.

sponsored entities—clearly the sessions are organized around institutions. In lieu of an institutional focus, which I think is somewhat mis-
guided, I think it would be more appropriate to focus on the functions
these institutions perform. Several colleagues of mine at the Harvard
Business School have recently written a book entitled "The Global
Financial System: A Functional Perspective" (Crane et al., 1995), in
which they describe and illustrate the functional approach to regulation. For those of you who have not read the book, I recommend it. To
be forward looking, the authors argue, one needs to take a functional
perspective because the boundaries between organizations, markets,
and countries are no longer as clear as they have been historically.
While the institutional framework is not an appropriate framework for
analyzing the future, it is more appropriate for analyzing the past.

Nevertheless, I think even when one studies history, it is important to think in terms of functions, which is what Dr. Kroszner's paper
illustrates. His paper about security issuance prior to the passage of
the Glass-Steagall Act of 1933 is not really about banks versus investment banks or about banking in general, but rather the function of
underwriting securities and the potential for conflicts of interest. I do
not mean to imply that historical institutional analysis cannot be
informative especially given the fact that I, too, have written about
historical banking regulation (Esty, 1998). In fact, this kind of
research reminds me of one of my favorite quotations. Like many
witty, insightful sayings, it is attributed to Mark Twain, who put a
wonderful twist on Santayana's admonition about history: "Those
who forget the past are condemned to repeat it." Twain wrote, "History does not repeat itself, but sometimes it rhymes."

Because the world has changed so dramatically since the
1920s—the advent and use of computer technology is just one example of change—history will not repeat itself. Yet, certain aspects of
history may shed some light on current regulatory debates, even
though one has to be careful with historical analysis and interpretation.

At the start of his paper, Dr. Kroszner writes, "Investigating this
historical episode (during the 1920s and 1930s) is crucial...because it
suggests how market forces may address conflict-of-interest issues..."
My concern is Dr. Kroszner's assumption that the markets were
"unregulated" prior to 1933, which is not the case. They were regu-

lated, just in a different fashion. Before one can make historical judgments about the period, never mind draw implications for regulating financial institutions in the modern era, one must have a solid understanding of the regulation that existed at the time.

In a recently published paper (Esty, 1998), I analyzed the impact of contingent liability on commercial-bank risk taking. Contingent liability was a critical aspect of the regulatory system in place prior to the passage of the Glass-Steagall Act of 1933. In a system with contingent liability, regulators could assess bank shareholders to cover shortfalls between assets and liabilities in the event of failure. Essentially, contingent liability was a way to prevent equity holders from maximizing the option value of their levered equity through risk shifting (see Green, 1984 or Esty, 1997). Among other things, I found that contingent liability was effective in limiting risk-taking incentives. Another important finding was the fact that most bank closures prior to 1920 were voluntary. In contrast, I do not think there has been a voluntary bank closure since the creation of deposit insurance almost 65 years ago.

Contingent liability is relevant to Dr. Kroszner's paper because it provides an alternative, untested hypothesis. Because I do not know what kind of liability rules were placed on investment banks (possibly limited liability?), yet I know that all New York commercial banks were subject to double liability, it is possible that commercial banks were subject to stricter liability rules. As a result, banks chose to hold and underwrite safer securities, which is consistent with the paper's findings.

Failure to analyze and control for differences in liability rules creates an omitted variable bias that may or may not affect the results. In the next version of the paper, I would like answers to the following questions: What were the liability rules for investment banks and for bank affiliates? Before we declare universal banking a good thing based on evidence from 1920-1930, we need a better understanding of the existing regulatory structures because part of the outcomes may be attributable to other forms of regulation, such as contingent liability.

I have two other suggestions regarding additional analysis that I think might strengthen the paper. First, I would like to see an analysis of default rates, not just a comparison of yields, for bank affiliate groups versus internal bank underwriting groups. Are internal groups, in fact, underwriting riskier securities as measured by actual performance—though I recognize *ex post* performance is not always a good measure of *ex ante* risk? Second, I think a more direct test of the "naïve investor hypothesis" would be to analyze what issuers do with the proceeds. If the "naïve investor hypothesis" is true and if banks are subject to a conflict of interest, then issuers should use the proceeds to repay bank debt. Is this the case? What do issuers do with the proceeds?

I turn now to the second paper by Dr. Lown et al., which examines the impact of capital regulations on bank lending and concludes that curtailed lending by the largest banks contributed to the slowdown in economic activity in the early 1990s. Besides an historical note that relates to a similar comment made above, I have three empirical suggestions for this paper. Before the authors can credibly conclude correlation, not to mention the implied causality between lending and macroeconomic performance, additional empirical analysis is required.

In Figure 1, the authors note the gradual decline of capital ratios from 1863 to 1935, exactly the period when contingent liability was in effect for banks. In effect, bankers chose to maintain additional capital to prevent future assessments. In my 1998 *Journal of Financial Economics* paper (Esty, 1998), I find that banks subject to stricter liability rules have higher capital ratios. And when capital disappeared through losses, bankers chose voluntary liquidation often before the market value of net worth became negative. Yet, after gradual elimination of contingent liability beginning in the 1930s, it was rational to increase leverage. My point here is simply that one has to imbed such historical analysis in the regulatory framework in place at the time and not just assume that either market forces or "informal" (the authors' term) policies were at work.

In terms of empirical analysis, I propose an alternative hypothesis for the decrease in bank lending that merits further analysis. It is possible that the slowdown in lending was not in response to stricter capital standards, but rather a decline in banks' investment opportunity set. If the attractiveness of lending opportunities decreased as the country entered a recession, then it would be rational, and optimal, for banks to curtail lending. Viewed in this light, the recession caused the decrease in lending, not the other way around as assumed in the paper.

What I am highlighting is a problem of endogeneity in both the hypothesis and the empirical analysis.

To test this alternative hypothesis and to address the econometric problem of endogeneity, I suggest the authors rerun the analysis in Table 2 in terms of changes on changes (alternatively, they could run two-stage least squares). The current regression specification has the *change* in lending as a function of the initial *level* of leverage. To conclude that changing capital had an effect on bank lending, this regression should use the change in leverage as an independent variable instead.

I also have an alternative hypothesis for the results shown in Figures 2 and 3—the findings that undercapitalized banks charged higher rates because of stricter capital standards. The theory of risk shifting predicts that leverage increases the incentive to invest in risky assets. Thus, we would expect undercapitalized banks (i.e., more highly leveraged banks) to invest in more risky assets, which is exactly what the authors find. These banks are not charging higher rates because of capital requirements, but rather investing in risky assets, which shows up as higher portfolio yields. I am not sure how to distinguish these two theories because they both generate similar empirical predictions. Even so, I suggest the authors consider other tests that might be able to discriminate between the two.

In conclusion, I enjoyed both papers, but remain a little skeptical about their conclusions in the absence of further analysis. The process of regulation or deregulation is about "picking poisons." There are always benefits and there are always costs. The key is to make sure one has accurately incorporated the major benefits and costs.

References

Crane, Dwight B., et al, 1995, *The Global Financial System: A Functional Perspective*, Harvard Business School Press (Boston, MA).

Esty, Benjamin C., 1998, "The Impact of Contingent Liability on Commercial Bank Risk Taking," *Journal of Financial Economics* 47, 189-218.

Esty, Benjamin C., 1997, "Organizational Form and Risk Taking in the Savings and Loan Industry," *Journal of Financial Economics* 44, 25-55.

Green, Richard C., 1984, "Investment Incentives, Debt, and Warrants," *Journal of Financial Economics* 13, 115-136.

Kroszner, Randall S., 1998, "Restructuring Bank Regulation: Conflicts of Interest, Stability, and Universal Banking," University of Chicago mimeo, March.

Lown, Cara S., 1998, "Capital Regulation and Depository Institutions," Federal Reserve Bank of New York Working Paper.

President's Commission on Financial Structure and Regulation, 1971, Final report, Chairman Reed O. Hunt (Hunt Commission), December 22.

Arthur W. Leibold Jr., Esq.

If your experience on "regulation versus the free market" over the last 25 years results from dealing with the Federal Home Loan Bank Board and the Office of Thrift Supervision, the free market wins every time. If, in fact, this even means lawsuits by stockholders dealing in terms of Dr. Kroszner's issues about the Bankruptcy Act and securities laws, even though I've been on the defense side rather than the plaintiffs' side, I believe that the free market, including lawsuits, is superior to regulators.

Now, someone at some point, whether it be James R. Barth [formerly Chief Economist at the Office of Thrift Supervision, now Senior Finance Fellow at the Milken Institute] or someone else, may analyze the consequences of the mutual operations of the segment of the savings and loan industry, because the Federal Home Loan Bank Board's analyses and actions stem very significantly from dealing with no stockholders, but rather dealing with so-called "mutual institution owners." For those of you who are acquainted with Original Sin, I think that the Bank Board's philosophy is an example, because the Bank Board's concept of conflict of interest was controlling people of mutual institutions versus the depositors and versus the government. Then, when the Bank Board took into account stockholders, the element of alleged greed became involved.

Nonetheless, Bank Board policy had a tremendous overhang of mutuality. Then one proceeded, of course, to the Financial Institutions Reform, Recovery and Enforcement Act (1989), and Congress giving substantial power to agencies to sue people, whether administratively or in civil courts. We do not have the time to get into that in detail, but again, we had a form of regulation in which, instead of using a "free market of lawsuits," the Congress proceeded with a sledgehammer approach to government agencies. At some point, we will possibly be able to analyze the results of that tremendous grant of power to federal agencies such as the Federal Deposit Insurance Corporation and others.

My own reaction to Glass-Steagall was that for many purposes, it has not existed for quite some length of time, other than being there in name. There have been ways of avoiding it, possibly even evading it.

At some point, Congress, even though it may create a political problem for some members, probably will recognize that it is appropriate to repeal Glass-Steagall.

João A. C. Santos[1]
Economist
Bank for International Settlements

The paper by Randall S. Kroszner reviews the empirical evidence on two issues—conflicts of interest and the stability of banks—that are at the center of the ongoing debate over expanding the powers of commercial banking organizations to include investment banking and equity ownership.[2] He relies on recent studies of banks' investment-banking activities prior to Glass-Steagall to support the repeal of that act and to argue that market forces, rather than regulations, should dictate the organizational structure of banking conglomerates.

The location of the investment banking activities in the organizational structure of a banking conglomerate has now moved to the center of the debate over repealing the Glass-Steagall Act because of the different proposals put forth by the agencies charged with regulating and supervising banks. These agencies all agree on allowing commercial banking companies to reenter the investment banking business provided they house the securities activities in a separately capitalized unit. However, they have argued for different regulations on the location of the securities unit in the conglomerate. The Office of the Comptroller of the Currency and the Federal Deposit Insurance Corporation have manifested their preference for a regulation allowing banks to undertake such activities in one of their subsidiaries or in a subsidiary of a holding company that also owns the bank. The Federal Reserve System has expressed its preference for a regulation requiring banks to adopt the holding company model to combine commercial banking with investment banking.

In the United States, banks' securities powers and the organizational models that they are allowed to adopt in order to offer securities services vary with the bank charter. Since the enactment of the Glass-Steagall Act in 1933, banks have been permitted to undertake only a very limited set of securities activities in-house. State-chartered mem-

---

1. The views stated herein are those of the author and are not necessarily the views of the Bank for International Settlements.
2. See Rajan (1996) or Santos (1998a) for a review of the literature on the potential effects of commercial banks' expansion into investment banking.

ber banks can offer some additional securities services if they situate them in a subsidiary of a bank holding company (BHC). National banks and state-chartered nonmember banks are also allowed to offer a broader set of securities services if they situate them in a separate unit, which can be a subsidiary of a BHC or a subsidiary that they own.[3]

Dr. Kroszner argues, based on pre-Glass-Steagall evidence, that banks value the ability to choose where to locate the securities activities in their organizations. International evidence on the predominant organizational model in each country appears to corroborate that claim and to indicate that banks prefer to undertake their securities activities either in-house or in one of their subsidiaries.[4]

Table 1 presents that information for several countries. It highlights two important facts. First, the vast majority of the countries considered allow banks to offer securities services either in-house or through their subsidiaries. Second, in countries where banking companies have more freedom to choose where to locate the securities activities, they choose in most cases to locate them within the bank. When they opt to implement corporate separateness, they prefer to offer such services through one of their subsidiaries. The holding company model does not appear to be frequently used abroad to combine commercial banking with investment banking. In considering the international evidence, however, one should take into account two important caveats. Factors idiosyncratic to each country may influence banks' choices of the organizational model and, if there are market imperfections, a certain model may predominate, not because it is the most efficient, but because it is, for example, the best organizational structure for extracting rents.

---

3. See Pollard, Passaic, Ellis, and Daly (1988) for a detailed presentation of the U.S. regulations.
4. See Santos (1998b) for a discussion of the advantages and disadvantages of the various organizational models most frequently adopted to combine commercial banking with investment banking.

Table 1: Permissible Corporate Organizational Forms[a]

Countries	Bank Holding Company Permitted	Securities Activities[b]			
		Directly In The Bank	Bank Subsidiary	Bank Holding Company Subsidiary	Most Frequently Conducted In
Austria	Yes, but infrequently used	Yes	Yes	Yes	Bank[c]
Canada	No	No	Yes	No	Bank subsidiary
Finland	Yes, but infrequently used	Yes	Yes	Yes	Bank
Germany	Yes, but infrequently used	Yes	Yes	Yes	Bank
Greece	No[d]	Yes[e]	Yes	No	Bank subsidiary
Ireland	Yes, but infrequently used	Yes	Yes	No	Bank subsidiary
Italy	Yes, widely used	Yes	Yes	No	Bank
Luxembourg	No[f]	Yes	Yes	No	Bank
Netherlands	Yes, widely used	Yes	Yes	Yes	Bank
Portugal	Yes, but infrequently used	Yes	Yes	Yes	Bank & bank subsidiary
Spain	Yes, but infrequently used	Yes	Yes	NA	Bank & bank[g] subsidiary
Sweden	No	Yes	Yes	No	Bank
Switzerland	Yes, but infrequently used	Yes	Yes	Yes	Bank
United Kingdom	Yes, but infrequently used	Yes	Yes	Yes	Varies

Source: Barth, Nolle, and Rice (1997).

a. Information as of January 1997.
b. Securities activities include underwriting, dealing and brokering in all kinds of securities and all aspects of mutual funds business.
c. Securities activities fall under the banking activities provisions of Section 1 of the Austrian Banking Act. Hence, such business may be conducted exclusively by a bank.
d. Holding companies may own the majority of shares in a Greek bank, but there is no specific legal framework referring to such companies.
e. Only underwriting and custodian services
f. Pure holding companies are permitted to incorporate under Luxembourg law, but the statute of a BHC does not exist. This type of company is not submitted to any prudential control by any authority.
g. Public debt directly in bank and stock exchange in bank subsidiary.

With respect to the second topic of Dr. Kroszner's paper, the possible expansion of commercial banks' powers to include ownership of nonfinancial companies' equity, the author discusses the negative impact that the doctrine of equitable subordination is likely to have on U.S. banks' incentive to take equity positions in these companies. Besides that disincentive, which also exists in other countries such as Britain, the current proposals would still introduce a regulation significantly more restrictive than those in force elsewhere (see Table 2). The current U.S. regulations generally prohibit national and state member banks from making direct equity investments in voting or nonvoting stock. State nonmember banks are generally limited to investments that are permissible for national banks. With respect to BHCs, they are limited to investments that do not exceed 5 percent of a nonfinancial company's capital. The proposals under consideration to change the existing regulation would relax the conditions under which BHCs can invest in nonfinancial companies, but they would still prohibit banks from taking equity positions in such companies.

Table 2: Commercial Banks' Investments in Nonfinancial Firms

Countries	Regulations
Austria	Complies with the EC Second Banking Directive.[a]
Belgium	A single share holding may not exceed 10% of a bank's own funds and such holdings may not exceed 35% of a bank's own funds on an aggregated basis.
Canada	Limited to 10% of outstanding shares of a nonfinancial firm, with aggregate holdings not to exceed 70% of bank capital.
Denmark	Complies with the EC Second Banking Directive. However, a bank may not hold a permanent decisive participation in nonfinancial firms.[a]
Finland	Complies with the EC Second Banking Directive.[a]
France	Complies with the EC Second Banking Directive.[a]
Germany	Complies with the EC Second Banking Directive.[a]
Greece	Complies with the EC Second Banking Directive.[a]
Ireland	Complies with the EC Second Banking Directive.[a]
Italy	Most banks are subject to an overall investment limit of 15% of own funds (7.5% in the case of unlisted firms) and to a concentration limit of 3% of own funds in each holding in nonfinancial firms or groups.
Japan	A single bank's ownership is limited to 5% of a nonfinancial firm.
Luxembourg	Complies with the EC Second Banking Directive.[a]
Portugal	Complies with the EC Second Banking Directive.[a] However, a bank may not control more than 25% of the voting rights of a nonfinancial firm.

**Table 2: Commercial Banks' Investments in
Nonfinancial Firms** *(continued)*

Countries	Regulations
Spain	Complies with the EC Second Banking Directive.[a]
Sweden	Investments on an aggregated basis are limited to 40% of a bank's own funds. Ownership in a firm is limited to 5% of this base and it cannot exceed 5% of the firm's voting rights.
Switzerland	A single participation is limited to the equivalent of 20% of the bank's capital. However, the Swiss Banking Commission can allow this limit to be exceeded.
United Kingdom	Complies with the EC Second Banking Directive.[a] However, an ownership share of more than 20% requires that the investment be deducted from the bank's capital when calculating its capital adequacy. Otherwise, the investment is treated as a loan.

Source: Barth, Nolle, and Rice (1997).

a. The EC Second Banking Directive limits each qualifying investment (defined as a direct or indirect holding in a firm equal to at least 10% of its capital or voting rights) in a nonfinancial firm to no more than 15% of the bank's own funds, and the total qualifying investments to no more than 60% of the bank's funds. These limits may be exceeded, but the amount by which they are exceeded must be covered by the bank's own funds and these funds may not be included in the solvency-ratio calculation.

The debate on the expansion of commercial-banking company powers to include equity investments has focused on the potential impact of this expansion on banks' stability. The implications of allowing commercial banks to take equity positions in nonfinancial companies, however, go far beyond that impact. Such investments will affect, among other things, the nature of the relationship that banks have with their borrowers, including banks' monitoring in normal periods and in periods of financial stress, and the design of the contracts that banks can offer borrowers. These effects will in turn influence borrowers' incentives and the availability and cost of funds.

Research does show that banks' investment in borrowers' capital is beneficial for these companies.[5] It is possible to achieve part of these benefits even when banks do not take equity positions because banks will, for example, design covenants to the debt contracts in an

5. See Saunders (1994) or Santos (1998c) for a review of the literature on banking and commerce.

attempt to replicate the contracts that would be available to them if they could use equity in addition to debt to fund companies. However, because they will not be able to span that space of contracts without using equity contracts, the prohibition to take equity positions in non-financial companies will be costly. Therefore, it would seem important for lawmakers to consider such costs together with the potential impact on banks' stability when deciding the conditions under which commercial banks will be allowed to invest in the capital of nonfinancial companies.

Like Dr. Kroszner's paper, the paper by Cara S. Lown, Stavros Peristiani and Kenneth Robinson also focuses on banking regulation, in particular the side effects that arise when there is a change in a regulation. The authors illustrate these effects through the study of the implementation of the 1988 Basle Accord on capital standards. They claim that the introduction of the new capital regulation had an adverse effect on banks' lending and it led to an increase in the interest rates charged on automobile and personal loans. They also claim that the new regulation influenced the monetary aggregate M2.

There has been an important debate about the possible causes of the credit slowdown that occurred in the United Sates in the late 1980s and early 1990s. Part of it has focused on the potential causes of the slowdown, in particular on whether it was mainly driven by demand or supply factors. The implementation of the Basle Accord has been frequently indicated in that debate as a key contributor to the reduction in commercial banks' lending. As mentioned above, the paper by Dr. Lown and her colleagues also defends this view. Furthermore, the writers claim that larger banks were the main contributors for that reduction.

The identification of the banking segment most responsible for the credit slowdown is important because of the difference in the portfolio of companies that usually do business with small and larger banks. Small companies raise most of their funding from the banking sector, particularly from smaller banks. Larger companies also raise funding from the banking sector, but mainly from larger banks (see Table 3). There are several reasons for that pattern. Small companies depend on banks because of the problems they have accessing capital markets. In addition, because small companies are less well-known and have problems providing the information that a standard loan evaluation procedure requires, they tend to do better with banks that are willing to invest heavily in information gathering. Large companies are not subject to such problems. As a result, they are able to raise funding from capital markets, and they do well with banks that have a standard loan evaluation model.

Table 3: Outstanding C&I Credit (June 1993)[a]

Bank size by assets	Number of banks	Portfolio of shares of outstanding C&I credit by bank size			Proportion of outstanding C&I credit by credit size		
		≤ $1 M	> $1 M	Total	≤ $1 M	> $1 M	Total
0–50M	5,333	0.980	0.020	1.000	0.073	0.001	0.028
50M–250M	4,927	0.917	0.083	1.000	0.266	0.014	0.107
250M–1B	937	0.693	0.307	1.000	0.183	0.047	0.097
1B–10B	350	0.347	0.653	1.000	0.300	0.329	0.318
>10B	53	0.145	0.855	1.000	0.178	0.609	0.450
All Banks	11,600	0.368	0.632	1.000	1.000	1.000	1.000

a. All computations based on Call Report data. T-thousands, M-millions, and B-billions of U.S. dollars respectively.

With respect to banks, although large banks can service both small and large companies, they tend to prefer the latter. These companies are better known, and some even have credit ratings, thus requiring less information gathering and making it easier to evaluate their risk. In addition, these companies give banks the opportunity to explore the scale economies of granting and administering large loans. Small banks, however, concentrate on small companies. They do not offer the pool of services demanded by large companies, and have problems giving large loans because of the difficulties these create for their diversification objectives and for their compliance with the regulation on risk exposure.[6]

Given that pattern of relationships, one would expect that a credit slowdown in the large bank segment would mostly affect large companies, giving them an added incentive to raise funding from alternative sources. As a complementary test to that adopted by the authors, it would be interesting to study the composition of large companies' sources of funding following the introduction of the Basle Accord.

6. Banks are required to limit their exposure to any single borrower to 15 percent of their capital.

Another side effect of the new bank capital regulation mentioned by the authors of that paper is the establishment of a permanent link between bank capital and bank lending. While that linkage was probably strong in the period immediately following the introduction of the new standards, its strength, however, tends to decrease with time. As happened with other regulations, whenever they started preventing banks from exploring potentially profitable opportunities, banks developed instruments to sidestep them, which in some cases prompted further action by regulators. This interaction between banks and their regulators sometimes resembles a cat-and-mouse game, or what Professor Edward Kane has termed the "regulatory dialectic."[7] Banks, for example, avoided deposit-rate ceilings by making implicit interest payments (they offered free gifts to depositors). They avoided the prohibition on interstate branching by creating BHCs with banks in multiple states. They circumvented the Glass-Steagall Act by developing new financial products, such as market-indexed deposit accounts. In the case of capital regulation, banks have avoided some of the burden it imposes on them by securitizing certain classes of loans, thus reducing the strength of the capital-lending relationship noted above.

In conclusion, the insights of the two papers discussed here are particularly timely because of the ongoing debate over reforming the Glass-Steagall Act. Among other things, they suggest that lawmakers consider the market forces and the banks' incentives when hammering out the final provisions of the reform bill. Otherwise, we should not be surprised to observe some unintended effects arising with the implementation of that bill, and to see banks challenging the new regulation.

References

Barth, J. R.; Nolle, D. E.; and Rice, T. N. (1997) "Commercial Banking Structure, Regulation, and Performance: An International Comparison." Comptroller of the Currency, Working Paper No. 7. Washington, D.C.

---

7. See Kane (1981) and Santos (1996).

Kane, E. (1981) "Accelerating Inflation, Technological Innovation, and the Decreasing Effectiveness of Banking Regulation," *Journal of Finance* 36, 335-67.

Pollard, A. M.; Passaic, J. G.; Ellis, K. H.; and Daly, J. P. (1988). *Banking Law in the United States.* Boston: Butterworth Legal Publishers.

Rajan, R. G. (1996) "The Entry of Commercial Banks into the Securities Business: A Selective Survey of Theories and Evidence," in *Universal Banking: Financial System Design Reconsidered*, (I. Walter and A. Saunders eds.), Chicago, Irwin, 282-302.

Santos, J. A. C. (1998a) "Commercial Banks in the Securities Business: A Review." Forthcoming in the *Journal of Financial Services Research.*

Santos, J. A. C. (1998b) "Securities Units of Banking Conglomerates: Should Their Location be Regulated?" Forthcoming in the *Cato Journal* 18 (1).

Santos, J. A. C. (1998c) "Mixing Banking and Commerce: A Review," Mimeo Bank for International Settlements.

Santos, J. A. C. (1996) "Glass-Steagall and the Regulatory Dialectic," *Federal Reserve Bank of Cleveland, Economic Commentary*, February 15. Also in the *1997 Readings to The Economics of Money, Banking, and Financial Markets*, (J. W. Eaton & F. S. Miskin eds.), Massachusetts, Addison Wesley, 155-162.

Saunders, A. (1994) "Banking and Commerce: An Overview of the Public Policy Issues," *Journal of Banking and Finance* 18, 231-254.

Section Two

Regulatory Capture at the U.S. Securities and Exchange Commission

Susan E. Woodward
Economics Professor
Stanford Law School

Economists have not been shy in their efforts to explain government decision-making. The optimistic "public interest" approach begins with the proposition that the notion of externalities serves to define the proper role of government and emphasizes the government's role in correcting market imperfections that result from externalities. In this view, regulatory agencies may or may not be well-informed, but they are well-intentioned. An alternative, the "capture" view, focuses on the role of interest groups in shaping public policy.

The more cynical "regulatory capture" intellectual tradition has deep roots. Some have argued that big business sought and paid for control of important economic institutions. Others have argued that even small-business industries could capture their regulators. There is a theory of collective action, which predicts that for a given issue and its interested parties, the smaller the group and the higher the per capita stake, the more likely the group will be successful in organizing and effectively influencing regulatory outcomes. Noting the emergence of powerful consumer groups in the 1970s, some have extended the theory of collective action to incorporate these groups as well, and saw a role for government officials to weigh competing interests and not always choose an outcome that favors business. Still others have emphasized the importance of the complexity of the issue and the resulting information asymmetries among the various interest groups and between the interest groups and the bureaucrats who decide their fate in determining the regulatory outcome.

The U.S. Securities and Exchange Commission is not exempt from these forces. Indeed, if anything the SEC is a more likely candidate for capture for two reasons. First, the lawyers (the majority of SEC professional staff) who work in the regulation-writing divisions often find their best, and best by a wide margin, post-SEC employment opportunities working for the regulatees, and must change fields completely if they go elsewhere. Second, the inherent complexity of the institutions of the securities industry and its regulatory apparatus create substantial fixed costs that purveyors of influence must conquer in order to be effective.[1] These two factors make for powerful forces that push the SEC in the direction of rule changes that help rather than hurt the powerful incumbents of the securities industry.

The SEC is not captured by a single group of regulatees but rather by groups in three areas corresponding to its realms of regulation, each defined by one of the central pieces of enabling legislation that define the SEC's mission:

- The Division of Corporate Finance writes and administers the rules pursuant to the Securities Act of 1933, which provide for disclosure regarding the character of securities sold to the public.
- The Division of Market Regulation writes and administers the rules pursuant to the Securities and Exchange Commission Act of 1934, which provide for the regulation of securities exchanges and dealer markets to prevent unfair practices.
- The Division of Investment Management writes and administers the rules pursuant to the Investment Company Act of 1940, intended to provide for registration and regulation of mutual funds and investment advisers.

Occasionally an issue arises that affects two constituent groups and hence two divisions of the SEC, for example brokers and mutual funds or issuers and mutual funds.

Division of Market Regulation

Market Regulation is the division of the SEC that writes and administers the rules concerning stock trading. This division is captured by the two large incumbent organizations that trade stock: the National Association of Securities Dealers (NASD) and the New York Stock Exchange (NYSE).

The New York Stock Exchange is the venue where the shares of most large public companies are traded. The NYSE sets its standards for companies that can list on its exchange so that only the largest and most successful companies are found there. The NYSE is mainly an auction market, with trading centralized on the floor of the exchange,

---

1. In 1992, the Shadow SEC Committee, a group of academics who are interested in SEC issues, held one of its public meetings to consider several issues before the SEC. The committee voted in favor of recommending that financial disclosures expense stock options granted to employees. The committee chose not to vote on the issue of "payment for order flow," having determined after several hours of discussion that the members would need further study of the institutions before they could decide which policy option (ban or permit payment for order flow) was preferred.

and requires its members to bring or send most customer orders to the exchange floor for execution.

The NASD maintains markets for smaller companies, although many companies that were once small but have grown large, notably the Microsoft Corporation, have chosen to remain listed with the NASD rather than move to the NYSE despite being eligible. The NASD is a dealer market, and member dealers can make a market in any registered stocks they choose. The NASD does maintain central facilities for disseminating dealer quotes in all stocks and for reporting trades in all stocks, but there is no facility like the floor of the NYSE to which all orders are brought. Many members of the NASD are not market makers, but simply order takers who then route customer orders to other members who are market makers. The NASD and NYSE compete for listings (companies that list with them and pay a listing fee to have their stock traded) and also as trading venues, because NASD members are allowed to make a market in NYSE-listed stocks and do attract considerable business away from the NYSE.

The capture of the division of Market Regulation by these two entities manifests itself in barriers to the entry of additional competitors. There are two notable cases that merit extended discussion.

Instinet

Instinet is a computerized trading system. It gives its subscribing members a computer terminal and allows them to place their buy and sell stock-trading orders in the system. These are all in the form of "limit" orders, that is, offers to buy (or sell) a given amount of stock at a given price. The book of prevailing offers to buy and sell in a given stock can be seen by all members, but no names are attached; the orders are anonymous. When an order to buy matches an order to sell, the orders execute automatically. Instinet charges a commission on trades consummated on its system. The size of the commission depends on how much business the member does with Instinet.

Instinet has been a huge success, and even by 1995 was executing 20 to 25 percent of all volume of the National Association of Securities Dealers Automated Quotations (Nasdaq). Instinet began its business by signing up only institutional investors—pension and mutual funds. It was an institutional network. The institutional members valued it for its anonymity (they could not be front-run[2] by Instinet the way they could by placing their order with a live broker-dealer who could trade for his own account), but still did much of their business through traditional brokers because a counterparty was not always available in Instinet.

After much deliberation, Instinet invited the broker/dealer community to join to create a thicker market and found that these members valued their anonymity in Instinet at least as much as the institutions did. Broker/dealers' quotes in the Nasdaq system—their main means of quote dissemination prior to Instinet's invitation—were accompanied by identities, and even the NASD systems that display just the inside quotes (highest bid to buy, lowest offer to sell) identify the dealers at the inside quotes. In addition, the brokers who solicited the day traders who trade through the Small Order Execution System (SOES)[3] were excluded from Instinet. Thus a broker/dealer could not only put a quote outside of the inside quote in the NASD system, which SOES could not access, but put a quote at the inside in Instinet, where it was unreachable by SOES traders.

Instinet is a NASD member—but only a broker, not a dealer or a market maker, and certainly not an exchange. Instinet holds no inventory and does not trade with customers; it merely offers customers a facility to trade with each other and provides clearing services. Hence, it is subject to SEC regulation only as a broker. It is not regulated as a market maker or as an exchange. Yet the services that it

---

2.   Large orders to buy or sell often move price. A broker who gets a large order to buy could first buy some stock himself, then begin working his customer's order, anticipating the rise in price, and then finally sell the stock he bought at a profit. This is called front-running. It is illegal, but it is very difficult to detect, and it is unlikely that institutions would have such a strong preference for anonymous trading venues if it did not happen with some frequency.

3.   The SOES system was put in place after the 1987 crash in order to give small investors, who could not get through to their brokers on the phone, instantaneous access to the market for small sized orders. It was expected that the orders executed on the system would be mainly retail, uninformed trades. Instead the system attracted day traders who watched screens looking for markets with stale quotes, that is, where an unalert dealer had allowed the market to drift away without changing his own quote. SOES traders were notorious for choosing their times to trade adversely to the interests of the market makers, and studies of their trades confirm that on average, dealers lose money on SOES trades.

offers are very exchange-like. It is a venue where stocks are exchanged.

This gave rise to the cry on the part of the NYSE and NASD that Instinet should be regulated as an exchange and that it was unfair to the traditional exchanges that they bear the burden of exchange regulation and Instinet escape it. The level playing field called for imposing greater costs on Instinet. There were at least three efforts on the part of the Division of Market Regulation to impose new regulations on Instinet that would seriously damage its business. One was made by the division to recommend the adoption of proposed Rule 15(c)-2-10 in the Market 2000 report (killed by the Commission); the second was proposed Rule 17(a)-23 (never adopted by the Commission); and a third was the original version of the proposal for the new Order Handling Rules that became effective in January 1997 (modified by the Commission).

The two proposed rules would have imposed on Instinet three requirements devastating to its business. First, it would have to submit all of its rules and rule changes to the Commission for review and approval. Second, it would have to announce a set of requirements for membership, subject to Commission review, and take everyone who qualified and wished to subscribe as members. Third, and perhaps least burdensome, it would have to surveil its customers affirmatively for violations of federal securities laws. The first two requirements would have impaired Instinet's ability to provide a trading venue mainly free of undesirable counterparties.

The proposed 1996 Order Handling Rules would have forbidden broker dealers to put a better offer into Instinet than into the NASD system. It also would have allowed any broker/dealer, and hence, under the new rules, any customer who placed a limit order with that broker, to execute with an Instinet counterparty, even though not a member of Instinet. This also would have impaired Instinet's ability to provide a trading venue free of undesirable counterparties.

The public interest that the Division of Market Regulation was purporting to promote was one of fairness. The regulators argued that since the prices in Instinet were accessible only to Instinet members, and were usually better than those offered over the NASD's own system, accessible by the public, the system was unfair to the nonmembers of Instinet.

This view of Instinet misunderstands, perhaps deliberately, the nature of stock markets. Among the various costs of doing business for a market maker is the chance that the market maker will trade with someone who knows something the market maker does not. That is, the market maker sells to a customer who knows that the price is to rise, or buys from one who knows the price will fall. The prices at which market makers trade must on average cover the cost of such losses. If dealers can discern which customers are knowledgeable and which are not, they can offer better prices to the customers who impose lower costs on them—the ones who know less. Thus, when dealers advertise the quotes at which they are willing to trade, these quotes should be interpreted as the price at which the dealer is willing to trade with the highest-cost (best-informed) customers. Customers who do business regularly with a given market maker and have a reputation with that dealer for not being so well informed can negotiate a price better than the quote.

The dealer market has always been a negotiated market.[4] Of the trades for 500 shares or more, 30 to 40 percent take place at prices inside the prevailing quotes. This demonstrates that the quotes are often not the best price available, but rather the price at which negotiation begins. If Instinet's limited access is unfair, then the negotiated market is also unfair.

It was not really the unfairness of the Instinet system, but rather that it was taking over the NASD's traditional business and escaping the burdens of regulation that was so objectionable. So far, Instinet's anonymity and shelter from undesirable counterparties has been preserved, but a new threat looms: the NASD's own new proposal for an NASD-run centralized limit order book (in which all customer limit orders would be entered and interact with each other). If adopted, it would put the NASD in direct competition with its own members, including the traditional broker/dealers, but especially with Instinet, whose system is explicitly a "members-only" open limit order book.

---

4. The NYSE is also a negotiated market in the sense that as the specialist and floor traders learn more about the identity and nature of a particular order, they often are willing to "step inside the quotes" by placing a better offer to take a particular trade, and then step back again and wait for the next order. NYSE TORQ data reveal systematic differences in execution quality by customer class. See Angel [1996].

The vested interests align as follows: the broker/dealer members of the NASD generally oppose the establishment of a NASD centralized limit order book (CLOB). The institutional traders, including institutional subscribers of Instinet, support the CLOB, but only if they have anonymous access to it. If their orders are seen by a broker/dealer in the CLOB, they regard it as no better than the current system. They are hoping for a deeper, cheaper Instinet.

This brings us to the force that protects Instinet: customers like it and it has clear benefits for them. The broker/dealer users of Instinet are of two minds. On the one hand, they would like to retake the business they have lost to Instinet. On the other, Instinet's presence lowers the cost of doing business with their remaining customers. If the other dealers use it, an individual dealer cannot afford not to use it. On net, the traditional brokers would be better off without Instinet. But the members of the Commission listen to the customers as well as the NASD and the NYSE, and while the Commission will lean in the direction of rules that erode Instinet's competitive advantage, they are unwilling to go so far as to adopt rules that will kill it.

Another SEC rule change whose impact on Instinet may be profound is the recent change in the Order Handling Rules, which began in January 1997. A possible interpretation of these rules is that they were intended to force the traditional broker/dealers to be more competitive with Instinet. Indeed, the public statements that led to the rules complained that broker/dealers were placing better-priced offers in Instinet than in the NASD's own system. Rather than allow competitive forces such as the further growth of Instinet to pressure the NASD into change, the Commission chose to apply the pressure itself.

The new rules require that market makers display the prices of customer limit orders in their quotes if these orders are priced better than the dealer's own quote. The new order-handling rules have resulted in a substantial narrowing (25 percent to 35 percent) of quoted and effective spreads in thickly traded stocks (with some increase in volatility and a decline in the depth of the quotes measured as the number of daily quote changes divided by daily volume), but much smaller narrowing in thinly traded stocks. Precisely how Instinet executions compare with ordinary NASD executions, including commissions, is not known, and under the current regime, undiscoverable, because the relevant data is Instinet's proprietary data and Instinet does not share it.

AZX

The Arizona Stock Exchange (AZX), formed in 1990, is another alternative trading system that has encountered the resistance of the Division of Market Regulation. AZX's system offers investors what is known as a call market. This marketplace accumulates orders to buy and sell to a specified moment in time, and executes at that time at the price that then equates demand and supply. Prior to the market's close, the system displays the prevailing demand and supply, and shows the price at which trades would execute if no more orders are entered. Customers are encouraged to submit orders early by higher commissions and coarser tick sizes for late entered orders. Like Instinet, AZX customers trade without a middleman and pay no spread. Instinet offers continuous trading, with all of the consequent short-run variability in price related to order size. AZX instead offers agglomerated trading at a point in time, which, in principle, ought to afford considerable protection to customers with very large orders, and indeed ought to create a venue where such large orders could be placed "in the sunshine" to attract counterparties. Like Instinet, AZX has no inventory and does not trade with customers.

In principle, customers who know they have no special information, whether their orders are large or small, should be "patient" traders. That is, they should be willing to wait for the call market, in which they can transact without paying a spread, rather than trade immediately in the continuous market, where they will almost certainly pay a spread. Another way to say this is that they should have no demand for immediacy. This set of "no special information customers" should in principle include all retail trades (trades of individual investors), as well as nearly all of the institutional trades.[5]

---

5. The original research by Jensen [1965] as well as the most recent research by Carhart [1997] indicates that the average mutual fund does a little bit worse than the market; the more funds spend on research and trading, the more they do worse than the market; and there is no serial correlation in fund performance. Thus, it must be the case that these institutions have no better information than does the rest of the market.

Evidence of how efficient a call market can be lies in the experience of the NYSE with its informal call markets now held on triple witching days. When Standard & Poor's 500 futures contracts and options contracts were introduced, these contracts, plus the options on the larger stocks among the S&P 500 all expired simultaneously at the moment of close, for settlement at the closing price on particular Fridays. For those who were delivering or paying stock in these contracts, a particular movement in the price of the larger stocks in the index could be quite profitable. To attempt to influence these prices, the holders of large positions would send their traders to market to attempt to "bang the close"—to place orders for a few thousand or tens of thousands of shares in order to move the price at which millions of shares would then trade. Hence the witch in "triple witching."

Responding to the negative publicity surrounding triple witching, the NYSE changed the expiration of these contracts from the close to the open of the same Friday. It then instructed the specialists in the larger S&P 500 stocks to conduct an informal call by advertising order imbalance at the price that resulted in the least order imbalance for the hour prior to the market's open. With the informal call, there is no opportunity to "bang the open." An order for a few thousand shares added to the call market cannot move the price at which millions of shares are already poised to trade. As a result, the options and futures on the S&P 500 and the options on the stocks all expire simultaneously, and millions of shares change hands with no particular uproar.

Instinet registered as a broker/dealer when computers were slow and clunky and it traded a nonthreatening volume. Then, as computers got better, it grew quietly inside the NASD, in a sense a stealth exchange. In contrast, AZX, since it had "exchange" in its name, attempted to cooperate with the bureaucracy of the Division of Market Regulation. It was rewarded with a "small-exchange" exemption from the full regulatory requirements of a NYSE, but was hobbled by a restriction that precludes any significant growth: its call cannot be held during NYSE trading hours, and in fact was assigned the hour of 5 p.m., Eastern Standard Time.

AZX's threat is that it is a price-discovering system. It is not a "crossing" network such as Posit, which matches customer buy and sell orders at a price determined in another venue, either the NYSE or

Nasdaq. The staff of the division of Market Regulation is concerned that AZX would discover a price that would be outside the prevailing NYSE quotes at the same moment. This concern reflects the division's belief that if there are multiple prices at the same time, someone is being cheated. By assuring that there is only one prevailing price at any moment, no such inference can be drawn. The division is most vexed when a non-NYSE member, third-market dealer such as Jefferies reports a trade in a NYSE stock at a price outside of NYSE quotes, even if it is for a far larger quantity of stock than is being offered at the NYSE. Somehow those who had offers to trade at better prices at the NYSE (the extant limit orders at the NYSE) should have had their orders filled, and would have if the division's opinions regarding the centralization of trading had prevailed everywhere. The division's rationale for consigning AZX to the hours when most traders were tired and or had gone home was the fear that this upstart system would "trade through" the NYSE and do it for a volume large enough to call into question whose price was more legitimate.

Had AZX not been so devoted to the notion of being an exchange, had registered as a broker/dealer instead of an exchange, and operated its system as a NASD broker, perhaps it could have chosen a more popular trading time (for instance, every day at the NYSE open). Perhaps it would be a major venue now, or perhaps its growth and the competition it offered would have prompted the NYSE to run its own call. But at this point, the NYSE has introduced only enough of a call to avert the adverse publicity of triple witching. It is easy to see why the NYSE resists a call: any business that a call would take away from its more profitable continuous trading business would make the NYSE less valuable. But by choosing to try to cooperate with the staff of Market Regulation, rather than taking the stealth approach of Instinet, AZX seems unlikely to ever grow large enough to incite the division to attempt to put it out of business by rulemaking.

Division of Investment Management

The Division of Investment Management is captured by the trade group that represents mutual funds, the Investment Company Institute (ICI). The incumbent companies in the industry are, not surprisingly, largely content with the status quo. The status quo is one in which the central legal document and sales brochure, the mutual fund prospectus, is mainly impenetrable to investors. The SEC's own research (which I had more than a hand in designing) shows that while investors feel they absolutely must have the fund prospectus, they learn very little from it. This is not unsatisfactory to the mutual fund sponsors. Investors are somewhat baffled by investments generally and by mutual funds in particular, and as the SEC survey of fund investors demonstrated, are indeed poorly informed about them. It is certainly in the interest of both the ICI and the brokerage community to leave investors with the notion that investment decisions are very complex and that one needs to be a professional in order to make wise choices. This attitude is well borne out in the ICI's position on risk disclosure for mutual funds. The capture is seen in the SEC's tepid response on the issues.

The controversy over fund-risk disclosure has arisen from two important changes that have occurred over the past 20 years. First is the change in the demographics of responsibility for investment choices. As of 1980, only about 10 percent of the households in the United States had ever directly purchased a security. By 1995, this figure had grown to 35 percent, almost entirely through the growth in mutual fund sales, mainly through defined-contribution pension vehicles (401ks, Keoughs, IRAs, etc.) as defined-contribution plans supplanted the traditional corporate defined-benefit pension plans. Some of the increase was also due to mutual fund sales through banks.

This important change in the demographics of participation in the securities markets coincided with the introduction of "structured" securities. The first big wave of structuring in securities came quickly after the introduction of mortgage-backed securities. Securities that represented pools of mortgages, usually single-family residential mortgages, were separated into parts, with different parts sold to different parties. For example, a simple but representative structuring of a mortgage-backed security would be to assign the first half of the mortgage principal payments (including prepayments), along with accompanying interest to the date of prepayments—whenever they occurred—to one group, and the remaining half of the principal payments to a second group. These are known as prepayment *tranches*.[6] Another standard structuring is to divide the payments from a mort-

---

6. *Tranche* is French for "slice."

gage pool or a bond into just the interest payments and just the principal payments, known as interest-only strips and principal-only strips. By structuring a security, one can create subclass securities that have either much less risk or much more risk than the underlying security.

Traditionally, words have been used to describe risk in mutual fund prospectuses.[7] To the degree that investors in mutual funds were the same people who were investors in stocks and bonds, and familiar, for example, with what a 20-year BB bond was, this was relatively satisfactory. With the introduction of structured securities, information contained in simple words such as stock, bond, and for bonds, maturity date and default-risk rating, became much less indicative of how much risk was involved in a particular investment.

The introduction of structured securities thus stimulated organized objection to mere words for describing risk. The bond rating agencies, notably Standard & Poor's, were concerned that their bond ratings, designed to indicate risk of default, were being misused to indicate overall risk by some mutual funds. For example, a mutual fund could hold principal-only strips in long-term AAA-rated bonds, and advertise itself as an AAA bond fund with an exceptionally high yield, failing to emphasize that the interest-rate risk in the fund was far greater than that of an AAA-bond fund holding the better-known whole AAA bonds. Similarly, some bond funds were advertising themselves as "government guaranteed" or "United States Treasury" bond funds with exceptionally high yields. The government funds were not S&P's particular problem, but as long as it was going to tackle mutual fund risk, the decision was to tackle it all.

After considerable market research, S&P decided to attach letters similar to its default-risk letters to mutual fund risk because it found investors paid little attention to anything else. When S&P experimented with numbers for fund risk, if any default risk letters, such as AA or BB were also displayed, investors gave far greater weight to the letters. Only when overall mutual-fund risk was reported also with letters did investors realize that AAA default risk could be accompanied by BB overall risk. Indeed, a portfolio of 10-year Treasury bonds

---

7.   A notable exception is the Vanguard complex, which has reported the standard deviation of return, normalized to a portfolio of half bonds and half stocks, for all of its funds for many years.

would be assigned a BB overall mutual fund risk rating by the S&P method.

S&P's method is, in the first and last analysis, a standard deviation approach. Even if applied crudely, this approach should be very successful. When standard deviations calculated on three years of monthly mutual fund returns are regressed on the standard deviations similarly calculated for the subsequent three years, these cross-sectional regressions produce explained variation statistics (r^2) of .80 to .90. Mutual fund risk, measured as standard deviation, is highly stable. In fact, S&P's approach is more sophisticated than this, because it is based on funds' current portfolio holdings instead of simply past returns and has "judgment" added. Just what "judgment" means is not so clear, but presumably it has been empirically judged to be at least as good as a simple projected standard deviation, which we already know is very good. S&P's approach to mutual-fund risk is essentially the same as that of the major investment banks in assessing their derivative positions; the options exchanges in evaluating their customers' risk exposure, and the approach used by recent Nobel Prize-winning financial economists.

Now this sounds like a story that should promptly end happily: The demographics of the market changes, and the market itself becomes more complicated. A private free-market solution, researched and refined for digestibility, is produced with alacrity. Problem solved.

This is not what has happened. In order for any materials to be given by brokers to investors, the NASD must approve these materials. This includes the S& P mutual-fund risk ratings. In order to get its materials approved, S&P must apply to the NASD to change its rules. Twice S&P was turned down on the basis that the risk ratings might mislead investors more than inform them. As of the third application, the materials were approved on an experimental basis, with the strict caveat that the risk ratings cannot be called risk ratings, but must be called volatility ratings. The NASD decision will then proceed to the SEC for its review, as all NASD rule changes must be approved by the SEC. The SEC will approve the rule, (the SEC must be given credit for pressuring the NASD into finally approving the volatility ratings) grumbling because the disclosure is not as informative as it could be, but will, I expect, take no action to improve it.

This skirmish over risk ratings takes place against a broader discussion of a more thorough revision of the basic prospectus, including the possibility of a one-page summary prospectus that could be printed as an advertisement and would suffice as the disclosure required for a sale. Currently, an investor must possess a prospectus before the fund can legally take the investor's money. On the one hand, the fund sponsors face the possibility of substantial savings from the printing and mailing of prospectuses. The danger to the funds is that the more succinct prospectus, if it contained the most relevant information, might just reveal to investors what mutual funds do and do not have to offer them. I do not regard this as a threat to the size of the mutual fund business, but it certainly is a threat to its nature.

Thirty years of research on mutual fund performance has told essentially the same story. The basic results that emerge from this research are that the average fund does just a little bit worse than the market; the more investors' money that funds spend on "research" and trading, the more they do worse than the market, and there is no serial correlation in fund performance.

This does not imply that mutual funds are a bad deal for investors. On the contrary, they can provide thorough diversification, an improved risk-return tradeoff, even for small investments at a low price. They can deliver substantial savings in transaction costs. But their advertising is almost entirely in terms of performance, a quality that the research says they cannot deliver.

Could a one-page prospectus provide what investors need to know about a mutual fund in order to evaluate it? Basically, yes. The main evidence of this is that the Morningstar one-page fund summaries contain every fact that most financial economists would regard as relevant to mutual fund investment decisions (plus a lot of information that is not relevant, or is at least redundant). But the format of the Morningstar summary is very challenging for the ordinary investor. Indeed, the aspect of it most salient to the ordinary investor is the Morningstar star ratings, which indicate, by assigning between one and five stars, the past performance of the fund compared to similar funds. Yet the scientific research indicates that there is no serial correlation in fund performance and even Morningstar will emphasize that its stars do not predict fund performance.[8] The stars should be ignored.

Here is a case where the optimistic public interest view of government action could be very helpful. There are certain pieces of information about mutual funds that are essential, such as risk, return, expenses and load fees (tax basis, and logistic details such as minimum initial and additional investment, check writing, etc., are also essential but deserve less emphasis). A standardized format for reporting them would help investors not only to assess a given fund, but also, through use, would teach them to better understand their investments as they became familiar with the format. The notion of externalities essential to efficient government action is indeed present here: information is valuable to everyone, and a standardized format for all funds makes them all easier to comprehend. This is the philosophy behind the Federal Trade Commission's standardized disclosure on appliance efficiency and nutrition labels for packaged food.

What is the difference between the securities industry and the food industry that we have a clear, standardized nutrition label, but still struggle with the impenetrable, and often not meaningful mutual fund prospectus?

Perhaps part of the answer lies in the absence of a competing regulator. The Department of Commerce is generally regarded as the province of corporations, representing them in opposition to the Department of Labor. The Department of State has numerous small offices of experts in the affairs of other nations, largely representing the interests of these nations, and is poised in opposition to the Department of Defense, which represents the interests of the domestic military establishment. The Department of Agriculture represents the interests of farmers and food manufacturers, often opposing the Food and Drug Administration, which represents consumer interests. We might expect more balanced and efficient rulemaking with competing agencies. Instead, at the SEC we have the Commissioners themselves taking into account the interests of the investing public to some

---

8.　Investors disbelieve this to such a degree that the NASD pressured Morningstar to produce star ratings based on one year of performance, when it had been producing only three, five, and 10-year stars. Morningstar resisted, and its head, Don Phillips, flatly stated that the one-year stars would be meaningless. Upon the threat of removing Morningstar's NASD blessing as material that could be given to investors, Morningstar relented and produced a one-year star to help brokers encourage investors to churn their mutual funds.

degree, but also under pressure from the regulatees, and the Commission staffs captured by the regulatees.

Part of the difference may also lie in the complexity of securities institutions. Most people, even without studying nutrition, have a good idea that fruits and vegetables are healthy foods and that butter and ice cream are not. But how many people know the three basic results (reported above) about mutual funds? According to the SEC survey of fund investors, almost none. A simpler standardized disclosure would help them but the prevailing forces at the SEC, forces of regulatory capture, have prevented it from happening.

Division of Corporate Finance

The division of the SEC that oversees prospectuses for new securities issues and regular disclosures for companies with publicly traded stock is not captured by the companies who issue securities, its direct regulatees. Instead, it is captured by the lawyers who prepare their disclosures and the underwriters who take them public. This capture is easy to understand. The lawyers and underwriters are far less numerous than the issuers, and far better informed as well.

The result of this capture seldom produces a good yarn about a specific issue, like that of Market Regulation and Investment management, but instead just a quiet hum of rent seeking. The 1933 act bar prefers that the regulations for disclosure remain complex, obscure and in flux. Because the regulations are complex, the barrier to entry is high. Because the regulations are obscure, every issuer needs a lawyer who is familiar to the staff of the division and can interact with them to get the client's materials approved. The rules are sufficiently unclear that it is very seldom that the division reviews a filing and requests no changes and because the rules are in flux, only those who practice regularly are qualified to do the work, providing another barrier to entry.

The situation in this division is the most stable of the SEC rule-writing divisions. There have been no demographic or technological changes that have altered the issues or the politics facing the division.[9] While this division, like investment management, oversees pro-

---

9.   Although stock offerings through the Internet may prove to be the force disrupting this division.

spectuses and other disclosures, investor protection never relied on investors actually reading and understanding these documents. Instead, class-action lawyers and security analysts read the prospectuses. The information in them is promptly reflected in prices, and if it is wrong, suits are promptly filed. When issuers complained to Congress that the suits were too numerous and too costly, Congress obliged with the Securities Litigation Reform Act of 1996. This act seems to have had little impact on the frequency of disclosure-related suits.

Final Thoughts

Despite the various complaints here regarding SEC decision making, I must join the rest of the world in acknowledging that the securities markets of the United States have been dazzling in their effectiveness at raising capital and assisting in the creation of value. But it is very difficult to know why. Has the regulatory apparatus of the securities markets contributed to their integrity, and thus to their success? Or is the apparatus itself just a manifestation of the underlying commercial ethics and contracts that make for such a great volume of mutually beneficial transactions?

It is very difficult to know. But as I support my economist colleagues in promoting the view of regulatory capture at the SEC, I would be remiss if I did not also indicate what policy choices I believe are efficient. There are changes that would promote efficiency. Until the pension landscape changed to directly involve most working people in the securities markets, disclosures accessible only to investment professionals did not have a high social cost, because most decisions were delegated to professionals anyway. But now many individuals must make their own decisions and collective action could help considerably in promoting standardized and simpler disclosure of the facts that are the most important. As new technology offers us less-costly systems for trading stock, these systems should be allowed to offer their services and, if found satisfactory, allowed to grow.

We should expect these changes both to be made eventually. The regulatory capture view of economic institutions does not suggest that regulatory outcomes are always inefficient, but that there are forces, such as costly information and costly organization, that lean against efficiency. Each of these changes is sufficiently important that the resources necessary to produce them will be forthcoming.

Comments on...

Regulatory Capture at the U.S. Securities and Exchange Commission

Roberta Romano, Esq.
Allen Duffy/Class of 1960 Professor of Law
Yale Law School

My comment will focus on two important insights in Susan E. Woodward's paper: her microanalytic approach to the capture theory of regulation and her view of the benefits of regulatory competition.

Capture Theory

Dr. Woodward's paper is a nice sketch of the complexities of applying a regulatory capture theory to the decisions of an agency such as the SEC. With an insider's perspective, she breaks down the agency into distinct regulatory fiefdoms and provides examples of how the different divisions' rulemaking tends to shore up the competitive positions of their particular regulatory charges: the Market Regulation Division's efforts to impose costs on alternative exchanges, and the Investment Management Division's slowness on simplifying mutual fund disclosures. This is a regulatory capture process that might be obscured if one simply looked at the agency as an undistinguishable black box.

To emphasize the value in this microanalytical approach to the institutional structure of the agency, let me provide an example where the setup may be useful in explaining SEC policy that might otherwise seem inconsistent from a capture theory perspective.

This is the SEC's disclosure policy with respect to sales of securities: the expanding exemptions from 1933 act disclosure requirements via Rule 144A and Regulation S simultaneously with the insistent strict application of 1934 act disclosure requirements in the agency's opposition to the New York Stock Exchange's desire to list foreign issuers without their having to reconcile their accounting statements with Generally Accepted Accounting Practices (GAAP).

The former exemptions have the benefit of protecting U.S. underwriters' competitive market shares (from erosion due to Eurobond market competition) and perhaps of facilitating their entry into foreign issuer markets—a group with whom Dr. Woodward describes the Corporate Finance Division is aligned, whereas the latter proposal does not clearly assist underwriters' business. The stocks that can list on the NYSE are not new issues but large companies seeking secondary trading markets, and any underwriting accompanying their exchange listing would not appear to be as lucrative as the underwritings involved in the exempt securities case.

The beneficiaries of reducing foreign companies' disclosure requirements are: 1) the NYSE, whose regulatory influence Dr. Woodward identifies with the Market Regulation Division and not the Corporate Finance Division that controls the relevant regulatory agenda, 2) foreign issuers, who would have no internal influence channel, and 3) U.S. investors who will be able to acquire such companies more cheaply than through direct foreign investment. The losers, if any, would be U.S. issuers, who are selling shares in the same market subject to more costly accounting disclosure requirements, and whose interests would be represented by the lawyers filing disclosures, a clientele Dr. Woodward identifies as aligned with the Corporate Finance Division.

Dr. Woodward's interest group capture analysis thus helps to explain the division's inaction, although there are some puzzles. The costs to U.S. issuers of following GAAP are sunk, and it is unlikely that the additional cost compared to a non-GAAP-compliant foreign issuer would diminish U.S. investors' demand for U.S. stocks. The home-bias of investor portfolios is well known (French and Porterba). In addition, underwriters should at best be indifferent to an easing of the listing requirement because such domestic trading would not appear to bear directly on the profitability of underwriting new issues. Depending upon how much U.S. issuers actively lobbied against altering the disclosure requirements for foreign issuers, one possibility is to interpret her thesis as implying that divisions only react to pressure from their specific constituents. Another possibility is that the Corporate Finance Division is in this instance acting as a Niskanen-type regulator, seeking to expand its jurisdictional territory, independent of the interests of the groups by which it is captured. SEC disclosure policy remains globally dominant when foreign companies seeking to list in the United States must comply with SEC disclosure requirements. It is also possible that accountants benefit from the reconciliation requirement, a group whose status is similar to the professionals (lawyers and underwriters) that Dr. Woodward emphasizes as central to the work of the Corporate Finance Division.

It would be interesting to know whether the NYSE has tried to rally its support in the Market Regulation Division to assist it in making its case to the Corporate Finance Division. In the congressional arena, although difficult to do successfully, when a committee with whom an interest group has no tie has jurisdiction over matters of importance to them, the group attempts to change the relevant policy venue and use its other congressional connections to affect that committee.[1]

This inquiry leads to the obvious institutional point that significant policy changes must be approved by the top of the agency, the Commissioners, who may not simply rubber-stamp the divisions' policy recommendations. The interests of the groups represented by the different divisions must be aggregated by the Commissioners in some way when they conflict, or when adversely affected groups are not the controlling division's specific "wards."

It would be interesting and helpful if Dr. Woodward would flesh out some of that process for us. For instance, what kind of interaction is there across divisions in the policymaking process and how does that get played out at the Commissioner level? More specifically, for instance, what stopped the Market Regulation Division's adoption of the most destructive rules regarding Instinet (rather than their more incremental attack), action that she suggests occurred at the commissioner level? Such a discussion would round out our understanding of the extent of regulatory capture.

Benefits of Competitive Regulation

Dr. Woodward further makes the valid and important point that regulatory competition tends to produce better regulatory policy than a monopolist regulator in her discussion of the inadequacies in mutual fund disclosure compared to food and drug labeling.

---

1. See Romano (1997) (describing efforts of securities industry and SEC to use banking committee members to affect agriculture committees' bills in order to alter CFTC's jurisdiction over equity derivatives). This is not a common occurrence (hence success is rare) because most typically, interest groups will have close ties to the legislators whose committees have jurisdiction over matters of importance to the group's livelihood. Baumgartner and Jones (p. 19) detail, however, instances where interest groups are successful at achieving significant policy change by redefining a policy issue so as to shift the policy-making venue to a more favorable decision maker.

I am very sympathetic with this claim. Taking her mutual fund disclosure example, for instance, it strikes me that not all mutual funds benefit from obscurity in prospectuses or in having customers believe that investing is so complex that they need a broker. This may be the position of the funds that dominate the Investment Company Institute, but, the Vanguard Group, for one example, surely does not benefit from such policies. It is probably no coincidence that the Vanguard Group is identified by Dr. Woodward as having provided better risk information concerning its funds' performance than other funds for a long time.

Accordingly, if there were not a monopolist regulator mandating the disclosure format but a competitive regulatory setting, flexibility would be introduced across regimes to meet the diversity in funds' disclosure preferences. Funds like Vanguard would be able to introduce a simpler disclosure format in order to increase their sales by registering under the securities regulator that permitted such disclosures. Furthermore, their simpler disclosure documents might force funds that do not get similar benefits from the simplified format to adopt it in order to compete for investors who prefer to obtain such information.

There is, in fact, some limited evidence concerning the SEC's behavior that supports Dr. Woodward's thesis. In the context of the regulation of new financial products, the SEC faces competition—the Commodities Futures Trading Commission—and here it has shifted its regulatory stances from an initial position hostile to innovation in the 1970s, to one, by the 1990s, of actively encouraging the stock exchanges' foray into innovative products.[2]

Yet when it comes to public equity, where there is no competition, the SEC has been less responsive to competitive concerns of exchanges and issuers, continuing to expand its regulatory requirements. In particular, it has been insensitive to competitive concerns in registrants' complaints regarding derivatives disclosure (where there is no competing regulator).[3]

---

2. See Romano (1997, pp. 354-58) (tracing SEC's opposition to stock options before the creation of the CFTC and its opposition to futures on securities after the CFTC's initial establishment, to its promotion of index participation units in the 1990s political battle to obtain jurisdiction over equity derivatives).

Competing divisions within the agency are not enough: although exclusive, rather than overlapping, jurisdictions appear to be a necessary feature in order to foster product innovation through regulatory competition (see Romano, 1997, p. 370), it is also true that overlapping jurisdiction increases the opportunities for companies to take advantage of regulatory competition to reduce regulatory costs (Kane 1984). Moreover, the objects of the regulatory competition must be substitutes rather than complements for competition to produce optimal regulation (Albrecht, et al., 1996, p. 27). That is not the case for the targets of the differing divisions' regulation.

Let me conclude by attempting to extend Dr. Woodward's insight to its ultimate implication, which is to support regulatory reform in the securities context that is directed at eliminating the SEC's regulatory monopoly.

This is easiest to implement for 1933 and 1934 act matters regarding issuers. Regulatory competition could be achieved by letting states compete with the SEC in providing securities regimes (disclosure and antifraud regulation) to issuers under a jurisdictional rule in which the regulator depends on the domicile of the issuer, rather than on the site of the sale of the security, and hence is chosen by the issuer.

This arrangement will produce securities regimes most favorable to investors because investors' preferences will dictate issuers' domicile choices in the competitive capital market. Institutional investors buying securities will be able to process information concerning securities regimes and incorporate it into the stock price. Companies choosing the regimes most preferred by such investors will lower their cost of capital.[4]

It is more difficult to implement competition for 1940 act matters, given the different mix of mutual fund investors compared to direct stock investors. With fewer or no institutional investors, it is possible that the marginal fund share purchaser will not be able to incorporate securities regime value into the price. In addition, the selectors of the regime, the fund owners, are not the regime's supposed beneficiaries,

---

3. For example, in its derivatives disclosure release, the SEC made only very minor changes in response to comments raising proprietary concerns and provided a very superficial cost-benefit analysis of the proposal (see SEC, 1997, pp. 6054-62).

4. For the elaboration of such a reform see Romano (1998).

the fund customers. These two differences may render regulatory competition through mutual funds' choice of regime less effective compared to the issuer context. But, while it may take more care in determining how to operationalize regulatory competition in the mutual fund setting, it is, in my view, a more propitious route than what Dr.Woodward's paper appears to support: reliance on the SEC to set the right disclosure policy for mutual funds.

Finally, stock exchange regulation under the 1934 act is a middle case, as issuers may adequately police exchange rules to ensure the highest value of their listings.[5] This would suggest that opening up regulation of exchanges to a self-chosen overseer, state or SEC, would work; or that one could go further and eliminate governmental oversight of the exchanges, subjecting them to the discipline of the market forces governing issuer listing choices. Although I am agnostic concerning the most effective approach, I am convinced that either would be an improvement over the existing arrangement of the SEC's monopoly, which permits, as Dr. Woodward details, the exchanges' capture of the relevant agency decision maker, to the detriment of the investors whom the laws were intended to protect.

References

Albrecht, W., C. Bronfman and H. Messenheimer (1996), "Regulatory Regimes: The Interdependence of Rules and Regulatory Structure," in A. Lo (ed.), *The Industrial Organization and Regulation of the Securities Industry.* University of Chicago: Chicago, pp. 9-33.

Amihud, Y., and H. Mendelson (1996), "A New Approach to the Regulation of Trading Across Securities Markets," *New York University Law Review,* 71, 1411-66.

Baumgartner, F. and B. Jones (1993), *Agendas and Instability in American Politics.* University of Chicago: Chicago.

French, K. and J. Poterba (1991), "Investor Diversification and International Equity Markets," *American Economic Review,* 29, 237-64.

Kane, E. (1984), "Regulatory Structure in Futures Markets: Jurisdictional Competition between the SEC, the CFTC, and Other Agencies," *Journal of Futures Markets,* 4, 367-84.

---

5. This may require issuers' approval of listings (see Amihud and Mendelson, 1996).

Romano, R. (1997), "The Political Economy of Derivative Securities Regulation," *Yale Journal on Regulation,* 14, 279-406.

Romano, R. (1998), "Empowering Investors: A Market Approach to Securities Regulation," *Yale Law Journal,* 107 (2,359-2,430).

Securities and Exchange Commission (1997). Disclosure of Accounting Policies for Derivative Financial Instruments and Derivative Commodity Instruments and Disclosure of Qualitative and Quantitative Information about Market Risk Inherent in Derivative Financial Instruments, Other Financial Instruments, and Derivative Commodity Instruments, Release No. 33-7386, Federal Register, 62, 6044 (to be codified at 17 C.F.R. pts 210, 228, 229, 239, 240, and 249).

Kevin E. Villani
Executive Vice President and Chief Financial Officer
Imperial Credit Industries Inc.

I have drifted in and out of public policy [Federal Home Loan Mortgage Corporation, Federal Reserve Bank of Cleveland], of academe [University of Southern California, George Mason University, University of Pennsylvania, Perdue] and of the business sector [Imperial Corporation of America, Imperial Credit Industries]. So I have learned most of what I know about the types of models that Susan E. Woodward is talking about—regulatory capture, adverse selection, moral hazard, go-for-broke—through practical experience, usually after the fact, trying to explain what just happened to me.

In fact, some of you may not know that Dr. Woodward had a job—Deputy Assistant Secretary for the Office of Economic Affairs at the Department of Housing and Urban Development—that I had in the late 1970s early 1980s. John C. Weicher [now a Senior Fellow at the Hudson Institute] had that job before I did.

I can recall, in the case of Fannie Mae, having a discussion that Dr. Weicher may or may not recall, in 1975. At the time, we knew that Fannie Mae was a government institution, that—it had been argued in the 1930s, and we now had strong statistical evidence—could, if it continued to be a major force in the capital markets taking the risks that it did, undermine the savings and loan industry, and that is a story that we will talk about and hear about later.

We knew the political economy of the institution. We could see on the horizon the types of options risk that it would take. Incorrectly pricing options led to losses in the 1970s, using round government figures, $10 billion. We could see the "adverse selection" and "go-for-broke" possibilities of the early 1980s, where Fannie Mae—again, using round numbers—presumably, taking credit risks to bail itself out of past losses, lost another $10 billion.

And so, given that it was a small institution at the time, given that we had already trashed the "counter-cyclical and public policy arguments" at the time, we said now is the time to take this agency out of the public sector and subject it to market discipline. HUD was the regulator; the HUD secretary was technically appointed, but she appointed the general counsel of HUD to be on Fannie Mae's board. So Fannie Mae did the only thing that it could do at the time—it hired HUD's general counsel. And that is how I happened to learn about the way the "regulatory capture" model worked.

Not to get too far away from Dr. Woodward's story, but I think it is all related. Marvin Phaup [Deputy Assistant Director, Special Studies, U.S. Congressional Budget Office] is sitting next to Dr. Weicher, and Dr. Phaup and I go way back to the days of the Fed.

But Dr. Phaup, in my view, deserves the award for the most memorable title to a memorandum written for the bureaucracy. I still remember it, written in 1982. It was subsequent to the Boston Fed Conference in 1982, when we were examining if the savings and loan industry was insolvent to the tune of $150 billion or $200 billion. We had done these calculations and it was one or the other, or someplace in that range. Dr. Phaup's memo was titled, "The Savings and Loan Industry: Will it Go Out With a Bang or a Whimper?" And I still remember that, because nobody knew, or at least the public did not know, that the industry was under water by $200 billion, and we certainly, as public officials, were not going to tell them that.

The industry, of course, had not lost that money on its own account—it was all a matter of systemic risk or political risk. Or to put it another way, we believed our interest-rate forecasts, embedded in the yield curve. The savings and loan institutions had been doing what they had been forced to do as a matter of public regulation—that is, make long-term, fixed-rate loans and fund them with short-term deposits. Now the money was lost. We, as a political class, had made great promises to depositors as well as promises to mortgage borrowers, and we could not deliver on those promises.

I think it is particularly ironic now, since we knew that the savings and loan industry was a great example of crony capitalism, that Bill Clinton of Whitewater and savings and loan fame, is now leading the charge against crony capitalism internationally. But the real point of the savings and loan debacle was, "Do government officials and politicians have the incentives to make financial information the most transparent? Because ultimately, that is what we are going to argue is the Security and Exchange Commission's (SEC) primary role.

I think that Gerard Caprio Jr. [Research Manager at the Development Research Group of the World Bank] can tell you, looking at the experience with deposit insurance and the associated regulatory systems around the globe, that deposit insurance systems are used as mechanisms for getting cheap government debt, or the equivalent of an implicit tax on depositors, as opposed to an explicit tax.

And I think the same has been true in the United States. In fact, I think political risk is another term for systemic risk. Whether political regulation is generally cause or cure, systemic risk is still open to question. Politicians and regulators have spoon-fed contemporary historians with the positive view of the role regulation played in the savings and loan crisis. In large measure, the regulations that we have today come out of the 1930s, and I think we are still trying to determine what actually happened in the 1930s, and why we do things the way we do.

Accepting the historical view of regulation as a positive force mitigating systemic risk, several previous speakers have invoked Mark Twain and Santayana to stress the fear of repeating history.

I do not subscribe as much to Mark Twain's or Santayana's view of history as I do to Friedrich A. Von Hayek's—that historians are usually looking and writing about the tremendous civilizations created by the kings, when in fact, what actually happened is that through free individual action, tremendous wealth was created by previous societies and kings came along and expropriated it and built monuments. Historians write about the kings, and not about how the value was created. This, it seems to me, may provide a better explanation of our current positive view of financial market regulation.

To put it in broad terms, the two greatest areas of financial regulation in the public interest relates to deposits and to retirement savings. There are a whole bunch of papers at the Conference about the scale and magnitude of retirement savings.

I think the government's historical track record for transparency on the deposit issue is questionable at best. When it comes to the transparency of retirement systems, as I recall, we passed the Employee Retirement Income Security Act (ERISA) to try to get better management, largely by state and local, as well as private pension funds, and to obey certain principles in terms of funding pension savings. If you applied those same principles to Social Security, we'd be locking up a lot of politicians and bureaucrats right now.

I understand that Social Security is a pay-as-you go system, but we have excess right now. We claim to be investing it, but in fact, we're not investing it; we're funding deficit spending, which is current consumption, and we're calling that savings.

I would say that Dr. Woodward's model of regulatory capture does not end with bureaucrats. In large measure, we're asking, "Are the bureaucrats ultimately going to make financial information transparent?"

Ultimately, bureaucrats are subject to political will. As Ed Gray, who was a "captured regulator" if ever there was one, learned the hard way, he ultimately had to respond to and be accountable to Jim Wright, as did the whole system.

Let me turn to the three divisions within the SEC that Dr. Woodward talked about. I will not say much about the area of market regulation, but the notion that government bureaucrats can regulate prices and try to determine the price at which securities should trade is not novel, but it's counterintuitive.

I remember being with the Hungarian Finance Minister—I think it was 1992—and I complimented him on the tremendous contribution that Hungary had made to the world. Because as you know, Hungary in 1968 introduced their "market-oriented principles," which, implemented by bureaucrats, largely became the notion that prices count, so we'll have bureaucrats set them. I pointed out to him that Poland had introduced true price reform just six months earlier and the Polish economy had passed them in six months. Hungary taught the world how not to do it. Bureaucrats are just not going to get prices right.

When it comes to the Division of Investments, I think it is actually helpful to know that in the mutual fund area, it has been benign—that is, no positive impact. We have killed a lot of trees to produce prospectuses since the 1930s, but we've provided no useful information. As we all know, performance is based on real productivity, and we really cannot say much about it.

My personal experience with this type of disclosure goes back to 1969. I had just passed the exams to become a registered representa-

tive and was trying to market mutual funds. We had the 1968 performance books, and I can remember that they showed what happened to
an investment of $10,000 held for 10 years and 15 years. Of course,
they had skyrocketed, based on 1968 performance, but in 1969, you
lost virtually all of the historical gain (though you were much better
off buying at the bottom of the market in 1969 than in 1968).

I was just learning sales techniques when Paul Samuelson wrote
an article saying exactly what Dr. Woodward said. That is, there's no
difference in performance other than the fact that when guys like me
sell it, we get paid 1 percent, and if you buy it out of the paper, you
save the 1 percent.

I went to the sales manager, and I said, "How can I possibly sell
these funds? Look what my hero, Paul Samuelson, said."

My sales manager said, "Ah, if anybody asks you, just tell 'em
you never saw the article and you don't read the newspapers."

When it comes to the Corporate Finance section, my experience
is a little more recent. This section deals with new-issue disclosure.

I noticed the same fellow at my office always showing up, and
people disappearing—my general counsel going to lunch and my
controller going to lunch. I said, "Well, who is this fellow?"

They said, "Oh, he's the president and owner of the L.A. printing
firm."

I said, "Well, how much business do we do with him?"

They said, "You want it annually, in round numbers, in millions
of dollars? We've made the firm. We spend millions and millions just
for the printer every year. For disclosure, about once a week, we have
drafting sessions, rooms about this size, of lawyers, at about $300 an
hour, drafting disclosure for public securities that we'll issue."

It is probably the least productive activity that one will ever see—
an ultimate example of rent seeking. It has nothing to do with public
policy. These are people writing the risk section of the securities that
we will file, and none of them are trained in risk management or measurement as we would know it or define it, and they know nothing
about Merton Miller [winner of the 1990 Nobel Prize in Economics
and author of "Merton Miller on Derivatives"]. They know one guy,
William S. Lerach [one of the leading securities lawyers representing

shareholders]. They need him desperately, because otherwise, why would we pay them $300 an hour to get together once a week just to draft the language? Short of a Shakespearean solution, I see no way out of this particular form of rent seeking; it will probably outlast India's caste system.

I'd like to make two closing comments.

I think that public agencies and bureaucrats do not really have the incentives that we are talking about for transparent financial disclosure and risk-taking, and even if they did, they could not do the job.

I know I'm speaking very broadly, but in a society in which—people argue about exact amounts—42 percent of household income goes directly to tax, individuals, if you surveyed them, would not think they were getting 42 percent of their value from government. Therefore, the pressure is to make the cost nontransparent. Herein we tax through regulations, we tax in distorting ways, we tax through inflation and this will be a continuing problem.

Interest-only (IO) regulation happens to be one of those examples. It was one of these things mortgage bankers used to produce loans at a loss. Well, it was an accounting loss, but they created a contract that was called a "servicing contract," which we now view as an IO strip, as value. This process allowed them to always accelerate their expense and defer their income when calculating tax liability. But they wanted to be able to book the value of this on the balance sheet, partly to satisfy government agencies such as Ginnie Mae, to show that they really had net worth. So we created a sort of IO strip, based on a tax distortion in the system.

Now you take this IO strip. You say, well, it is really a series of cash flows, the way we look at it, but it has got enormous prepayment risk.

Let me just translate how one of these examples had tremendous impact on the Japanese banking system. Economists would view an "interest only strip" as simply an investment in an instrument that generated cash flows with enormous prepayment risk. The companion derivative security is a principal only (PO) security, whose cash flow is derived purely from what accountants call "the underlying principal" of the mortgage loans. IO's and PO's trade at prices that reflect a discount rate, or expected yield on the underlying cash flows. But what economists call the underlying principal and interest in an IO or PO is different than the labels of accountants reflecting the underlying mortgage collateral. Herein lies the potential for regulatory obfuscation.

Here is an example of what some Japanese banks do. Take IOs and POs—maybe we invest 50 cents on the dollar for an IO and 50 cents on the dollar for a PO, but the IO has no "notional principal." So, we attach 2 percent of what we call the "notional principal" to the IO, and 98 percent of what we call the "notional principal" to the PO. Then we will sell the IO. We will get 50 percent of our cash back, because that's what we spent for it, but we'll only call 2 percent of the IO "notional principal." We will report a gain—we say we make about 25 times our money, if I did the math right. We will not report the $0.48 loss on the other side. This simple trick, done with the full knowledge of Japanese financial regulators, allowed underwater Japanese banks to book tens of billions of dollars in regulatory capital.

We will continue to see those types of transactions. The asset-backed securities market is now bigger—the below-investment grade segment—than the corporate finance market. There are more issues of the BBs and BBBs in the asset-backed market and we will continue to misclassify what is true risk because, as Dr. Woodward explained, the rating agencies determined credit risk in an environment where prices were relatively stable. It did not work for rating agencies when prices went down a lot in the 1930s. The calculated gains due to falling rates could not be realized because companies could not pay. Price gains were more than offset by credit losses. It did not work going the other way either. When you had inflation, credit risk declined as companies paid in deflated dollars, but investors again lost due to falling bond prices. So, it is very difficult to put these systemic risks of interest rate and of options pricing into a credit-rating-agency type environment, and therefore, difficult to regulate risk.

Similarly, with respect to embedded options, we have been dealing with embedded options in mortgage contracts that have had huge amounts of value since the 1970s. Accountants will never get options right. Even if you price them right, they will never account for them right. They have now begun to account for separately traded options premiums not as earned income, but when an option is embedded in a contract, people tend to record the income first and not look at the out-of-the-money-put element of it. That is going to continue to create problems.

That is, you can continue to report performance that does not exist because you have written options and you are taking the premium into income, but the potential expense comes later. It has distorted the entire financial sector.

Regulators are looking to Generally Acceptable Accounting Practices financial accounting—which was never intended as a risk measurement tool—to look at the value of financial institutions. The financial companies that have used gain-on-sale accounting have reported income that they have not earned—that typically they may never earn. We have seen enormous losses of hundreds of millions of dollars by reversing previously reported income that will not be earned because of this embedded option in contracts.

At least in Japan, when out-of-the-money options contracts eventually come due, resulting in insolvency, the incentive for regulators is that somebody has to commit suicide. I mean, it happens occasionally. It is a very low-probability event, but should discourage such regulatory risk-taking. We do not have that culture in the United States, so it seems to me that our regulators have a totally different perspective on this.

To summarize, I do not share Merton Miller's conclusion that there's no regulatory capture at the SEC, but maybe there's more benign neglect. That is, I think deposit regulation and retirement saving regulation is much more pernicious, in the sense that we tend to allocate savings to consumption in the government sector. When the government sector gets involved in capital allocation, it does an extremely bad job. Productivity, no matter whether you add on social productivity or not, has been extremely poor in all countries that do this. So, to the extent we drive money to the capital markets away from the regulated banking sectors and continue to disintermediate, we're better off.

It does not mean that there is any net positive benefit to the SEC's role in trying to regulate the pricing of securities markets or in disseminating information, but it may be a less detrimental role than in deposit markets.

The globalization trends that you talked about at your previous conferences probably undermine the banking system, in a sense that they disintermediate and they probably drive the funds more toward the capital markets. The SEC's objective, while it may not be any more achievable than the Federal Reserve's objective that you listed, is at least more simple—they want to make the information more perfect. If they don't achieve it, then their failure is less in scope than that of other regulatory agencies.

The issue is one of political economy, not of economics. And economists, especially those limited by our neoclassical models, are somewhat limited by this, because we tend to too easily accept government solutions when practical experience tells us that they don't work.

I don't know what the solution is—I know that movies continue to glorify politicians and government regulations, although at least on TV, *The X-Files* has taken on bureaucrats and undermined their credibility. So maybe we should start a movie industry and try to at least get a more balanced historical perspective on the role of financial regulation in society.

Section Three

Regulating Mutual Fund Investor Knowledge: Policy Fantasy or Reality?

Gordon J. Alexander
Professor of Finance
Carlson School of Management
University of Minnesota*

Jonathan D. Jones
Senior Financial Economist
Risk Management Division
Office of Thrift Supervision*

Peter J. Nigro
Senior Financial Economist
Economics and Evaluation
Office of the Comptroller of the Currency*

*The first two authors were previously affiliated with the Securities and Exchange Commission. The Securities and Exchange Commission, the Office of Thrift Supervision, and the Office of the Comptroller of the Currency as a matter of policy disclaim any responsibility for any publication or statements by any of their employees. The views expressed herein are those of the authors and do not necessarily reflect the views of these agencies, or of the authors' colleagues on the staffs of the agencies. The authors thank the Investment Company Institute, especially Sandy West and Vicki Chambers, for helpful comments and providing the data related to the mutual fund industry.

Abstract

This paper presents a general overview of the mutual fund industry and examines several regulatory concerns that are increasingly important in light of the continuing mutual fund boom and resulting heightened focus by regulators on investor protection, investor knowledge, and disclosure. Recent survey data compiled by the Office of the Comptroller of the Currency and the Securities and Exchange Commission are used to examine mutual fund investors' general investment knowledge, their beliefs about risks and costs, and their sources of information used in making fund investments. Given that mutual funds are sold through several major types of distribution channels, differences in mutual fund investor attributes across the various channels are examined in order to detect whether any of the channels pose unique regulatory concerns. One conclusive result is that the overall level of investor financial literacy is low. While recent "plain English" and profile prospectus initiatives of the SEC are sensible, it is highly unlikely that more regulation of disclosure of information at the time of sale will alleviate these shortcomings. Future research should involve examining various mechanisms to improve investors' level of financial literacy, including those being put forth by the private sector.

Introduction

Over the past 20 or so years, mutual funds have become an increasingly popular investment vehicle.[1] Household ownership of stock, bond and money market mutual funds rose from 6 percent of U.S. households in 1980 to more than 37 percent in 1997.[2] During the same period, employers began relying more heavily on mutual fund companies to manage the nation's retirement assets.[3] Given these two

---

1. There are numerous reasons for the popularity of mutual fund investments including their: (1) accessibility and offering of various investor services; (2) allowing investors to benefit from professional management and ownership in a well-diversified portfolio; (3) offering numerous investment objectives to choose from; and (4) having high liquidity.

2. See Investment Company Institute (February 1998), p. 1.

3. According to the Investment Company Institute, retirement plan holdings accounted for 35 percent of all mutual fund assets in 1996, while in 1983, using a slightly different definition, they comprised only 9.9 percent; see Investment Company Institute (1997c), p.1 and (Winter 1994/1995), p.67.

major developments in conjunction with an unparalleled bull stock market, the total assets held by mutual funds soared by more than 3,200 percent, from $135 billion in 1980 to roughly $4.5 trillion at the end of 1997. This made the mutual fund industry the second-largest and fastest-growing sector of the major financial intermediaries.[4] As recently as the end of 1990, mutual fund assets stood only fifth among major financial intermediaries, while at the end of 1997 mutual funds stood only second to commercial banks in terms of balance-sheet assets.[5] Today, the mutual fund industry plays an important role in facilitating capital flows and promoting economic growth in the United States.

The purpose of this paper is to present a general overview of the mutual fund industry and provide perspective on several regulatory concerns regarding this industry in light of the heightened focus by regulators on investor protection, investor knowledge and disclosure. Recent survey data compiled by the Office of the Comptroller of the Currency (OCC) and the Securities and Exchange Commission (SEC) are used to examine mutual fund investors' general investment knowledge, beliefs about risk and costs and sources of information used in making fund investments. Because mutual funds are sold through several major types of distribution channels, differences in mutual fund investors attributes across the various channels are examined to detect whether any of them pose unique regulatory concerns.

The remainder of this paper proceeds as follows. Section II provides an historical overview including the growth in fund complexes, fund offerings, the types of funds, and the assets held by funds. This section also provides descriptive information on the typical fund-owning household and discusses whether the mutual fund boom is unique to the United States. Section III examines regulation of the various distribution channels. It also presents results from the OCC/SEC survey that relate to mutual fund investor knowledge, the beliefs about risks and costs, and the sources of information used in making

---

4.   See the Investment Company Institute (1997b), p. 60, and the ICI's web page at http://www.ici.org/about shareholders/fund_owner_figures_95-96.html.

5.   At the end of 1997, mutual fund and commercial bank assets totaled $4.5 trillion and $4.8 trillion, respectively, for a gap of $.3 trillion, while in 1990, the gap was $2.2 trillion. The slower growth of bank assets is due to much more modest price appreciation and the lack of inclusion of off-balance sheet assets; see Boyd and Gertler (May 1994).

mutual fund investments. Special attention is focused on two distribution channels that are subject to slightly different regulatory frameworks: the bank and pension distribution channels. Section IV discusses two issues related to the mutual fund industry that will likely become increasingly important to financial regulators in the near future. Finally, Section V discusses some policy implications.

Mutual Fund Industry

Mutual funds are not new to our financial system. Indeed, mutual funds have existed in the United States since the 1920s.[6] The size and complexity of the mutual fund industry, however, have evolved dramatically with economic events, financial innovations, changing demographics and changes in the legal landscape. This section concentrates primarily on the past 20 years, a period of the greatest growth in fund assets.

What Is a Mutual Fund?

A mutual fund is an investment company that pools money from investors and invests in a diversified portfolio of securities. Each investor holds a number of shares that reflects his or her ownership portion of the pool. Basically, the investment company itself does not pay taxes on its earnings as long as they are passed on to its investors, who must themselves treat these earnings as taxable income. Investment companies fall into one of three categories: open-end investment companies, closed-end investment companies and unit investment trusts.[7]

---

6. The mutual fund industry traces its roots back to 19th century Britain, where the Foreign and Colonial Government Trust formed in London resembled a mutual fund; see Investment Company Institute (1997b), p. 16.

7. This paper only examines "open end" funds, since they comprise the majority of the market. Closed-end funds often hold less liquid securities and comprise a very small percentage (about 4 percent) of the overall market. Source: Investment Company Institute (1997a), p. 3 and (1997b), p. 21.

An open-end mutual fund continually issues and redeems its shares at a price that equals the fund's net asset value (less any one-time fees, known as loads), which is calculated daily after security markets close.[8] A board of trustees elected by shareholders manages mutual funds. The board's purpose is to ensure that fund assets are managed according to the policies and restrictions specified in the prospectus. Among the most important duties of the board is the selection, subject to shareholder approval, of an investment advisor who oversees daily operations of the fund. The investment advisor ensures that the fund is making appropriate investments and usually receives an annual fee based on the fund's annual average net assets. The board also contracts out most other fund activities. These contracts include those with the 1) sponsor, who organizes the fund at its inception, 2) the distributor, a registered broker-dealer, who serves as investment banker and is also responsible for issuing new shares, 3) the administrator, who is responsible for administrative services, such as accounting, 4) the custodian, who is responsible for keeping records of securities held and their prices as required by law, and 5) the transfer agent, who is responsible for fund shareholder records and handles sales and redemptions of fund shares.

Growth in Number of Mutual Fund Complexes

In response to the strong demand for the investment management services provided by mutual funds, the industry has been growing rapidly. Although the industry has experienced several mergers in recent years, the number of start-up companies far outweighs the effects of consolidation. Figure 1 shows that the number of mutual fund complexes has grown from only 123 in 1980 to more than 400 in 1997.[9] The recent growth can be attributed to banks that have found it beneficial to start their own funds and managers of defined contribution pension funds that have also begun to offer their own funds.

Table 1 reports the Top 25 mutual fund complexes ranked by assets.

---

8. Mutual funds meet redemptions by holding a percentage of very liquid "cash equivalent" assets (such as Treasuries), drawing on lines of credit from commercial banks, or through interfund lending; see Fortune (July/August 1997).

9. A mutual fund complex is a group of funds under substantially common management (or distributorship), and is composed of one or more family of funds.

Figure 1: Number of Mutual Fund Complexes

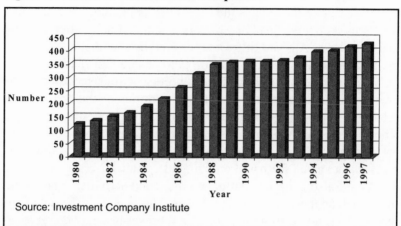

Source: Investment Company Institute

Table 1: Top 25 Mutual Fund Complexes: Assets and Market Share

Rank	Mutual Fund Complex	Assets 12/31/97 ($Mil)	Market Share 12/97	Market Share 12/96
1	Fidelity Distributors	$374,244	12.34%	12.45%
2	Vanguard Group	285,263	9.41	8.55
3	American Fund Distributors	220,432	7.27	7.20
4	Franklin Distributors Inc.	162,212	5.35	5.60
5	Putnam Financial Services	150,858	4.98	4.61
6	Merrill Lynch Asset Management	81,410	2.68	3.06
7	T. Rowe Price Investment Services	78,095	2.58	2.57
8	AMEX Asset Management	67,637	2.23	2.33
9	AIM Distributors	60,005	1.98	1.93
10	Oppenheimer Investor Services	55,104	1.82	1.72
11	Dean Witter Reynolds, Inc.	54,781	1.81	2.02
12	American Century Investment	52,535	1.73	1.84
13	Janus Funds	47,481	1.57	1.40
14	Massachusetts Financial Services	44,113	1.45	1.37
15	Fidelity Advisors	43,813	1.44	1.44
16	Smith Barney Advisors	39,457	1.30	1.45
17	Van Kampen Morgan Stanley	36,068	1.19	1.27
18	Zurich Kemper Investments	32,743	1.08	1.20
19	Prudential Securities	32,396	1.07	1.22
20	Dreyfus Service Corp.	32,063	1.06	1.28
21	PIMCO Advisors	30,632	1.01	1.05

Table 1: Top 25 Mutual Fund Complexes: Assets and Market Share *(continued)*

Rank	Mutual Fund Complex	Assets 12/31/97 ($Mil)	Market Share 12/97	Market Share 12/96
22	Federated Securities Corp.	25,858	.85	.92
23	Scudder Investor Services	24,032	.79	.84
24	Alliance Fund Distributors	23,453	.77	.76
25	John Hancock Funds	23,356	.77	.70

Source: http://www.mfcafe.com/pantry/msp_top50_0298.html.

These accounted for 68.5 percent of the industry's assets in December 1997, with the top 50 complexes accounting for more than 80 percent.[10] Concentration in the industry appears, on the surface at least, to be quite high, with 29 percent of market share accounted for by the top three complexes. By antitrust standards, however, the concentration ratio as measured by the Herfindahl-Hirshman Index is roughly 329, which is quite reasonable for an unconcentrated industry.[11] Given the number and size distribution of fund distributors and the relative ease of entry and expansion, the mutual fund industry can be considered competitive from a regulatory standpoint. This has caused regulators to devote most of their focus to ensuring adequate disclosure of business and financial information to investors.

Number and Types of Mutual Funds

Although there has been a substantial increase in the number of investment company complexes, growth in the number of funds offered has been much more dramatic over the past two decades. The following discussion concentrates on the three basic types of mutual funds offered: stock (also called equity), bond and money market funds. Figure 2 shows that the number of these funds grew more than tenfold, from 564 to 6,809 funds between 1980 and 1997, with the growth in long-term funds (i.e., equity and bond funds) being the

---

10. See http://www.mcafe.com/pantry/msp_top50_0298.html.
11. The Herfindahl-Hirshman Index (HHI) was constructed by squaring the market share of each independent fund management company in the marketplace and summing all of these squared figures. The Department of Justice Merger Guidelines describe a market with HHI below 1,000 as "unconcentrated" and one with a HHI between 1,000 and 1800 as "moderately concentrated." See Investment Company Institute (March 1998), p. 11. See also White (1992).

greatest.[12] Within these broad categories, the number of investment objectives has also increased. In 1976, there were only eight main categories of mutual funds classified by objective. Currently, the mutual fund trade group, the Investment Company Institute (ICI), lists more than 20 types of mutual funds classified by investment objective.[13] These more-specialized fund types, targeting specific geographic areas and industry sectors and offering diverse investment strategies, have emerged over time to meet a growing variety of customer demands.

Figure 2: Number and Types of Mutual Funds

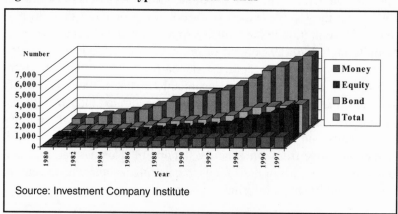

Source: Investment Company Institute

Mutual Fund Assets

Figure 3 illustrates the spectacular growth in total assets held by mutual funds, which soared by slightly more than 3,200 percent, from $135 billion at the end of 1980 to roughly $4.5 trillion at year-end 1997. The recent growth in fund assets can be attributed to price appreciation, net new cash flow and newly reporting funds. In 1997, 56 percent of the growth was attributable to price appreciation, while

---

12. Investment Company Institute (1997b), p. 61 and conversations with Investment Company Institute personnel.

13. These investment objectives include: aggressive growth, growth, growth and income, precious metals, international, global equity, income equity, option income, flexible portfolio, balanced, income-mixed, income-bond, U.S. government income, Ginnie Mae, global bond, corporate bond, high-yield bond, national municipal bond, state municipal bond, tax-exempt money market-National, tax-exempt money market-State, and taxable money market. Source: Investment Company Institute, (1997b), pp. 24-25.

44 percent was attributable to net new cash flow and newly reporting funds.[14] A major reason for the growth that stems from net new cash flow involves the growth of pension assets invested in mutual funds. The overall level of U.S. retirement assets increased from $1.67 trillion in 1983 to $5.35 trillion in 1995, giving U.S. households more pension assets than in all other industrialized countries combined, excluding Japan.[15] From 1992 to 1996, the years in which there exist comparable data on pension assets invested in mutual funds, retirement holdings of mutual fund assets in the United States grew from $776 billion, or 25 percent of the total market, to more than $1 trillion, or 35.7 percent of the industry's total assets.[16] Using a slightly different definition of retirement assets, the ICI estimated that, as recently as 1983, pension assets comprised only 9.9 percent of all fund assets.[17]

Figure 3: Total Industry Net Assets

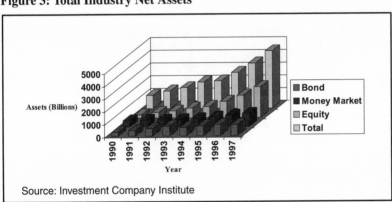

Source: Investment Company Institute

Several reasons account for the growing importance of mutual funds as investment vehicles for pension assets.

First, tax-deductible Individual Retirement Accounts (IRA) became available to all Americans in 1981. This change permitted U.S. workers to invest a fixed amount each year in nontaxable invest-

---

14. Investment Company Institute (1997b), p. 103 and conversations with ICI personnel.
15. See Investment Company Institute (Winter 1994/1995), p. 58 and (1997b), p. 51.
16. See Investment Company Institute (1997b), pp. 51-54.
17. See Investment Company Institute (Winter 1994/1995), p. 65.

ment vehicles of their choice.[18] Despite a major curtailment of the eligibility rules of deductible IRAs in 1986, the IRA market has undergone rapid growth, and today represents the largest portion of the mutual fund industry's pension assets.[19] At year-end 1996, IRAs held around $1.35 trillion in assets, about 38 percent of which was invested in mutual funds.[20]

Second, the tremendous increase in the number of defined contribution (e.g., 401(k) and 403(b)) plans has fueled a corresponding rise in mutual fund investments.[21] The ICI estimated that 210,000 corporations sponsored 401(k) plans in 1993 that had about 18 million active participants.[22] In 1994, the Department of Labor estimated that defined contribution plans represented 43 percent of total private plan assets in the United States, up from 29 percent in 1980.[23] In terms of the number of plans, defined benefit plans dwindled from 168,000 in 1984 to 78,000 in 1995, while defined contribution plans increased from 436,000 to 660,000 over the same period.[24] As shown in Figure 4, the share of 401(k) assets invested in mutual funds increased from 8.4 percent in 1986 to 38.7 percent in 1995.[25] Prior to this dramatic shift to defined contribution pension plans, most pension assets were invested in guaranteed investment contracts (GIC).[26]

---

18. As more workers retire or change jobs, a significant portion of the IRA market is coming from pension rollovers into IRAs. For example, in 1993, 28.9 percent of the total IRA assets invested in mutual funds came from rollovers. See Investment Company Institute (Winter 1994/1995), p. 77.

19. At year-end 1996, IRAs accounted for 14.4 percent of all mutual fund assets and 27.5 percent of all shareholder accounts; see Investment Company Institute (1997b), pp. 60-61, 92.

20. Investment Company Institute (1997b), p. 53; note that the 38 percent figure represents direct holdings only, and hence does not include certain brokered and trusteed accounts. See also Investment Company Institute (Winter 1994/1995), p. 76.

21. In a defined contribution plan, an employee's pension income is linked to the level of employee contribution and to the performance of the portfolio chosen by the employee. Alternatively, in a defined benefit plan, an employer agrees to pay a fixed retirement benefit that usually depends on the employee's salary during his or her last years of service and the overall tenure of service.

22. See Investment Company Institute (Winter 1994/1995), p.17

23. See Department of Labor (April 24, 1995), p. 11.

24. See Inglis (1997) pp.123, 124.

25. See Investment Company Institute (1997b), p. 54.

26. See Wyatt (October 1995).

Figure 4: 401(k) Assets Invested in Mutual Funds

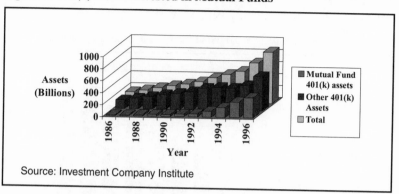

Source: Investment Company Institute

Although the United States has experienced the most dramatic growth in mutual fund assets during the 1990s, mutual fund assets have also grown in other parts of the world. Foreign countries including France, Japan, Germany, Luxembourg, Britain and Canada each reported amounts of fund assets in excess of $200 billion at the end of 1996. Indeed, worldwide mutual fund assets (excluding the United States) have grown from $1.5 trillion at the end of 1991 to $2.9 trillion at year-end 1996.[27] This increase corresponds to an annual growth rate of 14.5 percent, while the comparable rate for the United States is 20.5 percent. It should be noted, however, that cross-country comparisons are difficult to make because there are reporting differences and definitions that are not consistent from one country to the next. Nevertheless, it can be concluded that the recent mutual fund boom is a worldwide phenomenon.

Household Ownership and the Typical Mutual Fund Shareholder

The ICI reports that at year-end 1996, households held 74.2 percent of all mutual fund assets, while fiduciaries and other institutional investors held the remaining 25.8 percent.[28] Figure 5 shows the num-

---

27. Investment Company Institute (1997b), p. 48.
28. See Investment Company Institute (1997b) p. 35. In conversations with ICI personnel, they claimed the year-end 1996 percentages were 75 percent and 25 percent respectively.

ber of households owning mutual funds increased from 6 percent in 1980 to slightly more than 37 percent in 1997.[29]

Figure 5: Percentage of U.S. Households Owning Mutual Funds

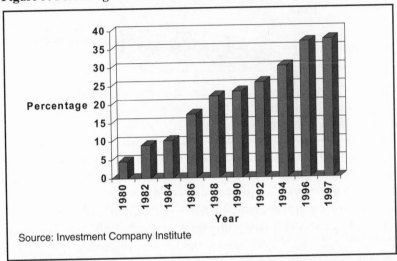

Source: Investment Company Institute

Given this dramatic increase in household ownership of mutual funds, in 1995 the OCC and SEC jointly surveyed 2,000 randomly selected mutual fund investors in order to gather data. The survey collected information on, (1) their demographic, financial and fund ownership characteristics, (2) their familiarity with the costs and certain investment risks associated with mutual funds, and (3) the sources of information that they used to learn about these costs and risks.[30] Six distribution channels, including stockbrokers (both full-service and discount), banks, mutual fund companies, insurance companies,

---

29. There has been a corresponding increase in the number of mutual fund accounts; see Investment Company Institute (1997b), p. 63.

30. The data employed in this paper is from a joint OCC/SEC survey that was conducted between June 28 and August 4, 1995. To qualify for inclusion, respondents needed to be (1) the principal financial decision makers, (2) 18 years or older, and (3) a member of a household owning mutual funds. A total of 32,075 telephone calls resulted in 2,019 completed interviews, of which 19 were not included in the analysis because respondents provided inaccurate information on the types of mutual funds purchased. The sample of mutual fund shareholders was drawn from a nationally representative sample of telephone numbers. All telephone numbers in the nation, whether listed or not, had an equal probability of being selected. For more on how the survey was administered, see Market Facts, Inc. (September 1995).

employer-sponsored pension plans and "other" (e.g., financial planners) were considered. These distribution channels were not mutually exclusive.[31] That is, an investor who purchased a mutual fund directly from a fund company may have purchased another one from a bank or a brokerage firm. As a result, the percentages reported in any given row in the following tables frequently total more than 100 percent.[32]

Demographic Characteristics

The major demographic characteristics considered in the survey include age, income, education, investor seasoning, and gender. Table 2 presents the median age, median income, and the percentages of respondents with a college education or graduate training by distribution channel.

Table 2: Demographic Characteristics

Demographic Characteristic	Distribution Channel Used						Total
	Bank	Broker	Pension	Direct	Insur.	Other	
Median age	45*	47*	41*	44*	44	44	43
Median income	$55,200	$67,600*	$62,100*	$67,000*	$59,200*	$58,400	$58,800
Gender: male	50.0%*	62.5%*	62.3%*	69.4%*	54.9%*	57.6%	58.6
College graduate	59.3	62.8	57.5*	68.5	55.3	52.2	54.6
Some graduate school	21.1*	32.0*	27.7	37.7*	27.5	24.4	26.5
Seasoned investor[a]	69.7	76.9*	65.6	75.4*	74.6*	64.7	66.3

Because the distribution channels are not mutually exclusive, a chi-squared statistic is used to test for significant differences in the percentages between bank and nonbank purchasers, broker and nonbroker purchasers, pension and nonpension purchasers, and so on. To save space, the cell values corresponding to nonbank purchasers, nonbroker purchasers, non-pension purchasers and so on are not reported in the table. The complete set of results is available from the authors upon request. A A*≅ denotes a cell value that is statistically significantly different, at the five percent level, from the corresponding value for all other purchasers not using the particular distribution channel being examined. Nonparametric tests for differences in the percentage values yield similar results and are not reported. A nonparametric test for median values is used to test for significant differences in the median age between bank and nonbank purchasers, broker and non-broker purchasers, pension and nonpension purchasers, and so on.

a. Purchased mutual fund prior to 1993.

---

31. Because distribution channels are not mutually exclusive, a chi-squared statistic is used to test for significant differences between bank and nonbank purchasers, broker and non-broker purchasers, pension and non-pension purchasers, and so on. Except where otherwise indicated, statements about statistical significance are based on a chi-squared statistic.
32. The demographic and financial characteristics of sample respondents in the survey are very similar to those reported in various ICI reports on mutual fund investors, suggesting the respondents are representative of the population of mutual fund owners.

The median age of a mutual fund shareholder is 43 years, which is greater than the median age (38 years) of the United States voting-age population.[33] Bank, broker and direct fund company purchasers are significantly older, and pension purchasers are significantly younger, each as a group, than are their counterparts who purchase their mutual fund shares elsewhere. Although not reported, elderly purchasers (65 years or older) make up slightly more than 9 percent of the sample, and banks have a significantly larger base of elderly shareholders (16 percent) than nonbank purchasers do.

In terms of household income, mutual fund investors have a median household income of $58,800. This income level is substantially higher than the 1994 median household income of $38,782 reported by the U.S. Census Bureau, but close to the median household income of fund owners reported elsewhere.[34] Mutual fund purchasers using brokers, those buying directly from the fund company, and those buying through pension plans report significantly higher median incomes than those purchasing through other distribution channels.

Table 2 also presents data on the percentage of survey respondents who are college graduates, male, and seasoned.[35] Mutual fund investors are well educated, with 54.6 percent having at least completed college, compared with 39.4 percent of the U.S. voting-age population.[36] Broker and direct fund company customers are more likely to have at least a college degree than customers are in the other distribution channels.

---

33. The U.S. median age figure is calculated from U.S. Bureau of the Census (1996), p. 289. A 1996 survey of mutual fund shareholders conducted by the Investment Company Institute reports that the median age of mutual fund shareholders is 44 years; see Investment Company Institute (May 1996), p. 53.

34. See Investment Company Institute (May 1996), p. 53.

35. When conducting research, the Investment Company Institute (May 1996, p. 15) "routinely defines shareholders who purchased their first fund in the two years preceding the survey as 'new' shareholders." Since the current survey was taken in 1995, 1993 was used here as a cutoff date for defining a mutual fund shareholder as "seasoned" in order to be consistent with ICI's definition.

36. See U.S. Bureau of the Census (1996), p. 289. According to the Investment Company Institute, (May 1996), p. 53, 58 percent of mutual fund shareholders completed college or postgraduate training.

As shown in the table, 58.6 percent of survey respondents were males, whereas males represent 48 percent of the U.S. voting-age population.[37] Investors who purchased mutual funds directly from a fund company were significantly more likely to be male (69.4 percent). In contrast, survey respondents who purchased mutual funds through banks were equally divided between male and female, again indicating that banks reach a somewhat different segment of the population than that reached by other mutual fund providers. Finally, most mutual fund investors were not new to investing in mutual funds, since 66.3 percent were seasoned investors. This was particularly true for investors using the broker, direct, or insurance distribution channels to make their purchases.

Financial Characteristics

Panel A of Table 3 presents data on the types of mutual funds owned by purchasers using the various distribution channels. Each type, or category, of fund represents a different combination of possible risk and return.[38] More than 72 percent of respondents own stock mutual funds and nearly 40 percent own bond or money market mutual funds or both. Direct, broker, and pension plan purchasers were significantly more likely to own stock funds, whereas bank and insurance company purchasers were significantly less likely to own them. In contrast, bank and insurance company customers were significantly more likely to own money market mutual funds than were the customers using other sales channels.[39] Lastly, broker, pension, direct, and insurance customers were significantly more likely to own bond funds than are other sales channel customers. Panel A also reveals that the median number of funds owned by the respondents is three.[40] The median number of funds owned was significantly greater

---

37. See U.S. Bureau of the Census (1995), p. 289. According to the Investment Company Institute (May 1996), p. 53, males make up 57 percent of all mutual fund shareholders.

38. There is also a wide range of risk-return tradeoffs within each of these broad categories.

39. This information on bank purchasers is consistent with bank call report data that indicate over 90 percent of mutual fund sales activity by banks is in money market mutual funds. See Figure 9A, derived from the Federal Deposit Insurance Corporation *Call Reports*.

40. A median of three funds owned is also reported by the Investment Company Institute (May 1996), p. 54.

for broker, direct, and pension investors relative to nonbroker, nondirect and nonpension purchasers.

Panel B of Table 3 presents the type of mutual fund in which the respondents hold their largest investment. The largest fund type may indicate some measure of the risk preferences of investors, or alternatively, the knowledge of investors. More than 63 percent of the respondents reported that their largest investment was in a stock fund. Broker, direct, and pension plan purchasers were significantly more likely to have their largest investment in a stock fund. On the other hand, bank and insurance purchasers were significantly less likely to have their largest investment in a stock fund. Bank purchasers were the largest investors in money market funds with a percentage (25.3 percent) significantly greater than that for nonbank purchasers (14.7 percent).

Panel C of Table 3 presents data on the other types of financial assets owned by the survey respondents. The typical mutual fund shareholder owned several other types of financial assets besides mutual funds. About 50 percent owned individual stocks, 30 percent owned individual bonds, 35 percent owned Certificates of Deposit (CD), and 40 percent had money market deposit accounts (MMDA).[41] More than 80 percent of the sample owned their primary residence, compared with 64 percent of the U.S. population.[42] Purchasers of mutual funds from brokers were significantly more likely than all other purchasers to own individual stocks and bonds.[43] Those purchasing through brokers were also significantly more likely to own all of the other types of assets listed, including their residence. In contrast, bank purchasers were significantly less likely to own individual stocks, which is consistent with the earlier observation that these customers were less likely to own stock funds. Bank purchasers were significantly more likely to own CDs and MMDAs, however, which is also consistent with economic intuition, given these are major products offered by banks.

---

41. MMDAs are insured bank accounts offering a rate of return that is tied to the rate of return on short-term debt instruments.

42. See U.S. Bureau of the Census (1996), p. 736.

43. Brokers, especially full-service ones, are known for giving investment advice on individual stocks and bonds. As noted, the survey does not distinguish between full-service and discount brokers.

In summary, the demographic and financial characteristics of mutual fund investors are notably different from the population at large. Furthermore, there are notable differences in several of these characteristics across the distribution channels.

Table 3: Financial Characteristics

Panel A: Fund Type Owned	Distribution Channel Used						Total
	Bank	**Broker**	**Pension**	**Direct**	**Insur.**	**Other**	
Stock	64.8%*	82.3%*	80.1%*	85.3%*	58.5%*	75.9%	72.9%
Bond	40.3	45.6*	39.3*	39.7*	41.0*	34.5	36.1
Money market	44.6*	39.4	39.1	38.8	65.5*	32.8	39.2
Other	15.5	19.1	12.4*	21.8*	28.6*	20.7	14.6
Median Number of Funds Owned	3	4+*	3*	4+*	3	3	3
Panel B: Largest Fund Type							
Stock	49.8%*	69.7%*	68.0%*	73.9%*	59.5%*	59.3%	63.8%
Bond	14.7*	11.6	8.1*	7.9*	9.0	20.4*	10.6
Money market	25.3*	11.6*	14.1*	9.7*	20.1*	13.0	16.3
Other	10.2	7.3*	9.8	8.5	11.3	7.4	9.3
Panel C: Other Financial Assets							
Individual stocks	44.6%*	72.6%*	51.8%	58.4%	47.4%	42.4%	50.8%
Individual bonds	34.4	39.0*	30.4	33.4	34.4	29.4	31.1
CDs	47.6*	41.7*	30.8*	34.3	36.3	28.3	34.9
MMDAs	50.7*	46.2*	36.5*	37.3	36.3	38.0	38.3
Annuities	31.0	31.0*	25.1	25.0	45.5*	25.0	26.7
Primary residence	77.6	88.6*	81.0	82.1	84.6*	71.7*	80.9
See notes to Table 2.							

Regulation and the Role of Mutual Funds in the U.S. Economy

The SEC has jurisdiction over the administration and enforcement of the federal securities laws with respect to all individuals and companies, including banks.[44] Banks and pension funds, however, are subject to supplementary forms of regulation, or in the case of banks, guidelines.[45] This section examines the regulatory framework for investment companies and provides some descriptive evidence on several regulatory concerns related to mutual funds. The first section concentrates on SEC regulation of the industry, while the remaining

---

44. See Martha L. Cochran and David F. Freeman, Jr. (1997), particularly pp. 518-522.

two sections concentrate on the nuances and policy issues related to the regulation of the bank and pension distribution channels.

SEC Regulation of the Mutual Fund Industry

The 1929 stock market crash and the Great Depression prompted Congress to enact the first laws protecting investors and regulating securities markets. The Securities Act of 1933 and the Securities Exchange Act of 1934 are the fundamental regulations governing issuance and trading of securities, respectively. Of particular relevance for the mutual fund industry are two subsequent pieces of federal legislation: the Investment Company Act of 1940 and the Investment Advisors Act of 1940.[46]

The primary focus of most of the regulation of mutual fund activity involves ensuring adequate disclosure.[47] Both the amount and type of information that existing and prospective shareholders receive is under close scrutiny by the SEC, whose underlying mission is investor protection. A smaller percentage of regulation related to mutual fund activity deals with safety considerations that limit the types and maturities of assets a portfolio may hold.[48] The rationale for all the

---

45. Banks selling mutual funds are all subject to the *Interagency Statement on Retail Sales of Nondeposit Investment Products* issued by the Federal Reserve Board, Federal Deposit Insurance Corporation, Office of Thrift Supervision, Office of the Comptroller of the Currency, and National Credit Union Association (1994). A limited number of banks, however, with sales agents that are bank employees have a "bank exemption" and are subject only to these guidelines. The number of banks using the bank exemption in securities activities is estimated to be less than 300 and the number of sales personnel is estimated to be only a few thousand (see General Accounting Office (September 1995)). In recent years, bank regulators have successfully proposed that all these employees currently selling securities under the bank exemption pass comparable examinations (i.e., Series 6 and Series 7) as their counterparts in the securities industry.

46. The SEC delegates significant regulatory authority to a number of private member-owned and member-operated securities industry organizations, including the National Association of Securities Dealers (NASD). NASD responsibilities include establishing rules governing its broker/dealer members' business conduct; setting qualifications standards for securities professionals; examining operational conditions and compliance with regulations; responding to inquiries and investigating potential violations of securities laws; and disciplining violators of applicable rules.

47. Harvard Law School Professor Howell E. Jackson (1997), p. 535 states that "the 1940 Act relies on disclosure based regulation more than any other comparable regulatory structure in the United States."

regulation of the securities industry, in general, rests on the belief that the market, if left to its own devices, will not provide sufficient information to permit suitable investment choices.

The National Securities Market Improvement Act of 1996 further redefined the regulatory framework for mutual funds and was the first major overhaul of securities law in the United States in more than 50 years. In particular, the act for the most part eliminated state regulation of mutual funds and gave full regulatory authority to the SEC. Other important elements of the legislation included: 1) eliminating the 1940 act's Section 12(d)(1)(B) that prohibited a fund from creating "a fund of funds" by purchasing shares of other mutual funds," 2) providing the SEC with additional funding to supervise investment advisors, 3) loosening the requirements to qualify as an unregistered private investment pool, and 4) providing for the establishment of a database that tracks the disciplinary records of investment advisory firms.[49]

Because the Investment Company Act of 1940 tries to ensure that investors receive the information that is necessary to make informed judgments, it is important to seek answers to a number of related questions:

- What sources of information are useful to investors?
- How well do they understand key disclosure issues, such as fund expenses and risk?
- How financially literate are mutual fund investors?
- What changes could be made to improve or enhance investor knowledge?

Much of the regulation involved with the investment company industry deals with ensuring adequate disclosure through the mutual fund prospectus. However, just how useful is the prospectus? Table 4 indicates that the mutual fund prospectus was the single most widely used source of information, with 57.7 percent of respondents having cited it as a source of information in making their most recent mutual fund purchase.[50] Survey respondents also reported that they relied

---

48. See Howell E. Jackson (1997), pp. 538-539.
49. See Fortune (July/August 1997), pp. 50-51.
50. In an ICI survey (see Investment Company Institute (May 1996), p. 23), 50 percent of mutual fund shareholders said they consulted the prospectus before purchasing their latest fund.

heavily on financial publications (i.e., newspapers and magazines), employer-provided printed materials, family or friends, and meetings or presentations at work in choosing their most recent mutual fund investments. About a third of the survey respondents stated that brokers provided information that they used in making their most recent mutual fund investment decisions. For those who purchased mutual funds directly from a fund company, the prospectus and financial publications were by far the most widely cited sources of information. Not surprisingly, broker, bank and pension-channels purchasers were much more likely to cite brokers, bankers and employers, respectively, as sources of information than purchasers who used other distribution channels.

Table 4: Information Sources Used in Purchasing Most Recent Mutual Fund

Information Sources	Distribution Channel Used						Total
	Bank	Broker	Pension	Direct	Insur.	Other	
Prospectus	51.2%*	56.5%	60.8%*	74.0%*	59.1%	49.4%	57.7%
Broker	27.4	61.6*	24.8*	29.6	31.7	31.8	31.0
Family or friends	40.4	34.3*	33.6*	30.5*	42.4*	36.5	37.6
Financial publications	41.4	49.8*	41.3	67.9*	39.7	34.1	42.0
Banker	41.1*	6.9*	7.0*	4.3*	10.5	4.7	10.3
Insurance agent	0.0*	0.6*	0.6*	0.5*	6.0*	0.0	1.6
Fund company	0.0	0.2	0.3	0.7*	0.0	0.0	0.3
Employer	34.4*	23.3*	65.0*	25.9*	35.6*	35.3	44.5
Meeting/Presentation	23.9*	18.3*	46.6*	17.1*	31.1	27.1	33.5
Other	4.6	4.8*	3.5	5.9*	3.5	5.9	3.5
Total	100.0%	100.0%	100.0%	100.0%	100.0%	100.0%	100.0%
Number of Respondents	285	627	1,105	561	514	85	1,956

See notes to Table 2.

Although the prospectus is heavily cited as a piece of information, it is not cited as the best source by fund investors. Table 5 presents respondents' perceptions of the best source of information for their most recently purchased mutual fund. Generally, shareholders cited the information source most closely associated with the distribution channel used in making the purchase as the most important. For example, a significant percentage of bank (19.4 percent), broker (39 percent), and pension purchasers (39.3 percent) named banker, broker and employer, respectively, as the best information source, consistent with earlier observations on the results presented in Table 4. These results are a major reason for the SEC move toward the profile prospectus and "plain English" disclosure proposals.[51]

Table 5: Best Source of Information Used in Purchasing Most Recent Mutual Fund

Best Source of Information	Distribution Channel Used						Total
	Bank	Broker	Pension	Direct	Insur.	Other	
Prospectus	13.9%	13.0%	16.8%*	20.5%*	17.4%	13.4%	15.2%
Broker	11.0*	39.0*	11.7*	14.9	16.0	22.0	16.9
Family or friends	20.9*	13.3*	10.9*	12.6*	20.4*	24.4*	16.3
Financial publications	13.6	21.6*	16.6	36.7*	12.6*	14.6	17.1
Banker	19.4*	2.0*	1.9*	0.9*	4.4	1.2	4.2
Employer	18.7*	9.1*	39.3*	10.9*	21.4*	23.2	26.7
Meeting/Presentation	0.4	0.2	0.7	0.2	0.8	0.0	0.6
Insurance agent	0.0	0.3	0.1*	0.0	1.6*	0.0	0.4
Other	2.2	1.6	2.0	3.3	5.2*	1.2	2.6
Total	100.0%	100.0%	100.0%	100.0%	100.0%	100.0%	100.0%
Number of Respondents	273	608	1,080	542	499	82	1,897
See notes to Table 2.							

Investor Knowledge of Risk and Expenses

Given that the primary goal of investment company regulation is investor protection, how well do investors understand expenses and risk? Table 6 presents data on mutual fund investor awareness of certain investment risks involved with stock, bond and money market mutual funds. Most mutual fund purchasers know that it is possible to lose money in stock, bond, and money market mutual funds (94.0 percent, 71.8 percent, and 63.9 percent know this, respectively) with little difference across distribution channel. However, the observation that only 72 percent of investors realize they can lose money in a bond fund is surprising and of concern, particularly in light of bond fund investors' bad experience during early-1994's run-up in interest rates when many bond funds dropped significantly in value.

---

51. The survey is referenced in, for example, the Office of the Federal Register (March 10, 1997). The survey has also been cited in the popular press as a reason for the move toward the profile prospectus. See, for example, Wyatt (March 11, 1998).

Table 6: Investor Knowledge of Risk Associated with Mutual Funds by Type of Fund

Type of Fund		Distribution Channel Used						Total
		Bank	Broker	Pension	Direct	Insur.	Other	
Stock Fund	Yes	93.9%	96.9%*	94.6%	97.9%*	92.3%	92.4%	94.0%
	No	2.7	0.9*	1.5	0.5*	2.5	2.2	2.0
	DK/Refused	3.4	2.2*	3.9	1.6*	5.2	5.4	4.1
	Total	100.0%	100.0%	100.0%	100.0%	100.0%	100.0%	100.0%
Bond Fund	Yes	72.8%	79.5%*	73.6%*	85.6%*	68.7%	67.4%	71.8%
	No	13.3	8.2*	12.1	6.2*	13.2	18.5	12.3
	DK/Refused	14.0	12.4*	14.3*	8.3*	18.0	14.1	16.0
	Total	100.0%	100.0%	100.0%	100.0%	100.0%	100.0%	100.0%
Money Market Fund	Yes	64.0%	63.0%	64.9%	67.5%*	66.8%	64.1%	63.9%
	No	20.1	23.0	20.3	21.8*	20.0	19.6	20.5
	DK/Refused	16.0	14.0	14.9	10.7*	13.2	16.3	15.7
	Total	100.0%	100.0%	100.0%	100.0%	100.0%	100.0%	100.0%
Number of Respondents		294	638	1,118	569	521	92	2,000

See notes to Table 2. DK denotes "don't know."

As shown in the table, the percentage of investors who believe that mutual funds can lose money is lower for bond funds than stock funds (71.8 percent and 94.0 percent), and even lower for money market mutual funds (63.9 percent). The difference in the stock and bond fund percentages is statistically significant, as is the difference in the percentages for bond and money market funds. Furthermore, the differences between the stock and bond fund percentages are alike across all distribution channels. A similar observation can be made when the bond and money market fund percentages are compared, except for the insurance and "other" distribution channels where the differences are small and insignificant.

Table 7 presents the reasons given by those respondents who believe that one cannot lose money in a money market mutual fund. The reason that was cited most often (26.8 percent) was that money market mutual funds hold only safe assets. Under applicable SEC rules, money market funds are indeed limited to holding debt instruments that could be correctly characterized as safe.[52] The second most commonly cited reason (19.5 percent) was that money market mutual funds are insured, which is an incorrect reason.

---

52. Rule 2a-7 under the Investment Company Act restricts the holdings of money market mutual funds to high-quality, short-term debt instruments that have low volatility.

Table 7: Why Investors Believe One Cannot Lose Money in a Money Fund? (Asked only of those respondents who believe one cannot lose money.)

A. Can You Lose Money in a Money Market Mutual Fund?	Distribution Channel Used						Total
	Bank	Broker	Pension	Direct	Insur.	Other	
No	20.1%	23.0%	20.3%	21.8%*	20.0%	19.6	20.5%
B. If No, Why Do You Think So?							
Insurance	16.9%	23.8%	18.9%	17.7%	17.3%	11.1%	19.5%
Holds safe assets	35.6	23.1	29.5	30.6	28.8	44.4	26.8
Bailout funds	1.7	2.0	2.2	3.2	4.8*	0.0	1.9
Principal and/or interest guaranteed	8.5	4.8	8.8	6.4	10.6	11.1	8.3
Other	13.6*	27.2	20.7	30.6*	24.0	16.7	23.7
DK/Refused	28.8	25.8	27.3	16.9*	24.0	27.8	27.3
Total	100.0%	100.0%	100.0%	100.0%	100.0%	100.0%	100.0%
Number of Respondents	59	147	227	124	104	18	410

See notes to Table 2. DK denotes "don't know."

Table 8A reports data on investor familiarity with mutual fund operating expenses. The table presents information on the percentage of respondents who could provide some expense estimates for the mutual fund in which they have their largest investment. As shown in the table, the level of annual expenses did not seem to be an important factor in the purchasing decision of many respondents. Only 18.9 percent of the respondents could give an estimate of expenses for their largest mutual fund, although broker and direct purchasers were significantly more likely to be able to do so. The percentage of respondents who could provide even an approximation of actual expenses was even smaller. Respondents earning less than $75,000 were significantly less likely to provide an expense estimate. Males and college graduates were significantly more likely to provide an expense estimate.

Table 8A: Knowledge of Largest Mutual Fund's Annual Expenses

Knowledge of Expenses?	Distribution Channel Used						Total
	Bank	Broker	Pension	Direct	Insur.	Other	
Yes	15.3%	23.0%*	19.8%	35.0%*	20.7%	17.4%	18.9%
No	84.7	77.0	80.2	65.0	79.3	82.6	81.2
Total	100.0%	100.0%	100.0%	100.0%	100.0%	100.0%	100.0%
Number of Respondents	294	638	1,118	569	521	92	2,000
See notes to Table 2.							

Respondents who could not provide an expense estimate for their largest fund were asked if they knew any of their largest fund's expenses at the time of purchase. Table 8B reports that only 43 percent of the respondents claimed to have known any of their largest fund's expenses at the time they first invested in the fund. Broker, direct, and insurance purchasers were significantly more likely to have claimed to have known the annual expenses of their largest funds at the time of initial purchase. College graduates and males were significantly more likely to have responded that they knew the fund's expenses.[53]

Table 8B: Knowledge of Any of Largest Mutual Fund's Expenses at Time of Purchase

Knowledge of Expenses?	Distribution Channel Used						Total
	Bank	Broker	Pension	Direct	Insur.	Other	
Yes	46.1%	49.5%*	40.5%*	59.7%*	47.8%*	28.0*	43.0%
No	53.9	50.5*	59.5*	40.3*	52.2*	71.9*	57.1
Total	100.0%	100.0%	100.0%	100.0%	100.0%	100.0%	100.0%
Number of Respondents	204	406	748	308	343	57	1,348
See notes to Table 2.							

Pension purchasers, in contrast, were significantly less likely to have known their largest funds' annual expenses. However, annual expenses of funds may be of less significance to mutual fund shareholders who purchased their shares through employee pension plans because a participant in a typical defined contribution plan is presented with a limited choice of funds. Since this choice is generally

---

53. Of those survey respondents who cited financial publications and the prospectus as the best sources of information, 66.5 percent and 58.3 percent of them were knowledgeable about their fund's expenses, respectively. The percentages of those having knowledge of expenses were lower for the other best sources of information cited by respondents.

designed to allow the employee to allocate assets among broad categories of investments (e.g., stocks, bonds, or money market investments), the employee is not presented with a choice of different funds with the same objective. As a result, the cost of holding a particular fund would appear to be of lesser importance to an employee purchasing fund shares through an employee pension plan than to an investor purchasing funds through other distribution channels.

Investor Beliefs about Costs and Performance

Table 8C reports investors' beliefs about the relation between expenses and mutual fund performance. Almost 20 percent of the survey respondents believed that mutual funds with higher expenses produced better results, while 64.4 percent believed that funds with higher expenses produced average results. Only 15.7 percent of the survey respondents believed that higher expenses led to lower-than-average returns.[54] Bank customers were significantly less likely than nonbank customers to expect an inverse relation, which is surprising since most bank customers buy money market funds where the inverse relation is strong, while direct fund purchasers were significantly more likely to expect an inverse relation.

Table 8C: Expected Performance of Fund with Higher than Average Expenses

Expected Fund Performance	Distribution Channel Used						Total
	Bank	Broker	Pension	Direct	Insur.	Other	
Above average	23.8%	19.3%	19.7%	16.6%	22.9%	20.3%	19.9%
About average	66.5	63.3	64.4	62.9	63.6	56.3	64.4
Below average	9.7*	17.4	15.9	20.6*	13.5	23.4	15.7
Total	100.0%	100.0%	100.0%	100.0%	100.0%	100.0%	100.0%
Number of Respondents	206	420	756	350	363	64	1,364
See note to Table 2.							

---

54. In general, there is an inverse relationship between fund performance and expenses for bond and money market funds, but it is neither clearly negative nor positive for stock funds.

Table 9 reports investor perceptions about the year-to-year performance of mutual funds. Mutual funds frequently use historical fund
returns in their advertisements and many investors tend to choose
mutual funds solely on the basis of past performance. Empirical evidence on the historical relation between returns in successive years is
mixed.[55] Indeed, mutual funds are required to disclose in the prospectus that past performance is no indication of future performance.[56]
Approximately 24 percent of the respondents believe that a fund that
has performed well last year will have an above-average return this
year; 70.6 percent believe the fund will have an average return; and
5.3 percent believe the fund will have a below-average return. Direct
purchasers are significantly more likely than nondirect purchasers to
believe that returns in successive years are positively related.

**Table 9: Expected Performance of Fund with
Good Performance Previous Year**

Expected Fund Performance	Distribution Channel Used						Total
	Bank	Broker	Pension	Direct	Insur.	Other	
Above average	19.5%	24.9%	25.3%	29.8%*	27.3	23.6%	24.1%
About average	75.6	68.0	68.8	62.2*	69.1	69.4	70.6
Below average	4.9	7.1*	5.9	8.0*	3.6	6.9	5.3
Total	100.0%	100.0%	100.0%	100.0%	100.0%	100.0%	100.0%
Number of Respondents	246	491	885	423	418	72	1,595
See notes to Table 2.							

Panel A of Table 10 presents results on whether an investor's
knowledge that stocks have a higher average return than Treasury
bills over the long term was related to the type of mutual fund held by
the investor. As shown in the table, mutual fund investors who owned
stock and bond funds were significantly more likely to know that
stock market returns tend to exceed the return on U.S. Treasury bills.
College graduates, males and respondents earning more than $75,000
annually were significantly more likely to believe that the rate of
return on stocks is greater than that on Treasury bills.

Panel B of Table 10 presents results on whether an investor's
knowledge of the rate of return differential between stocks and U.S.

---

55. This is particularly so for stock funds. See, for example, Brown, Goetzmann,
Ibbotson, and Ross (1992); Grinblatt and Titman (1992); Hendricks, Patel, and Zeckhauser (1993); Goetzmann and Ibbotson (1994); Malkiel (1995); and Carhart (1997).
56. See NASD Rule IM-2210-3c4.

Treasury bills is related to the largest type of fund held by the investor. Mutual fund investors whose largest fund was a stock fund were significantly more likely to know that stock market returns on average exceed the return on Treasury bills. Investors whose largest fund type was a bond or a money fund, however, were significantly less likely to know that the average rate of return in the stock market is greater. Of concern is that about one out of every three of these investors do not realize that over the long term, stocks have a higher average return than Treasury bills.

Table 10: Investor Knowledge of Rate of Return: Stock Markets vs. U.S. Treasury Bills

A. Type of Fund	Stock (non-stock)	Bond (non-bond)	Money (non-money)
Number of investors purchasing fund type	n=1119 (n=598)	n=553 (n=1164)	n=607 (n=1110)
Percent who know on average that stock market return is higher	81%* (63%)	79%* (73%)	76% (74%)
B. Largest Fund Type			
Number of investors with largest fund type	n=879 (n=483)	n=140 (n=1222)	n=217 (n=1145)
Percent who know on average that stock market return is higher	82%* (69%)	66%* (78%)	65%* (79%)
*Signifies statistical significance at the five percent level. Comparison values are reported in parentheses. The effective sample size is given by n.			

Given that the vast majority of mutual fund investors surveyed (94 percent) knew that they could lose money in a stock fund, disclosure of this information appears adequate. Room for improvement exists, however, in investor knowledge of the investment risks associated with bond and money market funds since a significantly smaller percentage were aware that they could lose money in a bond fund (72 percent) or money market fund (64 percent).[57] Improvement is also needed in educating investors about the long-term investment performance of stocks and Treasury bills and about the relationship between fees and performance. Although expense information must be disclosed in the prospectus, the investors in the survey did not seem to view the level of expenses as a key factor in making their investment decision. Raising these percentages to higher levels will require inves-

---

57. A significant number of investors lost money in bond funds in 1994 and money market funds have been known to "break the buck"; see Edwards (1996), particularly pp. 74-80, 89-90.

tor education initiatives similar to the educational campaign by the SEC and other organizations, including some from the private sector. More regulation or disclosure requirements beyond the current "plain English" and profile prospectus ones are unlikely to be fruitful.[58] Instead, more reliance on the private sector to fill these investor needs is in order. [59]

Investor Financial Literacy

Although individual questions on investor knowledge provide useful information, constructing a broader measure of investor knowledge may provide even more useful information. In this section, the financial literacy of the mutual fund survey respondents is examined. The analysis is conducted in several steps. First, an aggregate measure of overall investing and mutual fund knowledge is constructed for each respondent. This measure is called the respondent's "quiz score." Then a multivariate analysis is conducted using a logit model to assess the factors that are most important in explaining differences in overall investor literacy as measured by the quiz score.

The quiz score should not necessarily be interpreted as indicating whether any particular financial intermediary has been more or less successful in educating investors. Quiz scores may show that in general more knowledgeable investors choose to purchase funds through particular channels. For example, the more financially literate investors are, the more comfortable they may be with the idea of purchasing directly from a fund company and the more likely they may be to maintain an account with a stockbroker. As a result, it can not be

---

58. It appears from the proposing- and final-rule releases that fear of legal liability was a primary reason why the private sector was unwilling to use "plain English" or the profile prospectus, hence necessitating regulation; see www.sec.gov/rules/proposed/34-38164.txt and www.sec.gov/rules/final/33-7497.txt.

59. One private sector initiative that has generated a lot of attention lately involves a product of Finance Engines, Inc., a firm co-founded by Nobel Laureate William Sharpe of Stanford University and others; see Quinn (March 2, 1998) and Bransten (February 23, 1998).

inferred that salespeople in these distribution channels necessarily do a better job of disclosing risks and costs.[60]

The measure of overall investor knowledge is based on the responses to a subset of questions in the mutual fund survey. The quiz consists of nine questions and the number of correct responses is called the quiz score. The quiz score is an aggregate measure of overall investor knowledge and measures investing knowledge in general and mutual fund investment knowledge in particular on the part of mutual fund shareholders. The questions involve the respondents reporting whether or not they know:

1. That it is possible to lose money in a stock mutual fund;
2. That it is possible to lose money in a bond mutual fund;
3. That money market mutual funds are not insured;
4. That there are thousands of mutual funds to choose from in making an investment decision;
5. That stock market returns are, on the average, greater than the return on U.S. Treasury bills;
6. What the term net asset value means;
7. What redemption means;
8. What derivatives are; and
9. What present value means.

Quiz questions six through nine are relatively weak measures of investor knowledge, as respondents were given credit for those questions if they claimed to know what these various terms mean, even though no attempt was made to verify the accuracy of their responses. The results reported here, however, are essentially unchanged when quiz scores are based solely on the responses to the first five questions.

Table 11A presents the mean and standard deviation of the quiz score. The results are reported for the total number of survey respondents, as well as by distribution channel. Also reported are the results

---

60. In fact, Alexander, Jones and Nigro (1998) find that investors "self select" into distribution channels based on their level of financial literacy. In other words, more financially literate investors purchase funds directly from the fund company or a broker, while less financially literate investors' make purchases through banks and insurance companies.

of conventional tests of the equality of mean quiz scores for each type of distribution channel.

Table 11A: Mean and Variance of the Quiz Score by Distribution Channel

Distribution Channel	Purchased yes/no	Mean	Standard Deviation	t-statistic
Bank	Yes	4.77	2.09	2.10*
	No	5.08	2.16	
Broker	Yes	5.48	2.06	6.21*
	No	4.81	2.17	
Direct	Yes	6.26	1.88	17.44*
	No	4.50	2.04	
Pension	Yes	5.14	2.17	2.39*
	No	4.89	2.13	
Insurance company	Yes	4.82	2.09	2.38*
	No	5.11	2.17	
Other	Yes	4.92	2.11	0.42
	No	5.04	2.16	
Total		5.03	2.16	

*Signifies statistical significance at the five percent level. A difference in means test is used to test for significant differences in quiz score that adjusts for unequal variances when necessary. Absolute values of the t-statistic are reported.

The typical mutual fund shareholder had a quiz score of five out of a possible nine.[61] Investors purchasing directly from fund companies scored much higher than any other fund group. Broker and pension plan purchasers also scored significantly higher than those buying mutual fund shares through other distribution channels. However, bank and insurance company purchasers received significantly lower mean quiz scores than other survey respondents.

Table 11B presents the mean and standard deviation of the quiz scores for each distribution channel where the respondents who reported using a given channel were broken down into two groups. The first group consists of those respondents who indicated the given channel was the only distribution channel that they used to purchase mutual funds; the second group consists of those respondents who purchased funds not only through the given channel, but also through

61. Recently, *Money* magazine and the Vanguard Funds Group conducted a 20-question survey of 1,467 mutual fund investors, and arrived at results similar to those reported here; see Walter L. Updegrave (February 1996). Similar results are also reported from a recent survey by Investor Protection Trust; see Albert B. Crenshaw (May 19, 1996).

at least one other distribution channel. Overall, the results reveal a significant difference in the quiz scores between the two groups—investors who have purchased mutual funds through multiple channels have notably higher scores (5.70) than those who used only a single channel (4.44). Furthermore, the differences are significant for each channel, with the largest difference being in the pension channel (1.57).[62] This is of particular interest, given the recent rapid growth in 401(k) plans.[63]

Table 11B: Mean and Variance of the Quiz Score By Distribution Channel Broken Down into Two Groups: Single Channel Purchasers and Multiple Channel Purchasers

Distribution Channel	Number of Channels Used	Mean	Standard Deviation	t-statistic
Bank	Multiple	5.21	2.03	4.82*
	Single	3.93	1.96	
	Difference	1.28		
Broker	Multiple	5.81	1.97	6.37*
	Single	4.61	2.06	
	Difference	1.20		
Direct	Multiple	6.38	1.87	2.41*
	Single	5.92	1.90	
	Difference	.46		
Pension	Multiple	5.78	2.05	11.83*
	Single	4.21	2.01	
	Difference	1.57		
Insurance company	Multiple	5.17	2.02	6.37*
	Single	3.77	1.91	
	Difference	1.40		
Other	Multiple	5.80	2.17	4.03*
	Single	3.90	1.52	
	Difference	1.90		
Total	Multiple	5.70	2.05	12.69*
	Single	4.44	2.07	
	Difference	1.26		

*Signifies statistical significance at the five percent level. A difference in means test is used to test for significant differences in quiz score that adjusts for unequal variances when necessary. Absolute values of the t-statistic are reported.

62. Technically, the largest difference is in the "other" channel. However, since this involves a variety of alternative distribution systems, it is ignored here.
63. *The Washington Post* reported that the number of 401(k) participants in 1995 was approximately 22 million, compared to approximately 10 million in 1985; See Albert B. Crenshaw (June 12, 1996).

When performing multivariate analysis using a logit model, the results indicate that there is a significant positive relationship between the quiz score and five demographic explanatory variables: being a male; a college graduate; working at a financial institution; earning income greater than $75,000; and owning three or more funds. Furthermore, those respondents reading financial publications and mutual fund prospectuses earn significantly higher quiz scores, while those who relied on employer-provided materials score somewhat lower on the quiz.

The results presented in this section argue for an examination of disclosure rules, which has been completed with the passage of the "plain English" and profile prospectus initiatives of the SEC, and more financial education programs. As mentioned earlier, financial education should be left primarily to the private sector since neither investor knowledge nor understanding can be regulated.

Bank Regulation

In response to both the outflows of deposits and the desire to diversify, banks have begun to participate heavily in the mutual fund industry through the advising of mutual funds and through the brokering of mutual fund shares. A bank can participate in the mutual fund industry in several ways. First, the bank can offer funds advised by the bank, for example proprietary funds, directly to its customers. Second, the bank can offer its proprietary funds through an unaffiliated distributor. Finally, the bank can, acting solely as a broker, sell shares of nonproprietary funds.[64]

While it is only in recent years that banks have become actively involved in proprietary mutual funds, the involvement of banks with mutual funds is not a new development. As part of their fiduciary activities, banks have acted as investment advisor, transfer agent and custodian for third-party mutual funds for more than 20 years.[65] Banks

---

64. Most sales of mutual funds at banks appear to be conducted through an unaffiliated distributor. The General Accounting Office (September 1995) found that of the 2,400 banks providing retail securities brokerage services, 88 percent offered funds through registered brokerage subsidiaries or through arrangements with nonaffiliated registered securities broker-dealers.

65. Fiduciary exams conducted by bank examiners were designed to ensure compliance with 12 CFR 12, which specifies requirements for record keeping and identifies conflicts of interests for portfolio managers.

have also provided access to third-party mutual funds for customers through discount brokerage services and bank dealer departments. More recently, banks have used certain trust funds as seed money for proprietary mutual funds. Whenever these assets involved pension funds, IRAs, or other employee welfare benefit plans, bank regulators ensured compliance with Employer Retirement Income Security Act (ERISA) of 1974.[66]

In recent years, as core deposits migrated to mutual funds, more banks began to offer mutual funds and bank regulators began focusing on retail sales of these funds. The push of banks into the mutual fund arena is an attempt to diversify income streams away from interest income attributable to commercial lending while maintaining market share in a shrinking market. As shown in Figure 6, noninterest income as a percent of total income at banks grew until the end of 1993, where it has stabilized at about 22 percent to 23 percent. Fee-based income generated from mutual fund sales at commercial banks, as shown in Figure 7, is a major force behind this diversified income stream at banks. In terms of the percentage of banks offering funds, Figure 8 shows that it has been fairly stable at about 21 percent to 23 percent since this information began to be collected on *Call Reports* in 1994. However, Figures 9A and 9B show that the level of mutual fund sales has increased over time, mostly due to money market sales, as opposed to long-term equity, bond and other (e.g., mixed, international) funds. Finally, although fund sales at commercial banks have increased, Figure 10 shows that the bank share of total fund assets has remained small over the last few years, having stabilized at about 14 percent.[67]

---

66. Since most banks selling mutual funds are also subject to SEC oversight, in June 1995, the OCC and SEC entered into a formal agreement for a program of joint exams for a certain number of national banks.
67. See Quittner (February 12, 1998).

Figure 6: Noninterest Income to Total Income Percentage

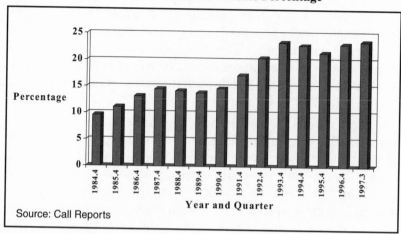

Source: Call Reports

Figure 7: Mutual Fund Income to Noninterest Income Percentage

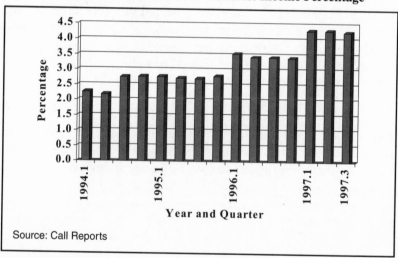

Source: Call Reports

Figure 8: Percentage of Banks Selling Mutual Funds

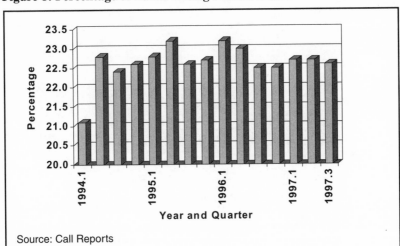

Source: Call Reports

Figure 9A: Commercial Bank Money Market Mutual Fund

Sales by Quarter

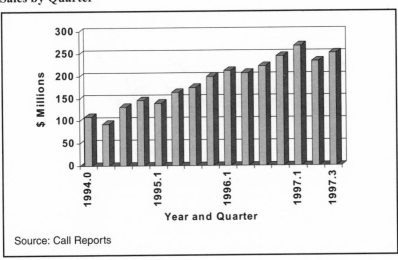

Source: Call Reports

Figure 9B: Commercial Bank Money Market Mutual Fund Sales by Quarter

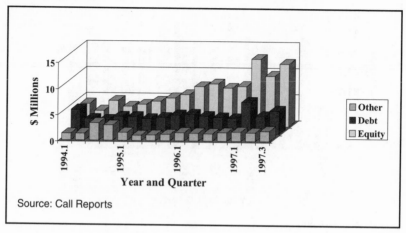

Source: Call Reports

Figure 10: Bank Related Fund Assets

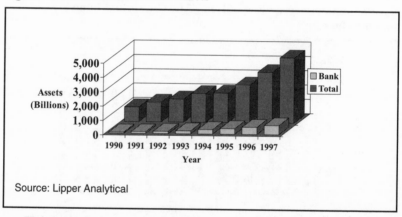

Source: Lipper Analytical

Heightened supervisory awareness evolved from the need for banks to comply with the *Interagency Statement on Retail Sales of Nondeposit Investment Products Statement* that was introduced 1994.[68] Retail sales of investment products in banks have added a new element of exposure to banks offering such products—the potential for customer confusion due to customers purchasing nondeposit investment products in banks and thinking that the investment is pro-

---

68. The *Interagency Statement* superceded *Banking Circular 274*, which was implemented in 1992 and addressed comparable issues.

tected by federal deposit insurance or backed by the bank.[69] The *Interagency Statement* requires that banks inform customers that the products are: 1) not insured by the Federal Deposit Insurance Corporation (FDIC), 2) not deposits or other obligations of the institution, 3) not guaranteed by the bank, and 4) subject to investment risks including the possible loss of principal. Even with these disclosures, the possibility of investor confusion presents a legal risk to banks in the form of potential customer litigation.[70] It remains to be determined whether this concern is a legitimate one.

Issues Related to Bank Mutual Fund Sales

It has been argued that bank sales of mutual funds pose special risks and regulatory concerns because of the presence of deposit insurance. This section examines investor perceptions of certain risks associated with mutual funds that are sold by banks, and issues related to investor beliefs that money market mutual funds are insured.

Fund Riskiness

Table 12 presents information on investors' perceptions of bank mutual fund sales. The table reports percentages of shareholders that believe that bank mutual funds are more risky, less risky, or have about the same risk as mutual funds sold through the other distribution channels. A large majority (62.6 percent) of all respondents believes that the risk is about the same, including 62.9 percent of those who purchased at a bank. Broker (66.3 percent) and direct purchasers (68.5 percent) are slightly more likely to expect funds sold through banks to have about the same risk as funds sold through other distribution channels.

---

69. On February 20, 1998, Comptroller of the Currency Eugene Ludwig urged fellow banking regulators to convert the voluntary guidelines on uninsured investment products to mandatory rules. His rationale was to give regulators enforcement capabilities beyond guidelines as banks continue to expand both their sales of mutual funds and insurance.

70. Another area of particular concern to bank regulators deals with fund liquidity problems that may occur when requests for redemptions of mutual fund shares are greater than the liquid assets of the fund.

Table 12: Knowledge of Risk of Mutual Funds Sold By Commercial Banks: Would You Expect Funds Sold Through Banks to Be More Risky, about the Same Risk, or Less Risky Than Funds Sold in Other Places?

Are Funds Sold Through Banks as Risky as Funds Sold in Other Places?	Distribution Channel Used						Total
	Bank	Broker	Pension	Direct	Insur.	Other	
More risky	5.8%*	9.1%	8.3%	10.2%	7.5%	6.5%	8.9%
About the same risk	62.9	66.3*	63.1	68.5*	62.0	64.1	62.6
Less risky	23.1	15.2*	20.1	13.5*	22.5	17.4	19.6
DK/Refused	8.2	9.4	8.5	7.7	8.1	12.0	9.1
Number of Respondents	294	638	1,118	569	521	92	2,000

See notes to Table 2. DK Denotes "don't know."

Survey respondents who thought that less risk was involved in bank mutual funds provided several possible explanations for their beliefs. As shown in Table 13, more conservative fund management was by far the most frequently cited explanation, followed by the beliefs that bank mutual funds are federally insured, and that banking is a regulated industry. Table 14 reports the source of information used by respondents who perceive bank funds as less risky. General knowledge or intuition is by far the most cited source of this information.

Table 13: Why Do You Believe That Bank Funds Are Less Risky? (Asked of those who believe that bank funds are less risky.)

Reason	Distribution Channel Used						Total
	Bank	Broker	Pension	Direct	Insur.	Other	
They have more conservative management	45.6%	68.0%*	58.2%	62.3%	59.8%	56.3%	56.3%
They are insured	13.2	10.3	12.9	10.4	15.4	12.5	14.1
They will be bailed out if necessary	2.9	3.1	3.6	2.6	1.7	18.8*	4.1
Banks are regulated	10.3	9.3	9.8	10.4	11.1	0.0	9.0
Other	22.1*	7.2*	13.8	14.3	14.5	12.5	14.1
Don't know	14.7*	8.3	7.6	6.5	4.3	6.3	8.2

See notes to Table 2.

Table 14: Sources Where People Learned That Bank Funds Are Less Risky (Asked only of those who answered less risky.)

Are Money Market Funds Insured?	Distribution Channel Used						Total
	Bank	Broker	Pension	Direct	Insur.	Other	
School	10.3%	5.2%	7.1%	7.8%	4.3%	0.0%	6.6%
Broker	2.9	3.1	2.7	3.9	2.6	6.3	2.8
Bank	8.8	9.3	5.8	6.5	9.4	12.5	7.7
Fund company	0.0	0.0	0.0	0.0	0.0	0.0	0.0
Insurance agent	0.0	0.0	0.0	0.0	0.0	0.0	0.0
Sales presentation	0.0	0.0	0.0	0.0	0.0	0.0	0.0
Prospectus	1.5	2.1	1.8	3.9	2.6	6.3	2.3
Book	4.4	3.1	4.0	5.2	2.6	6.3	3.1
Financial publications	3.1	2.2	3.1	3.2	4.4	3.3	3.0
Family or friends	10.3	5.2	9.8	13.0	9.4	6.3	9.5
Employer	2.9	2.1	4.4	2.6	3.4	0.0	3.3
General knowledge/ Intuition	55.9	61.9	61.8	53.2	54.7	68.8	58.6
Other	2.9	3.1	0.9	1.3	1.7	0.0	1.3
DK/Refused	4.4	3.1	4.4	3.9	3.4	6.3	4.9
Number of Respondents	68	97	225	77	117	16	391

See notes to Table 2. DK denotes "don't know."

Noninsurance Status of Money Market Funds

Table 15A indicates whether mutual fund owners believe that money market mutual funds are insured by the federal government. Although money market funds are required to invest in a diversified portfolio of liquid instruments subject to low credit risk, the funds are not insured by the federal government. As shown in the table, about one-third of the survey respondents believe money market mutual funds are insured.

Table 15A: Investor Knowledge of Whether or Not Money Market Funds Are Insured: Are Money Market Funds Insured?

Are Money Market Funds Insured?	Distribution Channel Used						Total
	Bank	Broker	Pension	Direct	Insur.	Other	
Yes	36.4%	35.3%	31.4%	22.7%*	35.7%	27.2%	33.1%
Number of Respondents	294	638	1,118	569	521	92	2,000

See notes to Table 2.

Mutual fund purchasers who bought directly from a fund company, or are college graduates or are male are significantly more likely to know that money market mutual funds are not insured. On the other hand, respondents earning less than $75,000 are significantly less likely to know that money market mutual funds are not insured. Table 15B shows that roughly one-quarter (27.5 percent) of those who thought that money market mutual funds are insured believe that these funds are insured by the FDIC. There are no significant differences in beliefs by age. Table 15C shows that those investors who believe money market funds are insured indicate that they learned this from a wide variety of sources, citing most often financial publications.

Table 15B: What Types of Insurance Do Money Market Funds Have? (Asked of those who believe that money market funds are insured.)

Type of Insurance	Distribution Channel Used						Total
	Bank	Broker	Pension	Direct	Insur.	Other	
SIPC	0.9%	4.0%*	2.0%	8.5%*	1.1%	0.0%	2.1%
FDIC	26.2	30.2	27.9	27.7	35.5*	36.0	27.5
Insurance against fraud	0.0	0.4	0.3	0.0	0.0	0.0	0.2
Insurance against bankruptcy	0.9	0.4	0.6	1.5	1.6*	0.0	0.6
Federal insurance	3.7	5.8	4.8	4.6	4.8	8.0	4.5
Other types of insurance	2.8	3.6	3.1	4.6	1.1	4.0	3.0
Bank and all other types of insurance	4.7	0.9	2.0	3.1	2.2	0.0	2.3
DK/Refused	54.2	41.3*	50.4	36.9*	46.2	48.0	50.5
Number of Respondents	107	225	351	130	186	25	662

See notes to Table 2. DK denotes "don't know." SIPC and FDIC are the Securities Investors Protection Corporation and the Federal Deposit Insurance Corporation, respectively.

Table 15C: Where Did You Learn That Money Market Funds Are Insured? (Asked of those who believe that money market funds are insured.)

Where You Learned	Distribution Channel Used						Total
	Bank	Broker	Pension	Direct	Insur.	Other	
School	6.5%	8.4%	9.1%	10.1%	9.1%	8.0%	7.9%
Broker	11.2	22.7*	8.8	10.9	12.9	12.0	10.7
Bank	27.1*	10.7	10.3	10.1	11.3	20.0	12.2
Fund company	0.0	0.4	0.0	0.0	0.0	0.0	0.2
Insurance agent	0.9	0.0	0.6	0.8	1.6*	0.0	0.6
Sales presentation	0.0	0.0	0.3	0.0	0.5	0.0	0.2
Prospectus	10.3	8.0	6.6	8.5	5.9	4.0	6.5
Book	7.5	5.8	6.6	12.4*	5.9	0.0	5.4
Financial publications	14.0	18.2	20.8	28.7*	22.0	20.0	19.6
Family or friends	10.3	9.8	11.1	10.1	15.6	16.0	12.5

Table 15C: Where Did You Learn That Money Market Funds Are Insured? (Asked of those who believe that money market funds are insured.) *(continued)*

Where You Learned	Distribution Channel Used						Total
	Bank	Broker	Pension	Direct	Insur.	Other	
Employer	12.2	8.0*	22.2*	6.2*	11.3	8.0	14.1
General knowledge/ intuition	10.3	15.6	13.1	14.0	17.2	24.0	14.7
Other	3.8	1.8	2.3	4.7	2.7	4.0	3.2
DK/Refused	13.1	10.7	9.1	7.8	7.0	8.0	10.3
Number of Respondents	107	225	351	129	186	25	662

See notes to Table 2. DK denotes "don't know."

Bank purchasers are less financially literate than more traditional channel purchasers are. Given this fact, both banks and their regulators should continue to undertake financial literacy initiatives and encourage compliance with the *Interagency Statement* since these efforts are more likely to be more beneficial in the long run than increasing disclosure regulation.[71]

Pension Channel Issues

The number of employees who must decide for themselves how to invest their pension plan assets has increased dramatically in the last few years as defined contribution plans have proliferated. As a result, both the burden and consequences of asset allocation and specific investment decisions has shifted from employers to employees. Given that overall investment performance is closely related to the asset allocation decision, it is imperative that employees be well informed about the basic investment principles needed to make this important decision.[72]

Since the asset allocation decision typically involves identifying which type of mutual fund to invest in, employees should also be

---

71. Several regulators have taken education initiatives. For example, the OCC has issued a brochure explaining risks, which is available to all national banks and on their Web page, and entitled "Deposits and Investments: There's a Critical Difference." The SEC, meanwhile, has conducted "town hall" meetings around the country to help educate investors and address the issue of financial illiteracy. See "SEC Issues Report on Financial Illiteracy" at http: //www.ici.org/issues /sec_ illit_ report.html. Finally, the theme of the ICI annual meeting to be held later in 1998 is "Building Investor Knowledge."

72. See Brinson, Hood, and Beebower (1986).

well-informed about the various features of mutual funds, such as historical performance and risks, fees and expenses, and investment objectives and styles. Recent research suggests that purchasers of mutual funds through employer-sponsored pension plans have neither the information nor the investment expertise necessary to make informed investment decisions. For example, a recent survey of 401(k) plan participants by John Hancock Mutual Life Insurance Company found that more than one-third of survey respondents believed it was impossible to lose money in a bond fund. An additional 12 percent were not sure. Another 12 percent believed it was impossible to lose money in an equity fund or said they did not know.[73] Furthermore, over 60 percent of all 401(k) funds are invested in fixed-income funds instead of equity funds, even though most workers are saving for retirement in the distant future.[74] This inefficiency in asset allocation has led some analysts to suggest that U.S. workers need to become much better educated about how their retirement savings are invested in mutual funds.

Section 404(c) of the Employee Retirement Income Security Act of 1974 (ERISA) is concerned with defined contribution pension plans that allow participants to self-direct their pension plan balances.[75] This section enables employers to shift investment responsibility for choices among a broad range of investment options to plan participants, thus limiting the potential liability of plan fiduciaries, including both sponsors and employers, for poor investment results. Compliance with Section 404(c) is optional and does not affect the sponsor's fiduciary responsibility for determining which investment

---

73. See Schultz (December 22, 1995).
74. See Brandt (May 2, 1994), p. 70. However, when looking at overall assets, households today have about 55 percent of their financial assets in higher risk asset classes (stocks and bonds), the highest level since the 1960s; see Sanford C. Bernstein & Co., Inc. (1995), pp. 51-58.
75. For more on Section 404(c), see Solomita (January 1994) and Investment Company Institute (1996), pp. 89-91. The regulatory effect of ERISA is discussed in Ippolito (1988).

options to offer.[76] Because sponsors retain a significant amount of fiduciary responsibility, they should consider the benefits of investor education. The cost of improving the education of participant plan investors has been estimated by experts as representing only 1 percent to 2 percent of a corporation's total outlay for managing its pension program.[77]

Alexander, Jones and Nigro (1997) found that employees whose only experience with mutual fund investing is through their pension plan particularly need to become better educated about a number of key investment concepts. The data show that pension plan investors are likely to use employer-provided printed materials and to attend meetings and presentations at work, suggesting that avenues for communicating educational materials to employees are currently in place. From this analysis it appears that employees, particularly investors whose only mutual fund purchases are through their employer, are not getting the requisite amount of information that they need to make sensible investment decisions.[78] This might be due to fears of legal liability by plan sponsors, as employers might be classified as investment advisors, depending on how much information they supply to their employees.[79]

Regardless of the reason for the apparent lack of investment knowledge on the part of employees, Alexander, Jones, and Nigro (1997) argue that public policy should be altered to hold employers responsible for providing some minimum level of information to ensure that employees' investment decisions take into account the tradeoff between risk and return and the impact of fund expenses and fees on portfolio performance. This can be accomplished by requiring employers to take steps to significantly increase the level of financial literacy of their employees. The interpretive bulletin on Section 404(c)

---

76. It should be noted that under all circumstances, fund management companies retain their fiduciary responsibility to ensure that funds entrusted to them are invested in accordance with the fund's stated investment objective. For more on ERISA and 401(k) plans, see Schmidt (1997) and Greenstein (1997).
77. See Brandt (May 2, 1994), p.72.
78. This involves a significant number of investors, since pension-channel-only investors amount to nearly 25 percent of all mutual fund investors in the survey. According to ICI research, there are 6.9 million investors whose only mutual fund was purchased through the pension channel (See ICI (May/June 1996), p.3).
79. See Zolkos (December 28, 1995).

of ERISA released by the Department of Labor represents a step in the right direction.[80] According to the interpretive guidelines, pension plan information, general financial and investment information, asset allocation models, and interactive investment materials can be used by plan sponsors to educate employees about their investment choices.[81] Ensuring the proper incentives are in place is a step in the right direction.

Other Topics of Importance to Financial Regulators

Two topics of concern to financial regulators that will become increasingly important in the near future are the privatization of Social Security and the short-term price effects of mutual fund cash flows. The level of investment knowledge displayed by mutual fund investors will determine to a large extent whether these two issues become regulatory trouble spots.

Although the pay-as-you-go Social Security system is currently solvent, by the year 2012, it is projected that benefit payments will exceed tax income under existing law, holding all else constant. In addition, as noted by Garner (1997), retirement of baby boomers, an increase in average life expectancy, and a decrease in fertility rates will all put substantial upward pressure on benefit payments in the next century. Clearly, changes will have to be made to the existing system to make it viable. Privatization of at least part of Social Security is one of the reforms that have been put forth to ensure its financial stability in the future. Reforms based on privatization typically involve replacing the current public retirement system with individual defined contribution plans in which employees invest in private securities and control the asset allocation decision as they do now in their private pension plans. Should such reforms be undertaken, the mutual fund industry will grow even bigger and control both private and public retirement funds.

Short-term swings in financial asset prices associated with the cash flows in and out of mutual funds in reaction to changing economic conditions is a second topic of concern (Edwards [1996]; Fortune [1997]). Recent concerns have been raised that the tremendous

---

80. See the Rules and Regulations section of the June 11, 1996 issue of the *Federal Register* and Greenstein (1997).
81. Ibid.

inflow of cash from mutual funds into the stock market has pushed stock prices far above the level justified by fundamentals, leading to the possibility of a severe market downturn. The view that mutual funds expose the financial system to increased fragility has grown as the industry's assets have increased and liquidity ratios have decreased. In addition, there is the perception by some that mutual fund investors engage in herd-like trading behavior, thereby exacerbating short-term movements in prices. These concerns are countered by those who argue that the typical mutual fund investor is patient and invests for the long term. It is evident that the level of investment knowledge displayed by mutual fund investors plays an important part in both of these regulatory issues, and that more knowledgeable investors will lead to a less fragile financial system.

Conclusions and Policy Implications

The mutual fund industry in the United States is thriving and will continue to do so. Substantial future growth in the industry will continue, particularly if the Social Security system is privatized. As a result, the mutual fund industry can be expected to play an even more important role in facilitating capital flows and promoting economic growth. Several important conclusions can be drawn from the OCC/SEC mutual fund survey. The survey shows that the typical mutual fund investor surveyed is older, wealthier, and better-educated than is the average American. However, the results of the survey suggest that investor knowledge of the interrelationship between mutual fund expenses, risks, and performance can be significantly improved. This is likely to become especially important in the future as less-well-educated individuals begin purchasing mutual funds, most likely through 401(k) plans. Although the average fund shareholder has invested in funds for several years, most fund shareholders do not appear to appreciate the relationship between fund expenses and performance. In addition, a substantial number of fund investors still believe they cannot lose money in a bond fund and do not realize that over the long-term, a well-diversified portfolio of stocks outperforms Treasury bills.

The survey results also suggest that more can be done to make mutual fund prospectuses more useful to investors. This suggests that the rules adopted by the SEC for the use of "plain English" and profile prospectuses are appropriate and timely, especially since the survey respondents considered the prospectus only the fifth-best source of information and more than 40 percent of them stated that they never used the prospectus.

Although broker and direct fund company purchasers are relatively more financially literate than are fund purchasers who did not use brokers and did not purchase directly, it is likely that investors self-select into the various distribution channels. Indeed, the authors found evidence that more knowledgeable investors seem more comfortable with the idea of purchasing from a fund company or a broker. As a result, salespeople at banks, as well as pension plan sponsors and employers, may face greater challenges in educating their typical mutual fund buyers since they tend to service less financially literate investors than other distribution channels. The survey should not be read as indicating that salespeople in broker and direct distribution channels necessarily do a better job of disclosing risks and costs than their counterparts in other channels.

The ongoing challenge of raising the level of investor comprehension of the costs and risks associated with mutual fund investments extends well beyond simply designing regulatory requirements. While regulators can ensure that there is adequate disclosure and dissemination of business and financial information to investors, it is impossible to regulate investor knowledge. Ultimately, the goal of improving investor education can only be achieved by a concerted joint effort of such private sector parties as plan sponsors, employers, brokers, fund companies and governmental regulatory agencies.

References

Alexander, Gordon J., Jonathan D. Jones, and Peter J. Nigro, "Mutual Fund Investing Through Employer-Sponsored Pension Plans: Investor Knowledge and Policy Implications," *Managerial Finance* 23 (1997), pp. 5-29.

Alexander, Gordon J., Jonathan D. Jones, and Peter J. Nigro, "Investor Self-Selection: Evidence from a Mutual Fund Survey," *Managerial and Decision Economics* (1998) forthcoming.

American Association of Retired Persons, Consumer Federation of America, and the North American Securities Administrators

Association, Inc., "Outline for Minimums for Hill Reform Action....Most Consumers Do Not Know Risk of Uninsured Investments at Banks," *Report* (January 1994).

Baumol, William J., Stephen M. Goldfeld, Lilli A. Gordon, and Michael F. Koehn, *The Economics of Mutual Fund Markets: Competition Versus Regulation,* Kluwer Academic Publishers, Boston (1990).

Blake, Christopher R., Edwin J. Elton, and Martin J. Gruber, "The Performance of Bond Mutual Funds," *Journal of Business* 66 (July 1993), pp. 371-403.

Bogle, John C., "Selecting Equity Mutual Funds," *Journal of Portfolio Management* 18 (Winter 1992), pp. 94-100.

Bogle, John C., *Bogle on Mutual Funds: New Perspectives for the Intelligent Investor,* Dell Publishing, Burr Ridge, IL (1994).

Boyd, John, and Mark Gertler, "Are Banks Dead? Or, Are Reports Greatly Exaggerated?" *Quarterly Review, Federal Reserve Bank of Minneapolis* (Summer 1994), pp. 2-23.

Brandt, J. H., "401(k) Requires Education," *Industry Week* (May 2, 1994), pp. 70, 72.

Bransten, Lisa, "Money-Management Start-Up to Offer Software on Internet to Aid Individuals," *Wall Street Journal* (February 23, 1998), p. B7A.

Brinson, Gary P., L. Randolph Hood, and Gilbert L. Beebower, "Determinants of Portfolio Performance," *Financial Analysts Journal* 42 (July/August 1986), pp. 39-44.

Brown, Stephen J., and William N. Goetzmann, "Performance Persistence," *Journal of Finance* 50 (June 1995), pp. 679-698.

Brown, Stephen J., William Goetzmann, Roger G. Ibbotson, and Stephen A. Ross, "Survivorship Bias in Performance Studies," *Review of Financial Studies* 5 (1992), pp. 553-580.

Capon, Noel, Gavan J. Fitzsimons, and Russ Alan Prince, "An Individual Level Analysis of the Mutual Fund Investment Decision," *Journal of Financial Services Research* 10 (March 1996), pp. 59-82.

Carhart, Mark M., "On Persistence in Mutual Fund Performance," *Journal of Finance* 52 (March 1997), pp. 57-82.

Cochran, Martha L., and David F. Freeman, Jr., "Functional Regulation," in *The Financial Services Revolution: Understanding the Changing Role of Banks, Mutual Funds, and Insurance Companies,* Clifford E. Kirsch, ed., Irwin Professional, Chicago (1997).

Collins, Sean and Phillip Mack, "Will Bank Proprietary Funds Survive? Assessing Their Viability Via Scope and Scale Estimates," *Finance and Economic Discussion Series* 95-52, Division of Research and Statistics, Federal Reserve Board, Washington, D.C. (1995).

Consumer Bankers Association, Consumer Investment Product Survey (November 1994).

Crenshaw, Albert B., "Before Risking the Money, Invest in Financial Literacy," *The Washington Post* (May 19, 1996), pp. H1, H4.

_____, "This Little Pennywise Piggy," *The Washington Post* (June 12, 1996), pp. F1, F7.

Department of Labor, "Pensions: Labor Department Cites Growth of Defined Contribution Plans," *Daily Labor Report*, Washington, D.C., No. 78 (April 24, 1995).

DeYoung, R., "Fee-Based Services and Cost Efficiency in Commercial Banks," Proceedings 30th Annual Bank Structure Conference (1994).

Edwards, Franklin, *The New Finance: Regulation and Financial Stability*, The AEI Press, Washington, D.C. (1996).

Elton, Edwin J., Martin J. Gruber, and Christopher R. Blake, "The Persistence of Risk-Adjusted Mutual Fund Performance," *Journal of Business* 69 (April 1996), pp. 133-157.

Federal Deposit Insurance Corporation, *Call Reports*, various years.

Federal Reserve Board, Federal Deposit Insurance Corporation, Office of Thrift Supervision, Office of the Comptroller of the Currency, and National Credit Union Association, *Interagency Statement on Retail Sales of Nondeposit Investment Products* (1994).

Fortune, Peter, "Mutual Funds: Part I: Reshaping the American Financial System," *New England Economic Review*, Federal Reserve Bank of Boston (July/August 1997), pp. 45-72.

Garner, C. Allan, "Social Security Privatization: Balancing Efficiency and Fairness," *Economic Review,* Federal Reserve Bank of Kansas City (Third Quarter 1997), pp. 21-36.

Gasparino, Charles, "Study Says People Who Purchase Funds at Banks Are Savvy," *The Wall Street Journal* (June 25, 1996), p. C26.

General Accounting Office, "Banks Securities Activities: Oversight Differs Depending on Activity and Regulator," Washington, D.C. (September 1995).

Goetzmann, William and Roger G. Ibbotson, "Do Winners Repeat?" *Journal of Portfolio Management* 20 (Winter 1994), pp. 9-18.

Greenstein, Mark, "Elements of the Regulatory Landscape Applying to Pension Plans," in *The Financial Services Revolution: Understanding the Changing Role of Banks, Mutual Funds, and Insurance Companies,* Clifford E. Kirsch, ed., Irwin Professional, Chicago (1997).

Grinblatt, Mark, and Sheridan Titman, "The Persistence of Mutual Fund Performance," *Journal of Finance* 47 (December 1992), pp. 1977-1984.

Hendricks, Darryll, Jayendu Patel, and Richard Zeckhauser, "Hot Hands in Mutual Funds: Short-Run Persistence of Relative Performance, 1974-1988" *Journal of Finance* 48 (March 1993), pp. 93-130.

Hensley, Scott, "OCC, SEC Find Bank Clients Up to Speed on Fund Risk," *American Banker* (June 25, 1996), pp. 1, 11.

Inglis, R. Evan, "Defined Benefit Plans Still Measure Up," *Pension Magazine* (June 1997), pp. 123-128.

Investment Company Institute, *Profiles of Mutual Fund Shareholders*, Washington, D.C. (Fall 1992).

_____, *Piecing Together Shareholder Perceptions of Investment Risk*, Washington, D.C. (Spring 1993).

_____, *Distribution Channels for Mutual Funds: Understanding Shareholder Choices*, Washington, D.C. (Summer 1994).

_____, *Profiles of First-Time Mutual Fund Buyers*, Washington, D.C. (December 1994).

_____, *Mutual Funds at Center Stage: Trends and Developments in the Mutual Fund Industry,* Washington, D.C. (Winter 1994/1995).

_____, *The Profile Prospectus: An Assessment by Mutual Fund Shareholders,* Washington, D.C. (May 1996).

_____, *FUNDamentals,* Washington, D.C. (May/June 1996).

_____, *FUNDamentals,* Washington, D.C. (December 1996).

_____, *A Guide to Closed End Funds,* Washington, D.C. (1997a).

_____, *1997 Mutual Fund Fact Book,* Washington, D.C. (1997b).

_____, *Retirement Plan Holdings of Mutual Funds,* 1996 Washington, D.C. (1997).

_____, *FUNDamentals,* Washington, D.C. (February 1998).

_____, *Perspectives,* Washington, D.C. (March 1998).

Ippolito, Richard A., "Consumer Reaction to Measures of Poor Quality: Evidence From the Mutual Fund Industry," *Journal of Law and Economics* 35 (1992), pp. 45-70.

Jackson, Howell E., "Strategies for Regulating Risk in Financial Intermediaries: General Approaches and their Application to Regulation of Investment Companies," in *The Financial Services Revolution: Understanding the Changing Role of Banks, Mutual Funds, and Insurance Companies,* Clifford E. Kirsch, ed., Irwin Professional, Chicago (1997).

Kahn, Ronald N., and Andrew Rudd, "Does Historical Performance Predict Future Performance?" *Financial Analysts Journal* 51 (November-December 1995), pp. 43-52.

Kimmelman, John, "Banks Best at Disclosing Risks, Study Finds," *American Banker* (June 9, 1995).

Malkiel, Burton, "Returns from Investing in Equity Mutual Funds 1971 to 1991," *Journal of Finance* 50 (June 1995), pp. 549-572.

Market Facts, Inc., "Mutual Fund Study Methods Report" (September 1995).

Market Trends, Inc., *Survey of Nondeposit Investment Sales at FDIC-Insured Institutions* (May 5, 1996).

Office of the Comptroller of the Currency, *Banking Circular* 274, Washington, D.C. (July 1993).

_____, *Interagency Statement on Retail Sales of Nondeposit Investment Products*, Washington, D.C. (February 1994).

_____, *OCC Quarterly Journal* 13, Washington, D.C. (September 1994).

Office of the Federal Register, *Federal Register* 62, No. 46, Washington, D.C. (March 10, 1997), pp. 10,898-10,692.

Plasencia, William, and Debra Cope, "Blasted on Mutual Fund Disclosure, Banks Hit Back," *American Banker* (January 19, 1996).

Quinn, Jane Bryant, "401(k)s: The Next Step," *Newsweek* (March 2, 1998), p. 57.

Quittner, Jeremy, "Banks Again Stuck at 14 Percent Share of Exploding Mutual Fund Market," *American Banker* (February 12, 1998), pp.1, 8.

Reid, Brian K., "Mutual Fund Developments in 1996," *Perspective*, Investment Company Institute, Washington, D.C. (March 1997).

Sanford C. Bernstein & Co., Inc., *The Future of Money Management in America*, 1995 Edition, New York (1995).

Schmidt, William A., "The Revolution in Retirement Savings: 401(k) Plans and Investment Intermediaries," in *The Financial Services Revolution: Understanding the Changing Role of Banks, Mutual Funds, and Insurance Companies,* Clifford E. Kirsch, ed., Irwin Professional, Chicago (1997).

Schonfeld, Victoria E., and Thomas M. J. Kerwin, "Organization of a Mutual Fund," *The Business Lawyer* 49 (November 1993).

Schultz, Ellen, "Helpful or Confusing? Fund Choices Multiply for Many Retirement Plans," *The Wall Street Journal* (December 22, 1995), pp. C1, C25.

Simon, Ruth, "How Funds Get Rich At Your Expense," *Money,* (February 1995).

Singletary, Michelle, "Survey Finds Fund Buyers Know Risks," *The Washington Post* (June 25, 1996), p. D4.

Sirri, Erik R., and Peter Tufano, "Buying and Selling Mutual Funds: Flows, Performance, Fees, and Services," *Working Paper*, Harvard Business School, Cambridge, MA (1993).

Solomita, A. F., "A New Generation of Plans: Banks With Mutual Funds Bidding For 401(k) Assets," *Pension World* (January 1994), pp. 18-20.

Taylor, Jeffrey, "SEC Approves Overhaul of Fund Rules," *The Wall Street Journal* (February 28, 1997), p. C25.

Testimony of Barry P. Barbash, Director of the Division of Investment Management of the Securities and Exchange Commission, and Eugene A. Ludwig, Comptroller of the Currency, Before the Sub-committee on Capital Markets, Securities, and Government-Sponsored Enterprises of the Committee on Banking and Financial Services of the U.S. House of Representatives (June 26, 1996).

Updegrave, W. L., "Fund Investors Need to Go Back to School," *Money* (February 1996), pp. 98-100.

U. S. Bureau of the Census, *The Statistical Abstract of the United States:1996*, Washington, D.C. (1996).

White, Lawrence, "Market Structure and the Regulation of the Mutual Fund Industry" in *Modernizing U. S. Securities Regulation: Economic and Legal Perspectives*, Kenneth Lehn and Robert W. Kamphuis, Jr., eds., Irwin Professional, Burr Ridge, IL (1992).

Wyatt, Edward, "Rules to Simplify Mutual Fund Documents," *The New York Times* (March 11, 1998), p. D6.

Wyatt, L., "401(k) Participation Up, GIC Investment Down," *Pension Management* (October 1995), pp. 8, 14.

Zolkos, R., "Investor Education Guidance Offered," *Business Insurance* (December 28, 1995), pp. 1, 16.

Comments on...

Regulating Mutual Fund
Investor Knowledge:
Policy Fantasy or Reality?

Michael Staten
Credit Research Center
Georgetown University School of Business

I come at this issue as someone who has spent a lot of time look-ing at consumer credit behavior, particularly as can be observed through consumer surveys. I can tell you that in the consumer credit arena, a great deal of regulatory hand-wringing has occurred over whether consumers really understand the terms and impact of the credit products they use. Even with the disclosure of loan terms (and, more recently, lease terms) the question, "Do they know what they are doing?" is often raised in reaction to rising aggregate debt levels. The same questions are now being raised about consumer investing.

Consequently, I think the authors have set forth an excellent premise for this paper: the idea that further efforts to provide more mutual fund product disclosure could be trumped by development of methods to improve financial literacy. This premise derives from a survey of mutual fund investors from which the authors conclude that many consumers do not have a sufficient general understanding of markets to effectively utilize disclosures. Therefore, the authors con-clude that general education would generate a higher yield than spe-cific disclosures.

My gut feeling is that the authors' conclusion is probably correct. The data from their survey make a suggestive but not compelling case. That said, the paper represents an excellent first step toward measuring literacy in such a way as to test the underlying premise regarding efficacy of general financial education versus specific prod-uct disclosures.

The survey seems to have been well executed. I will raise just three points with respect to interpretation of the results.

Response Rates

Given the nature of the authors' conclusions, it seems to me that we must worry a bit more than usual about the problem of sample nonresponse bias. However, the authors do not give us much informa-tion about response rates. We know from the paper that the survey had 2,000 completed interviews out of 32,000 randomly selected telephone numbers. Business numbers and households that did not own mutual funds were excluded from the respondent base, and therefore account for some of the dropout. However, we also know from other nationally representative surveys (most recently the Federal Reserve Board's Surveys of Consumer Finances) that about one household in three owns mutual funds. So the 2,000 completed interviews are, at best, only about 25 percent of what we would expect if the survey achieved perfect response from qualified households. This leads us to wonder about the characteristics of the three-quarters of telephoned households that did not respond to the request for an interview.

We know from other household surveys that response rates tend to fall with income. One of the authors' results was that higher-income people tended to score higher on the financial literacy test. Consequently, the nonresponse problem, if more prevalent among those higher-income households called, may be contributing to an understatement of true financial literacy because lower-income households are overrepresented in the sample. This is a problem that can be evaluated and addressed through comparison of the survey data to other detailed representative household surveys, such as the FRB's Surveys of Consumer Finances. It may be that the bias is not great, or can be corrected through appropriate weighting. However, without that additional analysis, the survey conclusions are weakened by the possibility of bias.

Of course, this problem affects only the projection of the survey mean values onto the general population. It does not weaken the observation that financial literacy rises with income. Since we know that the incidence of mutual fund ownership rises with income, in the coming years probably the largest single source of new participants in the mutual fund markets are going to be from the lower end of the income spectrum. So, regardless of whether the literacy of the existing population of fund owners is accurately measured by this survey, it seems likely that literacy will be diluted, other things remaining constant, as mutual fund companies broaden their marketing campaigns to reach a wider segment of households.

Questionnaire

Since the importance of the paper derives from its attempts to measure investor knowledge, the survey questionnaire itself is critical to an evaluation of the authors' conclusions. However, the paper does not contain a copy of the questionnaire. Phrasing of questions is critical. For example, people have a tendency not to respond to questions that appear intimidating, or appear to presume a correct answer. On the other hand, questions that are phrased so that an answer of "I don't know" reflects poorly on the respondent may not be answered truthfully. As I look at the tables of results I see a fairly high refusal rate or "don't know" response on a number of questions (perhaps 20 percent to 30 percent on some). Without seeing the question phrasing it is impossible to evaluate either the nonresponse or the positive answers.

Purchase Decisions

I would like to see more exploration of how the purchase decisions were reached within each distribution channel. I think this was a fascinating dimension to the project.

For customers who bought mutual funds from banks, the three most important sources of information were family and friends, the bank and the employer. These buyers apparently utilize a word-of-mouth network largely independent of written prospectuses. In contrast, consumers who bought funds from brokers relied on the broker, financial publications, and the prospectus. These consumers read and glean information. These are quite different avenues for going about making the decision of where to buy and what to buy, with quite different implications for the demand for additional written information and the likely effectiveness of required disclosures. This is a relationship that should be explored in greater detail, either within this survey or in future research.

Conclusion

In summary, the authors raise an excellent question, one that should be posed more often in discussions of disclosure regulations. Their methods are sound. The survey is well focused and the results suggest that further efforts at raising financial literacy would not be wasted. Although the authors may be premature (due to sampling problems) in concluding that the overall level of investor literacy is "low," their results do clearly suggest a literacy gap between high income investors and the growing number of households with moderate-to-lower incomes who find themselves making mutual fund decisions. That result is enough to suggest that further efforts at raising financial literacy would not be wasted.

Ingrid M. Werner
Associate Professor
Ohio State University

I would encourage everyone to read the paper by Alexander, Jones and Nigro. The paper provides fascinating and somewhat scary evidence on the financial literacy of the investing public. The survey results are truly eye-opening. Rather than discuss the specific findings, I will provide more of a background on mutual fund investing. I then will discuss some of the lessons that can be drawn from combining the development of mutual funds with the paper's findings.

We have seen a tremendous growth in the mutual fund industry in recent years and now have more mutual funds than individual exchange-listed stocks in the United States. Why do we need so many mutual funds? Some background might help answer this question. In the mid-1960s, Sharpe, Lintner and Mossin showed that if the market was working properly (loosely speaking) investors should only hold one portfolio (fund) of risky securities. They also showed that the one and only fund to hold is the market-capitalization-weighted portfolio of risky securities: the market portfolio. Their theoretical results are now known as the capital-asset-pricing model (CAPM).

The most common interpretation of the CAPM, both empirically and in the investment world, is to use the S&P 500 index as a proxy for the market portfolio. Several of the first mutual funds designed to imitate the return on an index (so-called index funds) were indeed based on the S&P 500 index. The fathers of the CAPM, however, envisioned a much broader set of securities, including smaller-cap stocks, bonds and real estate. After some hesitation, the money management industry eventually listened. Funds indexed to the total stock market as well as to subsets such as medium-cap stocks, small-cap stocks, micro-cap stocks, corporate bonds, municipal bonds, treasuries, real estate, etc., are now offered by practically all fund families.

In the mid-1970s, Ross developed a competing asset-pricing model, the arbitrage pricing theory (APT). The APT suggests that we should expand the set of risk factors beyond the market index already mentioned to, for example, industry portfolios. Mutual funds with industry focus have more recently become quite popular. Examples of such funds include those focused on health care, financial services, gold, telecoms, technology, computers and software. Black, Solnik and Stulz pioneered an international version of the CAPM in the early 1980s. It was not until the 1990s, however, that money managers started promoting international investment. Investors now have a wide choice of mutual funds indexed to individual foreign markets as well as to regions such as Asia, Europe, and the emerging markets.

These asset-pricing models have one basic message in common: investors should buy and hold indexed portfolios. The models say that investors should not expect an active portfolio manager to deliver better performance than that of an indexed portfolio with similar risk. Indexing guarantees a low turnover and hence ensures that trading related transaction costs are low. Index funds also have extremely low costs for research and as a consequence their management fees are very low.

If index funds are so great, why are there so many actively managed funds that focus on stock picking? It would be reasonable for actively managed funds to be popular if they consistently outperform index funds. However, a large body of empirical research from the academic community has clearly shown that actively managed mutual funds on average deliver worse risk-adjusted returns than indexed portfolios. Recently, actively managed funds on average do worse by about 200 basis points per year. It is thus truly a puzzle that so many investors favor actively managed mutual funds over indexed funds.

By contrast, I would argue that it is not a puzzle that actively managed mutual funds underperform their benchmarks. If markets are semistrong form efficient, all publicly available information should be reflected in prices. This does not mean that an investor cannot gain anything from investing time and resources into finding "undervalued" stocks (stock picking). The efficient markets hypothesis just says that the investor in expectation will get rewarded for the time and effort devoted to doing the valuation analysis. In the mutual fund industry, the costs of research are passed along to investors in the form of management fees. Fees on average simply eat up any of the benefits from stock picking.

With this background, I return to my original question. Why is there such a plethora of particularly actively managed mutual funds? I think the evidence reported in Alexander, Jones and Nigro on financial literacy combined with the recent growth in defined-contribution plans is the answer. After having read the evidence presented by Alexander, Jones and Nigro, I conclude that the public's understanding of investing is extremely limited. It therefore troubles me that the shift from defined-benefits to defined-contribution plans has placed the investment decisions in the hands of individual investors without proper education in basic finance. The survey evidence suggests that many investors are simply not equipped to manage their own retirement assets.

On the whole, the survey evidence paints a very grim picture of general financial literacy. It is clear that many of the respondents do not understand the concepts of risk and return. Admittedly, it takes a few weeks to teach MBA students risk and return, so I am not totally surprised that the average investor would be somewhat confused about these important basic concepts. What is more surprising is that the respondents do not understand what it means to pay a load fee of 5 percent. I also find it astonishing that investors do not know that the stock market on average has outperformed the bond market historically. Perhaps the most shocking result, however, is that such a large proportion of the survey's respondents think that mutual-fund investment is insured by the federal government. It is no wonder that actively managed funds can attract substantial investment—large groups of investors simply do not understand how to compare investment alternatives!

My conclusion from the evidence on financial literacy (or rather lack thereof) presented in this paper is that basic investment education is needed to prevent a disaster down the road. There is a danger that investors may make such poor investment choices that they end up without sufficient funds to retire. If this happens on a major scale, I predict that employers and ultimately the government risk getting roped into a bailout. This would obviously be undesirable. Not only would such a bailout cost taxpayer money, it would also undermine the whole idea of defined-contribution retirement plans.

Who should provide requisite basic investor education? In the short run, employers have to devote more resources to providing basic finance education to their employees. Granted, to implement such educational programs is difficult given current regulation. Many companies are worried that they will be held liable if investments that were made by their employees following company-provided recommendations fail to provide the employee with sufficient funds to retire as planned. Fearing that they will be perceived as performing the role of financial investment advisors, companies often go the safer route of providing little, if any, information to employees. To the extent that current regulation discourages or outright prohibits companies from providing basic investment education, the rules should be revised or scrapped completely.

Mutual funds can also do a whole lot more to promote investor education. A good start would be to use plain and simple language to communicate to investors as recently recommended by the Securities and Exchange Commission. Funds should illustrate the pros and cons of choosing between different alternatives much more clearly than they do today. Hands-on examples in dollar terms combined with simple illustrations would go a long way toward making investment less of a mystery to the average investor. For example, it is clear from the survey evidence that investors understand neither percentages nor fees. So why not make it simple? Tell investors that if they had $100,000 in their retirement account at the beginning of the year and they invested in a market index, they would own $120,000 at the end of the year—minus $200 in fees (0.2 percent). If, by contrast, they had invested the $100,000 in an actively managed mutual fund they would have $123,000 at the end of the year (supposing the fund manager was a decent stock picker)—minus $5,000 in fees (5.0 percent) to the fund manager. I bet every single investor would realize the difference between $119,800 and $118,000. Communicating the differences across alternative strategies in simple dollar terms would help a lot.

Since I predict that individual retirement investing is going to be increasingly important, I believe that even more comprehensive measures should be taken to promote investor education. I would argue that basic finance should be taught in high schools. Key concepts to convey are the time value of money and the tradeoff between risk and return. While augmented high school education does not remedy the deficiencies among current retirement savers, it might help increase the financial literacy of future generations. This is the only way we can hope to provide the general investing public with information about prudent financial investment strategies.

In conclusion, I really enjoyed this thought-provoking paper. Unfortunately, it did confirm my worst fears about the lack of financial literacy of the investing public. It also helped me understand why so many actively managed mutual funds are viable despite delivering poor performance—many investors simply do not understand how to compare investment alternatives. The paper clearly suggests that much more effort has to be devoted to investor education at all levels: through employer-sponsored education, through more straightforward mutual fund prospectuses, and through the educational system.

Ken Scott
Senior Research Fellow
Hoover Institution
and
Ralph M. Parsons
Professor in Law and Business
Stanford Law School

On a paper like this, how can any academic argue against the desirability of more education? It seems like it is a foregone conclusion. Nonetheless, I'd like to be something of an iconoclast, because I am a bit uncomfortable with both the diagnosis and the prescription for treatment.

We had a variety of numbers presented here to illustrate what investors knew or did not know. The paper cites some survey results—that 28 percent of bond investors think they cannot lose money. Some 20 percent to 25 percent do not know that stock market returns are higher than Treasury bill returns; 21 percent think you can not lose money in a money-market fund. They are not totally wrong: one might note that no retail investor ever has, in fact, lost money in a money-market fund (make that 99.99 percent of all investors). Some 24 percent believe in positive serial correlation in fund performance over time, and so on.

So you have these numbers. How do we know that those numbers are low? What is the standard, the implicit frame of reference, that we want to apply? Are those numbers substantial? What is your expectation? What expectations are reasonable when we are talking about these kinds of issues?

Well, let me look at a few survey polls of knowledge in other areas. Politics, for example: only 76 percent know that Al Gore is vice president. Science: only 43 percent know that electrons are smaller than atoms. Is that too tough? Well, how about, does the earth go around the sun or the sun go around the earth? Twenty-one percent think the sun goes around the earth, and another 7 percent are not sure on the matter. History: Did the United States use the atom bomb in World War II? Twenty-two percent are not aware of that.

Now here we are dealing, presumably, with an above-average subset of the population. Nonetheless, the point I want to make is that in percentage terms, polls usually show a substantial reservoir of ignorance on most fact questions. Indeed, to my mind, what is surprising is to find questions that practically everybody gets right—that 94 percent, for example, know you can lose money in stock funds. That is up there with the 96 percent who know Bill Clinton is president.

So, are the Office of the Comptroller of the Currency (OCC) poll numbers low? Do they urgently call for redoubled educational efforts, or are they in the range you have to expect and can really only do a limited amount to change?

Let me shift perspective, and try to frame this, a little differently. If, for any product, most customers have little or no information, how can markets function? We do not expect buyers of automobiles or VCRs to really understand the technology or how it works. What protects them in their purchases, if they are largely ignorant of basic facts? The seller has an interest in future transactions, of course. What else?

- Part of the answer lies in competition for the marginal customers—the ones who are knowledgeable and choose accordingly. The mutual fund industry is certainly competitive, as the authors note: the Herfindahl Index of concentration is a very low 329.
- Part of the answer lies in the development of informational intermediaries, who make a business of assessing complex information and transmitting it to customers: *Consumer Reports* for autos, or Morningstar for mutual funds.
- Part of the answer lies in the role of sophisticated agents acting on customers' behalf. Auto rental companies buy fleets and lease them to customers; employers structure pension plans for employees. All of these are mechanisms for overcoming the customer-ignorance problem. Therefore, if we are going to attack this problem, it seems to me, any response should focus on these as well—not just on investors alone.

But if you do want to expend resources on raising investor literacy, what is the way to go about it? On what do you wish to raise literacy, and how are you going to attempt to do it? Not, I would suggest, by following the route of the Securities and Exchange Commission (SEC) prospectus—a document that is shoved at purchasers on the theory that it contains all the information that they need in order to decide whether to pay the offering price for some security.

You know that is pure nonsense, and it has been pure nonsense ever since 1933. The prospectus contains mainly company information, not industry or economic information. Only a professional securities analyst could possibly use it to derive a price. The result is, of course, that most public buyers ignore it, quite wisely.

The mutual fund version, at least, deals with traded securities, not asset values, so pricing is much less of an issue. But the mutual fund prospectus, whether it is simplified or not, talks only about the broad category of securities the fund may buy, and something about expenses and past returns. Now it also has a crude diagram on risk. This is of quite modest value, and of course, it is all historical, all backward-looking. You are always more interested as a security investor in trying to be forward-looking.

I would suggest that a more promising route to investor literacy would focus on simply a few investment fundamentals:

- That there is a positive correlation between expected returns and expected risk. You know, we really ought to be teaching that from grade school on. I can think of no better inoculation against fraud than understanding the proposition that anybody who tells you that you are going to get a huge short-term gain is also telling you that you are bearing a huge short-term risk. It applies to Spanish prisoner swindle or the pigeon drop swindle. It would be wonderful if you could hammer this home in grade school: that when someone says, "Here's a deal," and "I'll double your money," then there is a very big chance you will not see your money again.
- That risk is reduced by diversification. Perhaps you could start hammering that in from maybe school on.
- That the attitude toward risk should be affected by the investor's time horizon. In other words, that there are lifecycle considerations in investing. Susan E. Woodward, in her paper, offered some additional candidates.

If you want to educate the mass of investors, I think this is the most you ought to aim at—a few very basic fundamentals. Suppose the SEC had devoted the past 60 years to these objectives, rather than turning out hundreds of thousands of company prospectuses? I think the public would be a lot better off.

Still, you will not reach everybody, especially in pension plans, for example. What I am suggesting is acceptance of a law of irreducible ignorance. For those you cannot teach, what do you do?

Well, let me offer a suggestion, and stick my neck out, rather than just playing the safe role of a critic. I would suggest not just more educational efforts, but a different approach, and that would be modal default rules.

For employees who do not want or know how to make their own choices, it might be interesting to try to develop a consensus set of default rules that would deal with the things we have just been talking about: rules about asset mix; about function of time to anticipated withdrawals; shifting allocations over time among categories; and a set of index funds chosen by employers as a method of achieving diversification within categories.

If employers could adopt default rules within some recommended parameters, and thereby discharge their fiduciary duties under the Employee Retirement Income Security Act (ERISA), they would have a large incentive to move in this direction. Employees, of course, could choose to drop out if they desired. That would be the whole point.

So, to reiterate, it seems to me you have to accept a sizable amount of ignorance or lack of interest among investors as normal, and find ways to accommodate it. Now, is a suggestion like this politically feasible? Or would the industry groups prevent it? On the political fronts, I am no expert; I defer to Dr. Woodward and others for that. I would offer just one point: that if you go the ERISA route, you are going through the Department of Labor, and you bypass the SEC and you bypass the Investment Company Institute and National Association of Securities Dealers capture structure that is already in place, at least to some extent.

Section Four

Pensions, Public Policy, and the Capital Market

Richard Ippolito
Professor
George Mason University
School of Law

Abstract

In this essay, I review the major historical developments in pensions that explain their role in today's financial markets and explore the deficiencies in pension policy that interfere with a fully efficient pension market. By that I mean one in which companies and workers are free to arrange pension rules that increase productivity and allow savings rates that are jointly optimal to the market participants. Other social goals for savings and retirement-income adequacy should be attained by modifying vehicles for universal coverage, such as Social Security. Toward this end, I make a series of proposals that encourage a free market for retirement savings. In my model, pensions are treated just like any other investment vehicle offered by other regulated financial institutions such as mutual funds, banks or insurance companies. Subject to the usual fiduciary rules and full reporting and disclosure, my model allows a full assortment of pension forms to develop, all with their own configurations of risks and rewards. I also advocate greatly expanded Individual Retirement Accounts, which ensure full and open competition for retirement savings. A corollary to this approach is that the distinction between pensions and other financial instruments is greatly diminished.

Introduction

Most large companies and public employers offer pension programs to their employees. There are two kinds of pensions: defined contribution pension plans and defined benefit plans. In a defined contribution pension plan, employers make contributions to individual accounts that effectively are owned by employees.[1] In a defined benefit plan, the employer promises an annuity at retirement often tied to final salary and service. In this kind of pension, employees accrue rights to a pension, but the employer has the responsibility of

---

1. Technically, the sponsor holds pension assets in trust for workers, and thus, my use of the word ownership is overly broad. For all intents and purposes, however, employer contributions and associated earnings belong to workers after they satisfy a vesting period, which by law is no more than five years. Usually, however, vesting in these accounts is faster than five years, and often occurs immediately for employer contributions (U. S. Department of Labor 1994). Sometimes, employees make contributions to these accounts, particularly in 401(k) versions of these plans (see later). These contributions are never subject to vesting rules.

accumulating assets in a separate trust fund to back at least some portion of the promised benefits.[2]

From a financial perspective, the assets that accumulate in either type of fund are loosely referred to as the pension industry. At the end of 1995, pension funds held $5.3 trillion in assets. Since pension promises often exceed fund assets in defined benefit plans, the present value of retirement income represented by pensions is considerably in excess of this amount.[3]

In addition, assets in Individual Retirement Accounts (IRA) and Keogh plans exceeded $1.2 trillion in the same year. While these accounts are not pensions as such (because they are not sponsored by employers), they often are considered as part of pension assets because they share both the tax-favored status and the retirement savings aspect of pensions.

The role of pensions in supporting retirement income is well known and is the subject of much public policy attention. The reason is apparent. In 1995, pension-plan payouts from private, state, municipal, and federal pensions exceeded $300 billion, an amount equivalent to payouts to retirees from the Social Security System.[4] These plans cover 23 million retirees (and their survivors) and 44 million workers.[5] Public policy also has importantly affected pensions as a vehicle for capital accumulation, however, and this paper principally addresses that issue.

---

2.   There are many rules that restrict the minimum and maximum amounts that private employers can contribute to the pension plan each period.

3.   On the assumption that Federal pensions were terminated immediately, liabilities exceed assets by almost $900 billion as of 1993 (EBRI 1997). On an ongoing basis (that is, recognizing that pensions for workers will be indexed to final wages), the deficiency is far greater. For private plans, underfunding on a termination basis was $64 billion in 1995 (PBGC 1997).

4.   In 1995, social security payments from the old age and survivors insurance trust fund and the disability insurance trust fund amounted to $332 billion (Social Security Administration 1997, Table 4.A3). Of all payments from pensions, about 60 percent are from private plans, while state and Federal payments account for about 20 percent each (EBRI 1997).

5.   I use state and local data directly from EBRI (1997) because it already adjusts for double counting for workers in more than one plan. I use EBRI federal participation numbers, except I adjust the data for double counting workers in both defined-benefit

Background

Historical Development

Pension tax policy in the United States generally follows consumption tax treatment. The Revenue Act of 1921 established the basic principles:[6] contributions to the pension are not subject to taxation to either the worker or the company; earnings accumulate in a tax-free trust fund and pension benefits in retirement are treated as ordinary taxable income. This tax treatment is favorable in comparison to tax assessments against earnings deposited in taxable savings vehicles that are subject to comprehensive income tax treatment.[7]

Interestingly, the contemporaneous effect of the act was small because in 1921 few individuals paid income taxes and marginal tax rates were inconsequential.[8] While some pensions existed from the late 18th century, coverage was not pervasive and funding was not a dominant characteristic.[9]

The economics of pensions changed markedly during World War II. The Revenue Act of 1942 expanded the personal income tax structure to resemble the institution as we know it today; most workers at that time paid income taxes, and (median) marginal tax rates increased five-fold to more than 20 percent. The change ensured that pensions would become important conveyors of investment funds to the United States and world capital markets.[10]

---

5.   and defined-contribution plans. For private participation, EBRI does not adjust for double counting in multiple plans. I therefore use PBGC estimates that show 27 million workers and 17 million retirees (and survivors) covered by private pensions. Comparable numbers for state and federal plans are 11.8 and 4.4 million workers, and 1.5 and 4.5 million retirees, respectively.
6.   Most pension provisions are found in section 401 and related sections of the Internal Revenue Code.
7.   Pensions are not unique in awarding consumption tax treatment. Most investments in personal homes are treated similarly. Other savings vehicles, like variable annuities, are given partial consumption tax treatment (in the sense that investment earnings are not taxed when they are realized, but at the time of withdrawal).
8.   In 1940, for every 100 workers, only 14 personal income tax returns were filed on which taxes were paid; the median marginal tax rate was 4.4 percent (Ippolito 1986).
9.   Pensions began appearing in the late 19th century in industries dominated by unions, particularly railroads. They were created as a way to encourage retirement, but were not notably funded. See Williamson (1992) and Latimar (1932).

In 1945, about one-in-five full-time workers in the private sector was covered by a pension; by 1960, the historical maximum coverage rate was attained, with almost one-in-two full-time workers covered by a pension plan.[11] As the system matured during the postwar period, and encouraged by tax-exempt status, pension funds began to accumulate large amounts of assets.[12]

Figure 1 depicts this growth. In 1950, pensions held $129 billion in 1995 dollars. By 1960, real pension assets had tripled to $469 billion, and increased another ten-fold in the ensuing 35 years: in 1995, pensions held $5.3 trillion. About two-thirds of these monies are held in private pensions.[13] Over the postwar period, for each civilian worker in the United States, pension assets increased from $2,000 to $42,000 in real terms.[14]

---

10. By 1945, there were 72 personal income tax returns on which taxes were paid for every 100 workers; the median marginal income tax rate was 23 percent (Ippolito 1986).

11. Taking into account that coverage increases with age, this coverage rate implies that about two-thirds of workers in the private sector expect to retire with a pension (Scheiber and Goodfellow 1994). Most uncovered workers are either young or are in the lower portion of the wage distribution, where Social Security replacement rates are high, and income tax advantages of pension savings are low. For a review of coverage statistics, see Fernandez et al. (1994).

12. With time, there are more retiree cohorts and more workers accumulating service accruals in the plan; and the sponsor gradually funds the obligations it has incurred.

13. Of the $1.7 trillion in public funds in 1995, only $375 billion were in the federal retiree funds for government workers. The rest were held by state and local governments (EBRI 1997).

14. Pension assets increased from less than 5 percent of gross domestic product in 1950 to 72 percent in 1995. National data on workers and output are taken from Council of Economic Advisors (1997); pension data are compiled from EBRI (1997).

Figure 1: Pension Assets, 1950 – 1995

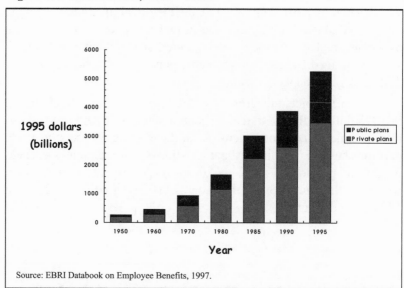

Source: EBRI Databook on Employee Benefits, 1997.

The relevance of the pension vehicle for financial markets is shown in Figure 2. In 1950, pensions held 13 percent of outstanding bonds (light color bars) and a negligible share of outstanding equity (black bars). In 1980, they held almost half of all outstanding bonds and almost 20 percent of outstanding equity. After 1980, a notable shift in favor of equities was in evidence; this shift, plus continued growth of pension assets, meant that by 1995, pensions held more than one-in-four dollars of outstanding equity and one-in-five dollars of all financial assets (solid line schedule).[15]

---

15. All data are compiled from the Federal Reserve Flow of Funds by the U.S. Department of Labor. Data prior to 1990 are found in U. S. Department of Labor (1992); data for 1995 are unpublished from the U. S. Department of Labor.

Figure 2: Pension Share of Financial Assets, 1950 – 1995

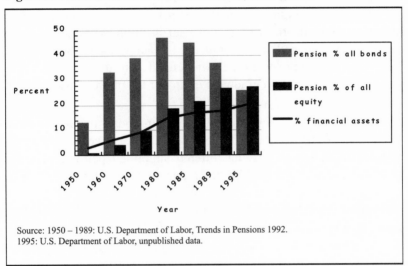

Source: 1950 – 1989: U.S. Department of Labor, Trends in Pensions 1992.
1995: U.S. Department of Labor, unpublished data.

These data do not include $1.2 trillion in assets held in IRAs and Keogh plans in 1995. IRAs are limited to $2,000 contributions per year.[16] Keogh plans permit contributions by self-employed persons equal to 25 percent of compensation (up to a maximum contribution of $30,000 per year).[17] In 1995, pension plans, plus IRAs and Keoghs collectively held assets totaling about 90 percent of gross domestic product.[18]

---

16. IRAs were created in the Employee Retirement Income Security Act of 1974. Originally, they were limited to workers who were not covered by a pension plan. In 1982, they were expanded to include all workers (and spouses) whether or not coverage was obtained at the job. Since 1987, covered workers' access to IRAs are subject to an income means test. Individuals who fall outside the income limits can contribute $2,000 of after-tax monies to IRAs, but enjoy only partial tax preference. Roth IRAs, which allow after-tax contributions (up to $2,000 per annum), but tax free buildup and withdrawals, are effective in 1998, but also are subject to a (different) income means test.

17. These plans, named after Congressman Eugene Keogh (Brooklyn), were created in the Self-Employed Individuals Tax Retirement Act of 1962. The Tax Equity and Fiscal Responsibility Act of 1982 eliminated the distinctions between Keogh plans and the qualified plans of corporations, which worked to increase the limits substantially.

18. Assets held by pensions, IRAs and Keoghs in 1995 were $6.5 trillion (EBRI 1997). Gross domestic product in 1995 was $7.2 trillion (Economic Report of the President 1997).

Investment Management

The pension industry is not a distinct entity in the sense that its assets are separate from other financial institutions. Some of these monies are managed by insurance companies, banks and mutual funds. Indeed, with the growth of defined contribution funds (see below), there has been a gradual merging of the pension industry and the mutual fund industry.

Traditionally, pension monies were controlled by two institutions: investment managers that offered customized services to pensions, and insurance companies that offered simplified pension plans to companies (assets were held in their general account). In 1980, these institutions controlled 70 percent and 20 percent of private pension plan assets, respectively. Mutual funds had less than 10 percent of pension assets (see black bars in Part a of Figure 3).[19]

By 1995, this pattern was markedly different. Traditional pension money managers held only 44 percent of private pension assets. While insurance companies continued to hold about 20 percent of pension assets in general accounts, they also managed 12 percent of pension assets in separate accounts.[20] Notably, mutual funds controlled more than 20 percent of pension fund assets (lighter bars in Part a of Figure 3).[21]

Similar changes occurred in IRA and Keogh plans. In 1985, banks, thrift institutions and credit unions dominated the market, controlling fully 60 percent of these assets. Mutual funds and brokerage firms each managed about one-sixth of these monies (black bars in Part b of Figure 3).

By 1995, the banking industry had lost two-thirds of its market share. Mutual funds and brokerage firms (self directed accounts) held 38 percent and 34 percent of these monies, respectfully (lighter bars in Part b of Figure 3). One important reason for the change is the

---

19. These data are found in EBRI (1997).

20. Separate accounts are managed for pension funds by insurance companies. They are not held to back pensions administered directly by the insurance company.

21. I base this estimate on data compiled by EBRI (1997), which differs somewhat from data published by the Investment Company Institute (ICI). According to EBRI compilations, mutual funds held $1,097 billion in both private pensions and IRAs and Keoghs in 1995. ICI puts the estimate at $997 billion (Reid and Crumrine 1997).

alteration in the market for pensions, notably a shift from defined benefit to defined contribution plans.

Figure 3: Asset Management

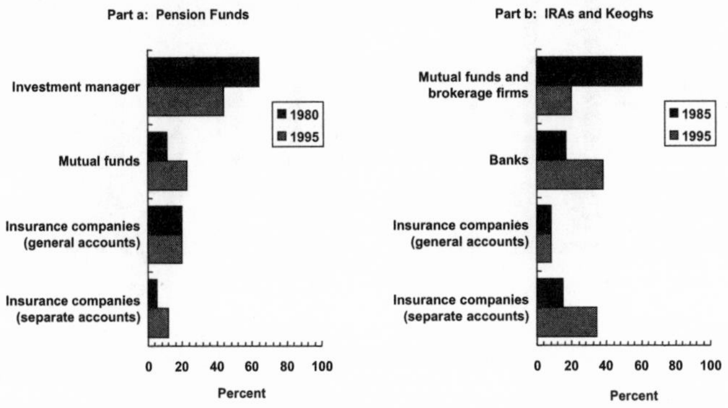

Source: EBRI Databook on Employee Benefits, 1997.

Trends in Pensions

The most important development in private pensions over the past 15 years has been the gradual shift away from defined benefit plans and toward defined contribution plans. Historically, defined benefit plans dominated primary pension coverage. In 1979, among workers covered by a pension plan, more than 80 percent were covered by a defined benefit plan. By 1998, this share was less than 50 percent (see Figure 4).[22]

Figure 5 illustrates the implications of this trend for asset management. The dark bars show assets in 1995 dollars held by defined benefit plans in the private sector. The lighter bars show assets held by defined contribution plans. The share of assets held in the defined benefit plans decreases to about 50 percent in 1995 (see the black-line schedule marked by closed circles), from 70 percent in 1981.

---

22. These data are taken from estimates of primary plan coverage (U. S. Department of Labor 1997, table E5), and their unpublished data and projections based on trends in the Form 5500 data and the labor force.

Figure 4: Share of Pension Coverage by Pension Type

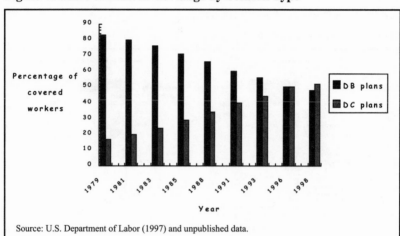

Source: U.S. Department of Labor (1997) and unpublished data.

Figure 5: Assets in Private Defined Benefit and Defined Contribution Plans

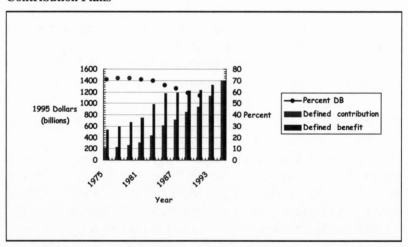

Employment shifts explain about half of the reduction.[23] Large unionized companies in the manufacturing sector—which traditionally had high defined benefit coverage rates—lost a significant portion of their employment to smaller, nonunion companies in the service sectors, where defined benefit plans traditionally had smaller market

23. Several studies have disentangled the employment effect from the preference change. See Gustman and Steinmeier (1992), Kruse (1995) and Ippolito (1998a).

shares. Increased regulatory costs for defined benefit plans can explain shifts among the smallest plans.[24] Even holding these factors constant, there has been a persistent and widespread trend in favor of defined contribution plans.

There are two prominent candidates to explain this pattern. One is legislation enacted in 1978 permitting the introduction of a new kind of pension plan—the so-called 401(k).[25] The other is an important change in tax policy toward defined benefit pensions, starting in 1986.

Causes of Decline in Defined Benefit Plans

New Competition: 401(k) Plans

Unlike traditional defined contribution plans, 401(k) plans permit workers to make tax-deductible contributions. The company can match these contributions within a wide permissible band.[26] Thus, within the same pension plan, contributing employees can receive matching contributions from the company, while noncontributors often receive no sponsor contributions. This is a dramatic departure from previous public policy toward pensions that tended to apply a similar contribution formula to all participants in the plan.[27]

The 401(k) plans have the obvious efficiency of aligning workers' desired savings rates with actual savings rates. In addition, sponsors

---

24. A study done by Hay Huggins Co. (1990) shows that relative per-participant cost of defined-benefit versus defined-contribution plans increased dramatically for very small plans (15 participants) but had little impact on plans with at least 100 participants. The reason is that many of the cost increases had a fixed-cost element that was inconsequential for larger plans.

25. The name refers to the section in Internal Revenue Code that permits these plans. Similar kinds of "thrift" plans were allowed prior to 1979. The tax treatment of thrifts, however, was parallel to the advantages afforded to IRAs today to individuals who do not qualify for before-tax contributions. Thus, the tax advantages of these plans were not as favorable to the individual as 401(k) plans.

26. The sponsor can, but is not required, to make unconditional contributions to employee accounts.

27. Pension policy encourages sponsors to have pensions that treat workers similarly, particularly across wage levels. Thus, for example, in a typical defined contribution plan, the sponsor might contribute x percent of pay into all workers' accounts. The 401(k) rules restrict the portion of pay that "highly-compensated" workers contribute to the 401(k) plans relative to contribution rates from the nonhighly-compensated workers. See Allen et al. (1997) and McGill et al. (1996).

can contribute different amounts to workers based solely on their pro-
pensities to save. That is, through matching, the employer pays savers
more than nonsavers, a feature that I have argued elsewhere aligns
pay with an unobserved productivity attribute.[28]

In any case, 401(k) plans have proved to be successful innovations in the pension market. Indeed, by 1995, about 35 million workers in the private sector were covered by a 401(k) plan;[29] almost a
third of pension-covered workers in the private sector had only a
401(k) pension plan.[30]

The data show that these plans have displaced both traditional
defined benefit plans and traditional defined contribution plans. Figure 6 shows assets held in private plans over the 1984-1995 period.[31]
The share held by defined benefit plans (dark solid line) is reproduced
from Figure 5; it is clearly in decline over the period.

The dashed-light-line schedule (with closed circles) denotes the
share of assets in traditional defined contribution plans; this share
exhibits a small negative drift over the period. 401(k) plans—denoted
by the lighter bars in the figure—clearly dominate pension asset
growth.[32] In 1984, these plans already had 10 percent of private pen-

---

28. More particularly, I argue that some companies prefer workers with low discount rates—because their long view makes them self motivated to do good work that
has longer-term rewards. High discounters tend to be harder to motivate and thus
require more supervision to obtain the same amount of output (Ippolito 1998a).

29. In 1993, there were 23 million workers in the private sector that had a balance in
a 401(k) plan, including 9 million who had no other plan (U.S. Department of Labor
1997 table D5); a reasonable extrapolation puts these numbers at 25 million and 11
million in 1995. These data do not count workers covered by a 401(k) plan, but who
opt not to contribute to the plan. Data reported in the Current Population Survey
(1993) show that about 30 percent of eligible workers in 401(k) plans choose not to
contribute (Ippolito 1998a). This estimate implies that about 35 million were covered
by a 401(k) plan in 1995, including about almost 16 million who had no other plan.

30. A reasonable extrapolation of 1993 data reported in U.S. Department of Labor
(1997), Table F4, puts the number of private workers covered by a defined-benefit
plan in 1995 at about 24 million, and about 26 million workers covered primarily by a
defined-contribution plan (including about 4 million in sole 401(k) plans that chose
not to contribute). Thus, since 16 million workers were covered only by a 401(k) plan
(see prior note), then of the approximately 50 million private covered workers, about
32 percent had only a 401(k).

31. U. S. Department of Labor (1997); the publication started the 401(k) asset series
in 1984.

sion assets. Four years later, their share doubled to almost 20 percent. By 1995, they had a 30 percent share. The trend seems apparent.

Figure 6: 401(k) Share of Private Pension Assets: 1984 – 1995

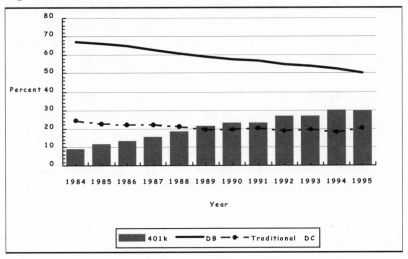

The rise of 401(k) plans is closely associated with growth in mutual fund assets. Figure 7 shows three data series. The first is the bar sequence: it represents the defined contribution share of private pension assets, minus its 28 percent share in 1975. Thus, this series is the increase in the defined contribution share of assets since 1975. This share did not change noticeably through 1981. By 1990, the share had increased by 15 percentage points (left hand scale); and by 1995, it had increased by about 21 points (for a total share of private plan assets of about 50 percent).[33]

---

32. Not all of this growth is attributable to new contributions (and investment earnings). Some (unknown) portion comes from plan amendments to old defined contribution plans to add a 401(k) component. For example, a profit sharing plan might be amended to allow workers to save some additional amounts of their own contributions in the same vehicle. When this amendment is made, the assets are counted in the 401(k) category on the Form 5500s.

33. Some also is attributable to a reduction in funding levels in defined benefit plans, as I discuss later. The share data are taken from U. S. Department of Labor (1997) and unpublished data from the Department of Labor.

The line schedule marked with asterisks shows the portion of mutual fund assets that come from employer-sponsored pensions (mostly 401(k) plans).[34] In 1981, pension monies accounted for about 5 percent of mutual fund assets (left scale); by the late 1980s, this share had grown modestly to about 9 percent; and since 1990 has increased to about 19 percent (Reid and Crumrine 1997). If monies from IRAs are added to this amount, then retirement monies account for about 35 percent of mutual fund assets (not shown). Mutual funds gradually are becoming a dominant vehicle for retirement savings.

This point is made dramatically by the solid-line schedule in Figure 7 (right-hand scale). It shows the ratio of the total mutual fund assets to total pension fund monies (private plus state and municipal).[35] In 1977, mutual fund assets were only 10 percent of total pension assets; by 1988, they were 40 percent, and by 1995, they were 70 percent.

With the rise of 401(k) plans, more decisions about asset allocation are being made by the participants themselves.[36] Often, this means that monies are invested through banks, insurance companies, brokerage firms and mutual funds. In many 401(k) plans, employers allow their employees to decide on their own asset allocation.

34. They also include 403b plans that are counterparts to 401(k) plans for nonprofit institutions.
35. These data are found in EBRI (1997) and the Mutual Fund Fact Book (1997).
36. The employer is responsible for providing a reasonable range of opportunities using various fiduciary investment vehicles; these often include bank certificates of deposits and or families of mutual funds, company stock and so on. Fully 86 percent of 401(k) participants can choose the asset allocation of their own contributions and 58 percent can allocate the employer's contribution (U. S. Department of Labor 1994).

Figure 7: Assets in Mutual Funds Versus Pensions

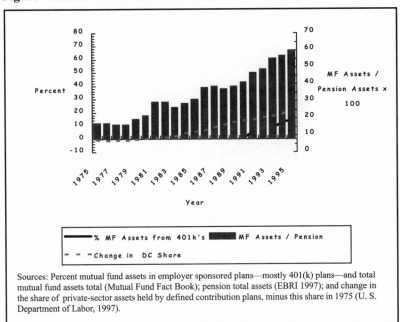

Sources: Percent mutual fund assets in employer sponsored plans—mostly 401(k) plans—and total mutual fund assets total (Mutual Fund Fact Book); pension total assets (EBRI 1997); and change in the share of private-sector assets held by defined contribution plans, minus this share in 1975 (U. S. Department of Labor, 1997).

This trend apparently does not portend dramatic changes for asset allocation. I use data compiled by the U.S. Department of Labor from a sample of annual Form 5500 reports.[37] The first two pie charts in Figure 8 show the allocations for defined benefit and defined contribution plans (inclusive of 401(k) plans) for the private sector in 1993; the third chart shows separately the allocation for those defined contribution plans that are 401(k) plans.[38] The share of equity in all the portfolios is remarkably similar; all of the plans exhibit stock shares in the range of 50 percent.[39]

---

37. They evaluated the components of all pooled funds for a sample of plans using attachments to the Form 5500s in the 1993 plan year. After allocating these pooled funds to their underlying components (equity, fixed income and other [including real estate, and so on]), they then compile the overall portfolio shares.

38. The 401(k) plan allocation excludes employee stock ownership plans that are in the 401(k) category.

39. I checked the 401(k) result with holdings in the federal thrift plan; this plan also reveals a portfolio allocation similar to the private-plan result shown in the figure.

Figure 8: Asset Allocation by Plan Type, 1993

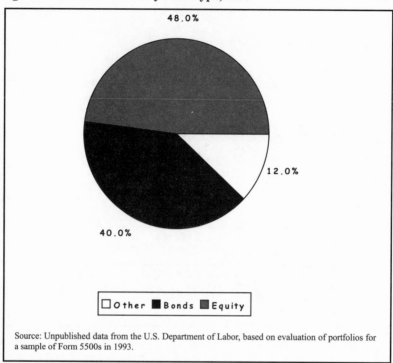

Source: Unpublished data from the U.S. Department of Labor, based on evaluation of portfolios for a sample of Form 5500s in 1993.

Changing Tax Policy for Defined Benefit Plans

Defined Benefit Plans

Private-sector defined benefit plans cover about 42 million participants, including 25 million workers.[40] Compared with defined contribution plans—which are often likened to tax-preferred savings accounts—defined benefit plans are more complex contracts. The value of these plans to a worker depends on the age and service level when he or she leaves the company; thus, they affect quit-and-retirement behavior.[41] Defined benefit plans also have a profit-sharing

---

40. Participants include workers, as well as separated vested workers, retirees, and survivors of deceased participants.

41. There are several reviews of the pension contract. See, for example, Gustman et al. (1994) and Quinn et al. (1990). The firm has wide latitude in how it sets up the incentives in these plans, and thus, can generate a wide range of age-service profiles in the firm (Ippolito 1998a).

aspect in the sense that the workers are more likely to receive the full value of the pension if the company is successful.

Projected Versus Accrued Benefits

In a defined benefit plan, the employer makes a promise to pay workers an annuity commencing at retirement. Often, the benefit is proportional to final tenure and pay.[42] These benefits, known as Projected Benefit Obligations (PBO), reflect a kind of real value of the pension promise.

If a plan terminates, however, the pension benefit is based on workers' wages at the time of termination, not at the time of retirement; workers lose any benefit of indexing in the interim. The present value of these benefits, known as Accrued Benefit Obligations (ABO), are a kind of nominal value of the pension promise.

Since PBO is based on projected wage and ABO is based on current wage, projected benefits are almost always higher than accrued benefits. Importantly, funding rules have permitted companies to fund for projected benefits, and thus, often, pension funds hold assets well in excess of accrued benefits—in which case they have "excess assets"; that is, they have a funding ratio for accrued benefits well in excess of 100 percent. Usually, this ratio is higher, the younger the work force covered by the plan.[43]

Implicit Pension Contract

Workers in defined benefit plans do not own pension assets, as such. Instead, they are like partly secured debtors: they hold the company's obligation to pay future pension benefits, usually in the form of an annuity during retirement.[44] The company retains the right to terminate the plan at any time.

---

42. An important exception is flat benefit plans in which all workers receive a fixed amount per year of service. Usually, these plans fund only for accrued benefits and thus are often underfunded for ABO.

43. The younger the workforce, the longer is the period of projection of wages to retirement age, and thus, the greater is the difference between projected and accrued benefits.

44. The promise is legally enforceable up to certain limits, and most benefits are guaranteed against employer insolvency by the Pension Benefit Guaranty Corporation.

Presumably, if the company is successful, it will not terminate the plan, and workers will receive the full value of their ongoing pension benefits; if the company encounters sufficient financial stress, however, it may terminate the plan, and pay workers their termination benefits.

We can think of the difference between ongoing and termination liabilities as contingent benefits, because their payment depends in part on the financial success of the plan sponsor. If the plan is funded beyond termination benefits, the company historically had the rights to excess assets; that is, the funding of contingent benefits did not trigger a requirement to pay benefits beyond the legal minimum (that is, accrued benefits).

Excise Tax on Reversions

In 1986, Congress enacted landmark legislation that changed the corporate tax treatment of excess pension assets that revert to the employer. It levied a 10 percent (nondeductible) excise tax on reversions from defined benefit plans;[45] increased the rate 15 percent in 1988, and finally, set a confiscatory 50 percent rate in 1990. In doing so it thereby affirmed the new ownership paradigm:[46] as long as liabilities beyond termination values were funded, the company's call on contingent liabilities was virtually valueless. Creditors' ability to access the excess assets to pay part of the company's unsecured debt also was reduced.[47]

If the plan has no excess assets then the new tax levy does not affect the company's option to default on contingent pension benefits. Companies with excess assets, however, lose the option to cut contingent benefits up to the amount of excess assets in the plan. The company can reclaim some of the value of its option by reducing excess assets in the plan by means other than reversion (notably by reducing its rate of contributions). In effect, the new tax provisions require that

---

45. The new law was triggered in part by reversions during the 1980s that were tied to various corporate restructurings.

46. If the sponsors contributes 25 percent of the reversion to another qualified pension plan covering the terminated employees, then the tax rate is reduced to 20 percent. In the event of bankruptcy and liquidation, the excise tax rate was set at 25 percent, not 50 percent.

47. Pension assets could never be used as collateral as such, but excess assets were available to settle debts of the plans sponsor.

companies cannot both have the advantage of tax-free buildup for excess assets, and keep the option value of defaulting on contingent benefits.

New Full Funding Limit

In December 1987, Congress took further action to reduce excess assets in defined benefit pension plans. Effective in 1988, the new law required that any pension plan with a termination funding ratio in excess of 150 percent of termination liabilities could not make tax-deductible contributions to the pension. Since benefit payments from plans would continue, the law anticipated that funding levels of over-funded plans would fall toward 150 percent.[48]

Impact on Funding

The data are consistent with the hypothesis that these tax changes had a dramatic effect on plan sponsors' target funding ratios. In fact, the reactions are sufficiently large so as to explain the entirety of the decline in funding ratios between the mid-1980s and mid-1990s (Ippolito 1998b). While I will not explain this study in detail here, the essence of the results are shown in Figure 9. This figure shows the distributions of funding ratios (on an accrued benefits basis) for the years 1986 and 1994, where liabilities in both years are calculated using the same 6.7 percent interest rate to discount future benefits.

---

48.   An interesting feature of the limit is that it can be moved over some range at the discretion of the plan sponsor. For example, the law permits the firm to calculate pension liabilities using an interest rate within 90 to 105 percent of a moving average 30-year Treasury rate. For purposes of the limit, they can use their own mortality assumptions (which can vary over a broad range). And sponsors are permitted to use the lower of "actuarial assets" or market assets—actuarial assets are smoothed market values that lag market values when investment returns are positive. Beginning in 1998, the limit is scheduled to increase gradually to 170 percent. However, because of redundant funding restrictions (notably those restricting sponsors from projecting wages), these increases are expected to have little impact. For convenience, I continue to refer to the limit as the 150 percent full funding limit, notwithstanding these scheduled increases.

Figure 9: Funding Ratios, 1986 Versus 1994

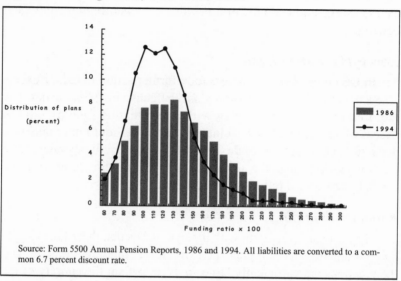

Source: Form 5500 Annual Pension Reports, 1986 and 1994. All liabilities are converted to a common 6.7 percent discount rate.

At the beginning of 1988, the distribution is diverse, as denoted by the black-line schedule with closed circles, reflecting the wide disparity of maturity levels in these plans. Despite excess investment returns on a balanced portfolio that were 6 percent per annum over the period—the distribution shifted noticeably to the left by 1994 (denoted by the solid-area distribution).

The study shows that the reduction in contribution levels started in 1986 with the advent of the reversion tax. While the new full funding limit imposed in 1988 exerted an additional impact on pension funding, it was of second-order magnitude: the decline was already well underway. In fact, companies seemingly intentionally set their assumptions to accelerate the decline in funding anticipated by the new limits.

Based on the estimation of a funding model over the period 1980-1994, I put the impact of both changes in tax policy at about $365 billion. Thus, while defined benefit plans held about $1.1 trillion in assets in January 1995, the estimates suggest that they would have held almost $1.5 trillion had tax policy not been modified. The reduction in tax advantages of defined benefit plans implied by these policies may help explain the rapid demise of defined benefit plans over the period. The combination of 401(k) plans building assets and plan sponsors defunding their defined benefit plans explains the rapidly changing assets shares in the private pension market (Figure 5).

Efficiency Issues

Regulatory Issues

Regulations of state and local pensions are in the jurisdiction of the 50 states. Since the enactment of the Employee Retirement Income Security Act (ERISA) in 1974, however, the federal government has had exclusive jurisdiction in the regulation of private pensions.[49] There are many regulations that affect pensions, but there are four main categories.[50]

Fiduciary rules ensure that pension trusts are used solely for the benefit of participants.[51] Reporting and disclosure rules require plans to issue periodic benefit statements to workers and to file financial reports with the federal government. Funding rules restrict defined benefit plans from being "too underfunded" or "too overfunded." Qualification rules include all the restrictions imposed by Congress as a condition to obtain tax-preferred status.

Fiduciary Rules

ERISA fiduciary rules are consistent with modern portfolio theory. Riskiness is not viewed in isolation, but rather in the context of the entire portfolio. ERISA follows the so-called "prudent man" rule: it allows pension plans to have portfolios that would reasonably be chosen by like professionals in similar circumstances.[52]

The trust fund must be administered for the sole benefit of participants. Generally, this rule is interpreted to mean that the plan fidu-

---

49. Prior to ERISA, funding rules were found in the Internal Revenue Code, but fiduciary regulations were under the jurisdiction of the states in which the plans operated.

50. For a list of regulations enacted since 1980, see Hay Huggins Co. (1991), and the ERISA Industry Committee (1996).

51. The regulatory structure is separated into three parts, each administered by a separate agency. Fiduciary rules (Title I of ERISA) are administered by the U. S. Department of Labor; mandatory pension insurance for defined benefit plans is administered by the Pension Benefit Guaranty Corporation (Title IV), which I ignore in this paper; and all rules that are prerequisites to having the tax benefits of pensions are administered by the Internal Revenue Service.

52. The rules are discussed in Allen et al. (1997) and McGill et al. (1996).

ciary should pursue the highest returns consistent with risk (in the "prudent man" sense). This requirement rules out self dealing with the plan sponsor, and "social" investments that sacrifice return. Put simply, fiduciary rules generally are not impediments to the flow of pension monies to their highest uses.

One oddity is that for many pension plans fiduciary rules permit no more than 10 percent of plan assets to be invested in the plan sponsor's own securities. This rule finds its genesis in "consumer protection" in the sense that it limits the risk to employees in their pension, though, since 1974, it mainly acts to protect the mandatory pension insurance program.[53]

In contrast, in defined contribution plans, Employee Stock Ownership Plans (ESOP) are permitted; these plans concentrate workers' pension exposure in their employer's financial success.[54] In addition, companies can set up profit-sharing-defined contribution plans, in which the flow of contributions can be entirely dependent on the financial performance of the plan sponsor.[55]

Reporting and Disclosure

Reporting and disclosure rules resemble those covering other fiduciary instruments. Just as publicly traded companies and mutual funds must issue a prospectus to new investors, so too, do pension plans issue summary plan descriptions. These documents outline the basic rules of the plan, including benefit accrual rates, conditions for receiving benefits, and so on.

Just as mutual funds issue periodic statements revealing share values, so too, do plans issue periodic (often annual) statements showing workers' accrued benefits in the plan. Pension plans issue annual reports showing portfolio composition, funding levels and so on.

---

53. Upon bankruptcy, an underfunded defined benefit plan can become a claim on the Pension Benefit Guaranty Corporation. If the plan invests heavily in its own stock, the funding status would deteriorate in the case of serious financial stress, leaving large potential claims for the insurance agency.

54. Once workers attain age 55 with 10 years of service, the sponsor must allow workers the option to move his or her monies to a self-directed diversified portfolio.

55. Contributions to these plans are limited to the maximum of 15 percent of compensation. In profit-sharing 401(k) plans, a sponsor can decide whether, and how much, its matching rate will be in the coming year. A typical plan of this kind is discussed in some detail in Kusko, Poterba and Wilcox (1994).

These reports are filed with the Internal Revenue Service and are available for inspection from the pension plan or the U.S. Department of Labor disclosure room.

Funding Rules

Defined contribution plans are fully funded by definition. The sponsor is responsible for making contributions. The account balance is determined entirely by the market value of the underlying securities. Thus, funding rules do not affect defined contribution plans.

In contrast, defined benefit plans are regulated by a voluminous set of funding rules. These rules have a dichotomous purpose. First, they regulate maximum contributions: these rules exist because of the special tax status afforded pensions, though, as I suggested above, they mostly have become redundant to the reversion tax. Second, they regulate minimum contributions. These rules are designed mainly for consumer protection, though they have become redundant to a mandatory insurance program enacted with ERISA; thus, the rules now can be viewed as a way to control pension insurance premiums.

Qualification Rules

Qualification rules generally constrain the characteristics of pension plans that will be allowed to enjoy consumption-tax treatment. These rules involve the details of the pension contract. Their general thrust is not principally oriented toward consumer protection, but more to controlling who receives the tax benefits. The aim of these rules seems to be to prod sponsors to award more benefits to the shorter-service, and lower-paid workers, and to reduce benefits to longer-service and higher-paid workers.

The rules regulate: participation; vesting; the disparity of pension accruals across workers in the company (nondiscrimination);[56] Social Security integration; spouse protection (mandatory joint and survivor annuities); defined benefit service accruals (cannot be too tilted to later ages, cannot vary across participants, cannot vary with company profits); limitations on benefits (projected wages above certain limits

---

56. Essentially, the rules are intended to have workers of different salary levels subject to the same or similar pension provisions.

cannot be reflected in the pension formula, annuities cannot exceed other limits); and so on.[57]

The rules tend to be inconsistent across different kinds of plans. For example, while all workers covered by 401(k) plans must participate after one year of service, fully 30 percent of all workers who participate in 401(k) plans in fact contribute nothing (and thus receive no matching), while in traditional defined contribution plans and defined benefit plans, all participants must receive the same accruals.[58] Similarly, in defined benefit plans, the pension formula cannot be too back loaded, but in defined contribution plans, age-service related formulas are permitted.

Even ignoring the implicit cost of the distortions imposed by these rules, Hay Huggins Co. (1990) has shown that the direct costs of regulations imposed by pension legislation throughout the 1980s eliminates a significant portion of the tax advantages of pensions, particularly for defined benefit plans sponsored by smaller companies.[59]

Tax Policy

How Pension Tax Policy Matters

In pension plans, ordinary income tax rules are modified to award "consumption tax treatment" of savings. Importantly, this treatment is availed mostly to individuals only through company-sponsored pensions.[60] To qualify for this treatment, plan sponsors must

---

57. Most of these rules are found in Section 401(a) of the Internal Revenue Code, and in code citations referenced in 401(a). They include a large portion of all pension rules, and comprise the majority of the IRS pension function. See note 77.
58. Plans are allowed some integration with social security benefits under section 401(l) of the code. If the sponsor uses this provision, accrual rates for lower-compensated employees can be lower than for highly compensated workers.
59. They estimated that the average annual pension contribution was $1,400 per worker in 1990 dollars. Perhaps 25 percent of this amount represents the tax advantage of pension tax treatment, or about $350. Hay Huggins showed that, since 1981, regulatory costs per annum for defined benefit plans increased by $394 per person (in 1990 dollars) for 15-person plans, $144 for 75-person plans, and $77 for 500-person plans. The increases were more modest for defined contribution plans: $112, $95 and $45 respectively.
60. When an individual is self employed, he is availed a Keogh plan, which is an exception of sorts to the rule. In addition, there is an exception for IRAs in the amount of $2,000 per annum, subject to certain income means-tested limits.

write pensions to conform to a myriad of rules in the Internal Revenue Code and in the ERISA statute.

The compelling case for consumption tax treatment of savings is that the effective tax rate on wages does not depend on the period in which the earnings are used to support consumption. Income tax treatment encourages workers to ignore their future consumption requirements, a problem of special magnitude during older ages when workers' productive capabilities typically wane.

One way to characterize income tax treatment of savings is as an extra income tax on wages at the time they are earned. In effect, there is a two-tier tax rate. If earnings are used to support current consumption, they are assessed a tax rate equal to the statutory rate proscribed in the Internal Revenue Code. If earnings are used to support future consumption, they are assessed at the statutory rate plus some increment.

For example, consider a 40-year-old person who considers either spending a marginal dollar of wages now, or saving it for later consumption at age 60. Suppose the interest rate is 6 percent, and the marginal tax rate (at all ages) is 40 percent. If he consumes his marginal earnings immediately, he incurs a tax rate of 40 cents, leaving him 60 cents to spend. If he saves his monies in a tax-exposed vehicle, he will not have 60 cents to spend at age 60 in present value terms, but only 37 cents.[61] The extra taxes are assessed on interest earnings, which are not earnings as such, but instead merely translate dollars across time in present value terms.

That is, if he uses his marginal wage to support current consumption, he pays the statutory income tax rate of 40 percent. If he spends the monies later, he faces the equivalent of a 63 percent tax on the same dollar of earnings (Figure 10). The higher tax rate applies if and only if he decides to postpone consumption. If the individual has

---

61. In the comprehensive income tax treatment, earnings saved for future consumption are subject to a so-called double tax; once when the wages are received, and again in the form of taxation of interest, which effectively taxes earnings a second time. To illustrate, consider a worker who decides to save $1 of current wages to support retirement consumption 20 years hence. Suppose that the marginal tax rate, denoted by t, is the same in both periods, and that the nominal interest rate is i. In 20 years, the $1 is worth $I_{20} = (1-t)\$1e^{i(1-.020)}$. If i is 6 percent and t is 40 percent then $I_{20} = \$1.23$. In year zero dollars, this amount is valued at $\$1.23\ e^{-i20} = \$0.37$.

access to a pension plan then he can eliminate the de facto surcharge: he faces a 40 percent tax on his earnings regardless of when he spends them.[62]

Figure 10: Tax Bias Toward Spending: Income Tax Treatment

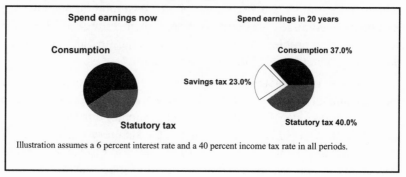

Illustration assumes a 6 percent interest rate and a 40 percent income tax rate in all periods.

Current Tax Policy

The United States has a hybrid income tax structure that broadly endorses comprehensive income tax treatment of savings, but allows substantial exceptions, including consumption-tax treatment of owner-occupied housing and pensions.[63] Oddly, in comparison to a comprehensive income tax system, a hybrid scheme may not affect marginal savings decisions, and thus, may not substantially increase the overall savings rate.[64] But it encourages substantial economic distortion that affects the flow of investments; for example, the decision between housing versus the productive capital stock, and between retirement savings versus precautionary savings, and so on.[65]

In addition, by selectively awarding consumption tax status, the Congress creates a reservoir of tax advantage to selected taxpayers. By then attaching conditions to obtain the tax benefit, Congress in

---

62. If the worker saves the $1 in a pension fund, the after-tax pension value in year 20 is $C_{20} = \$1\ e^{i\,20}\ (1\text{-}t) = \$2.05$ if t is .4.

63. There are many partial exceptions as well, including the exclusion of interest on municipal bonds, partial consumption tax treatment of variable annuities, and so on.

64. Individuals may simply move existing savings to the tax-preferred account. Savings is affected only if tax policy affects marginal savings decisions.

65. There are many other distortions in the current system, including the encouragement of too much investment in municipal versus private projects, decisions about stock versus bond financing, and so on.

effect can use some of this reservoir as a sort of off-budget source of financing to accomplish social objectives.

The equal application of a consumption tax across the economy eliminates these distortions: marginal investment dollars follow their highest-value uses. Most importantly, it eliminates the marginal incentive to use income to support immediate versus future consumption, and thus, works toward increasing the capital base. It also limits Congress from using special tax status as off-budget sources of financing.

Unraveling the Consumption Tax

Having ostensibly awarded consumption-tax status to pension plans, since 1982, the Congress has retracted at least some of these benefits, particularly for defined benefit plans. They have done this directly through explicit artificial limits on funding; by attaching confiscatory taxes on excess assets in the event of a plan termination, and by legislating restrictive pension rules that either impose direct regulatory burden on companies sponsoring pensions, or cause companies to distort their behavior (and the behavior of their workers) to comply with the rules, resulting in inefficiencies in the workplace.

There are other policies that work to dissipate the tax advantages of pension savings: notably the inclusion of pension monies for purposes of estate taxation, income means-testing of Social Security benefits, and asset means-testing of Medicaid benefits.

Estate Tax

The estate tax works to unravel the neutral savings feature of a consumption tax. If individuals knew their date of death beforehand then the estate tax biases only savings intended for bequests to non-spouse family members or other heirs.[66] But since the date of death is uncertain, accumulations meant for retirement consumption are often subject to an extra tax.

Currently, the federal government levies a tax rate of at least 37 percent on all estates in excess of $625,000,[67] with the maximum rate of 55 percent effective for amounts in excess of $3 million (I ignore addi-

---

66. The individual still can bequest monies to his or her spouse and/or to nonprofit entities without facing estate taxes.

67. Effective with 1997 legislation, the limit is now scheduled to increase gradually to more than $1 million over the next several years.

tional inheritance taxes levied by the state, which also can be considerable).[68]

Consider the example I used above (Figure 10): saving $1 of mar-
ginal wages in a pension plan results in a total tax bill of 40 cents in
present value terms. If the monies are saved outside the plan for 20
years, the worker faces a tax of 63 cents. But suppose that the individual who used the pension dies suddenly at age 60 before he has a
chance to spend his savings and suppose that either he is single or that
his spouse predeceases him. Further suppose that his estate is worth at
least $625,000 so that he faces a 37 percent estate tax.

Prior to 1982, the entirety of the pension balance would have
escaped the estate tax: it would be subject only to the income tax
(which I assume is 40 percent). His heirs could spend the same 60 percent share of his earnings, as before, thereby continuing pure consumption tax treatment of pension savings. Since 1984, the entire pension
balance is subject to the estate tax.[69]

In this case, the 37 percent estate tax is levied first; then the rest is
subject to the 40 percent income tax, leaving 38 percent for his heirs.
The de facto tax on his pension monies is 62 percent, almost identical
to the 63 percent tax that the individual would have paid had he faced a
pure income tax and spent the monies at age 60 just prior to dying. In
effect, the estate tax resurrects the double tax concept and subtly
biases the decision to spend monies faster than otherwise. (If the individual saves the monies outside the pension then dies, he would face a
triple tax on his wages, for a total tax of 77 percent.)[70] Figure 11 illustrates these tax rates.

---

68. A comprehensive evaluation of estate and income taxation of retirement monies,
including state taxes, is found in Shoven and Wise (1996).
69. The Tax Equity and Fiscal Responsibility Act of 1982 restricted the pension
exclusion to $100,000; the Deficit Reduction Act of 1984 eliminated the exclusion.
70. If he uses a tax-exposed vehicle, the double tax embedded in income tax treatment already reduces his balance at age 60 to 37 cents in present value terms (see
note 59); on top of this, he pays a 37 percent estate tax on the remainder, which
reduces the funds for his heirs to 23 cents in present value terms. In this case, the triple tax amounts to 77 percent. He can reduce his tax by investing in securities (or real
assets) that have little or no current yield, and instead pay a capital gain. In probate,
the cost basis of the asset is stepped up, and thus, the heirs avoid the capital gains tax,
but incur the estate tax. In this case, part of the hidden tax cost is in the distortion on
the individual's preferred risk-adjusted portfolio.

Figure 11: Tax Bias Towards Spending: Estate Tax Treatment

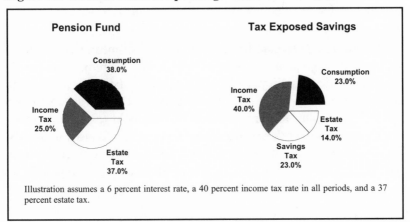

Illustration assumes a 6 percent interest rate, a 40 percent income tax rate in all periods, and a 37 percent estate tax.

Means-tested Social Security Benefits

The Social Security system is means tested against taxable income during retirement. Consider various couples who have earned a joint $12,000 Social Security annuity per annum. Assume that the relevant marginal income tax rate is 30 percent. Couples with taxable income less than $32,000 receive the benefits tax free; those with taxable income above $32,000 have to rebate $1,800 of their benefit to the Social Security Administration, and those with taxable income above $44,000 must rebate $3,060 of their benefit.

The problem with this means test is that other taxable income during retirement often reflects savings decisions made earlier in life. That is, other taxable income usually is attributable to the receipt of a pension annuity, withdrawals from defined contribution plans or IRAs, and/or earnings from other income-producing assets they accumulated for retirement.[71]

Three workers, each in the same job, with the same lifetime Social Security contributions and with the same family circum-

---

71. That is, in the first instance, 50 percent of the benefits, of $6,000, is subject to taxation. If the tax rate is 30 percent, then the couple sacrifices $1,800 of their benefits. In the second case, 85 percent of $12,000 is subject to a 30 percent tax, which amounts to a tax bill of $3,060. The tax revenue is sent directly to the Social Security trust fund, making the implicit means test explicit. In 1996, Social Security retrieved $6.4 billion of benefits paid through this provision (Social Security Administration 1997 table 4.A1).

stances, are treated differently based solely on taxable income during retirement. The means test creates a disincentive to save for retirement.[72]

In addition, Medicaid for the elderly is asset-means tested: those who save through pensions or other vehicles for retirement are penalized by Medicaid policy. Elderly individuals who have zero assets qualify for nursing-home care if they need it. Those who save more must dissipate any retirement accounts they hold (as well as other assets) and turn over their private pension annuities in order to qualify for the same nursing home care that automatically is given to those who have no savings. The means test in Medicaid discourages workers from accumulating private savings and earning pension annuities.

Some Policy Proposals

Tax Treatment

The above discussion suggests numerous policies that would reduce the economic distortions caused by current tax policy. My proposals encompass retirement income savings, broadly interpreted, and revolve around the efficiencies entailed by their consumption tax treatment. In a perfect world, the Congress would replace the current income tax code with a pure consumption tax.[73] The broad application of a consumption tax has several sources of efficiency.

- It eliminates the distortion in a comprehensive income tax that favors spending over saving.
- It eliminates the distortion in a hybrid tax scheme that favors some kinds of savings over others (savings for retirement, for example, over precautionary or bequest motives).
- The consumption tax leads to an efficient flow of monies to investment opportunities based on their underlying economic value, unfettered by their differential tax treatment (thus, housing and municipal projects are not favored over other productive investments).

---

72. Evidence on this point is reported in Hubbard, Skinner and Zeldes (1995); also see Burtless (1996).
73. Many alternatives are possible. Two are found in Hall and Rabushka (1995) and Bradford (1977).

- By eliminating the extra tax on savings, the capital stock increases, which results in higher wage levels and higher national income. This policy would have to encompass all tax law: estate taxation, for example, unravels the benefits of consumption tax treatment.[74]
- It redirects resources used to influence tax policy to more productive activities.
- The policy reduces the amount of off-budget financing to Congress.

In a consumption-tax arrangement, pensions are not favored institutions, and it is predictable that strident competition will arise across financial institutions to act as intermediaries between savers and investment opportunities. Pensions, as such, will survive only if they confer large efficiency gains.[75]

Short of the consumption-tax approach, several changes in tax policy could be made toward retirement savings that would improve the efficiency of this market. While the gains are not of the magnitude availed by the broad consumption tax, nevertheless, the payoff from a series of smaller changes could provide a substantial increase in efficiency over the current system.

These ideas entail the same principles of the consumption tax and the essence of a fully competitive market. One inefficiency is unavoidable: if Congress does not want a broad-based consumption tax then pension policy must have some additional regulations to reduce the possibilities for arbitrage that characterize a hybrid system.

Eliminate the Estate Tax

A significant step toward reducing the disincentive to save is the elimination of estate taxation. This action preserves consumption-tax treatment of pension savings and eliminates triple taxation of savings made in tax-exposed vehicles. If the government is concerned about "overuse" of the pension vehicle, it could attach the 10 percent excise

---

74. In addition, either the corporate tax assessment is dropped or integrated into the consumption tax system so as to prevent double taxation of investment earnings. Hall and Rabushka (1995) work through the details of one proposal.

75. For example, if the pension is the most effective way to reduce quits and manage retirement ages then it may survive full and open competition.

tax now applied to premature withdrawals as a way of recapturing some portion of the tax gains embedded in the pension fund.

Reduce the Reversion Tax

Reduce the current confiscatory 50 percent tax on asset reversions from defined benefit plans to 10 percent. This tax rate is consistent with excise tax assessments on premature withdrawals from other retirement accounts and recaptures a portion of the tax advantage embedded in excess assets.[76] The current confiscatory treatment of reversions has contributed to reductions in funding of these pensions by almost $400 billion.

Eliminate the 150 Percent Full Funding Limit

Currently, full consumption-tax treatment is afforded to defined contribution plans, but is restricted to defined benefit plans, particularly those offered by sponsors with lots of younger workers. The problem is easily redressed by reverting to pre-1988 policy to allow defined benefit plans to accumulate assets sufficient to pay projected benefits.[77] I also would eliminate auxiliary constraints that also artificially restrict funding for these benefits.[78]

Tax Social Security Benefits Like Pensions

Social Security benefits should be taxed on consumption tax principles, like pensions. Consumption taxes can be applied either when contributions are made (as in a Roth IRA) or when benefits are

---

76. For example, withdrawals from most IRAs prior to age 59', are subject to a 10 percent tax. In Roth IRAs, the contributions that are made after tax can be withdrawn without penalty.

77. In 1997, the Congress allowed a gradual phase in of higher limits to 170 percent, but since it did not relax auxiliary limits, some of which are redundant to the 150 percent limit (see next footnote), these changes alone are not expected to affect pension funding constraints.

78. As a corollary, I would eliminate other sections of the code that prevent actuaries from funding for full projected benefits. I would eliminate maximum allowable salary levels as recognized in the pension formula in IRC Section 415(b) ($160,000 in 1998), and maximum pension benefits in the Internal Revenue Code Section 401(a)(17) (in 1998, $130,000 per annum for an age-65 annuity—less for earlier ages). These rules also act to restrict funding for ongoing benefits, because they require actuaries to pretend that for all future periods, these (nominal) amounts also will prevail.

242

taken (as in a traditional IRA). Currently, 50 percent of Social Security contributions are taxed as ordinary income for most recipients.[79]

The problem is easily solved by including 50 percent of benefits as taxable income for all recipients. Normal exemptions, deductions and progressivity in the U.S. income tax code award older Americans with lower incomes the same favorable tax treatment as their younger counterparts with the same taxable income. I also would extend these principles to noncash Social Security benefits (notably, Medicare).[80]

Regulatory Reform

Disentangle Pensions from Employers

A central feature of pension policy in the United States is the bundling of retirement savings tax preferences with employer-sponsored pension plans. By creating this nexus, the federal government creates a reservoir of tax advantage that can be dissipated by direct and indirect regulatory burden. The likelihood that a free pension market would generate the pension outcomes we now observe is negligibly small. Without regulatory constraints, employers and workers would gravitate to a market characterized by a wide range of pension arrangements, one that would increase the efficiency of the system because they would encourage decisions based on desired savings rates and productivity-enhancing attributes of pensions.

---

79. As discussed earlier, a minority of recipients pay higher taxes on their Social Security benefits based on an income means test. These correspond to the so-called employee share of the contribution. The employer share is tax deductible to the employer but not taxable as income to the worker.

80. The current entitlement of the elderly to Medicare and old-age Medicaid (nursing home) should be ended in its current form. The main problem currently is that the size of the entitlement is entirely independent of contributions, thereby converting Medicare contributions to a pure tax on labor. In addition, the Medicaid benefits are asset-means tested, thereby discouraging savings for retirement. The problem is easily remedied by applying the formula for cash benefits to medical benefits as well, with identical tax treatment (see earlier). That is, workers would earn credits in return for contributions to the system. Workers should be free to use their earned credits during retirement to buy insurance from competing insurance carriers. These benefits would be invariant to other assets and income received by the elderly during their retirement and should be taxed on the same principles as cash benefits. An elaboration of this policy is found in Ippolito (1998a), along with numerous other proposals for Social Security reform.

Indeed, one argument for the rise of 401(k) plans is the freedom that they confer: freedom for workers to choose whether or not to save in the pension and freedom for companies to make different pension contributions to workers based solely on workers' revealed preferences for savings.[81] In addition, by making these plans profit sharing, the company can introduce flexibility in its benefit accruals, which is not a realistic alternative in defined benefit plans.[82]

Expanded IRA

The most effective way to eliminate the employer-pension nexus is to increase the limits on annual contributions to IRAs to 25 percent of wages, without regard to either income level or availability of pensions on the job.[83] This change has far-reaching implications for efficiency of the pension market. Once companies are required to compete with IRAs, only those pensions that impart large efficiency gains in the company will survive.[84]

---

81. They do this through the matching formula. I argue elsewhere that companies may attach more value to savers than nonsavers, which rationalizes companies' decisions to effectively pay higher wages to savers through the match formula (Ippolito 1998a).

82. Technically, the company can change pension generosity for future accruals, but this is a costly alternative and it is not a feasible alternative to effect every year. In an unregulated environment, the company can set a match rate that depends on its financial performance. In periods of poor performance, it can set a zero match rate. In periods of strong performance, it can set a relatively generous match rate. The value afforded to companies from contribution flexibility is developed in Petersen (1994).

83. This limit already is embedded in the Internal Revenue Code [Section 415(c)]. All other limits can be abolished. Taking into account a reasonable Social Security replacement rate, this savings rate is required to reach an adequate savings rate, assuming investment in riskless securities. Assume a work life of 40 years, and retirement period of 20 years. For simplicity, assume that real wages are flat over the lifetime. A 25 percent savings rate yields a per annum retirement flow equal to 50 percent of the wage. To enforce the rule, employers could include the contribution percent on employees W-2 form each year. In this way, the sum of company contributions to pension plans plus the individual's own contributions to IRAs could be effectively constrained by the limit.

84. Since workers have the option of saving in a tax-preferred account outside the company, they would require some premium to accept a retirement plan with cond-

Reduce Regulatory Burden

With the introduction of the expanded IRA, the demand for pensions at the company will be more sensitive to regulatory costs, which will exert a pressure on government to reduce them. Moreover, since the government will not require individuals to obtain their pensions at the workplace, the argument for strong regulatory oversight is greatly diminished. I would greatly reduce the regulatory burden on pensions.

Except for portfolio restrictions (which I would eliminate), I would retain most fiduciary rules, as well as most reporting and disclosure rules, comparable to those found in other financial institutions.[85] I would retain some regulations on maximum contributions (consistent with a maximum-contribution rule of 25 percent of wages)—otherwise, arbitrage will effectively transform the pension exception into a full-scale consumption tax.[86]

Most importantly, I would eliminate all tax qualification rules.[87] This change has large potential efficiency prospects: it allows companies to stylize pensions to its various workers, just as they do wages. Companies should be able to offer a variety of pension provisions to their various employees, and workers should be allowed to elect their

84. ditions, like a defined benefit plan. But if the company's productivity is substantially increased with this kind of pension (because, for example, it reduces quit rates and helps manage retirement ages), this gain can be used partly to finance the wage premium. I develop this point more fully in Ippolito (1998a). Companies can accomplish some of these objectives now for "top hat" individuals in the company, but are not availed consumption tax treatment. The revised rules allow flexibility across all workers in the company, and award full consumption tax treatment to contributions.
85. These requirements are not unlike those that govern mutual funds.
86. I also would eliminate most other funding rules, including amortization rules, deficit reduction contribution rules, and so on, on the condition that the plan's funding would be reported annually to participants. As a corollary, I would privatize pension insurance, and make it voluntary. Clearly, the cost of pension insurance would depend (among many other things) on the company's adherence to funding restrictions as set out in the policy.
87. Notably, I would eliminate IRC Section 401(a) and all code citations referenced in 401(a). In effect, I would adopt rules that now pertain to so-called top-hat plans except I would allow their full funding and award full consumption-tax treatment. When funded, these plans are subject to fiduciary rules and some reporting and disclosure. I would expand the disclosure rules for general application. For details on top-hat plans and discussion of the myriad of qualification rules, including 401(a) and cross references in the code, see Towers Perrin (1995), Allen et al. (1997) and McGill et al. (1996).

coverages from those availed to them by the sponsor. I would impose no restrictions on participation, vesting, benefit formulas, accrual rates and so on. In other words, companies are permitted to use pensions in ways that maximize their value to the company and workers.

From the perspective of workers, a pension is treated like any other investment, and so is regulated comparably. Workers can accept any pension contract, subject to full reporting and disclosure.

Upon hiring workers, companies would issue a summary plan description (the prospectus), which articulates the rules of the plan. Like any prospectus, the summary should spell out the rewards of the plan as well as all the attendant risk. The disclosure requirement would meet rigid criteria. Companies' pension promises would be enforceable in the courts like other contractual obligations.

Otherwise, the government would allow all types of pensions, just as they allow a wide variety of risk characteristics in mutual funds. Predictably, the market will be characterized by a large variety of competing pensions, including multiple pension types in some companies.

In consideration of the competing expanded IRA availed to all workers in this proposal, workers will not be attracted to company-offered pensions, particularly those characterized with high risk, unless they are adequately compensated.[88] These conditions will drive companies to economize on pension restrictions and to use only those restrictive criteria required to accomplish the productivity goals set by the company.[89] It will be up to market participants to decide which pension features prevail in the free market.

Conclusion

The United States has always been ambivalent toward the tax treatment of savings. Presumably motivated by concerns about income distribution, it has a long history in rejecting the pure application of a consumption tax, yet seems drawn to its positive influence on capital accumulation. Pension policy is an outgrowth of this ten-

---

88. Indeed, I have argued elsewhere that workers will not work in companies with defined-benefit plans without receiving a significant premium to compensate them for accepting a large portion of their wages in the form of a deferred pension that is conditional on completion of their entire tenure with the company (Ippolito 1998a).

sion. Its special treatment in the tax code explains why monies from the pension industry account for roughly 20 percent of financial assets in this country.

The dichotomous tax treatment of savings, however, has a downside feature: it creates a reservoir of special tax advantage that attracts regulation. In order to receive favorable treatment, invariably, various conditions must be satisfied. These conditions translate to regulatory burden. Put differently, the pension product is heavily regulated, both in its content and the coverage it entails.

Recently, defined benefit plans have been particularly disfavored. Burden on this product has been growing, and Congress recently has reduced its tax advantages, even as it created a new kind of pension, the so-called 401(k). These tax changes have fundamentally altered the private pension industry.

In municipalities and states, which are beyond the reach of much federal regulation, defined benefit plans still dominate coverage. In the private sector, however, there has been a strong trend toward defined contribution plans since the early 1980s, notably, the 401(k) variety. By 1995, fully 30 percent of covered private-sector workers had only 401(k) coverage; and assets in defined contribution plans began to overtake those in traditional defined benefit plans.

The trend provides an opportunity for far-reaching regulatory reform. The growing dominance of 401(k) plans makes it apparent that pensions are merely investments and, in fact, there has been a noticeable fusing of the pension and mutual fund industries. Workers in 401(k) plans can decide whether or not to participate, and they enjoy an opportunity to invest in a wide variety of investment vehicles, all with different risk and reward structures.

---

89. For example, in rare cases where patent developments or trade secrets might be important, the company may set a requirement that scientists leaving the company will forfeit their pension if they work for a rival company within 10 years. This provision clearly will entail a wage premium, and thus, the company will have no incentive to apply this criteria to other workers. Some companies may be substantially more productive if they can maintain their workers over long periods of tenure: In this case, a defined benefit plan might prevail, or a defined contribution plan with a long vesting period. The market will ensure that these companies pay a premium (financed by higher productivity) to workers to compensate them for the attendant risk, just as investors in stock issues receive a higher return over Treasury bill investments. See Ippolito (1998a).

By contrast, in traditional defined-benefit and defined-contribution plans, sponsors face strict regulations about the inclusiveness of coverage, and the risk attributes of the pension. The question is begged: why is any pension plan subject to rules about its risk-reward structure?

There is a large potential efficiency gain from expanding the opportunities for free competition in the pension market—in the form of more efficient savings decisions, less direct regulatory burden, and higher productivity resulting from the strategic application of pension plan provisions to the workforce.

Full competition can be created by making a simple change to the tax code: expand IRA contribution limits from $2,000 per annum to 25 percent of wages. All workers would have immediate access to retirement savings vehicles that are subject to consumption tax principles, without having their employers act as an intermediaries. Companies that want to use pensions must compete directly with workers' opportunities to invest retirement savings in other financial institutions.

To make the competition fair, I would free pensions from most of the regulatory burden now imposed on them, with the exception of fiduciary and reporting and disclosure regulations similar to those that cover other financial instruments. Pensions will survive if labor productivity (and thus the wage level) is sufficiently enhanced by the pension structure to make it worthwhile for workers to accept the attendant risk.

In this world, pensions would be treated like any other investment choice. Except for its role in Social Security, the government would stop trying to regulate savings behavior and pension risk. Once the risks and rewards are disclosed, workers would be free to enter the contracts of their choice.

Interestingly, similar ideas are being considered for the Social Security system. The current system is dominated by rules intended to make it mimic a risk-free instrument. The pay-as-you-go feature of the system, however, portends large political risk: forthcoming generations may balk at paying ever-higher tax rates to support the system.

The most important impact of the current arrangement is its negative impact on national income. It does this mostly by discouraging savings for retirement, depriving the capital markets of an important flow of new monies. Annual contribution to the entire system (inclusive of Medicare) approached $500 billion in 1996.

Recently, numerous scholars and the Social Security Advisory Council (1997)[90] have advanced various proposals to transpose at least part of the current system to a kind of defined contribution plan.[91] The new plans are characterized by higher investment risks and rewards, but award more control of savings to the individual and less to the government. In contrast to the private pension solution, however, I would maintain the required participation in the system, enforced by the federal government.[92]

The transition problems are daunting: paying off current obligations could involve the issue of $4 trillion to $5 trillion of debt by the year 2035 (1995 dollars). But the diversion of even 5 percent of projected contributions could result in retirement balances of $8 trillion in 1995 dollars by 2025 (Social Security Advisory Council 1997), and larger balances beyond.

The debate of these ideas will continue in many venues. For present purposes, I note two important aspects of the issue. First, the potential impact of Social Security reform on the wealth of the nation could well eclipse the potential gains from revamping pension regulation and tax policy. Second, the existence of a robust and unfettered pension market, and thus, the building of a higher private capital stock and more private savings, may be a prerequisite to a successful reform of the Social Security system.

References

Allen, E., Melone, J., Rosenbloom, J., and J. VanDerhei, Pension Planning. Homewood, IL: Richard D. Irwin, 8th edition, 1997.

---

90. There are three separate proposals in the report. I refer to the so-called Personal Savings Account Proposal advanced by members Bok, Combs, Schieber, Vargas and Weaver.

91. See Feldstein (1996), Feldstein and Samwick (1996), Social Security Advisory Council (1997), and Kotlikoff and Sachs (1997). Engen and Gale (1997) provide a good overview of various proposals, and offer some evaluation. For a review of some ideas to reduce some of the auxiliary benefits and the inefficiencies of the current system, without revamping it, see Ippolito (1998a). Social Security flow and stock data are found in Social Security Administration (1997).

92. Indeed, the floor benefit provided by Social Security is the basis for allowing a free market in private pensions.

Bradford, David, <u>Blueprints for Basic Tax Reform</u>. Washington, D.C.: U.S. Department of the Treasury, 1977.

Burtless, Gary, "The Folly of Means-testing Social Security," in Peter Diamond and David Lindeman, eds., <u>Social Security: What Role for the Future?</u>. Washington, D.C.: National Academy of Social Insurance, 1996, 172-180.

Clark, Robert, and Ann McDermed, <u>The Choice of Pension Plans in a Changing Environment</u>. Washington, D.C.: American Enterprise Institute, 1990.

Council of Economic Advisors, <u>Economic Report of the President</u>. Washington, D.C.: GPO, 1997.

Employee Benefits Research Institute, <u>Data Book on Employee Benefits</u>. Washington, D. C, 1997.

Engen, Eric, and William Gale, "Effects of Social Security Reform on Private and National Saving," Brookings Institution, 1997.

ERISA Industry Committee, <u>Getting the Job Done: A White Paper on Emerging Pension Issues</u>. Washington, D. C., July 1996.

Feldstein, Martin, "Social Security and Savings: New Time Series Evidence," <u>National Tax Journal</u> 49 (June 1996), 151-164.

_____, and Andrew Samwick, "The Transition Path in Privatizing Social Security," NBER Working Paper No. 6055, September 1996.

Fernandez, Phyllis, John Turner, and Richard Hinz, editors, <u>Pension Coverage Issues for the '90s</u>. Pension Benefit and Welfare Administration, U. S. Department of Labor, 1994.

Gustman, Alan, and Thomas Steinmeier, "The Stampede Towards Defined Contribution Plans," <u>Industrial Relations</u> 31 (Spring 1992), 361-369.

Gustman, Alan, Olivia Mitchell, and Thomas Steinmeier, "The Role of Pensions in the Labor Market: A Survey of the Literature," <u>Industrial Labor Relations Review</u> 47 (April 1994), 417-438.

Hall, Robert, and Alvin Rabushka, <u>The Flat Tax</u>. 2nd Edition, Hoover Press, 1995.

Hay Huggins Co., <u>Pension Plan Expense Study for the PBGC</u>, Final Report submitted to the PBGC, June 1990.

Hubbard, Glenn, Jonathan Skinner and Stephen Zeldes, "Precautionary Saving and Social Insurance," Journal of Political Economy, 103 (April 1995), 360-399.

Investment Company Institute, Mutual Fund Fact Book, 37th Edition, 1997.

Ippolito, Richard A., Pensions and Employee Performance: Evidence, Analysis and Policy. University of Chicago Press, 1998a.

_____, "The Decline in Pension Funding," mimeo, Washington, D.C., 1998b.

_____, An Economic Analysis of Pension Tax Policy in the United States. Homewood, IL: Richard D. Irwin, 1990.

_____, Pensions, Economics and Public Policy. Dow-Jones Irwin, 1986.

Kotlikoff, Lawrence, and Jeffrey Sachs, "It's High Time to Privatize," Brookings Review 15 (Summer 1997), 16-22.

Kruse, Douglas, "Pension Substitution in the 1980s: Why the Shift Towards Defined Contribution Plans?" Industrial Relations 34 (April 1995), 218-241.

Kusko, Andrea, James Poterba, and David Wilcox, "Employee Decisions with Respect to 401k Plans: Evidence from Individual-Level Data," NBER, Working Paper No. 4635, 1994.

Latimar, Murray, Industrial Pension Systems. New York: Industrial Relations Counselors, 1932.

McGill, Dan, K. Brown, J. Haley and S. Schieber, Fundamentals of Private Pensions, 7th edition, Pension Research Council, 1996.

New York Stock Exchange, Fact Book 199x, New York, 199x.

Pension Benefit Guaranty Corporation, Pension Insurance Data Book 1996, Washington, D.C., 1997.

Petersen, Mitchell, "Cash Flow Variability, and Pension Plan Choice: A Role for Operating Leverage," Journal of Financial Economics 35 (December 1994).

Quinn, Joseph, Richard Burkhauser, and Daniel Myers, Passing the Torch: The Influence of Economic Incentives on Work and Retirement. Kalamazoo, MI: Upjohn Institute, 1990.

Reid, Brian, and Jean Crumrine, "Retirement Plan Holdings of Mutual Funds, 1996," Investment Company Institute, 1997.

Scheiber, Sylvester, and Gordon Goodfellow, "Pension Coverage in America," in P. Fernandez, J. Turner, and R. Hinz, editors, <u>Pension Coverage Issues for the '90s</u>. Pension Benefit and Welfare Administration, U. S. Department of Labor, 1994.

Shoven, John, and David Wise, "The Taxation of Pensions: A Shelter Can Become a Trap," National Bureau of Economic Research, No. 5815, November 1996.

Social Security Administration, <u>Social Security Bulletin: Annual Statistical Supplement, 1997</u>, Washington, D.C., 1997.

Social Security Advisory Council, <u>Report of the 1994-1996 Advisory Council on Social Security</u>. Social Security Administration, Washington, D.C., 1997.

Towers Perrin, <u>The Handbook of Executive Benefits</u>. Burr Ridge, IL: Irwin Professional Publishing, 1995.

U.S. Department of Labor, <u>Employee Benefits in Medium and Large Firms</u>, Bureau of Labor Statistics Bulletin No. 2456, 1994.

U.S. Department of Labor, <u>Employee Benefits in State and Local Governments</u>, Bureau of Labor Statistics Bulletin No. 2477, 1996.

U. S. Department of Labor, Pension and Welfare Benefits Administration, <u>Private Pension Plan Bulletin</u>, 1997.

____, <u>Trends in Pensions</u>, 1992.

Williamson, Samuel, "U.S. and Canadian Pensions Before 1930: A Historical Perspective," in <u>Trends in Pensions</u>. U.S. Department of Labor, 1992.

Comments on...

Pensions, Public Policy, and the Capital Market

Jane Bozewicz
Accounting Faculty
Babson College

It is an honor to be invited here as a discussant on a paper by Richard Ippolito, whose work has informed so much research on pensions. Dr. Ippolito has provided a concise and comprehensive overview of the current status of retirement savings and offered quite a few suggestions that he believes would increase the efficiency of our retirement savings systems.

The policy issues Dr. Ippolito raises are of particular interest given the increase in retirement plans such as Individual Retirement Accounts and Keoghs and also in view of the changes in corporate-sponsored pension savings. In addition to sector shifts in employment, Dr. Ippolito puts forth two "likely candidates" to explain the movement away from defined-benefit plans toward defined-contribution plans. These are the introduction of the 401(k) plan and changes in tax policy toward so-called excess assets held by defined benefit plans.

Another explanation might pertain to the risk attributes of the two types of plans. Under a defined-benefit plan, absent bankruptcy or plan termination, the risk rests primarily with the plan sponsor. The benefit has been defined: it is the plan sponsor's responsibility to provide that benefit regardless of the final cost. If plan assets perform well enough to provide the benefits, fine; if not, the sponsoring company must increase its funding.

If there is uncertainty about actuarial parameters, inflation, if there is a COLA requirement, or payments from Social Security, if the plan is integrated, the associated risks affect the plan sponsor's obligation. With defined contribution plans, the story is over once the contribution to the plan has been made.

The benefit, in terms of the contribution and the sufficiency of the contribution to provide a given level of retirement income, is not a concern of the plan sponsor. Many corporations experienced a rude wake-up call with respect to their retiree health care promises in the late 1980s and early 1990s, which may have heightened their awareness of risk exposure related to defined-benefit pension obligations.

Perhaps the most important aspect to the shift from defined-benefit to defined-contribution plans has been the greater emphasis on the individual's responsibility for making the decision about how much to save, when to save, and how to allocate those savings. As we have seen with the evidence on mutual funds presented in an earlier paper, there may be limited public awareness concerning the realities of financial markets and investments. There may also be a widespread lack of awareness of the potential impact of retirement savings (and failure to save), particularly among younger workers.

Currently, income is unevenly distributed among the elderly. The trend toward self-directed retirement savings will likely increase this disparity. In particular, there are very high rates of poverty among elderly women. More than 20 percent of single (that is, never married, divorced and widowed) women are living in poverty (1993 Current Population Survey). The poverty rate for those divorced or separated is close to 30 percent. Many elderly women are dependent on retirement income (from both private pensions and Social Security) based on their husbands' employment and when widowed find their income decreased substantially. Although changes in female-labor-force participation rates will mitigate this somewhat in the future, it is important that policy be constructed to protect this segment of the population. Increased incentives for younger workers or lower-income groups should also be considered.

According to the most recent Survey of Consumer Finances, the number of families reporting "saving" in the prior year dropped from 57 percent in 1992 to 55 percent in 1995. The aggregate savings rate as reported in the national income and product accounts fell from 5.9 percent to 4.7 percent over the same period. As in the past, "liquidity," a category that includes a variety of precautionary motives, was the most common reason for saving. The percentage of families citing this factor has been relatively steady. However, families are increasingly reporting retirement, as the second most powerful savings motivation for savings (18.4 percent in 1989, 19.3 percent in 1992 and 23.5 percent in 1995).

As Dr. Ippolito has pointed out, incentives in the system may not affect marginal savings decisions and instead affect the decision between different types of savings. He supports a consumption tax as eliminating the marginal incentive to use income to support immediate versus future consumption, despite the fact that many architects of the tax-preferenced treatments for various types of retirement savings viewed them as having the same effect. And perhaps there is some support for this in the surprising amount of interest that has been shown in the Roth IRA. However, his assessment of the effect of the tax bias toward spending is itself affected by his assumption of a 40 percent income tax rate in all periods, rather than anticipating a decline in tax rate with retirement.

Unlike defined benefit plans, some defined contribution plans permit participants to borrow from their savings, which appears to be increasing (based only on anecdotal evidence). Is this feature good or bad and should it be restricted?

There has been a significant increase in savings among families with income less than $25,000 and some of this may be due to the increased self-financing opportunities these plans provide. In 1995, 24.2 percent of these families had retirement savings outside defined benefit plans, although the percentage of families with coverage from a current job has remained relatively constant at around 40 percent. But approximately a quarter of families eligible to participate in 401(k)-type plans did not do so in 1995, primarily in this income group. How can policies provide increased incentives for these families to participate?

If hybrid taxation continues and the effects of reform are largely marginal and participants continue to be allowed to borrow from their defined contribution plans, there may be no real increase in retirement security. Social Security should, I believe, as its architects envisioned, largely function as a safety net. What can we do to increase retirement security for those low-income workers who are essentially unable to participate in the new retirement savings vehicles? And how will these policies encourage small businesses (the weak link here) to make more retirement savings options available to their employees and make greater contributions on behalf of lower income employees?

My primary concerns are that regulatory reform: 1) provides more incentives for small businesses to provide retirement savings options for their employees; 2) provides more protection for the elderly poor, particularly elderly women, an astonishing percentage of whom live in poverty; and 3) provides increased employer incentives to contribute to and provide vehicles for retirement savings for employees with lower incomes.

Section Five

Derivatives Regulation:
Problems and Prospects

Christopher L. Culp*
Director of Risk Management Services
CP Risk Management LLC
and
Senior Fellow in Financial Regulation
Competitive Enterprise Institute

*Dr. Culp is Director of Risk Management Services at CP Risk Management
LLC in Chicago and Senior Fellow in Financial Regulation at the Competitive Enterprise Institute in Washington, D.C. He is grateful to participants of
the Milken Institute's conference on restructuring financial regulation for
their comments, but the usual disclaimer applies and the author alone is
responsible for the content.

Introduction

Behind the phrase "derivatives regulation" lies a world of complexity, in part because no single corpus of law defines the regulation of derivatives contracts and their users. Instead, derivatives regulation in the United States is comprised of a mixture of other legal fields, including banking, securities, commodities, and bankruptcy law. Any time multiple areas of law and regulation come together, complexities arise.

Derivatives regulation is also troublesome because significant jurisdictional ambiguities arise on a very regular basis both regarding derivatives as financial products and the users of derivatives. Certain types of derivative products are subject to stringent regulations, whereas others fall outside the jurisdiction of any regulatory agency. Similarly, some participants in derivatives activity are subject to duplicative and costly supervision by three or four agencies, while others are not regulated at all. Infighting among agencies vying for ill-defined and constantly changing regulatory turf further exacerbates these jurisdictional uncertainties.

This paper attempts to provide an overview of the U.S. regulatory landscape for derivatives today, as well as some comments on how that landscape might be improved.[1] The second section of the paper provides the necessary background on derivatives and their users. In the third section, the primary tenets of current derivatives regulations are reviewed. The fourth section then summarizes some problems with derivatives regulation and proposes several suggestions for how to improve the current system. The final section summarizes and concludes.

---

1.   This paper makes no attempt to address the regulation of derivatives outside the United States.

Derivatives and Their Participants [2]

One of the reasons that derivatives regulation is complex and often ambiguous is that derivatives themselves are actually quite hard to define. A financial instrument that cannot easily be defined cannot easily be regulated—at least not without a great deal of controversy, legal questions and jurisdictional infighting. Nevertheless, our discussion of derivatives regulation cannot proceed concretely without some attempt to define our subject matter.[3]

What Are Derivatives?

A derivatives contract is a financial contract that derives most of its value from some underlying asset price(s), reference rate(s), or index level(s).[4] Common types include futures, forwards, options and swaps. Derivatives can be based on one or more of virtually any "underlying," such as money market rates (e.g., 90-day London interbank offered rate), equity index levels (e.g., the S&P 500), commodity prices (e.g., the price of gold), and exchange rates (e.g., the Swiss franc/U.S. dollar spot rate). The most prevalent types of derivatives are swaps and futures based on interest rates and forward contracts on currencies.[5]

Derivatives contracts are bilateral and hence negotiated between two specific counterparties. Types of derivatives are often distinguished based on the manner in which they are negotiated. "Privately negotiated derivatives" are contracts that are negotiated outside the world of organized financial exchanges in an opaque, decentralized

2.   Portions of this section draw from Christopher L. Culp, *A Primer on Derivatives: Their Mechanics, Uses, Risks, and Regulation* (Washington, DC: Competitive Enterprise Institute, July 1995) (hereinafter "Culp (1995a)"), and Christopher L. Culp and James A. Overdahl, "An Overview of Derivatives: Their Mechanics, Participants, Scope of Activity, and Benefits," in *The Financial Services Revolution*, C.E Kirsch, ed. (Chicago, Ill.: Irwin Professional Publishing, 1997).
3.   The author has argued elsewhere that definitions of derivatives as financial products are useful only as pedagogical tools and not as the bases of regulations. For a discussion, *see* Culp (1995a), *op. cit.*, Culp and Overdahl, *op. cit.*, and Merton H. Miller and Christopher L. Culp, "Rein in the CFTC," *Wall Street Journal* (August 17, 1995).
4.   *See* Culp (1995a), *op. cit.*, Culp and Overdahl, *op. cit.*, and Christopher L. Culp, Dean Furbush, and Barbara T. Kavanagh, "Structured Debt and Corporate Risk Management," *Journal of Applied Corporate Finance* Vol. 7, No. 3 (Fall 1994).
5.   *Cf.* Bank for International Settlements, *Central Bank Survey of Foreign Exchange and Derivatives Market Activity, 1995* (Basel, May 1996).

environment of phones, faxes and quotation screens. As such, the two counterparties to a particular transaction may customize virtually any of the terms of that transaction (e.g., price, maturity, timing of payments, etc.).[6] Popular types of privately negotiated derivatives include swaps, forwards, and some over-the-counter options.

"Exchange-traded derivatives," as their name implies, are negotiated on organized financial exchanges, such as the Chicago Mercantile Exchange (CME) or the Chicago Board Options Exchange (CBOE). Unlike privately negotiated derivatives, the exchange that lists the contract for trading also determines most of the terms of the contract. The two counterparties to a trade thus generally negotiate only the transaction price, with terms such as maturity left to the listing exchange to define.[7] Exchange-traded derivatives include futures, options on futures and options on securities.

Participants in Derivatives Activity

Active participants in derivatives activity include commercial banks, investment banks, thrift institutions, insurance companies, manufacturing and other nonfinancial corporations, institutional investors and government-sponsored enterprises. To analyze how and why such institutions participate in derivatives, it is useful to consider privately negotiated and exchange-traded derivatives separately.

Participants in Privately Negotiated Derivatives Activity

Two types of institutions participate in privately negotiated derivatives: dealers and end users. Dealers act as economic agents for a variety of end user principals in privately negotiated derivatives transactions, generally standing ready to accept both sides of a transaction (e.g., long or short) depending on which is demanded at the time.[8] Privately negotiated derivatives dealers—often just called "swap dealers"—generally run close to a matched book, or a portfolio in which the cash flows on multiple transactions on both sides of a market net

---

6. Most privately negotiated derivatives are contractually documented under "master agreements," or *pro forma* documentation for the general terms of the transaction. The particulars of any deal can be customized within a master agreement, and additions to the master agreement also are possible.

7. Some newer exchange-traded products enable traders to negotiate terms other than just the price of the contract. "FLEX options," for example, allow traders to negotiate the option price *and* the option's striking price.

to a relatively small risk exposure on one side of the market. When exact matching is not feasible, dealers usually hedge their residual risk using other derivatives. Dealers in dollar-denominated interest rate swaps, for example, rely heavily on CME Eurodollar futures to manage the residual interest-rate risk of their dealing portfolios.

Because dealers act as financial intermediaries in privately nego-tiated derivatives, they typically have strong credit ratings, high capi-talization, good access to information about a variety of end user customers, and relatively low costs of managing the residual risks of an unmatched portfolio of customer transactions. As such, most active dealers are commercial banks, investment banks, and insur-ance-company affiliates.

End users of privately negotiated derivatives are those institutions that engage in derivatives transactions as principals for purposes of changing their risk profiles—e.g., reducing the volatility of funding costs. End users do not usually take both sides of a contract but instead enter into derivatives either as a long or a short to obtain or modify specific risk exposures. Dealers also often participate in deriv-atives as end users. Commercial bank swap dealers, for example, often use interest rate swaps to manage the interest rate risks arising from traditional bank asset/liability operations. Such swaps are typi-cally negotiated independently from swaps in dealing portfolios.

Participants in Exchange-Traded Derivatives

Two types of organized financial exchanges list derivatives for trading in the United States—securities exchanges and futures exchanges. Futures contracts and options on futures contracts trade only on futures exchanges such as the Chicago Board of Trade (CBOT) and the Chicago Mercantile Exchange (CME). Securities exchanges, such as the CBOE, the Philadelphia Stock Exchange and the American Stock Exchange list for trading products such as options on individual stocks, options on cash equity indexes, and options on foreign currency.

---

8. The terms "principal" and "agent" are used in the text with their economic mean-ing. Specifically, dealers serve the *economic* function of agents. In a legal context, however, dealers are principals to the transactions they negotiate with end users—i.e., they *do* bear credit risk and they *are* the counterparty of record in the transactions.

Futures Exchange Participants

Trading on a futures exchange is limited to members of that exchange. To become a member, a firm or individual must purchase a membership that gives it certain rights to trade. Memberships come in two varieties: those that grant owners access to trading in certain contract markets, and those that grant owners the right to settle their trades through the exchange's clearinghouse. Most memberships of the first type are offered for specific products or groups of products listed for trading by an exchange. A "full membership" on the CME, for example, entitles the seat holder to trade all CME futures and futures options, whereas other smaller CME memberships restrict trading to particular types of products (e.g., only financial futures and options). Benefits of holding such product-based memberships include direct access to the trading arena and reduced transaction fees.

Memberships that grant their owners access to a futures exchange clearinghouse are called "clearing memberships." A clearing member provides capital to back the clearing house in return for reduced clearing fees and less operational risk in the settlement process.[9]

Futures exchange members and clearing members may trade for their own account, for the account of another member, or for the account of a nonmember customer. The same member thus may trade as a principal in one transaction (e.g., to hedge its own risk exposures) and as an agent in another (e.g., to execute a transaction on behalf of a nonmember customer). Members and clearing members typically include commercial banks, investment banks, insurance companies and independent futures commission merchants (FCMs).[10]

---

9. For background on the exchange clearing process, *see* William J. Hanley, Karen McCann, and James T. Moser, "Public Benefits and Public Concerns: An Economic Analysis of Regulatory Standards for Clearing Facilities," Working Paper, Federal Reserve Bank of Chicago WP-95-12 (September 1995), and Bank for International Settlements, *Clearing Arrangements for Exchange-Traded Derivatives*, Report of the Ad Hoc Study Group on Exchange-Traded Derivatives of the Committee on Payment and Settlement Systems (Basel, December 1996).

10. FCMs are analogous to securities broker/dealers and are firms primarily in the business of executing transactions for nonmember customers, such as pension plans and mutual funds.

Securities Exchange Participants

As with futures exchanges, direct participation in the trading process on securities exchanges is limited to members. Unlike futures exchanges, however, securities exchanges often supplement the usual product-based memberships with a specific classification of membership called "market maker." One or several market makers on a securities exchange are obliged by exchange rules to buy or sell the listed contract at any time for a fair price, given demand for transactions by other members. Market makers can benefit from this privilege by earning profits on the bid-ask spread, but they in turn are generally expected to sell into a rising market and buy in a declining one to promote market stability.[11]

All nonmember customer trades on securities exchanges go through a broker/dealer with an exchange membership, which in turn executes its trades on behalf of the customer through a market maker.

Derivatives Regulation Today[12]

Derivatives are not specifically regulated per se—no commission or comparable body is charged with the supervision and regulation of derivatives.[13] That does not mean that derivatives and their users are unregulated. On the contrary, derivatives are regulated in essentially two distinct ways. First, certain institutions that are already subject to government regulation (e.g., banks and thrift institutions) may have their derivatives activities scrutinized by their institutional supervisors as part of the broader institution-specific regulations. Second, specific

---

11. As the October 1987 stock market crash demonstrated, however, market makers do not always engage in this "stabilizing" trading. *Cf.* General Accounting Office, *Financial Markets: Preliminary Observations on the October 1987 Crash* (January 1988).
12. Portions of this section are based on Christopher L. Culp, "Regulatory Uncertainty and the Economics of Derivatives Regulation," *The Financier* Vol. 2, No. 5 (December 1995) (hereinafter "Culp (1995b)").
13. Nor, in the view of this author, should such a regulator for derivatives exist. *See* Christopher L. Culp, "Regulation and the Growth of Derivatives in the Global Banking System," *Derivatives Quarterly* Vol. 1, No. 4 (Summer 1995) (hereinafter "Culp (1995c)"), and Christopher L. Culp, *Institutional vs. Functional Financial Regulation in Theory and Practice* (Washington, D.C.: Competitive Enterprise Institute, 1998) (hereinafter "Culp (1998)").

types of derivatives—namely, futures and certain options—are federally regulated as financial products.

Institutional Regulation of Derivatives

Certain institutions are regulated because they are perceived as
special. Banks, for example, are regulated because they take deposits
that are federally insured and because they often are perceived as
being systemically important. The derivatives activities of such special firms may be subject to specific regulations promulgated by their
institutional supervisors.[14] Institutions currently involved in derivatives activity that are regulated in this manner include nationally chartered and state-chartered commercial banks, bank holding companies,
thrift institutions, insurance companies, and some pension plans.

Because institutions are regulated—or not, as the case may be—
based on their type of corporate charter or firm classification, a derivatives user can be subject to multiple institutional regulators, most of
which oversee derivatives activities in slightly different ways. Regulators that have issued supervisory guidance on derivatives usage by
their constituent firms include the Federal Reserve, the Office of the
Comptroller of the Currency (OCC), the Federal Deposit Insurance
Corporation (FDIC) and the Office of Thrift Supervision (OTS). So, a
national bank affiliate of a bank holding company, for example, might
have to comply with both OCC and Federal Reserve regulatory guidance on derivatives activities.

Derivatives activities that are scrutinized by institutional regulators typically are subject to three types of supervision. First, regulators of these institutions often specify "permissible" activities for the
institution. This allows some firms to engage in derivatives while pro-
hibiting others from doing so.[15] In addition, some agencies allow derivatives to be used only in certain circumstances. Thrift institutions, for

---

14. Even if derivatives are subject to specific regulations adopted by the institutional
regulator, no institutionally regulated firm has derivatives activities that are unregulated.

15. Regulators often define the permissibility of an activity differently depending on
the nature of the entity being regulated. National banks, for example, were permitted
by the Office of the Comptroller of the Currency to engage in commodity futures
trading for many years before the Federal Reserve approved that activity at state-
member banks.

example, may engage in interest rate swaps, but only for the purpose of hedging or reducing their overall interest rate risk.[16]

Second, permissible derivatives activities are subject to prudential oversight. This oversight usually includes examinations of derivatives portfolios; risk management policies and procedures; risk limits administration and compliance; derivatives position and risk reporting, and related back office activities. Institutional regulators typically give their constituents a significant degree of autonomy in whatever derivatives transactions they are permitted to engage. For example, institutional regulators tend to "monitor" more than "regulate" once a derivatives activity has been deemed permissible.

Finally, institutional regulators may adopt special provisions for derivatives in any capital adequacy requirements imposed on their constituent institutions. Specifically, to the extent derivatives expose an institution to additional credit or market risk, the institution's regulator likely will demand additional capital to cover those risks.[17]

Product-Based Regulation

Unlike the regulation of derivatives activities at firms already subject to institutional government regulation, product-based federal derivatives regulations are targeted at the financial products themselves and, hence, any institution that uses them. Two types of derivatives are separately regulated as distinct financial products: futures and options.

Futures

In 1936, Congress amended the Grain Futures Act of 1922 and adopted the Commodity Exchange Act (CEA), which remains the primary statute underlying U.S. futures regulation today. The legislators' primary objective was to protect the integrity of markets whose main perceived functions were risk shifting and price discovery. The initial focus of futures regulation thus was to deter fraud and market manip-

---

16. *See* Christopher L. Culp and Robert J. Mackay, "Regulating Derivatives: The Current System and Proposed Changes," *Regulation* Vol. 4 (1994).

17. Capital requirements for users of derivatives often are unfortunately asymmetric—i.e., risk-increasing transactions usually result in higher capital requirements, but derivatives that reduce firm-wide risks often *do not* garner a break for the institution on its required regulatory capital.

ulation. Congress created the Commodity Exchange Commission to fulfill this legislative mandate. That commission delegated regulatory authority to the Secretary of Agriculture who, in turn, formed the Commodity Exchange Administration (later re-named the Commodity Exchange Authority).[18]

To promote the integrity of futures markets in practice, Congress relied heavily on a provision of the CEA known as the "exchange trading requirement."[19] This clause of the CEA provides that unless specifically exempted by the CFTC, a futures contract is illegal unless it is traded on a "board of trade."[20, 21] The term "futures contract," however, is never explicitly defined in the CEA. Instead, futures contracts are implicitly defined as "any transaction in, or in connection with, a contract for the purchase or sale of a commodity for future delivery."[22] The statute thus rests heavily on terms such as "commodity" and "future delivery," but those definitions, too, are far from straightforward in the CEA.

In 1974, Congress significantly revised the CEA in the Commodity Futures Trading Commission Act (CFTC Act). Among other things, the act ceded responsibility for futures regulation from the Secretary

---

18. *See* Jeffrey W. Markham, *The History of Commodity Futures Trading and its Regulation* (Praeger, New York, 1987).

19. *See* W.L. Stein, "The Exchange-Trading Requirement of the Commodity Exchange Act," *Vanderbilt Law Review* Vol. 41 (1988).

20. A board of trade is usually synonymous with an organized exchange, but not always. *Cf. Salomon Forex, Inc. v. Tauber*, 8 F.3d 966 (4th Cir. 1993), and *CFTC v. William C. Dunn and Delta Options*, 2 COMM. FUT. L. REP. &26,429 (2d Cir. June 23, 1995).

21. Two types of products that might be deemed "futures contracts" fall outside the CFTC's jurisdiction. The first are products that are excluded from the CEA by statute, including forward delivery contracts and contracts falling under the so-called "Treasury Amendment." The second are products that the CFTC has *exempted* from the CEA by decree—usually at the behest of Congress. Exempt products include certain swaps, hybrid securities, and oil delivery contracts. Unlike excluded products that have been proclaimed beyond the scope of the act by Congress, exempt products are exempted from regulation without a determination that the products are or are not futures. Also unlike excluded products, exempt products can later be determined to be nonexempt. For a good background discussion of these issues, see Mark D. Young, "The Quest for Legal Certainty: What Derivatives Are Subject to the Commodity Exchange Act?" in *The Financial Services Revolution*, C.E Kirsch, ed. (Chicago, Ill.: Irwin Professional Publishing, 1997).

22. 7 United States C. '6.

of Agriculture to the Commodity Futures Trading Commission, which was created in the 1974 act. The CFTC Act also expanded the definition of the term "commodity." Previously, commodities were limited to specific agricultural products, but the CFTC Act broadened the list to include a variety of unspecified financial assets. The resulting definitional ambiguity simultaneously broadened the jurisdiction of the CFTC and muddied the water concerning exactly what products fall under the purview of the CFTC.[23]

CFTC regulations now include significantly more than the antifraud and antimanipulation rules Congress originally envisioned. Today, the CFTC regulates almost everything having to do with futures and options on futures. CFTC regulations now cover a wide spectrum, ranging from delivery requirements for commodity futures to audit trail requirements on trading. One of the most notorious regulations obligates futures exchanges to obtain the approval of the CFTC in advance of listing a new futures contract. The approval process can take as long as two years, during which time privately negotiated derivatives dealers may offer a nearly identical product subject to no approval process.[24]

Although CFTC regulations are all based on products, those product-based regulations also affect institutions. Unlike institutional regulation, which targets only those institutions deemed "special," CFTC product-based regulations affect all institutions using "futures contracts" and options on "futures contracts."[25] Product-based regulations aimed at institutions include registration and capital requirements for FCMs; registration and permissible activity requirements on Com-

---

23. "Commodities" must underlie all futures contracts. So, for a contract to be subject to CFTC regulation, the asset underlying it first must be deemed a "commodity." By broadening the definition of a commodity, the 1974 act thus also broadened the definition of a "futures contract," *de facto* if not actually *de jure.*
24. Whether any advance approval process regarding new contracts serves a "social" purpose is far from clear. Some contend that such regulation exists only because some interest groups have successfully argued for "barriers to entry" on other groups in the form of product approval requirements. *See* Daniel R. Fischel, "Regulatory Conflict and Entry Regulation of New Futures Contracts," *Journal of Business* Vol. 59, No. 2, Pt.2 (1986).
25. Institutions using only exempt futures contracts or contracts that resemble futures but have not been legally classified as futures are not subject to CFTC regulation. *See* Young, *op. cit.*

modity Trading Advisors (CTAs); and risk management standards for exchange members.

Because all CFTC regulations ultimately trace to the definition of a "futures contract" and because that definition is itself ambiguous in the CEA, numerous institutions that are not actually CFTC-regulated live with the threat of possible CFTC regulation.[26] A firm that renders advisory services about privately negotiated derivatives, for example, may be called a CTA if the CFTC subsequently determines that the products in question actually were futures contracts. And sometimes it is not at all obvious just when the CFTC will make such a determination.[27] So, ambiguity about the legal status of a particular financial product also translates into ambiguity about the regulatory status of certain institutions.[28]

Securities

Various laws establish the regulatory framework for securities.[29] The Securities Act of 1933 ("33 Act") was enacted to regulate the public offering of securities, ostensibly because Congress deemed necessary the protection of capital formation in public markets. Unlike the CEA, which never explicitly defines futures, however, the 33 Act does explicitly define securities, including those securities exempt from the act.[30] The 33 Act also prohibits fraud in the public sale of securities and requires that any public offering of a nonexempt security be conducted through a firm registered with and regulated by the appropriate Federal agency.

The Securities Exchange Act of 1934 ("34 Act") elaborated on and broadened much of what was behind the 33 Act. The 34 Act

---

26. *See* Miller and Culp, *op. cit.*
27. *See* Miller and Culp, *op. cit.,* and Young, *op. cit.*
28. For background on this issue in the case of Bankers Trust, *see* Donald L. Horwitz, "P&G v. Bankers Trust: What's All the Fuss?" *Derivatives Quarterly* Vol. 3, No. 2 (Winter 1996).
29. Securities laws not discussed here that also are relevant include the Public Utility Holding Company Act of 1935, the Trust Indenture Act of 1939, the Investment Company Act of 1940, the Investment Advisors Act of 1940, and the Securities Investor Protection Act of 1970.
30. Exempt securities are products that fall under the legal definition of securities but are exempt from regulation under the act. A classic example are Section 144A private placements.

accomplished three primary objectives in securities regulation.

- It established the Securities and Exchange Commission (SEC) as a formal regulator of securities, securities markets and security market participants.[31]
- Second, the 34 Act established new regulations on the trading of securities in secondary markets.
- Third, the 34 Act expanded on the 33 Act by promulgating such regulations as prohibitions on market manipulation and fraud, registration requirements for broker/dealers, and permissible activities for broker/dealers. The 34 Act also established registration requirements and regulations for securities exchanges, clearing associations and transfer agents.[32]

Discussing securities law in a paper about derivatives regulation might seem strange. In fact, the SEC does regulate certain types of derivatives—listed options on nonexempt securities, to be precise. This jurisdictional oddity traces back to a long-standing dispute between the SEC and CFTC over financial products that have attributes of both a security and a futures contract.[33]

A clause granting the CFTC exclusive jurisdiction over futures was adopted in the CFTC Act of 1974. Because the 1974 act also widened and muddied CFTC jurisdiction by broadening the definition of commodities, the SEC demanded that Congress preserve its jurisdiction over securities that might also be deemed futures contracts or options on futures contracts. Accordingly, an SEC savings clause was included in the CFTC Act providing that

> ...nothing in this section shall (I) supersede or limit the jurisdiction at any time conferred on the Securities and Exchange Commission or other regulatory

---

31. The SEC's authority included not only the regulations adopted pursuant to the 34 Act, but also those adopted pursuant to the 33 Act that had previously been enforced by the Federal Trade Commission.

32. Clearing associations and transfer agents are discussed in Christopher L. Culp and Andrea M.P. Neves, "Risk Management by Securities Settlement Agents," *Journal of Applied Corporate Finance* Vol. 10, No. 3 (1997).

33. *Cf.* Christopher L. Culp, "Stock Index Futures and Financial Market Reform," *George Mason University Law Review* Vol. 13, No. 3 (Summer 1991), and Thomas A. Russo and Marlissa Vinceguerra, "Financial Innovation and Uncertain Regulation: Selected Issues Regarding New Product Development," *Texas Law Review* Vol. 69, No. 6, (1991).

authorities under the laws of the United States or of
any State, or (II) restrict the Securities and Exchange
Commission and other such authorities from carrying
out their duties and responsibilities in accordance
with such laws.[34]

Among other things, the inclusion of the savings clause was
intended to secure the SEC's jurisdiction over options on securities,
such as options on common stock.

A year after the CFTC Act was adopted, the scope of the SEC
savings clause was tested. Based upon a CFTC determination that
Government National Mortgage Association (GNMA) certificates
were commodities under the amended CEA, that agency approved the
listing of futures on GNMAs for trading at the CBOT. The SEC, however, argued that "GNMA certificates...are securities, as that term is
defined in the Federal securities laws. [The SEC] also believe[s] it to
be quite clear that contracts for future delivery of those securities are
also 'securities'."[35] The CFTC rejected the SEC's argument, and
GNMA futures continued to trade on the CBOT.

The SEC took its jurisdictional grievance to Congress in hearings
regarding the Futures Trading Act of 1978. The agency argued that
futures contracts on securities and options on securities were functionally indistinguishable. The SEC further maintained that because
the SEC savings clause gave it jurisdiction over securities options, it
should also have jurisdiction over futures on securities. Congress dis-
agreed and left the CFTC's exclusive jurisdiction intact over all types
of futures.

The burgeoning jurisdictional dispute was finally litigated in
Board of Trade of the City of Chicago v. SEC (hereinafter GNMA
Options).[36] This case arose after the SEC approved, in February 1981,
a proposal by the CBOE to trade options on GNMA certificates. The
SEC claimed that the products were options on securities and hence
were securities, protected under the SEC savings clause. The CFTC

34. *See* CEA '2(a)(1)(A)(i).
35. *See* Securities Exchange Commission-Commodity Futures Trading Commission
Jurisdictional Correspondence, compiled at [1975-1977 Transfer Binder] *Commodity
Futures Law Reporter* (CCH) & 20204 (N.D. Ill. 1975), at 20829.
36. *Board of Trade of the City of Chicago v. SEC,* 677 F.2d 1137 (7th Cir.), *vacated*
459 U.S. 1026 (1982) (hereinafter "*GNMA Options*").

and the CBOT, on the other hand, claimed that because GNMA futures had already been deemed futures by the CFTC, GNMA certificates had implicitly been deemed commodities, which made GNMA options equivalent to futures options under the CEA.[37] In November 1981, the Seventh Circuit Court of Appeals agreed with the line of reasoning presented by the CFTC and CBOT and granted a motion by the CBOT for a stay pending review, thereby blocking the CBOE from listing GNMA options on the grounds that GNMA options were futures options under the CEA.

Still unhappy with the jurisdictional uncertainty surrounding products with attributes of both futures and securities, the SEC and CFTC took matters in their own hands in December 1981 while GNMA Options was still pending. They reached an agreement called the Shad-Johnson Accord that provided four basic ground rules:

- The CFTC would regulate all futures and options on futures, even if the futures are based on securities
- The SEC would regulate all options on securities
- Futures on individual securities, such as stocks, were prohibited
- The SEC would play a formal role in the CFTC's approval of then-evolving stock index futures contracts

Shortly after the Shad-Johnson Accord, the GNMA Options decision called the accord into question, specifically noting that "the CFTC and SEC [cannot be allowed] to reapportion their jurisdiction[s] in the face of a clear, contrary statutory mandate."[38] Congress subsequently decided to give force to the accord, however, and enacted it into law almost verbatim in 1982.

The statutory adoption of the Shad-Johnson Accord left in place the central premise on which the Seventh Circuit based its final decision in GNMA Options: the CFTC has exclusive jurisdiction over any transaction that is both a security and a futures contract, unless that contract is an option on a security, in which case it is regulated by the SEC.[39] Judge Frank Easterbrook of the Seventh Circuit Court describes the result:

---

37. Section 2(a) of the CEA gives the CFTC jurisdiction over agreements including "any transaction which is of the character of, or is commonly known to the trade as, an 'option' ...involving contracts of sale of a commodity for future delivery..."

38. *GNMA Options*, p. 1142 n.8.

[T]he question a court must decide is the same as in GNMA Options: Is the instrument a futures contract? If yes, then the CFTC's jurisdiction is exclusive, unless it is an option on a security, in which case the SEC's jurisdiction is exclusive. So long as an instrument is a futures contract (and not an option), whether it is also a "security" is neither here nor there.[40]

Regulatory Paradigms and Prospects for Change[41]

Financial regulation may be functional or institutional. Functional regulation is the regulation of certain economic functions provided by the financial system, such as the provision of a secure payments system or the provision of risk-shifting opportunities.[42] In practice, such functional regulation translates into the regulation of specific financial markets and products.[43] Institutional regulation, by contrast, is the regulation of certain institutions because they are special. As noted earlier, banks, for example, are institutionally regulated because they are perceived as "systemically important" and because their demand deposits are federally insured. In institutional regulation, all activities and financial products in which the enterprise is engaged are regulated. In functional regulation, by contrast, all institutions participating in the regulated products are regulated.

---

39. For examples, *see* Culp (1991), *op. cit.,* Russo and Vinceguerra, *op. cit.,* and Culp (1995b), *op. cit.*

40. *Chicago Mercantile Exchange v. SEC*, 883 F.2d 537 (7th Cir. 1989), at 545. (hereinafter *"CME v. SEC"*)

41. Portions of this section are adapted from Culp (1995c), *op. cit.*

42. Other functions of the financial system are discussed in Robert C. Merton, "Operation and Regulation in Financial Intermediation: A Functional Perspective," Working Paper 93-020, Harvard Business School (1993).

43. *Cf.,* Merton, *op. cit.,* Chicago Mercantile Exchange, *Model for Financial Regulation,* White Paper (1993), Merton H. Miller, "Functional Regulation," *Pacific-Basin Finance Journal* Vol. 2 (1994), Myron S. Scholes, "The Future of Futures," in *Risk Management: Problems & Solutions,* W.H. Beaver and G. Parker, eds. (New York: McGraw-Hill, 1995), and Martha L. Cochran and David F. Freeman, Jr., "Functional Regulation," in *The Financial Services Revolution,* C.E Kirsch, ed. (Chicago, Ill.: Irwin Professional Publishing, 1997).

Problems with the Current "Hybrid" Regulatory System

Functional regulation in the United States consists mainly of securities and futures regulation. Judge Easterbrook characterizes the functional distinction between SEC and CFTC regulation as follows: "Securities usually arise out of capital formation and aggregation (entrusting funds to an entrepreneur), while futures are means of hedging, speculation and price revelation without the transfer of capital. So one could think of the distinction between the jurisdiction of the SEC and that of the CFTC as the difference between regulating capital formation and regulating hedging."[44]

As the previous sections suggest, the financial regulatory system in the United States is essentially a "hybrid" of institutional and functional regulation.[45] Derivatives bring to light some of the problems and asymmetries of this hybrid system rather dramatically. If a derivatives dealer or user happens to be regulated as an institution already, the derivatives activities of the firm are considered as part of the whole business enterprise. If the regulated institution also uses products that are subject to functional regulation, however, the firm is also subject to functional regulation. Bank-affiliated FCMs, for example, are institutionally regulated as commercial bank or bank holding company affiliates but are also subject to CFTC oversight because they use futures.

For firms not already regulated as an institution, any regulation to which they are subject depends entirely on functional regulation. The privately negotiated derivatives activities at a corporate end user, for example, thus may be totally unregulated. All activities of an investment bank using derivatives and underwriting securities, to take another example, may be regulated functionally, but the privately negotiated derivatives activities of its affiliates may be left unregulated.

As a result of this mixture of two essentially distinct regulatory paradigms, many institutions that use derivatives are regulated

---

44. *CME v. SEC*, at 543.

45. In some ways, the regulatory scheme classifications of "institutional" and "functional" are straw men, not observed in truly pure form anywhere. Nevertheless, most foreign financial regulatory systems tend toward being all-institutional or all-functional. Recent changes to British financial regulation, for example, have moved that regulatory system toward an almost entirely functional regulatory scheme.

both institutionally and functionally. Because privately negotiated derivatives are not themselves subject to any functional regulation, however, other participants in derivatives activity may be neither institutionally nor functionally regulated.

Some of the problems caused by this hybrid regulatory scheme include intense legal and jurisdictional uncertainty and high regulatory compliance costs, both of which act to discourage financial innovation and encourage firms to ship any of their creative financial activities off shore.[46] In addition, the unholy marriage of institutional and functional regulation creates serious competitive asymmetries between some market participants. Financial products may be privately offered by swap dealers, for example, with no intervention by a functional regulator like the CFTC. If a nearly identical product is offered by a futures exchange, however, the exchange, the product, and the users of the product all are subject to CFTC regulation—and to the CFTC's notorious contract approval process.

Toward a Less Hybrid System

Congress attempted in 1996 and 1997 to rectify some of the legal uncertainties and competitive asymmetries in U.S. derivatives regulation. The proposed legislation as originally contemplated would have partly deregulated futures markets and given their participants the same capacity to deal in a less regulated environment that swap dealers and end users enjoy. Unfortunately, many interest groups that engaged in the political debate over those reforms attempted to use the legislation to put competitors at a disadvantage rather than working to improve things for their own constituents.[47] Competing agendas—both in industry and between regulators—resulted in a deadlock: the reform bill faded into the policy background, and the

---

46. The hybrid system of institutional and functional regulation also has had some beneficial effects. *See* Culp (1995c), *op. cit.*

47. Such behavior is hardly surprising in light of the positive theory of economic regulation. Indeed, it is *to be expected.* Good discussions of this theory as it pertains to derivatives can be found in the chapters in Part II of Merton H. Miller, *Merton Miller on Derivatives* (New York: John Wiley & Sons, 1997). For a more general discussion of the positive theory of economic regulation, *see* George J. Stigler, "The Theory of Economic Regulation," *Bell Journal of Economics and Management Science* Vol. 2 (Spring 1971), and George J. Stigler, ed., *Chicago Studies in Political Economy* (Chicago: The University of Chicago Press, 1988).

futures industry remains in a competitive straightjacket relative to the privately negotiated derivatives industry.[48]

One solution to the problem of derivatives regulation is to move the financial regulatory paradigm toward one that is either entirely institutional or entirely functional.[49] Indeed, shifting the regulatory focus to a more orthodox one—either entirely institutional or entirely functional—would eliminate at least some of the overlaps, uncertainties, compliance costs, and anticompetitive biases of the current system.[50] Duplicative supervision of firms that are both institutionally and functionally regulated, in particular, would vanish.

Some overlaps and uncertainties would persist, of course. As illustrated by the dispute that culminated in the Shad-Johnson Accord, even functional regulators can argue among themselves. So, too, can institutional regulators, as regular disagreements between the OCC and the Federal Reserve demonstrate. But those overlaps and uncertainties almost surely would be less in a functional-only or institutional-only system than in a regulatory regime where institutions and products are both selectively regulated.

Reforming the financial regulatory system in this manner, however, does carry with it the risk that the new system would be worse than the present one. Three fallacies, in particular, must be avoided in reengineering the financial regulatory infrastructure:

- All firms and/or derivatives must be regulated
- A single regulator is better than multiple regulators
- Functional regulation is inherently preferable to institutional regulation

---

48. The author has argued elsewhere that futures should be deregulated and privately negotiated derivatives not subjected to greater regulation. In short, the justifications for the CEA are now essentially irrelevant in today's financial markets, and the *raison d'etre* for any regulation in this area is now questionable. *See* Culp and Mackay, *op. cit.,* Culp (1995a), *op. cit.,* Culp (1995b), *op. cit.,* Culp (1995c), *op. cit.,* and Miller and Culp, *op. cit.*

49. Such a regulatory reform would not just affect derivatives. To work, the entire system of financial regulation would need to be changed.

50. *See* Christopher L. Culp, *Institutional vs. Functional Regulation in Theory and Practice* (Washington, D.C.: Competitive Enterprise Institute, 1998) (hereinafter "Culp (1998)").

All Firms and/or Derivatives Must Be Regulated

A frequent criticism of current derivatives regulation is that some firms engaged in privately negotiated derivatives activity are totally unregulated. Separately capitalized broker/dealer and insurance company affiliates, for example, often operate as largely unregulated derivatives dealers. In like fashion, some even argue that the use of privately negotiated derivatives by corporate end users should be regulated.

No case for the regulation of these firms can be made, however, solely on the basis of supposed market failures. No evidence suggests that either type of firm is "systemically important" in any measurable way. These firms, furthermore, are already policed by the strong forces of competition. The unregulated dealers, for example, would have no customers were they not perceived as creditworthy enterprises. Privately negotiated derivatives transactions, after all, are highly credit-sensitive, giving market participants a much stronger incentive to detect potential problems than regulators. For these and other reasons, the goal of derivatives regulation should not be simply to regulate all users of and dealers in derivatives contracts.

A Single Regulator Is Better than Multiple Regulators

All discussions of financial regulatory reform must inevitably mention the recurring proposal that financial regulatory agencies all be lumped together in one super-regulator. Although the notion of moving to an all-functional or all-institutional paradigm might seem to be consistent with the idea of a single regulator, nothing could be further from the truth.

Competition between regulators helps reduce the costs of regulation.[51] Nothing faster precipitates the reduction in an agency's budget, after all, than a reduction in its regulated constituents. Competing regulators define a market in which competition among regulators tends to force regulation down to relatively manageable levels of cost.

---

51. *Cf.* Edward J. Kane, "Deregulation and Changes in the Financial Services Industry," *Journal of Finance* Vol. 38 (July 1984), Edward J. Kane, "Regulatory Structure in Futures Markets: Jurisdictional Competition between the SEC, the CFTC, and Other Agencies," *Journal of Futures Markets* Vol. 4 (1984), and Edward J. Kane, "Interaction of Financial and Regulatory Innovation," *American Economic Review* Vol. 78 (May 1988).

Surprising as it may sound, regulatory competition also benefits regulators. Some critics of regulatory competition argue that a "race to the bottom" results in a situation in which regulators are driven to underregulate as they try to steal market share from other agencies, hence justifying bigger budgets for themselves. Far from it, regulatory competition helps ensure that each regulator can develop specialized expertise about the institutions or functions it regulates, in turn allowing it to focus only on truly legitimate problems rather than on issues that do not actually warrant regulatory scrutiny. Central banks, for example, can easily justify their supervisory budgets by focusing on those banks perceived as sources of systemic risk. By comparison, smaller banks and holding company affiliates should—and do—receive relatively less supervisory scrutiny due to their lack of perceived systemic importance.

Regulatory competition, moreover, need not imply regulatory overlap. Banking regulation in the United States, for example, is presently characterized by both regulatory competition and regulatory overlap. Commercial banks with state charters, for example, are regulated by the Federal Reserve if they are members of the Federal Reserve System, by the FDIC if they are state non-member banks, and by state banking regulators in either case. A commercial bank can choose instead a national charter, in which case it is regulated by the OCC. This ability of banks to select a jurisdiction creates an important source of discipline on these agencies.

At the same time, commercial banks are often subject to duplicative regulatory overlap, in part because the Federal Reserve regulates all bank holding companies. The OTS, for example, regulates the holding companies that own thrift institutions. If a bank holding company owns a thrift institution, that bank holding company thus is subject to duplicative regulation both by the OTS and the Federal Reserve. Overlap, however, can be avoided by adhering to a simple principle: institutions should have at most one regulator but have a "choice" among several competing agencies to be that one regulator.

Functional Regulation Is Inherently Preferable to Institutional Regulation

Heralding functional regulation as greatly superior to institutional regulation has become quite fashionable in the last decade.[52]

The main ostensible benefit of functional regulation is that functions of the financial system are more stable than the institutions that provide those functions at any given time. Especially with somewhat arbitrary charter distinctions between institutions (for example, "banks" vs. "thrift institutions"), functions would seem to be a much more consistent target for regulation than institutions.

Functional regulation also is heralded for minimizing regulatory overlap. With a set of functions of the financial system that are defined exhaustively and mutually exclusively, no function should be regulated by more than one agency. That presumes, of course, that the functions of the financial system can indeed be defined mutually exclusively for regulatory purposes, which is not obvious.

A third ostensible benefit of functional regulation is that relatively few resources are allocated into regulatory avoidance and regulatory arbitrage. Whereas institutions are run by people that can consciously opt into another institutional category (e.g., bank charter switching), financial functions cannot opt into and out of jurisdictions. Consequently, proponents of functional regulation argue that time and resources are invested in avoiding the bite of regulation.

As enticing as it might seem, however, functional regulation also comes with some significant costs. By far the most significant drawback of functional regulation is the impracticality of the regulation of functions of the financial system directly. Instead, functional regulation must be implemented as financial product and market regulation. The operationalization of functional regulation at the financial product level leads to a number of problems, as the previous discussion of securities and futures regulation suggests.

1. First, even if functions of the financial system can be defined mutually exclusively, functions provided by particular financial products cannot. A bond issued for capital formation purposes may be purchased for interest rate risk management purposes, for example. Whether the bond should be regulated

---

52. *Cf.* Merton, *op. cit.,* Chicago Mercantile Exchange, *op. cit.,* and Scholes, *op. cit.*

as providing the capital formation or risk-shifting function of the capital market thus is not clear. This lack of clarity, in turn, engenders regulatory overlaps and legal and jurisdictional uncertainty for users of particular financial products.

2. A second problem with functional regulation is that it does not promote regulatory competition at the product level. As already noted, financial products cannot "choose" jurisdictions, unlike institutions operating in a competitive regulatory environment. Although this is viewed as a benefit inasmuch as rent-seeking behavior is reduced, the associated cost is that financial product regulators do not typically have much incentive to minimize the marginal costs of their regulations. Because their regulatory constituents are first financial products and then only second the institutions that design, issue, and use financial products, the primary constituents of the agencies are defined by law. With a captive marketplace of regulated financial products, cost minimization to attract regulatory constituents is not important, and functional regulators thus tend to make more costly and onerous regulatory decisions than institutional regulators.

3. Third, functional regulation greatly increases compliance costs for institutions by subjecting them to multiple regulators. A bank, for example, is likely to be engaged in activities and products that provide virtually all functions of the financial system. Unless a single functional regulator exists, the bank thus must contend with multiple functional regulators supervising its diverse activities and financial product market participation based solely on the perceived functions of those disparate activities and assets.

Finally, perhaps the greatest cost of functional regulation is the stifling effects on financial innovation resulting from uncertainties about particular product definitions. As the earlier discussion of the CFTC/SEC jurisdictional issues suggests, uncertainty about the legal classification of a financial product can create serious delays in bringing new products to market and can thoroughly discourage firms from engaging in innovative activities on U.S. shores.[53] Definitions of insti-

53. *See* Culp (1991), *op. cit.,* Russo and Vinceguerra, *op. cit.,* Miller and Culp, *op. cit.*, and Young, *op. cit.*

tutions, by contrast, are admittedly arbitrary, but at least no such uncertainty exists about them. Whether a product is or is not a futures contract, for example, is often extremely unclear, whereas whether a company is or is not a bank is entirely obvious from its charter.

On the whole, financial reforms designed to mitigate the current problems with a hybrid financial regulatory system will worsen rather than improve the status quo if those reforms lead to a greater emphasis on functional regulation. The normative goal of any major reform, then, should be to begin moving financial regulation in the United States toward an entirely institutional approach.[54]

Conclusion

The present state of derivatives regulation is an uncertain one principally because there is no uniform system of derivatives regulation. Nor is there a case to be made that derivatives or their users should be separately regulated. Unfortunately, the functional regulation of securities and futures combined with the institutional regulation of entities such as banks makes for a rather complicated mess when it comes to derivatives.

The result of the current hybrid regulatory system in the United States is a highly asymmetric and anticompetitive system of derivatives regulation that engenders numerous jurisdictional disputes and significant legal uncertainty, all of which discourage financial innovation. A move toward greater reliance on all-institutional regulation would be the preferred normative solution to these problems. Unfortunately, the competing interests of industry participants and regulators makes it unlikely that any major changes in the status quo can be expected any time in the foreseeable future.[55]

---

54. For a detailed discussion of how such a regulatory scheme might look, *see* Culp (1998).
55. *See* Miller, *op. cit.*

Comments on...

Derivatives Regulation:
Problems and Prospects

Joseph Cole
Chief Operating Officer
Hedge Financial Products Inc.
CNA Financial Corporation

Well, I appreciate the opportunity to visit with the Milken Institute again and talk to you about a subject that I hate to discuss: derivatives regulation. It is a topic that has dogged my professional life, especially in the development and trading of new products.

As I discussed with Christopher L. Culp beforehand, I would like to apply his paper to the arena of securitizing insurance risks in an uncertain regulatory environment.

First, I will present a brief discussion about insurance and insurance derivatives, and the amazing amount of new product development that we are seeing there. While it is very much constrained by the regulatory environment, I want to show you how we are adapting to that. Second, the use of accounting as a form of regulation and self-interest tool will be mentioned. Finally, the outlook: how do we move from the current environment to the next environment? Dr. Culp has spoken about that in his paper and in a prior piece. It is also one you should find of interest.

First, I would like to tell you a little story. This guy Bill Gates has more money than Ted Turner. This guy Scott McNeely wants some of that money. This is how they do it, sometimes, in Washington. I just have to tell you this story I heard.

After the Senate Judiciary Committee hearings, Scott McNeely, Michael Dell and Bill Gates went out for a beer. They said, "Well, let us get away; let us just go away and talk." They all went to the bar; each ordered a Guinness.

When the Guinesses arrived, each one had a fly in it, just by coincidence. Scott McNeely took a look at his beer and he said, "Bartender, there's a fly in my beer. Please, take it away, give me another one."

Michael Dell looked at his beer, saw the fly in there, tipped his glass a little bit, blew off the foam and started to quaff it down.

Bill Gates, the nerd that he is, of course, had a computer toolkit with him. He pulls it out, opens it up, takes out tweezers, takes the fly out, grabs it by the wings and says, "Spit it out, you bastard! Spit it out!"

All right, you had to hear that one.

More on topic, Dr. Culp has a nice overview in his paper about institutional versus product regulation and regulation by function versus institution. We are in the institutional area when it comes to regulation—that is, the insurance industry in particular.

Our industry is undergoing enormous convergence with the capital markets and insurance derivatives have been one of the precipitants. We started trading catastrophic insurance futures and options at the Chicago Board of Trade about four or five years ago. The success of that product opened up the eyes of many to a lot of other new products.

Unfortunately, if you think you have problems with regulation, I have to potentially deal with 50 commissioners at the NAIC. I also must be concerned with the SEC, Nasdaq and the CFTC. Furthermore, I have the self-regulatory element of each exchange and have off-shore regulators if I set up any off-shore trust. I personally have a Series 3, a Series 7, a Series 24. I'm a registered reinsurance broker, and I'm also a CTA.

Now, we used to joke in the office that sometimes we had more companies than people, in order to separate all the regulations. That is a very large burden.

If you asked me questions about insurance regulation, I would probably give you three answers if you wanted to know money-making specifics about the regulations. I would tell you, "Well, No. 1, I don't necessarily know the answer." Secondly, "The answer changes, depending upon which regulator you talk to." Or thirdly, "I paid good money for the right answer, so I'm not going to give it to you for free."

So there is this self-interest that is involved in doing new product development. But education is necessary since many potential investors do not understand the insurance and reinsurance industry. It is an enormous business, and some observers have said that nothing of significance gets done on the planet without insurance. For instance, you do not build plants without insurance; you do not utilize the factories without insurance; you do not hire workers without insurance. Even presidents are not inaugurated without event-risk insurance.

As an example of the insurance market, consider the following slide and assume you are a homeowner in California. You buy insurance from a primary insurer. That insurer often cedes the risk to the reinsurance market, and those reinsurers often cede part of that risk to the retrocession market. The reinsurance and retrocession market are, in essence, the dealer market for insurance risk, and they are beginning to trade these underlying insurance risks in the capital markets.

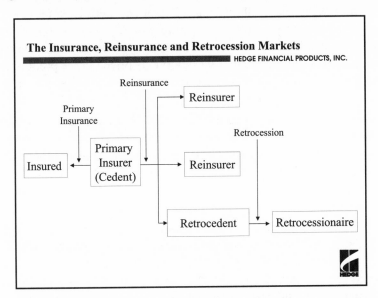

The Insurance, Reinsurance and Retrocession Markets
HEDGE FINANCIAL PRODUCTS, INC.

A good example of reinsurance trading has been provided by Warren Buffet. Warren Buffet, through the California Earthquake Authority, committed $1.5 billion of his own capital to reinsuring the California homeowners' earthquake fund. He received $590 million for that. He gave them a four-year contract, so the rate on line, or the rate of return, that he was getting on his exposure was almost 10 percent a year.

He will have to pay $1.5 billion of his own money if there is a single event in California that has an earthquake resulting in homeowners' losses being greater than $7 billion. The term, again, is four years, but the annual probability of this event is only 1.3 percent.

In the press, descriptions about this reinsurance capacity provided to the State of California often missed the point. A.M. Best described the bonds as "rolling the dice with God." An anonymous bond trader said, "Oh, an investor would need to become an expert in meteorology in order to invest in the CA's earthquake bonds."

I can tell you, this bond trader does not have a clue. If he did he would surely know the difference between meteorology and geology when it comes to forecasting earthquakes.

Consider further that this anonymous bond trader probably sits at the trading desk selling out-of-the money call options and doing gamma trading plays all day long. If you sell out-of-the-money call options, what are your odds of making money? They are one to one. In fact, it is a little bit less than that, when you bring in the commissions. That is the way their "fear of God" is priced in the premium by Black-Scholes or any other options model: essentially, it is a fair game with "even money" odds.

Warren Buffet is sitting there, on the other hand, and he's taking something like five-to-one odds. Remember? There's a 10 percent rate of return, and it's under 2 percent loss probability, adjusted per year. In other words, he's getting a five-to-one risk/reward ratio.

So, the perception versus the reality, which is a common theme that Mr. Milken often extolled at the High Yield Conferences, is out of line. The perception is that insurance derivatives are high risk, but the reality is, if you measure and compare the risk/reward characteristics, they represent a very good opportunity. Yet, there is so much earthquake risk that has to be moved from California through the capital markets that the price is paid at a five to one risk/reward ratio.

The reason the price is very high is that we have seen a substantial increase in insurable losses during the last 20 years. In fact, most people today think that the insurance industry is not equipped for a major catastrophe, that if we have a $25 trillion property market in the United States and there's only $235 billion of reinsurance capital that is available to that market, the implied 1 percent capitalization ratio is far too low.

We have also seen the U.S. population move into the high-risk areas over time, such that now, just California and Florida alone represent close to 18 percent of the population situated in areas very prone to earthquake and hurricanes. So, if you were managing this risk, especially if you are Allstate or State Farm, you could be 10 percent of the market in either of those locations. Thus, if you have a $5 billion industry loss, you take a $50 million hit to your balance sheet. Of course, it is hopefully covered by premiums elsewhere. By spreading through geographic and product diversification, your objective is to make money using the law of large numbers.

Insurance companies that are not diversified have a number of arrows in their quiver now to manage that risk: they can do reinsurance; they can use something that is known as industry loss warranties; they can go to the Chicago Board of Trade and do trade to CAT options; they can do over-the-counter CAT index swaps; and they can do 144(a) CAT bonds. To understand the economic equivalents of each one of these five tools, please realize that they are priced, not quite exactly, but fairly close to one another.

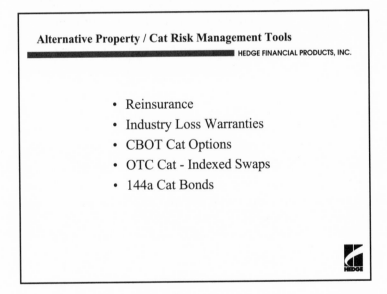

For example, an insurer may be concerned about an event and may want to cover the risk that the event might trigger industry losses in excess of $4 billion. If you try to cover, analyze and price that layer, the first thing to compute would be its expected loss over time. For instance, if this was Southeast wind—there have only been two events in history that would have attached or blown through these layers. These events would have been Hurricane Hugo and Hurricane Andrew, each would have caused losses greater than $4 billion for the industry. So, in only two out of the last 50 years, the insurer might have had losses in the Southeastern United States. But there is a price to trade this, and if you have a 10 percent market share, that implies that you have a potential $200 million loss. Insurance companies can cover this risk by any combination of the five prior tools that I just described.

The advantages of going to the capital market as an insurance-risk-management tool are that it is a capital source for hard-to-place risk. It increases your distribution of risk not going through the insurance community by tapping into different investor pools. Another advantage is the potential decrease in distribution cost.

Insurance companies can also increase their credit quality by tapping capital market sources, and there are huge potential price advantages. What many insurance and reinsurance companies are doing now is positioning themselves for the next catastrophe. These companies will be able to go out and retap the investor market, foregoing potentially high premiums of the other tools, if necessary.

From the investors' perspective, insurance derivatives represent a noncorrelated asset with a high Sharpe ratio. Investors can expand their efficient frontier with these new instruments, and it would make sense to have this in their portfolio. Investors are used to taking risk. Many times, however, they don't know how much that risk is.

**Investors Regularly Expose Themselves To Low Frequency /
High Severity Risk In The Form Of Default Risk**

HEDGE FINANCIAL PRODUCTS, INC.

Rating / Classification	One-Year Default Rate	Ten-Year Default Rate
Aaa	0.00%	0.74%
Aa	0.03%	1.13%
A	0.01%	1.73%
Baa	0.12%	4.61%
Ba	1.36%	20.94%
B	7.27%	44.31%
Investment Grade	0.05%	2.43%
Speculative Grade	3.93%	26.09%
All Corporates	1.12%	8.10%

Source: Moody's, 1938-1996 Default Rates

HEDGE

For instance, over a 10-year period, triple As will default at about a .75 percent basis; single Bs 44 percent of the time. The question is, are you getting paid for the amount of risk that you are taking?

We compared insurance-linked securities with the rest of the investment universe, and our numbers have been recently verified by Robert Litzenberger out of Goldman, Sachs, a Banker's Trust study, and a study done by Guy Carpenter. Insurance-linked securities have the highest Sharpe ratio in the industry. Thus they can be very useful for portfolio diversification.

So, we have a very useful security that benefits both the issuer and the buyer, and yet we have to walk our way through the regulatory morass in order to deliver the instrument. Despite that, we are being successful. There have been a number of catastrophic-linked issues, to the tune of about $1.5 billion during the last year, with, I understand, about 10 more on the slate here for this spring.

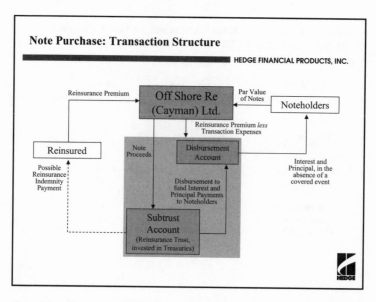

Consider the general structure for a 144(a)-type instrument that is set up as an off-shore company in order to manage and deliver this risk under the current regulatory scheme. For instance, I have Off-Shore Re in the Cayman Islands, set up in order to get reinsurance premium accounting for insurance clients. I take money from note holders and they receive securities at par value issuance. I put the note proceeds into a subtrust account. There is also a disbursement account for the interest. If there is no loss, I disburse the interest and the principal in the absence of a covered event. If there is a loss, the subtrust pays the reinsured instead, and the note holders potentially could lose all their interest and principal, depending on the type of structure that is assembled.

This securitization of insurance risk through 144(a) notes means high costs due to off-shore trust and legal fees, investment banking fees, rating agency fees and modeling agency fees. These costs run into the seven-figure range. In other words, you have to do a $500 million note at a time to make this worthwhile.

Now, a cheaper alternative is to use the Property Claims Services CAT options that trade at the Chicago Board of Trade. This market has been growing in terms of open interest. We currently have more open interest in these contracts than pork bellies. It has also been growing on the over-the-counter market versus the exchange-traded market. And, instead of after Hurricane Andrew in 1992 and 1993, when all of these insurance companies were set up off-shore, what we believe will happen after the next large catastrophe is that investors are going to snap up these various securities right and left because they are efficient capital-delivery mechanisms.

In essence, the convergence underway of the insurance and capital markets is reflected by insurance companies taking these supposedly diversifiable risks, acquiring these risks as insurance policies, packaging them as reinsurance and beginning to index it for investors. So when insurance risk aggregates on their books, and if the insurers can trade it back to investors, they are essentially securitizing and returning to the market portfolio risk that was originally company-specific in a CAPM sense.

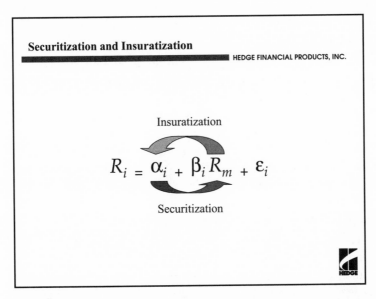

Convergence is also creating something called insuratization. I am running out of time to describe it, but insuratization is a movement of a capital market type (such as interest rate risk, commodity risk, other types of risk) into insurance policies. That transformation really runs into some accounting issues that are fundamental, especially when it comes to the dreaded "bifurcation rule" in accounting for derivatives.

The advantages of insuratization are basically as a cash flow management tool, since policyholders do not have to set up their own trading shop. They have low management control costs as a result. In addition, there are no rogue trader concerns and they do not have to deal with the pejorative term that derivatives sometimes represents to the Board of Directors.

The federal government is the largest issuer of insuratized policies that I am aware of. They have something known as crop revenue coverage, which started about two years ago. When it first came out, in Iowa and Nebraska, half of the farmers switched over to a policy that compensated them not only on yield losses, but also price changes as reflected by futures contracts at the Chicago Board of Trade. In actuality, the federal government has a futures contract pricing term embedded as an index in the insurance policy. Homeowners insurance with replacement cost has been around for a long time. Equity-linked GIC's and health care indices linked to medical inflation also exist.

We see this as a growing area, but there are a number of accounting hurdles that have to be overcome in order to deliver this product to the market. On the accounting side, there is a proposed derivatives accounting rule by FASB that has been floating around for several years now. A year ago last winter there were maybe five or six new products specifically defined as a derivative in the proposal, and how to account for it.   There was also a discussion about how insurance policies were excluded from this. Suddenly, last summer, the proposed rule changed so that "nontraditional" insurance would not be exempt if policies included currency options.

The reason that came about is intriguing. One of the first large insuratized transactions was done by A.I.G. for Honeywell that same summer, and it embedded currency fluctuations in an integrated-risk package that combined self-insured retention with workman's comp and property catastrophe losses and other items. I do not know, to this date, who put that change into the proposed rule. That change caused me about six months' extra work in order to dance through the regulatory loopholes. I have the suspicion that it was put in by a money center bank that was trying to protect their currency hedging turf.

Finally, because I have run out of time, I would like to give you the regulators' motto: Give them ambiguity or give them something else.

Todd Petzel
Executive Vice President and Chief Investment Officer
The Common Fund

Whenever we have alignment of interests, we have no need for regulation. Obviously, in the area of derivatives, there is somebody out there who thinks that there are many misalignments of interest, and hence, we need all kinds of derivatives regulation. Christopher L. Culp has articulated a lot of that very well.

I highly recommend to you Dr. Culp's discussion of regulatory competition, because that is a key discussion here.

When I was working at the exchange community, we called ourselves self-regulators. When I look back on how much time I spent actually self-regulating, I am a little bit embarrassed, because the ratio of fending off my regulator, other people's regulators and every other thing that was going on far exceeded my energy in the pure self-regulatory area. So that is kind of a sad comment, but it is true. We frequently found ourselves in the very schizophrenic position of fighting hard against the Chicago Futures Trading Commission (CFTC) because we perceived it to be working against the exchange's best interest, and then turning around and defending the CFTC against encroachments by the Securities and Exchange Commission (SEC) and the banking community and everybody else, because we figured they were better than any other alternatives. So that is a very significant part of this dynamic, and it is an important dynamic.

I am going to give two examples of areas where it is very difficult to come down to a simple solution and say regulatory competition will always work and will always help you out. The first is risk-based capital.

I am not going to go into detail here, but if you have studied capital rules for regulated financial institutions, they are astonishing.

The simplest example I can give you is, take two broker/dealers, SEC registered broker/dealers. There are formulas that are used to calculate the regulatory capital, and let us say, for purposes of this example, it is $50 million for each company. Company 1 is a pure broker/dealer—does nothing in derivatives. Company 2 is also a futures commission merchant (FCM). Then, they face another set of rules for regulatory capital for the CFTC. Suppose that company's regulatory capital requirement on that side of the sheet is $45 million. Okay? Two very different companies, in terms of what they do. What is the regulatory capital for each? Fifty million dollars. Because the rule says if you are both an FCM and a broker/dealer, you calculate the two numbers and you pick the higher number for your capital.

Now, I bet your intuition tells you that that is probably not the right number, if you are trying to match the capital up with the risk of the company. Your intuition may actually say that the second company should have capital of $95 million, but you have made an important assumption. That is, that these risks are additive.

You could set up the risk of the company in such a way that the positions on the securities side are all exposed to losses from rising interest rates, and that the risk on the derivatives side are all exposed to losses from declining interest rates. Just a hypothetical example.

You do not need to know a lot about investments in this example, but one thing you do need to know is that interest rates do not simultaneously go up and down. In such a world, the capital required for the risk of that second company may be only $5 million—the net—plus, let us say, $2 million or $3 million or $5 million more to cover basis relationships, if those instruments move slightly differently with the movement of interest rates.

What I'm trying to say here is that our system of risk-based capital is hardly that at all. While I agree with the comment this morning that it is difficult to measure risk, it is not impossible. The exchange clearing house community has been doing it for decades. My old exchange, the Chicago Merc, has never had a clearing member default in its almost 100-year history; the Chicago Board of Trade had one, when a local company blew up a few years ago.

But the bottom line is that the reason those organizations work, in terms of monitoring risk, is that they have an alignment of interests. That is, the members of the clearinghouse have a strong self-interest to find the right capital to make sure that the risk is covered, that you are playing on your own nickel, and not the clearinghouse's.

I am not sure precisely what the regulatory rules are at this point in time, in America, for risk-based capital, but the one thing I do know is that every time it tries to get rationalized by thoughtful discussion, the largest companies step up to the plate and say, "No. You don't understand the true risks of this business. I think you should keep it the way it is."

Which I always translate to mean, "If I have got enough capital left over from my credit card receivables or whatever else, I would just as soon keep the barriers to entry fairly high." I see that going on all the time.

The second issue that I wanted to raise was accounting rules. I am not an accountant, and I hope that the accountants in the room will bear with me on this. The Financial Accounting Standards Board (FASB) has worked extremely hard over many, many years to try to come up with meaningful accounting rules for derivatives. The current chairman, Edmund L. Jenkins, is as thoughtful and hard-working a person as I have ever come across. The reality is, that whenever the FASB tries to rationalize the accounting rules for derivatives, it runs up against some serious problems.

A couple of years ago, the FASB had a proposal on the table that basically said, "Let's do everything on a cash flow basis." So when you realize your profit or loss in terms of cash, you will account for it on the balance sheet. That meant any company that hedged or speculated with exchange-traded futures would have to account for it on a daily basis, theoretically, because we have not only mark to market, but variation payments that go through the system.

For a company that did the exact same hedging program with off-exchange derivatives that were mark to market every six months, every year or every two years, the company would not have to account for any change in the value of those products. You could have this very odd situation in which Company A was a pure speculator in exchange-traded products. It would look exactly the same, from an accounting standpoint, as a company that had the same futures positions for hedging, and both companies would look completely different from a company that used an off-exchange instrument, where there were not daily cash flows. This would be a very odd accounting rule. But that is the kind of situation FASB had to deal with, because you can measure these flows, and that was one solution. The exchanges and others argued against that.

From a public policy standpoint, what you want to do on the accounting rules is just have as clear a picture of what the company is doing as humanly possible. I am now an investor; I like to have good information. You might think that that is a public policy good. We have to give the true nature of what the company is doing.

I am also trained at Chicago, and believe that people who dig in among the facts and sort out the truth ought to be rewarded. I do not think everything needs to be disclosed perfectly in your accounting statement—I think it just needs to be accurate and complete. So that is not the issue here.

The issue that I think needs to be addressed is, can we have confidence that our accounting rules are not shaping the competitive framework? If that FASB rule from a couple of years ago had been put into law, I could guarantee you, within days, you would not have six-month resets on swaps—you would have two-year resets on swaps, so that people would not have to realize cash over an accounting cycle. The kind of games that we heard about this morning with the Japanese companies doing IOs and POs with their creative pricing would become part of our culture, and we would have disinformation rather than information in terms of understanding the balance sheets.

So those are a couple of the challenges.

Regulatory competition—I honestly do not think I want to have competing accounting frameworks out there from which I can pick and choose. That does not serve me well as an investor. I do not think risk-based capital should be done on an industry-by-industry or group-by-group basis, where you can pick your choice there. These areas have to have an integrated approach, and those are some of the challenges that we face as we move toward more use of derivatives.

Section Six

Financial Derivatives, Systemic Risk and Central Banking

William C. Hunter*
Senior Vice President and Director of Research
Federal Reserve Bank of Chicago

David Marshall*
Economic Advisor
Federal Reserve Bank of Chicago

*The views expressed in this paper are those of the authors and not necessarily those of the Federal Reserve Bank of Chicago or the Board of Governors of the Federal Reserve System.

Introduction

Innovation is the hallmark of financial markets around the world. This characteristic of modern financial markets is epitomized by the rapid evolution of financial derivatives. Indeed, the explosive growth in exchange-traded and over-the-counter (OTC) financial derivatives since the early 1980s has been one of the most profound structural developments in U.S. financial markets since the 1920s. These new instruments have proven to be important tools for businesses, financial institutions, and individual investors, among others, who use them for risk management and as investment vehicles.

The importance of financial derivatives as flexible and cost effective instruments for managing risks is typically evidenced by reference to their explosive growth. For example, in the area of exchange-traded interest-rate derivatives alone, the total volume of trades in these instruments in their initial years approximated less than 10,000 trades per month on the Chicago Board of Trade. Today, monthly trading activity in these instruments has increased by a factor of more than 800. Similarly, the volume of OTC swap transactions (interest rate swaps, currency swaps, and options on interest rates) reported to the International Swaps and Derivatives Association, increased from about $866 billion of debt being hedged using these instruments in 1987 to more than $15 trillion of hedges in place today.

This dramatic growth has also raised concerns in some quarters regarding the complexity of these instruments and the ability of managers, regulators and market participants in general to understand the risks associated with their use. This concern is justified in that these new instruments and products present a significant challenge to existing regulatory, supervisory, accounting and legal frameworks. These frameworks were designed for a world of on-balance sheet finance and are not well suited to deal with the rapid and frequent transformations of the characteristics of a company's financial claims and obligations. In particular, the traditional supervisory and regulatory structures for wholesale banks focus on periodic examinations of on-balance sheet transactions. This approach is ill-equipped to deal with an environment in which intraday on-and-off balance sheet positions change so rapidly that end-of-day positions are no longer sufficient statistics for projecting the evolving risk profile of an institution.

In addition to these concerns, there is also a growing perception that as a result of rapid innovation: 1) these markets have become less transparent and more interconnected; 2) that the derivatives business is unduly concentrated in a small group of dealer banks; and 3) that these markets are prone to systemic disturbances that threaten the real economy, thereby complicating (or at least fundamentally changing) the conduct of monetary policy and central banking.

In this paper, we focus on this latter premise. That is, we: 1) review the literature examining the notion of systemic risk; 2) evaluate some arguments that assert that the proliferation of derivative instruments and markets and the advent of systemic crises (perhaps induced or magnified by derivatives) have fundamentally changed the manner in which central banking and/or monetary policy should be conducted; 3) outline what we consider to be reasonable requirements for a coherent equilibrium model of systemic risk, and 4) evaluate the sources of systemic risk cited in the literature in light of these requirements.

We first discuss the concept of systemic risk because it is the key notion that directly or indirectly connects financial derivatives to central banking practice and monetary policy.

Characterizing Systemic Risk

In broad terms, systemic risk can be defined as a risk that can shock the financial system that significantly impairs crucial functions such as asset valuation, credit allocation, payments and settlements and that imposes significant costs to the real economy.

This characterization, while quite general, captures the spirit of many of the formal definitions of systemic risk in the published literature. Most of these definitions center on the efficient design of financial market regulation, particularly in the banking industry.[1] Kaufman (1994) and the Bank for International Settlements (BIS) offer typical definitions. Kaufman defines systemic risk as the probability that cumulative losses will occur from an event that ignites a series of successive losses along a chain of institutions or markets comprising a system. The Bank for International Settlements (BIS) defines sys-

---

1.   See, for example, Bordo (1986), Kaufman (1994), Eichengreen and Portes (1991), and Calomiris and Gorton (1991), among others.

temic risk as the risk that the failure of a participant to meet its contractual obligations may in turn cause other participants to default, with the chain reaction leading to broader financial difficulties. More specifically, in its Promisel Report (1994), the BIS defines a systemic crisis as a disturbance that severely impairs the working of the financial system and, at the extreme, causes a complete breakdown in it. Furthermore, it defines systemic risks as those risks that have the potential to cause such a crisis.

The U.S. General Accounting Office (GAO, 1994) in discussing systemic risk offers a definition tied to the notion that the abrupt failure of a large derivatives dealer could undermine the stability in several markets, simultaneously leading to a chain of market withdrawals, or possibly company failures, and a systemic crisis. Other definitions offered by various policy makers also center on the notion that the risk of a bank's default may cause a chain reaction of failures and even threaten the solvency of nonfinancial institutions.[2]

Discussions of systemic risk often focus on banking system crises even when the event precipitating the crisis originates outside of the banking sector. This is due to several reasons: 1) banks are thought to be special in the sense that their failure is more costly to society than the failure of nonbank companies; 2) banks are thought to be more fragile in the sense that they are more highly leveraged than are nonbank companies that is, they operate with low cash-to-asset ratios (as a result of the fractional reserve banking system); and 3) banks operate with high ratios of short-term debt-to-total debt with many of their short-term liabilities payable on demand (implying a high potential for bank runs). These characteristics are thought to make banks more susceptible to systemic crises than other companies. While it is probably true that banks are more fragile than nonbank companies, this does not mean that banks inherently have higher failure rates than other companies. As argued by Kaufman (1995), if banks are more fragile then they should be handled with more care. That is, regulation of banks should be designed in a manner consistent with this fact and that promotes proper risk-taking and adequate market discipline.

In summary, systemic risk is best thought of as the probability that a systemic event can occur. A systemic event is best thought of as

---

2.   See the speech by Robert Parry (1996). An alternative definition has been offered by Bartholomew et al. (1995)

an event having the ultimate effects contained in the definitions offered by Kaufman and/or the BIS and summarized above. In the discussion below, we follow the extant literature and use the terms systemic risk and systemic event interchangeably.

Practical and Political Concerns

As is evident from the above discussion, much attention has been directed toward establishing a workable definition of systemic risk. It is only natural to ask why it is important to settle upon a definition of systemic risk. The answer seems straightforward. If certain central banking and regulatory actions are to be justified on the basis of eliminating or containing systemic risk, the definition of systemic risk will be a key determinant of which types of regulatory or central bank interventions should be permissible. As noted by Federal Reserve Board Chairman Alan Greenspan, it would be useful to central banks to be able to measure systemic risk accurately since they are typically charged with monitoring it and engaging in actions to eliminate or mitigate its effects.[3]

A related question is why should central bankers and their regulators be so concerned about systemic risk. Again, the answer seems fairly obvious. Systemic events are usually characterized by a systemwide reduction in liquidity. In particular, liquid institutions may be reluctant to provide short-term financing to temporarily illiquid but solvent institutions. In such a situation, the central bank, as the only infinitely liquid institution in the economy, has a crucial role to play. It can serve as the ultimate provider of liquidity, either by acting as the lender of last resort or by increasing the appropriate supply of liquid assets in the economy (this latter strategy was used by the Federal Reserve in October 1997).

While many different (and often mutually contradictory) characterizations of systemic risk have been proposed, the fact that we do not have a consensus as to what systemic risk is in a quantitative sense does not mean that financial market regulators and central banks are unjustified in their keen interest in the potential risks that derivatives may pose to the financial system.

---

3.   See Greenspan (1995).

Regulators of financial markets and central banks face the challenge of balancing social and private costs and benefits with regard to regulatory and monetary policy intervention into financial institutions and markets. While derivative markets have flourished as a means of more efficiently sharing the risks flowing from changing asset prices and as an efficient mechanism for disseminating new information about asset prices, many derivatives represent highly leveraged positions that can disrupt markets in times of rapid change or turmoil.

This controversial point has been a much-debated rationale for more derivatives regulation. A more subtle concern is how the presence of a lender of last resort can affect the incentives of private agents operating in these markets. That is, the notion that the presence of a lender of last resort will induce moral hazard and excessive risk-taking under the presumption that the lender of last resort (i.e., the central bank) will step in during a crisis and engage in monetary policy operations that provide the needed liquidity to the system. Whether the perception is accurate or not, if market participants believe that the central bank will step in during a financial crisis, institutions may choose to hold less capital as a safety cushion than they otherwise would, and in effect the central bank and indirectly the taxpayer is pushed into assuming the cost for safeguarding the derivatives markets.

Are Derivatives Special?

As noted in the introduction, derivatives are often thought to play a special role in either initiating or magnifying systemic risk. Much of the recent concern regarding the role of derivatives in inducing or propagating shocks stems from the large losses suffered by the users of OTC derivatives and the fear that the failure of a large OTC derivatives dealer could set off a chain reaction of defaults that would culminate in a collapse of the international financial system. Feeding these concerns is the fact that these instruments and the markets in which they trade are thought to be excessively leveraged, less transparent, more interconnected, excessively concentrated and inadequately regulated, among others. These characteristics are said to make derivatives markets prone to disturbances and/or to make them key propagators of disturbances (and because most of the large derivatives dealers are banks, defaults on OTC derivatives could undermine the solvency of major banks, with potentially serious consequences for the banking system).

As argued by Edwards (1997) and Hentschel and Smith (1997), many of these fears regarding derivative dealers and markets do not appear to be well founded.[4] For example, as reported by Edwards, data published by the GAO suggest that U.S. derivative markets are not particularly concentrated. For example, the largest eight U.S. dealers account for only about 33 percent of the worldwide notional amounts held by dealers. Furthermore, the largest U.S. derivatives dealer holds only 6 percent of the total. Similarly, while it is true that derivatives have increased the linkages among financial markets, it is not obvious that such linkages have increased the likelihood of a systemic crisis. As markets become more interlinked, market participation widens, resulting in greater market liquidity. The more substitution there is among assets, the more elastic the demand for those assets, so that a demand or supply shock should result in smaller (not greater) price changes. Thus, rather than exacerbate market disturbances, it can be argued that increased market linkages should cushion financial disturbances by spreading price shocks over many markets.

Hentschel and Smith (1997) argue that defaults across derivative markets are not likely to be adversely correlated. Instead, they note that there are strong reasons to expect that defaults on derivatives contracts are approximately independent across dealers and over time. Their argument is based on two facts:

- Dealers have powerful incentives to assess default risks of their customers. Thus, in cases where dealers are evaluating taking the other side of a transaction with a lower-rated counterparty, extensive efforts will be made to assess the counterparty's exposure to interest rates and to ensure that the transaction is being used to offset, not magnify, risk exposure.
- Companies using derivatives to hedge their exposures are most likely to become insolvent precisely when their derivatives are in-the-money. Thus, shocks to the price of the asset underlying the derivative do not cause these companies to default on the derivative. In terms of excessive leverage and

---

4.   This discussion draws directly from Edwards (1997) and Smith and Hentschel (1997).

defaults within derivative contracts, defaults are negatively correlated. That is, at any point in time, only the side of a derivative that is in-the-money can lose from default and that party's losses represent equal and offsetting gains to the counterparty in the transaction. This negative correlation of the risks is due to the zero net supply of derivatives. For this reason, a simple summation of derivatives positions across the economy overstates total default risk.

In regard to the so-called gap in the regulation of nonbank derivatives dealers (dealer banks are subject to extensive regulation) and the risk this poses to the financial markets, there is no significant evidence that nonbank dealers take more risks or are more vulnerable to counterparty defaults than are bank dealers. Indeed, there is evidence that nonbank derivatives dealers are subject of substantial market discipline (see GAO, 1994).[5]

In terms of opaqueness and transparency, over the last several years many regulatory bodies have increased the level of public disclosure required in derivative transactions. The requirements by the Financial Standards Advisory Board and the bank regulatory agencies in the United States are but two of many examples.

Based on these types of arguments, the possibility of widespread default throughout the financial system stemming from the use of derivatives appears to be somewhat overstated. This is due to the fact that many analysts fail to recognize that the traditional measure of derivatives exposure notional value overstates the amount of capital at risk. Nevertheless, it must be recognized that derivatives are not without problems. In particular, the high leverage and infrequent payments associated with some derivatives make more careful internal controls especially important in the management of derivatives risk.

---

5. For additional arguments refuting the risk of derivatives and derivative dealers to the financial system, see Edwards (1997) and Hentschel and Smith (1997).

Derivatives, Systemic Risk and the Conduct of Monetary Policy

There is general agreement among central bank analysts that the growth of derivatives has affected the manner in which monetary policy is conducted. Clearly, derivatives have had a fundamental impact on traditional quantity indicators of monetary policy such as monetary and credit aggregates (BIS, 1994; Townsend, 1995; and Deutsche Bundesbank, 1994).

First, derivatives have altered the demand for money. By providing for the efficient management of risks and innovative investment strategies tied to market events, the transactions have reduced speculative demands for money. In addition, derivatives have contributed to the reduction of transaction costs in financial markets, allowing economic agents to operate with lower transaction balances. A major cost of trading in financial markets is the bid-ask spread. As is well known, informational asymmetries and trading volume are important factors in determining the spread. Derivative markets, by attracting information-motivated traders because of the higher leverage in derivatives, allows traders' private information to be transformed into publicly observable prices. Furthermore, since arbitrage between the derivative and underlying cash market keeps prices in these two markets linked, the information of derivatives traders is also reflected in the underlying cash market. As a result of the migration of informed traders to the derivatives markets, the spread in the underlying cash market is reduced and arbitrage simultaneously increases the volume of trading. Both of these factors reduce transaction costs and the demand for narrow money. As is well known, uncertainty about the demand for money function complicates the traditional conduct of monetary policy.

The general usefulness of the broader monetary aggregates has also been adversely affected as derivatives markets have grown. The low cost of hedging the price or interest-rate risk of government bonds, for example, has reduced the risks associated with these securities and transformed them into keen competitors with the traditional interest bearing components of the broad monetary aggregates. These developments have clearly been one key factor eroding the previously stable relationship between the monetary aggregates and nominal gross domestic product. For more than a decade, this has been apparent in the United States with respect to narrow aggregates such as M1 and broader aggregates such as M2 and total credit. Similar developments have occurred in Germany with respect to M3 and the relevant German macroeconomic targets.

Based on these developments, it seems clear that the advent of derivatives has made the conduct of monetary policy more difficult in terms of the usefulness of some monetary indicators. However, the development of derivatives markets should not affect the ability of central banks to establish the desired level of short-term interest rates. This is because the existence of derivative instruments does not alter the central bank's monopoly position as the supplier of the ultimate means of settlement: central bank reserves. Because of their pervasive influence in financial transactions, derivatives have likely altered banks' demand for central bank reserves requiring a recalibration of monetary policy actions. However, as long as there is a positive demand for central bank reserves, the central bank should have a means to control short-term interest rates and hence, an effective policy instrument.

There is much disagreement on the overall effectiveness of monetary policy in a world of sophisticated financial derivatives. It could be that the existence of derivatives, in addition to making for more complicated monetary policy as noted above, may also reduce the force of such policies on real economic activity (that is, a given amount of monetary policy stimulus may have a smaller effect). For example, the existence of foreign exchange derivatives may reduce the ability of central banks to influence exchange rates. Since money should be neutral in a frictionless economy, the sources of monetary nonneutrality must lie in economic frictions such as informational imperfections and transaction costs. By increasing the liquidity, depth, flexibility and transactional efficiency of financial markets, derivatives have increased the speed with which monetary policy actions are transmitted throughout the financial system. As noted above, lower transaction costs and reduced frictions resulting from derivatives activities increase the rate at which new information, including policy actions, is impounded into market prices.

Since derivatives markets reduce these sorts of frictions, they provide a more efficient mechanism for price discovery, speed up information transmission and reduce informational asymmetries. It follows then that by reducing frictions, derivatives markets reduce the real effects of monetary policy actions. Furthermore, derivatives markets act as a mechanism for spreading shocks across the economy as a whole. As discussed earlier, this spreading of shocks across the economy can be viewed as an advantage or disadvantage with respect to systemic risk (see Edwards, 1997 and GAO, 1994 for opposing views).

To the extent that derivatives reduce the force of monetary policy, monetary policy may become a weaker tool for counter-cyclical stabilization policy. However, if derivatives do provide the economy with the benefits cited by their proponents, i.e., a more efficient, more self-correcting, and more shock resistant economy, then there should be less of a need for counter-cyclical monetary policy. Stated differently, derivatives activity might actually reduce the incidence and severity of business cycles themselves, rendering monetary policy less important.

Modern business cycle theory focuses on the impulse that precipitates a downturn, and the propagation mechanism that translates the impulse into a contraction in economic activity. While there is much controversy over the nature of cyclical impulses, some of the more notable downturns in the United States, for example the 1929 stock market crash, appear to have been instigated by disturbances in the financial sector. The propagation mechanism may also involve the financial sector in a significant way, for example the massive bank failures in the early 1930s. Thus, to the extent that derivatives markets provide greater resiliency in the financial services industry, better allocation of risks in financial markets, and easier international and cross-market diversification, business cycle disturbances arising from the financial services sector would be less severe.

Lender-of-Last-Resort Function

The interaction among systemic events and the central bank's lender-of-last-resort function is important. This is because the presence of a lender of last resort may induce moral hazard and excessive risk-taking under the presumption that during a crisis the central bank, using its monetary policy operations, will come to the aid of the system. This may induce institutions to hold less capital than they otherwise would, exacerbating the likelihood and costs of a systemic crisis.

In the modern era, financial policy on the part of the U.S. central bank and its regulators in the face of systemic crises has most often involved use of the discount window and in the case of large banks, blanket coverage of all depositors. It has been argued that this mixing of bank closure policy with appropriate responses to systemic events is inappropriate to the extent that it increases moral hazard and closure costs without reducing the costs of systemic events.[6]

Normally, it is generally accepted that in the absence of a systemic crisis, the central bank should lend only to solvent but temporarily illiquid institutions. However, as Smith and Wall (1992) argue, in crisis situations where central bankers have private information that suggests that an individual bank is viable even though market-based financing is unavailable, discount window lending should be made available. Furthermore, they argue that in extreme circumstances where the real economy is threatened, discount window lending should be made available to secondary institutions that are nondepository intermediaries. Although the central bank is typically thought not to have an informational advantage over market participants when in comes to nondepository institutions, the central bank may nonetheless feel that failure to assist these companies could threaten the stability of the real economy.[7]

Modeling Systemic Risk

It is clear that systemic risk can be modeled in several ways. In this section we outline what we think are reasonable requirements for any rigorous equilibrium model of systemic risk.

Requirements of a Reasonable Model of Systemic Risk

While the general usage of the terms systemic crisis, systemic event and systemic risk refer to a shock to the financial system that impairs crucial functions of the system (such as asset valuation, credit allocation and payments), to date our view is that a complete, internally consistent, equilibrium theory of systemic risk has not been

---

6.   See Smith and Wall (1992) for a comprehensive review. See also the papers by Flannery (1991), Kanatas (1986), and Schwartz (1988).
7.   In such cases, Smith and Wall recommend that the central bank work through the commercial banking sector to provide the liquidity since the banks are typically better able to evaluate the solvency of the illiquid firm.

fully articulated. Despite this gap in the literature, it seems reasonable from our discussion to this point that such a model should, at a minimum, incorporate the following elements:

- A systemic crisis originates in, or is substantially magnified by financial markets. More precisely, systemic risk must originate in the process of financing. That is, the capital needed by a company is provided by investors outside the company. According to this property, systemic risk would not be present if all companies were purely financed internally.
- A systemic crisis involves contagion. That is, problems in one institution (company, country) cause (or at least, appear to cause) insolvency (distress, bankruptcy) in other, otherwise healthy, institutions.
- A systemic crisis involves a "loss of confidence" by investors. Usually, this means that investors or financial institutions cut back the amount of liquidity they are willing to provide to companies or other financial institutions. This loss of confidence has the connotation that the withdrawal of liquidity is not due to any objective deterioration in the quality of the borrower companies, but is more a function of investor psychology.
- A systemic crisis involves substantial real costs in economic output and/or economic efficiency. For example, a stock market crash is not necessarily a systemic crisis. If the crash simply redistributes wealth from speculators on the losing side (the ones who sold low) to the speculators on the winning side (the ones who bought low) without affecting real economic activity, it could not be regarded as a systemic crisis. Crises must hurt Main Street, not just Wall Street.
- A systemic crisis calls for a policy response. In particular, a systemic crisis must result in a Pareto-suboptimal allocation. This may be due to some externality, or to the presence of multiple equilibriums that can clearly be ranked from a welfare standpoint. The Diamond/Dybvig (1983) model is an example of the latter, for example. In Logunoff and Schreft's (1998) model of financial fragility, the resulting equilibrium is Pareto optimal: given the structure of the model, their "fragile" equilibrium is the best possible outcome of the

economy. If a particular definition of systemic risk does not imply costs in terms of economic efficiency (and therefore the possibility of corrective policy action), it would not correspond to a useful characterization of systemic risk for regulatory purposes.

In addition to these characteristics, another aspect of systemic crises that bears noting and that may be a significant feature in any modeling effort is that the crises or event can often seem to arise almost spontaneously. The recent Asian crisis provides an example.

It is generally agreed (*ex-post*) that there are obvious structural problems in many Asian economies: including a high reliance on external capital; a poorly developed banking system (with an even more poorly developed regulatory apparatus); cronyism between the financial sector and high government officials, and a remarkable lack of transparency in the workings of financial institutions. However, to some extent, all of these problems were well known during the period before the crises when these economies were performing very well. Foreign investors were perfectly willing to provide capital during this period. What happened to shift the confidence of foreign providers of capital dramatically and so quickly?

Radelet and Sachs (1998) argue forcefully that the crisis caught the financial world completely by surprise. For example, interest-rate spreads between the sovereign debt of key countries in the Asian crisis and U.S. Treasury debt declined between mid-1995 and mid-1997. Similarly, credit ratings of these countries' sovereign debt remained unchanged through June 1997 (the only exception was the Philippines, whose credit rating was actually upgraded in early 1997). In addition, Krugman (1997) notes that macroeconomic fundamentals were strong in all these countries. The governments were in fiscal balance, there was no irresponsible credit creation or monetary expansion, and inflation and unemployment rates were low. The closest one can find to a triggering event was the failure of Finance One, the largest Thai finance company. Why should this failure induce a profound plunge in the level of economic activity in five countries? The economic response seems wholly disproportionate to the size of the apparent triggering shock.

This lack of a clear cause characterizes many other systemic crises. Neither the 1929 nor the 1987 stock market crashes had an obvious precipitating event. No war was started; no high official was shot. (This is in contrast to the sharp market declines in the fall of 1973 or 1980, which were caused by the Organization of Petroleum Exporting Countries' announcement of its oil embargo and the fall of the Shah of Iran, respectively). Similarly, the 1992 crisis in the Exchange Rate Mechanism and the recent Mexican crisis did not have a clear trigger. Of course, foreign exchange traders might respond that there was a clear event that instigated the Asian crisis: a run on the Thai currency. But this just restates the puzzle: a run on the currency is simply a visible expression of a loss of confidence. What happened to cause a 180-degree change in investor confidence?

This lack of a causative event presents a real challenge to theorists. In the standard model, the value of a company is the present value of the net cash flow generated by the company. Similarly, the value of a national economy is the present value of the cash flow generated by the total economic activity of that country. In the standard model, one thinks of this as the "fundamental value." The market value of the company should be the best guess, given current information about this fundamental value. Similarly, a country's currency represents a claim to the current and/or future output of that country's economy. The value of this currency should in some sense reflect the fundamental value of the country's productive capacity. A sudden, precipitous drop in the value of a country's asset markets or currency would then mean that either: 1) the market's precrisis assessment of fundamental value was too high ("irrational exuberance"); or 2) the market's postcrisis assessment of fundamental value was too low ("irrational pessimism"); or 3) the crisis was precipitated by the arrival of new information that caused rational investors to change their assessment of this fundamental value.

If, as seems to be the case in many financial crises, the third alternative is difficult to sustain, then the standard model seems to force one to choose the irrationality embedded in either the first or the second alternative.

Cataloging the Sources of Systemic Risk

Recently, several efforts have been made to catalogue and clarify the various sources of systemic risk, along with the related (and perhaps equally ambiguous) notions of financial fragility and financial bubbles.[8] Although the literature detailing the potential sources of systemic risk is voluminous, in this section we summarize a number of proposed sources of systemic risk.[9] For each source, we ask whether it is adequate in scope to form the basis for a reasonably complete model of systemic risk relative to the modeling criteria discussed in the last section.

Excessive Debt

Minsky (1982), Bernanke and James (1991), Kindleberger (1978), and Feldstein (1991), among others, attribute systemic risk to an irrational piling-on of debt. In particular, companies finance capital investment with ever-increasing leverage ratios, stimulated in some sense by a vast increase in the money supply. Eventually, this debt level becomes "unsustainable," leading to an inevitable collapse.

This theory relies explicitly on irrationality: during expansions, companies become overly optimistic about their debt capacity. "Greed overcomes fear and individual investors take greater risks in pursuit of greater returns. A shock occurs and the market prices of assets begin to collapse. Bankruptcies...follow. The resulting failure of the payments mechanism and the inability to create credit bring on an economic collapse." (Feldstein, 1991, quoted in Benston and Kaufman 1995.) We regard theories based fundamentally on investor irrationality to be methodologically unsound. However, even if one were to accept this idea in principle, the policy implications are not credible. Presumably the government should impose regulations to keep these exuberant companies from overleveraging. In other words, the companies whose money is at stake cannot determine the proper level of debt, but government bureaucrats somehow can.

Furthermore, there is no basis for regulatory action if the costs of default induced by this excessive debt are borne primarily by the company and creditor. Bankruptcy is a transfer of assets from debtor to creditor in the event of default. Unless there are substantial costs

---

8.   See Davis (1992), Kaufman (1995), and the special issue of the *Journal of Financial Services Research* published in 1995 devoted to the subject of systemic risk.

9.   Eisenbeis (1997) identifies the following sources of systemic risk: random shocks and financial fragility, asymmetric information, and network failures and transmission difficulties.

borne by third parties, there is no rationale for government action to prevent this transfer. An example of poor policy induced by a misunderstanding of the nature of bankruptcy is the Chrysler Corporation bailout in the United States. At the time, it was justified by the idea that "jobs were at stake." Of course, this is not what bankruptcy is. The productive capital represented by Chrysler's plant, equipment, know-how and marketing network would not have disappeared in the event of bankruptcy, nor would the jobs of those needed to run this productive capital. It would have been transferred to new owners. If there was a need for capacity reduction, this would (and did) happen regardless of whether Chrysler went through the formal bankruptcy procedure.

Moral Hazard

There is an alternative notion of "excessive debt" that has a theoretically sound foundation. There may be an externality that drives a wedge between the privately optimal debt level and the debt level that is optimal for society as a whole. An obvious candidate is the moral hazard induced by a government-provided safety net. Under this explanation "systemic risk" is a state of overleveraging due to perverse incentives of the safety net, and "systemic crises" occur when, due to an external adverse shock, there are excessive defaults (relative to the number of defaults one would expect in the absence of the safety net). The externality is that the costs of default are borne in part by the taxpayers who provide the safety net.

The issue of moral hazard has potential implications for regulating derivatives usage. The danger here is that unhedged derivatives exposures by banks and other institutions protected by the government-provided safety net may be improperly accounted for in determining capital requirements. In particular, methodologies such as value-at-risk are not well suited for evaluating the risk of securities, such as derivatives, with highly nonlinear payoff functions. One important regulatory proposal that potentially can better account for the risk of derivatives portfolios is the Board of Governor's precommitment proposal.[10] Precommitment is an incentive-based approach to capital regulation, in which the bank chooses its own level of capital

---

10. The precommitment proposal is described in Federal Register, Vol 60, No. 142, pp. 38142-38144.

for its trading portfolio. However, penalties are assessed against the bank if ex post this capital level proves inadequate (in a well-defined sense). This places the responsibility for determining the risk of a derivatives portfolio squarely with the bank itself, which arguably has the best risk-assessment technology.

This problem of moral hazard is a well-articulated and precisely modeled issue in public policy. If systemic risk or systemic events involve solvent, prudent financial institutions being endangered by the failure of some other large institution, the optimal policy response may well be to bailout the failing institution in an effort to contain the contagion or domino effects, i.e., the systemic event or risk. If however, the source to the systemic risk or event is the moral hazard engendered by the implicit "too-big-to-fail" doctrine, the appropriate policy response would be laws preventing the bailout of large institutions. As mentioned above, the optimal policy response to the problem of systemic moral hazard is to reduce safety-net provisions, thereby forcing private companies to internalize more of the costs of excessive debt financing. In contrast, the usual response to systemic risk is to increase provision of the safety net. These conflicting policy prescriptions reemerged in discussions about the role of the International Monetary Fund in alleviating the Asian financial crisis. The standard argument is that this is a systemic crisis requiring an IMF "bailout." The alternative position, that IMF bailouts increase the possibility of systemic crises by exacerbating the moral-hazard problem, has received a scant hearing.

Complex Internetworking Among Counterparties

A bank has both direct exposure to the credit-worthiness of its direct counterparties, and indirect exposure to the credit-worthiness of its counterparties' counterparties, and so on. These indirect exposures render a bank vulnerable to disruptions caused by the failure of an institution with which it has no direct exposure. The size and complexity of these interlinkages has increased enormously as banks expand their activity in derivatives trading and market-making.

Undoubtedly this is an accurate description of financial markets, but it is not clear why this state of affairs calls for any policy response. Why is this different from a steelworker noting that his personal solvency is affected by problems suffered by the General Motors Corporation, a company with which he has no direct contractual relation. In both cases we have a chain of contractual relations, where, if one contractor fails, all contractors are potentially affected. In neither case is there necessarily an externality that calls for government intervention.

Furthermore, creditors should internalize all risks both direct and indirect. "Know thy counterparty" requires an assessment of all factors that could impair the counterparty's credit-worthiness, including his exposure to other companies' distress. The fact that a bank may have incomplete information about its counterparties' exposure to other institutions does not change this conclusion. Incomplete information is always associated with risk. Institutions should manage the risk associated with these informational lacuna in the same way they manage other types of risk. Formally, the probability that a bank will be impaired by the failure of its counterparties' counterparties can be computed as a compound probability. Unless banks are unable to estimate such compound probabilities, this notion of systemic risk reduces down to ordinary credit risk.

A major application of this notion of systemic risk is in the area of interbank payments.[11] The volume and complexity of these payments has grown enormously in recent years. Humphrey (1986) estimated that the failure of one major U.S. bank could saddle up to 50 banks with net settlement obligations at the end of the day in excess of their capital. However, while interlinkages are becoming more complex, the computing power to handle these complexities has grown in train. The main societal costs associated with this version of systemic risk are the costs of unwinding obligations in a net settlement system. These costs are borne not only by the direct participants in the system, all individuals in the economy who need to make payments suffer if the payments system (which acts as a classical "common carrier") shuts down. However, while these costs are large, it is not clear that the heavy superstructure of financial regulation is the best policy response. A better response is to reduce the costs of unwinding. This could be done either by moving to real time gross settlement system (RTGS), or, if this is deemed too costly in liquidity requirements, to move to a "virtual" RTGS. The latter would involve a computer keeping track in real time of what the positions of clearing

---

11. See also the papers by Smith (1991), Bhattacharya and Gale (1987), and Chari (1989).

members would be if real time gross settlement systems were in place. Then, in the event of a default, it would be straightforward to reconstruct the day's trades with the trades of the defaulting party eliminated. The resulting final positions would be the desired outcome after "unwinding" is completed.

Freeze-Up of Trading

The 1994 GAO report on financial derivatives gives a stark description of this scenario. The fear of an abrupt withdrawal or failure of one major dealer causes many dealers to withdraw, leading to a chain of defaults that shuts down the entire OTC derivatives market. It is unclear what mechanism could generate this result. In particular, the role of prices is ignored. Why don't prices adjust to avoid freeze-up? Presumably, there is some price at which banks would be willing to lend and dealers would be willing to trade. While some such event may be possible, the burden is on those who propose such a scenario to formulate an internally consistent model that supports this sort of outcome.

While economic theory may have difficulty modeling this sort of gridlock, central banks must consider the possibility that dealers in derivatives and other securities might be unable to trade due to a lack of liquidity. The central bank is the only infinitely liquid institution in the economy, so it has a key role in alleviating liquidity shortages in financial markets. We do not envision direct discount-window loans to nonbank derivatives dealers. However, the central bank could play a role similar to that performed by the Federal Reserve in the aftermath of the October 1987 crash: increase the total volume of liquidity via open market operations, and encourage large banks to channel this liquidity to illiquid dealers as needed.

Failure of Central Bank to Provide Liquidity

Schwartz (1986) traces the following chain of events as a template for systemic crisis. A financial crisis induces a banking panic (i.e., public loss of confidence in banks), implying a flight to currency and (with fractional reserve banking) widespread default. This does not explain why there is a sudden loss of confidence in the first place that generates the shortfall of liquidity. It may well be the case that, for many models of systemic risk, the optimal policy response involves provision of liquidity by the central bank, either through open market operations or through targeted lending via the discount window, and that a failure to do so prolongs the crisis. Still, Schwartz's characterization does not tell us why the liquidity crisis starts, so it is at best incomplete.

Adverse (Bad) Shocks

Benston and Kaufman (1995) argue that a prominent cause of bank failures is "shocks originating outside banking system" (e.g., an exogenous withdrawal of reserves). This may be so, but it does not necessarily imply a policy role. If the original "withdrawal of reserves" is an optimal response to some real exogenous shock, there need not be an externality calling for government intervention. Furthermore, we argue that the term "systemic crisis" should be reserved for crises originating in, or greatly propagated by the financial system. What is the mechanism that magnifies the initial shock? Without answering these questions, the role of government is unclear.

Knightian Uncertainty

Frank Knight, in his influential *Risk, Uncertainty, and Profit* (1921), argues that there is a fundamental difference between risk, which involves future possibilities that can be described by objective probability distributions, and uncertainty, which involves future events so different from the past that they cannot be assigned objective probabilities. Meltzer (1982) and Crockett (1995) argue that systemic crises can coincide with the appearance of these "uncertain" events. More precisely, "Systemic stress generally arises when an unexpected event occurs against the background of pre-existing contractual behavior predicated on its non-occurrence" (Crockett, 1995).

This idea is intriguing, but its public policy implications are decidedly unclear. Why does the possibility of "something completely different" call for government action? As with the "excessive debt" story, why is it not in the company's interest to prepare, as best it can, for "totally new" shocks? Will the cost of failing to prepare be borne by the company and its contracting parties? If not, where is the externality that imposes costs on society as a whole? It is (by definition) difficult for a company to prepare for the "totally new," or to guess at the costs of failing to prepare. Is the government any better at making these assessments? In short, it is not clear why this story differs from a more prosaic "bad shock" discussed in the previous subsection.

If shocks external to the financial system are a source of systemic risk, the derivatives market may have an important salutary role in avoiding systemic crises. Derivatives provide a means of hedging the risk of adverse shocks, reallocating this risk to those market participants best able to bear the risk. As such, the growth of new, innovative derivative products reduces the danger of systemic crisis due to adverse shocks. To the extent that this theory of systemic risk is empirically important, it represents a strong justification for regulators not to impede innovation in financial engineering.

Bank Runs

The Diamond and Dybvig (1983) model of bank runs is the most rigorously formulated model of systemic risk in the literature. Banks provide households with insurance against liquidity risk by pooling these risks, and by offering households financial assets redeemable upon demand at par. At the same time, banks provide borrowers with long-term loans. This duration mismatch makes the bank vulnerable to runs. In particular, all depositors are better off if no one runs the bank, but there is no mechanism in which depositors can coordinate their actions and mutually agree not to run the bank. If a run occurs, then it is individually optimal for everyone to run the bank. If a run on one bank acts as a coordination mechanism for depositors to run a second bank, then a wave of contagious bank runs could severely damage the banking system as a whole.

While the Diamond and Dybvig (1983) model is theoretically attractive and intuitively plausible, several empirical studies of the banking industry before deposit insurance cast doubt on whether any waves of bank failures actually were characterized by widespread bank runs. (See Benston and Kaufman, 1995, Calomiris and Gorton, 1991, Calomiris and Mason, 1994.) In particular, it appears difficult to find support for a direct link between bank runs and widespread bank failures. Rather, it appears that depositors generally can distinguish between sound and insolvent banks. The banks that are run in most cases are those that are truly insolvent due to nonperforming loans.

While this direct link between bank runs and bank failures may not characterize the historical record, the notion of a coordination failure remains a useful basis for a theory of systemic risk. The potential for a Diamond/Dybvig crisis arises any time there is a duration mismatch between short-term liabilities and long-term assets. Radelet and Sachs (1998) document that, in the East Asian countries most affected by the recent crisis, the ratio of short-term loans to short-term assets had exceeded 1.0 for several years. Note that the risk here is that of overleveraging. Derivatives contracts per se do not add to this risk. However, derivatives provide an easy way for institutions to rapidly increase their effective leverage, should they choose to do so. The Orange County, California, bankruptcy serves as a textbook case on how the improper use of derivatives to increase leverage can dramatically boost an institution's vulnerability.

Conclusion

As can be garnered from this tour through alternative characterizations of systemic risk, we are a long way away from a consensus theory. Serious research on the systemic effects of financial innovations, such as the growth of complex derivative instruments and derivatives trading strategies, is hampered by this theoretical vacuum. It is clear, however, that the role of central banks in heading off and mitigating systemic problems will continue to be central. Since competition and financial innovation best flourish within the context of a safe and sound financial system, this need for systemic supervision by central banks and their regulatory affiliates seems to be a legitimate one.

References

Akerlof, George (1979). The Market for Lemons: Qualitative Uncertainty and the Market Mechanism. *Quarterly Journal of Economics* 84:488-500.

Bank for International Settlements (1992). *Recent Developments in International Interbank Relations.* Report prepared by a working group established by the Central Banks of the Group of Ten Countries (also known as the Promisel Report). Basel: Bank for International Settlements, October.

Bartholomew, Philip F., Larry R. Moe, and Gary Whalen (1995). The Definition of Systemic Risk. Office of the Comptroller of the Currency. Presented at the 70th annual Western Economic Association International Conference, San Diego, California, July.

Bartholomew, P., and Whalen, G. (1995). Fundamentals of Systemic Risk. In G.G. Kaufman (ed.) Research in Financial Services 7:3-18. Greenwich: JAI Press.

Benston, George J., and George G. Kaufman (1996). The Appropriate Role of Bank Regulation. *Economic Journal* 106: 688-97.

―――――――――――――――――――――――――――. (1995). Is the Banking and Payments System Fragile? *Journal of Financial Services Research* 9 (December): 209-40.

―――――――――――――――――――――――――. (1988). Risk and Solvency Regulation of Depository Institutions: Past Policies and Current Options. *Monograph Series in Finance and Economics.* New York University: Salomon Center for Graduate School of Business.

Bernanke, Ben. S. (1983). Non-Monetary Effects of the Financial Crisis in the Propagation of the Great Depression. *American Economic Review* 73 (June): 14-31.

Bernanke, Ben, and Harold James (1991). The Gold Standard, Deflation, and Financial Crisis in the Great Depression: An International Comparison. In *Financial Markets and Financial Crises*, edited by R. Glenn Hubbard 33-68. Chicago: University of Chicago Press.

Bhattacharya, Sudipto, and Douglas Gale (1987). Preference Shocks, Liquidity, and Central Bank Policy. In *New Approaches to Monetary Economics*, edited by William Barnett and Kenneth Singleton, 69-88, New York: Cambridge University Press.

Bordo, Michael D. (1990). The Lender of Last Resort: Alternative Views and Historical Experience. *Federal Reserve Bank of Richmond Economic Review* 76 (January/February): 18-29.

Calomiris, Charles W., and Gary Gorton (1991). The Origins of Banking Panics: Models, Facts, and Banking Regulation. In *Financial Markets and Financial Crises*, edited by R. Glenn Hubbard, 109-73. Chicago: University of Chicago Press.

Calomiris, Charles W., and Charles M. Kahn (1991). The Role of Demandable Debt in Structuring Optimal Banking Arrangements. *American Economic Review* 81 (June): 497-513.

Calomiris, Charles W., and Joseph P. Mason (1994). "Contagion and Bank Failures During the Great Depression: The June 1932 Chicago Banking Panic," *NBER Working Paper No. 4934.*

Chari, V.V. (1989). Banking without Deposit Insurance or Bank Panics: Lessons from a Model of the United States National Banking System. *Federal Reserve Bank of Minneapolis Quarterly Review 13* (Summer): 3-19.

Crockett, Andrew (1995). "Financial Fragility: Sources, Prevention, and Treatment," in *Coping with Financial Fragility and Systemic Risk*, edited by Harald A. Benink. Boston: Kluwer Academic Publishers.

_____. (1997). The Theory and Practice of Financial Stability, Princeton Essays in *International Finance*, No. 203, April.

Davis, E.P. (1992). *Debt, Financial Fragility and Systemic Risk.* Oxford: Oxford University Press.

Deutsche Bundesbank Monthly Report (1994). The Monetary Policy Implications of Increasing Use of Derivative Financial Instruments. November.

Diamond, Douglas, and Philip Dybvig (1983). Bank Runs, Liquidity, and Deposit Insurance. *Journal of Political Economy* 91 (June): 401-19.

Edwards, Franklin R. (1996). *The New Finance: Regulation and Stability* (American Enterprise Institute).

Eichengreen, Barry, and Richard Portes (1991). The Anatomy of Financial Crises. In *Financial Markets and Financial Crises*, edited by R. Glenn Hubbard, 10-58. Chicago: University of Chicago Press.

Eisenbeis, Robert A. (1997). Bank Deposits and Credit as Sources of Systemic Risk. *Economic Review* (Federal Reserve Bank of Atlanta) Third Quarter: 4-17.

Feldstein, Martin (1991). The Risk of Economic Crisis. *NBER Conference Report*. Chicago: University of Chicago Press.

Financial Accounting Standards Board (1994). Proposed Statement of Financial Accounting Standards: Disclosure of Derivative Financial Instruments and Fair Value of Financial Instruments. *Financial Accounting Series* No. 136-B, April.

Flannery, Mark J. (1991). *Debt Maturity and the Deadweight Cost of Leverage: Optimally Financing Banking Firms.* University of Florida Working Paper, July.

General Accounting Office (1994). Financial Derivatives: Actions Needed to Protect the Financial System. *Report to Congressional Requestors*, GAO/GGD-94-133. Washington, D.C.: Government Printing Office, May.

Gorton, Gary, and Richard Rosen (1995). *Banks and Derivatives.* Wharton School, University, University of Pennsylvania, photocopy.

Gorton, Gary (1987*). Banking Panics and Business Cycles: Data Sources, Data Construction, and Further Results.* The Wharton School, University of Pennsylvania, photocopy.

Greenspan, Alan (1995). Remarks at a Conference on Risk Measurement and Systemic Risk. Washington, D.C.: Board of Governors of the Federal Reserve System.

Kanatas, George (1986). Deposit Insurance and the Discount Window: Pricing under Asymmetric Information. *Journal of Finance* 41 (June): 437-50.

Kaufman, George G. (1996). Bank Failures, Systemic Risk, and Bank Regulation. *Cato Journal* 16, No.1 (Spring/Summer):17-46.

Kaufman, George G. (1995). Comment on Systemic Risk. In G.G. Kaufman (ed.) *Research in Financial Services* 7: 47-52. Greenwich: JAI Press.

_____. (1994). Bank Contagion: A Review of the Theory and Evidence. *Journal of Financial Services Research* 8:123-50.

_____. (1992). Bank Contagion: Theory and Evidence. Federal Reserve Bank of Chicago, *Working Paper Series*, No. 92-13, June.

_____. (1988). Bank Runs: Causes, Benefits, and Costs. *Cato Journal* 7 (Winter): 559-87.

Kindleberger, Charles P. (1978). *Manias, Panics, and Crashes*. Mac-Millan: London.

Knight, Frank H. (1921). *Risk, Uncertainty and Profit, Boston*: No. 16 in series of reprints of scarce texts in economics, London School of Economics, London.

Krugman, Paul (1998). What Happened to Asia. *Working Paper.* MIT.

Logunoff, Roger D., and Stacey L. Schreft (1998). "A Model of Financial Fragility," *Federal Reserve Bank of Kansas City Research Working Paper* No. RWP 98-01.

Meltzer, Allan H. (1982). "Rational Expectations, Risk, Uncertainty, and Market Responses," in *Crisis in the Economic and Financial Structure*, edited by P. Watchel. Salomon Bros. Series on Financial Institutions and Markets. Lexington, MA: Lexington Books.

Minsky, Hyman P. (1982). The Financial Instability Hypothesis: Capitalist Processes and the Behavior of the Economy. In *Financial Crises: Theory, History, and Policy,* edited by Charles Kindleberger and Jean-Pierre Laffargue, 13-38. Cambridge: Cambridge University Press.

_____. (1982). Financial Stability Revisited: The Economics of Disaster, in Board of Governors of the Federal Reserve System, *Reappraisal of the Federal Reserve Discount Mechanism,* vol. 3. Washington, D.C.: Federal Reserve Board, pp. 95-136.

Mishkin, F. (1991). Asymmetric Information and Financial Crises. In R.G. Hubbard (ed.) *Financial Markets and Financial Crises,* 69-108. Chicago: University of Chicago Press.

Parry, R. (1996). Global Payments in the 21st Century: A Central Banker's View. *FRBSF Economic Letter,* Federal Reserve Bank of San Francisco, 3 May.

Schwartz, A. (1986). "Real and Pseudo-financial Crises." *In Financial Crises and the World Banking System*, edited by Forrest Capie and Geoffrey E. Wood. London: Macmillan, pp. 11-31.

Radelet, Stephen and Jeffrey Sachs (1998). "The East Asian Financial Crisis: Diagnosis, Remedies, Prospects," working paper, Harvard Institute for International Development, Harvard University.

Schwartz, A. (1995). Systemic Risk and the Macroeconomy. In G.G. Kaufman (ed.) *Research in Financial Services* 7: 19-30. Greenwich: JAI Press.

_____. (1986). The Lender of Last Resort and the Federal Safety Net. *Journal of Financial Services Research* 1 (January): 1-18.

Smith, Bruce D. (1991). Bank Panics, Suspensions, and Geography: Some Notes on the Contagion of Fear in Banking. *Economic Inquiry* 29 (April): 230-48.

Smith, Stephen D., and Larry D. Wall (1992). Financial Panics, Bank Failures, and the Role of Regulatory Policy. *Economic Review* (Federal Reserve Bank of Atlanta), January/February: 1-11.

Townsend, John (1995). Derivatives and Monetary Policy: A Central Banker's Perspective, speech at ISDA 10th Annual Conference in Barcelona, March 23, 1995.

Comments on...

Financial Derivatives, Systemic Risk and Central Banking

Roger Craine
Department of Economics
University of California, Berkeley

William C. Hunter and David Marshall tackle one of the most important topics in financial policy: systemic risk. This is a preliminary analysis and they do an excellent job of defining the problem and stating why it is so difficult. There are no easy answers—or this would not be an issue. My comments expand on their basic theme.

I will start with a prelude to put their paper and my comments in the larger framework of this conference. The conference topic is "Restructuring Regulation and Financial Institutions." A basic question is why do we need regulation, or why can't the market do it? There are two types of regulatory policy: 1) regulations and enforcement to make sure the players follow the rules, and 2) proactive policy to overcome a market failure.

Regulation to enforce rules is easy to understand and analyze, at least at a conceptual level. All games have rules and so must a well-functioning economy. Professional baseball has umpires that enforce (although they sometimes make mistakes) the rules of the game so that a competitive outcome should determine who wins. Modern versions of the famous Arrow-Debreu model of complete markets competitive equilibrium give a fully articulated description of an economy that functions perfectly. The model incorporates uncertainty, dynamics and capital accumulation. Arrow-Debreu securities can be packaged in portfolios that replicate the payoff on stocks, bonds, risky debt and derivatives—almost any instrument we see in modern financial markets. In this model, however, there are no institutions—no financial intermediaries, no companies and no government—the market does it all. A competitive equilibrium is Pareto optimal. Even this abstract model, however, requires a regulator that enforces the rules. The hypothetical "Walrasian auctioneer" enforces contracts. A risky debt contract permits default, but the "Walrasian auctioneer" checks that the collateral asset actually exists. Agencies such as the Securities and Exchange Commission enforce rules in the U.S. economy. They demand disclosure and monitor the accuracy of financial statements. One can debate how well they do their job, like how well do baseball umpires call strikes and balls, but not whether they serve a necessary function.

Analyzing systemic risk is inherently much more difficult. There is no systemic risk unless there is a market failure. Again a baseball analogy is useful. If a hit to the outfield bounces into the stands, the hitter gets a double. But in a perfect (complete markets) field the hitter might reach third base or even score. This could change the outcome of the game. The arbitrary "ground rule double" rule in baseball releases umpires from the responsibility (and retributions) of making a difficult subjective decision. The economy is much more important and (rightly so) has no "ground rule double" rule. Policy makers have to decide whether or not to intervene. They should intervene if there is a market failure (the hitter would have gotten to third base), but should not intervene if there is no market failure (it's a double.) But this is not so easy.

The problem is that actual economies, like baseball parks, are not perfect. Dr. Hunter, et al., astutely realize that even defining systemic risk is difficult. They review several definitions that I believe capture the essence of systemic risk. They use Kaufman's definition that systemic risk is the probability of cumulative losses. And they add Bartholomew's condition that the cumulative financial loss exceeds the fundamental loss due to a market failure and it feeds back on the real (nonfinancial sector). The crucial problem, which Hunter et al., emphasize, is that there is no mechanical rule for sorting out fundamental losses from systemic failures. I will illustrate with an actual (nonbaseball) example that Dr. Hunter uses in the presentation and that I worked on.

Systemic risk is usually associated with a sequence of bank failures that collapse the financial intermediation structure leading to losses in the real economy. It is also possible that a shock could collapse an exchange, which would interrupt securities trading and would lead to real losses. David Bates and I[1] examined the exposure of the futures market during the 1987 market crash. The futures market clearinghouse guarantees all contracts. On that October 19 the stock market recorded the largest daily price decline in its history. The

---

1.   Bates, David and Roger Craine (1998), Valuing the Futures Market Clearinghouse's Default Exposure During the 1987 Crash, forthcoming *Journal of Money, Credit, and Banking*.

price of a Standard and Poor's futures contract declined by 29 percent—the margin was approximately 3 percent. Long positions had to ante up 26 percent overnight. The futures market clearinghouse did not have sufficient liquidity to make up the entire shortfall. Massive defaults would have collapsed the exchange.

So here is the policy dilemma: if it is a liquidity crisis—the long positions have sufficient wealth to cover their losses, but not liquid wealth that can be converted to cash overnight—then, easy credit provides the needed liquidity and the crisis is aborted. But if the long positions are insolvent—they do not have sufficient wealth to cover their losses—then the defaults should occur even if it temporarily shuts down the exchange. The losers are forced out of the market and creditors claim the losers' assets. Easy credit, if the losers are insolvent, creates a moral hazard opportunity that allows the losers to continue playing with no downside risk.

Choices under these conditions are not easy or obvious. It is very hard to sort illiquid from insolvent. The Federal Reserve encouraged easy credit in the 1987 market crash and no clearing members of the Chicago Mercantile Exchange defaulted.

Lalita Ramesh
Research Associate
Milken Institute

William C. Hunter's paper addresses an issue that is becoming increasingly critical as capital flows within and across countries in greater volume and with increasing speed than ever before. The paper addresses the question of whether these flows should be regulated to avoid systemic crises. Such crises clearly have the ability to seriously disrupt capital flows. Do these disruptions have real effects? If so, are these effects serious enough to warrant regulation or intervention of some sort? The current theoretical literature on the subject provides few insights.

The paper is motivated by the need to design appropriate regulation in order to avoid the negative externalities arising from systemic risk. Appropriate regulation of course, requires an understanding of systemic risk, its origins and transmission.

Defining Systemic Risk

The first issue that arises is the identification of systemic risk. According to Dr. Hunter, "In broad terms, systemic risk can be defined as the risk that a shock to the financial system...significantly impairs crucial functions such as asset valuation, credit allocation and payments and settlements and...imposes significant costs to the real economy."

Does a Financial Crisis Have Real Effects?

The Keynesian view is that, in general, the path through which an economy evolves over time is determined by the interaction of investment demand, financing conditions, income distribution and aggregate demand. According to this theory, changes in monetary and financial institutions affect the economy through rigidities in nominal contracts (interpreted by Neo-Keynesians as arising from information deficiencies) and through stock-flow relationships (a thorny issue from a modeling point of view). The Post-Keynesian interpretation of a systemic crisis is that it occurs as a cumulative outcome of these real-financial interactions resulting in turbulent conditions and incoherent behavior (Minsky, 1994).

Aglietta (1996) summarizes the monetarist position on the basis of a paper by Schwartz (1992), who distinguishes financial crises from bank runs on the grounds that financial crises (unlike bank runs) do not have the potential to induce a global contraction of liquidity in the banking system and are therefore considered to be pseudo-crises. According to Dr. Hunter, empirical studies have cast doubt on whether bank failures are accompanied by bank runs, leading him to conclude that, on the whole, depositors seem to be discriminating and run on only those banks that are truly insolvent. However, monetarist theory does not address, to any satisfactory conclusion, the issue of "what if" there is a systemwide reduction in liquidity. This is the question that is the subject of Dr. Hunter's investigation.

If a systemic crisis is so crucially important in its impact on the economy, then how does one explain the vacuum in the literature? The real problem is that any model— monetarist or Keynesian—that assumes money is exogenous cannot, for obvious reasons, explain a widespread liquidity crunch with real effects, except as some sort of short-run adjustment to an exogenous shock.

In the absence of a clear exogenous event that would trigger a crisis, Dr. Hunter raises the question of whether the origins of a crisis could be due to irrational optimism or pessimism. Perhaps an alternative explanation for such irrational behavior is that it arises as an expedient (or optimal) response by boundedly rational agents to incentives arising out of information deficiencies (reflected in contracts; regulation; opaqueness in government and corporate decisions, and the institutional framework more generally). Modeling behavior in this way would be able to portray the idea that systemic risk arises from overleveraging due to perverse incentives. This might ultimately induce an endogenous contraction in liquidity, as bad investments begin to default and investors become more cautious as a result of being unable to distinguish between good and bad investments in an uncertain environment. Such a situation can only be interpreted as a coordination failure or a disequilibrium phenomenon. The resulting contingencies might, in an extreme case, necessitate a net infusion of liquidity from an outside source (such as a central bank).

Risk and Regulation

Is such an infusion of liquidity an appropriate regulatory response in the event of a systemic crisis? The answer would depend on what the source of risk is perceived to be.

If excessive debt arises from irrational exuberance (Minsky, 1982), Dr. Hunter argues against regulation for two reasons. The first is that if companies cannot determine the proper level of debt ex ante, neither can government bureaucrats. The second reason is that there is no rationale for government action unless there are substantial costs associated with the crisis ex post, that are borne by third parties.

If excessive debt arises as a result of moral hazard incentives created by regulation such as a government safety net, or by past infusions of liquidity by a lender of last resort, then further lending might only provide a temporary reprieve while worsening the underlying problem. This is because such actions, if undertaken often, could act as a signal to financial institutions that their downside risk will always be insured by such bailouts—an argument currently being used to discourage International Monetary Fund lending to Russia and the East Asian economies in crisis[1].

Who Should be Regulated?

As discussed in the paper, systemic risk is associated with banking crises for two reasons. First, banks are special in that their failure is considered costly to society. Second, banks are more fragile and highly leveraged (low cash to asset ratios, high short term to total debt and liabilities payable on demand at par value) than nonbanks and therefore more susceptible to problems.

More recently, the derivatives market has also been viewed as a potential source of systemic risk because of its concentration, lack of transparency and interconnectedness. All of these features, along with uncertainty in valuing credit risks, can potentially lead to liquidity problems in securities markets.

---

1. For a discussion of some of these issues, see "The Role of Governments and Markets in International Banking Crises: The Case of East Asia" by Barth, Brumbaugh, Ramesh and Yago, forthcoming in *Research in Financial Services*, JAI Press Inc., 1998.

In relation to derivatives however, Dr. Hunter asserts that the low cost of hedging risk has made them a competitive alternative to more traditional interest-bearing securities. He argues that bid-ask spreads have declined, indicating greater liquidity in the derivatives market, citing a study that shows that markets are not particularly concentrated (Edwards, 1996) and defaults are independent across dealers and over time. Since nonneutralities arise due to informational deficiencies and consequently high transaction costs, derivatives tend to reduce the impact of monetary policy (as it would when money is assumed to be neutral).

Can systemic risk propagate through the markets for derivatives as well? This issue is still unresolved and there is some concern that insofar as banks participate actively in securities markets, they would be adversely affected by a liquidity crunch in these markets. Depositors might also doubt the solvency of their bank under such conditions.

Aglietta, for instance, makes the point that market illiquidity can force banks acting as market makers to rely on dynamic hedging and to effectively transmit the liquidity gap to underlying markets. According to him, "The most insuperable difficulty to reach a correct estimate of credit losses is the fact that the correlation between the stochastic processes governing default probabilities and financial market variables is unknown." This has led Duffee (1994) to conclude that the joint stochastic behavior of defaults and credit exposure could result in a serious underestimation of credit risk. With respect to the Barings crisis of February 1995, Aglietta also observes that "absent actions by regulators, uncertainty could have induced dealers to forfeit their positions causing SIMEX to collapse; which would have provoked a slump in the Japanese Stock Exchange, thus worsening insolvency problems of Japanese banks." Aglietta also refers to the finding of the Fisher Report of September 1994, which acknowledged a widening gap between the ability of financial firms to manage their own risks and their inability to assess the riskiness of other participants.

Dr. Hunter would argue that regulators are not much better at doing this.

Instead, he suggests regulation such as the Federal Reserve Board of Governor's precommitment proposal. This proposal provides an incentive-based approach to capital regulation, in which banks themselves choose the level of capital suitable to their portfolio. A penalty is assessed if this level of capital is inadequate ex post. In this way, regulators can utilize the existing risk assessment technology of banks while providing banks with an incentive to monitor themselves.

To the extent that the potential for a crisis exists, Dr. Hunter suggests that there is indeed a role for regulation, if only to provide a framework within which agents have an incentive to form a realistic assessment of their risks. Active intervention is only advocated in situations in which negative externalities or the cost to society are likely to be significant.

Conclusion

The paper by Dr. Hunter points to the inadequacy of the theoretical literature with regard to the role of evolving financial institutions and their impact on economic growth. An understanding of these interlinkages would help in the design of appropriate regulation, which—if applied in the wrong context—could inhibit growth. Dr. Hunter also highlights the essential elements of a theory that could incorporate a systemic crisis, and suggests regulation to better deal with the problem.

References

Aglietta, M. (January 1996), "Financial Market Failures and Systemic Risk," CEPII Working Paper No. 96-01.

Duffee, G. (1994), "On Measuring Credit Risks of Derivatives Instruments," Federal Reserve Board, September.

Fisher Report, 1994, *Public disclosure of market and credit risks by financial intermediaries,* BIS, September.

Minsky, Hyman P. (1994). "Financial Instability and the Decline (?) of Banking: Public Policy Implications." Working Paper No. 127, The Jerome Levy Economics Institute of Bard College.

Schwartz A., 1992, Real and pseudo financial crises, in M. Bordo ed, *Financial Crisis,* vol I, chap 1, Cambridge University Press.

Systemic Risk, Contagion, and the East Asian Financial Crisis

Philip F. Bartholomew*
Chief Economist, Democratic Staff
Committee on Banking and Financial Services
U.S. House of Representatives

Gerard Caprio Jr.*
Head, Financial Sector Research
Development Research Group
World Bank

*Philip F. Bartholomew is Chief Economist on the U.S. House of Representatives' Committee on Banking and Financial Services. Gerard Caprio Jr. is Head, Financial Sector Research in the World Bank's Development Research Group. Any views expressed are those of the authors and do not necessarily reflect those of the Committee on Banking and Financial Services or the World Bank. The authors thank Sarah C. Clark and Kori L. Egland for research assistance.

During the 1980s, considerable attention was given to the U.S. thrift institution crisis and problems in commercial banking both in the United States and in a variety of industrial and developing countries. In the literature concerned with regulatory reforms proposed to fix many of the problems that contributed to these financial difficulties, interest developed in two related subjects. There is considerable literature that was developed by economists focusing on the causes and consequences of the banking crises that occurred in many countries during the 1920s and 1930s. Many of the reforms implemented in the 1930s were aimed at preventing recurrence of these crises, but these reforms also may have unnecessarily restricted activities or unwisely channeled activities of financial institutions. To those considering reforms in the 1980s and 1990s, it was therefore important to understand better the causes and consequences of financial crises so that any reforms would not make the financial sector susceptible to financial crisis while improving its efficiency and effectiveness.

Financial markets were subsequently deregulated in the 1980s and 1990s in an attempt to make them more market oriented. During this time, and seemingly in response to advocates of a market approach to reform of the financial sector, some regulators began to warn of systemwide problems or risks inherent in banking. The term systemic risk was eventually adopted to refer to the threat of systemwide failures that could lead to a collapse of public confidence, serious economic downturns and other macroeconomic ills. This threat was associated with regulatory closure of banks or other depository institutions. But until the early 1990s, little was written on the subject of systemic risk. As is discussed below, a number of studies directly address systemic risk, its definition, its causes and consequences, and possible means of addressing systemic risk and systemic events.[1]

The study of systemic risk is slightly different than the study of financial crisis. The consequence of a systemic event is a financial crisis. Those examining systemic risk, however, generally approach the

---

1.   See, for example, Davis (1992), Baer and Klingebiel (1995), Bartholomew (1998), Bartholomew and Whalen (1995), Bartholomew, Mote, and Whalen (1995), Caprio and Klingebiel (1996), Eisenbeis (1997, 1995), Goldstein (1995), Gup (1998), Kaufman (1995, 1996), Mishkin (1995), Schwartz (1995), Lindgren, Garcia, and Saal (1996).

subject in response to those that argue market orientation for financial regulatory reform has dangerous consequences. Many of the tools for reducing systemic risk, such as deposit guarantees, or for addressing systemic events, such as the central bank lender-of-last-resort facility, have undesirable consequences such as moral hazard. If, in order to maintain public confidence in a financial system, government-provided safety-net tools transfer risk from the risk-taker to the government, then the risk-taker has an incentive to undertake greater risk. A better understanding of systemic risk and systemic events is necessary, therefore, in order to construct a regulatory framework that both reduces the threat and consequences of systemic risk while not creating more risk or unduly or unfairly subsidizing players in financial markets.

Events over the past several months have refocused attention on financial crisis. In East Asia, these events in 1997-98 involve the financial sector as well as the real sector, and certainly appear to qualify as systemic, in at least one of the senses developed below. It is important, however, to more fully understand problems in Thailand, Korea and Indonesia in the correct context of systemic risk and financial crisis, or subsequent problems with substantial consequences could occur.

Systemic Risk

Although the term systemic risk seems widely used in discussion of banking and finance, there is no clear consensus regarding the precise definition of the term.[2] There are a few aspects of its definition, however, on which there appears wide agreement. First, a systemic event involves some element of externality (i.e., it entails costs to parties other than the stockholders, depositors and other creditors whose financial decisions may have contributed to the event). Second, a systemic event must have a sizable effect on the real economy, resulting in a loss in aggregate output.

---

2.   Although the term systemic risk has been used fairly widely since the early 1980s, no works can be found addressing it specifically until the 1990s. Davis (1992), Bartholomew and Whalen (1995), Bartholomew, Mote, and Whalen (1995), Gup (1998), Kaufman (1995, 1996), Mishkin (1995), Schwartz (1995), and Eisenbeis (1997), present overviews of systemic risk, suggest alternative definitions of the term, and relate systemic risk to the more-often discussed term financial crisis. What emerges from this literature, however, is that there is disagreement over its definition.

Bartholomew, Mote, and Whalen (1995) offer the following definition: "In very general terms, systemic risk is the risk of a collapse or major malfunctioning of the banking or financial system that results in significant costs to the real economy, as opposed to the failure of one or a few individual banks." This definition argues that there are two types of a systemic event.

Contagion

The first type of systemic event is contagion. In the parlance of banking economists, contagion refers to widespread bank runs. A general definition of bank contagion is where a disturbance at one financial institution (or in a financial market) is transmitted with deleterious and real economic consequences to one or more other financial institutions (or financial markets). Contagion is well discussed in the literature (see, for example, Gilbert [1988], Kaufman [1986, 1992]), and some argue that it represents the only type of systemic event (see Kaufman [1995]).

Collapse

Bartholomew and Whalen (1995), Bartholomew, Mote, and Whalen (1995), and Caprio and Klingebiel (1996) suggest another form of systemic event not associated with a contagion but fitting the aforementioned definition. Financial crises can be said to have occurred where a substantial portion of an economy's financial sector has developed problems sufficiently significant as to render the sector insolvent, meaning that net worth is zero or negative. In this type of "silent" banking crisis, there may or may not be individual or systemwide liquidity shortages, but the crisis is real in that the negative net worth is the financial counterpart of a real sector misallocation of resources. These events, such as those occurring in the Nordic countries and in numerous developing economies in the late 1980s and early 1990s, had as proximate causes exogenous shocks (such as a decline in the terms of trade) or some internally generated over-investment (typically related to real estate finance). As noted by Schwartz (1995), internally generated events are typically the result of a too-easy monetary policy that results in price inflation and high nominal interest rate volatility. If such an event is accompanied by real effects, the event may be considered systemic since it affects the entire system.

Widespread banking panics and bank runs, whether resulting from or causing contagion or merely the result of systemwide collapse of a substantial portion of the banking industry, are at the heart of systemic risk. A systemic risk must also involve real economic consequences from a financial sector disruption in order to be truly systemic.

Factors Affecting Severity of Systemic Risk

According to Bartholomew and Whalen (1995) and Bartholomew, Mote, and Whalen (1995), there are several factors that affect the severity of systemic risk. These include the degree to which financial markets are connected. The connectivity of financial markets domestically and internationally has increased dramatically and should be expected to further increase. But connectivity is only a means by which problems are transmitted. It is not clear that increased connectivity increases systemic risk. In fact, because of the nature of financial market efficiency, it is also possible that increased connectivity, when accompanied with better information and greater diversification, will reduce systemic risk.

Two other factors affecting systemic risk are somewhat related to each other. First, most would argue that portfolio concentration can contribute to increases in the likelihood of systemic events. An example of this has been financial difficulties in the United States, Canada, the Nordic countries, Thailand and Japan in commercial real estate markets; more broadly, Caprio and Wilson (1997) find portfolio concentration a leading proximate cause of banking crises, and Barth, Caprio and Levine (1998) find that countries in which banks are allowed to have broader powers are less likely to undergo a banking crisis.

Another critical factor affecting systemic risk is information. In fact, Mishkin (1995) suggests that discussion of systemic risk should focus on potential disruptions of information flows rather than financial flows. Information has both costs and benefits. As greater information is available in markets, financial efficiency should increase. However, as greater information is made available, new areas requiring information may develop. This can increase systemic risk if the required information cannot service the increasingly financial sector.

One point on which there is some consensus on systemic risk is that it can be increased by uncertainty. In normal times, players in a financial market are comfortable with the set of risks to which they are exposed. If a new instrument is introduced or a new market arrangement is established, financial participants tend to become more conservative until the new development is best understood. Uncertainty can be created by banking authorities by their actions in supervising or closing troubled financial institutions.

Addressing Systemic Events

Regardless of the ultimate consensus on the term systemic risk, both types of events have occurred and are safety and soundness issues (see Lindgren, Garcia, and Saal [1996]). Both require intervention techniques once they have occurred, and the risk of either may be reduced through static or dynamic bank regulation and supervision. However, the different types of systemic events require different methods of intervention and probably require different, possibly conflicting, strategies for risk reduction *a priori*.

Central bank liquidity support can deal with most contagions. Although there are disagreements over the efficiency of different tools that can deliver this liquidity, central bank capacity to deal with a contagion is fairly well established. Because the public does not rely solely on central banks for dealing with contagion, government guarantees (typically in the form of deposit insurance) are used to reduce the threat of a collapse of public confidence, thus reducing systemic risk. Both central-bank-liquidity support, a means to address a systemic event, and deposit guarantees, a means to reduce systemic risk *a priori*, have the negative consequence of potentially creating a moral hazard that can prove costly to regulators. As Bartholomew and Whalen [1995] and Bartholomew, Mote, and Whalen [forthcoming] point out, however, bank supervision can be used to reduce or contain this moral hazard.

It is less clear how to deal with exogenous shocks or internally generated financial bubbles. Certainly, monetary policy targeted at overall price stability contributes to a reduced risk of financial bubbles, but it is unclear that it is a general panacea. Moreover, once a financial collapse has occurred, it is less clear what general policy or policies exist for dealing with the consequences. If a substantial portion of a financial sector becomes insolvent, it is possible that temporary nationalization of some or all of the financial sector is best—but this is unclear. If there is a collapse of financial-asset prices, it may be that reflation of those prices is warranted—but this is unclear as well. Unfortunately, too little study has been devoted to these possibilities. It does seem evident, however, that policies and tools devised for dealing with contagion types of systemic events are not necessarily applicable. Far more study of systemic risk and systemic events is required.

There does appear to be consensus on some policies that can help reduce systemic risk, in addition to sound bank regulation and supervision, the lender-of-last-resort facility, and deposit guarantees. But these policies also do not represent general solutions. For example, invoking a stable monetary policy can structurally reduce systemic risk, but it is less clear what role monetary policy should take once a systemic event has taken place. Greater disclosure by market players may also increase information and reduce uncertainty. But many argue that less disclosure is warranted in dealing with a systemic event. This is especially true when considering that many policies such as providing liquidity support or offering government deposit guarantees can create a moral hazard that has its own cost implications.

Finally, although a fixed and well-known closure rule for failed institutions seems to make prudent sense for a well-supervised and regulated financial system, it is also important to explore the consequences of such a rule if a substantial portion of a financial sector is in trouble. It can be argued that closure of problem institutions can be accommodated through sale to other parties, but this may not be feasible if the economy is too weak. Moreover, reliance on foreign investment in the banking or financial sector could result in a host of undesirable problems for economies suffering a financial crisis.

The Asian Crises: Contagion?

Many commentators of the recent financial crises in the Asian countries of Thailand, Korea and Indonesia make overall reference to the "Asian contagion." Such reference implies that events in one country led to deleterious events in the other countries. Some commentators even suggested that problems in these three countries could spread to Japan. Unfortunately, such references misrepresent recent problems in Southeast Asia and Japan, and could lead to development of an inappropriate policy response.

Contagion Versus Spillover

Although it is unclear that economists have formally defined either term, and it is true that definitions are unfortunately arbitrary, the terms contagion and spillover seem to have particular meanings to economists. Both may be related to systemic risk and financial crisis, but they are certainly not synonymous.

To students of banking, contagion has a very specific meaning. As discussed above, contagion refers to the transmission of a financial disturbance from one financial institution, market or other arrangement to other financial players. Such disturbances may or may not have subsequent long-term effects, but the disturbance affects financial activity and there are probably at least short-term consequences.

A contagion, in financial terms, relates to a collapse of confidence by creditors to financial intermediaries. Absent deposit guarantees or other regulatory safety nets, if a single bank runs into financial difficulty, its depositors would be rational to withdraw their funds as soon as possible in order to assure themselves that the troubled institution would make good on the deposit. This isolated bank run turns into a contagion if the failure of one institution undermines depositor confidence in general and runs ensue at other institutions.

Such a contagion can occur at nonbank financial institutions or in financial markets where information is asymmetric. For example, if the collapse of the Thai banking system undermines creditor confidence in other countries with regard to their banks, then it can be said that there is a contagion. But, if banking systems in both countries were insolvent or in serious trouble in the first place, then it cannot be said that the collapse of one caused a collapse of public confidence

leading to the collapse of the other. There appeared to be a simultaneous rush by investors to exit these economies, but one event did not
cause the other, it only happened to precede it.

If, on the other hand, devaluation of the Korean currency, the
won, reduced confidence in other Southeast Asian currencies, it could
be said that the Korean devaluation had a contagion effect. Such an
effect, however, should be distinguished from the expected adjustments in foreign exchange markets.

If one country's interest rates and/or exchange rates adjust, there
will be consequences to its trade and capital flows. Depending upon
the volume of flows, countries with trade and financial relationships
with the devaluing country will suffer spillover effects. Spillover
effects can be considered the indirect consequences of an economic
action. In the case of the Southeast Asian financial crisis, spillover
effects from the devaluation are not yet fully realized because
exchange rates in these markets have not yet stabilized.

An alternative explanation for the Asian contagion is that the
economies in Thailand, Korea and Indonesia were suffering speculative bubbles that finally burst. All three economies suffered these bubbles and their financial sectors were weak and vulnerable to shocks.
There were spillover consequences from the economic problems and
devaluations of mid-1997, but there might not necessarily have been
any spread of the problem—all three suffered similar problems in the
first place. Similarly, Caprio (1998) shows that all three compared
unfavorably with a sample of East Asian and Latin American countries in the adequacy of their financial regulatory environment,
another problem in common.

The exchange rates relative to the United States of Korea, Japan,
Thailand and Indonesia are shown in Figure 1. Korea, Thailand and
Indonesia obviously devalued from a pegged or managed-pegged
exchange rate regime. It is unclear, however, from looking at
exchange rates alone that the devaluations were related in a causal
sense or whether they moved together.

Figure 1: Daily Exchange Rates

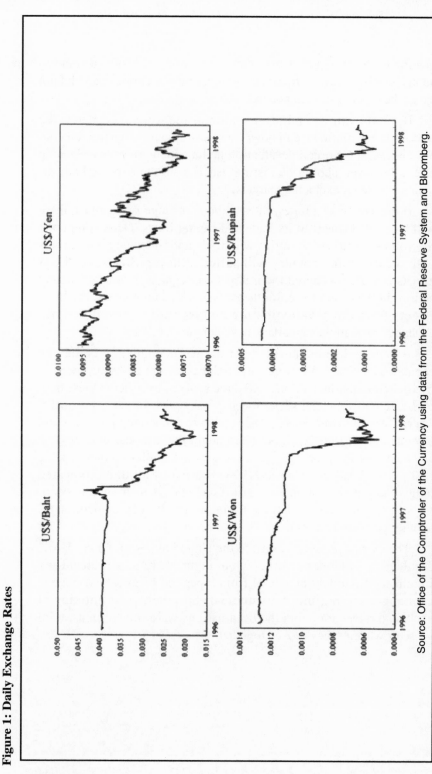

Source: Office of the Comptroller of the Currency using data from the Federal Reserve System and Bloomberg.

Figure 2 shows the coefficient of variation for the same currencies. Except for Japan, it seems that in general the variation in these exchange rates were fairly harmonious. One should expect that if a contagion had occurred, substantial variation would be seen in one market before being transmitted to others.

A similar analysis can be made using information on the same four countries' stock markets. Figure 3 shows declines in the stock market indices of Korea, Japan, Thailand and Indonesia. Figure 4 shows the coefficient of variation associated with the movements of these indices. Again, it can be seen that except for Japan, the indicator in the three countries moved together; the decline of the yen, as well as the banking crisis in Japan (usually dated as having commenced in 1991), clearly preceded the Thai crisis.

Financial Collapse and the Role of External Lending

More detailed analysis is required to fully sort out how the exchange rates and stock markets of Korea, Thailand and Indonesia moved over time during the crisis. Certainly, it is probably the case that because of information disruptions and experience gained with this crisis that Southeast Asian markets will suffer some contagion effects. For example, disturbances occurring well into the crisis will probably cause some confidence loss to varying degree in all Southeast Asian financial markets. Such contagion effects may dissipate if greater information about these markets is obtained by financial players, depending of course on how it compares with what is already discounted in the market.

The Southeast Asian crisis may better be explained looking at the role external lending had on the three economies. The three countries were some of the world's largest borrowers.

As of June 30, 1997, with $103 billion borrowed, Korea was the largest borrower from the Group of 10, European Monetary Union and Scandinavian countries (not considering borrowing from these lending countries). Thailand was the third-largest borrower ($69 billion) behind Brazil. Indonesia was the sixth-largest borrower ($59 billion) behind Russia and Mexico.

Figure 2: Monthly Coefficient of Variation for Selected Asian Daily U.S. Dollar Exchange Rates 1996 to Present

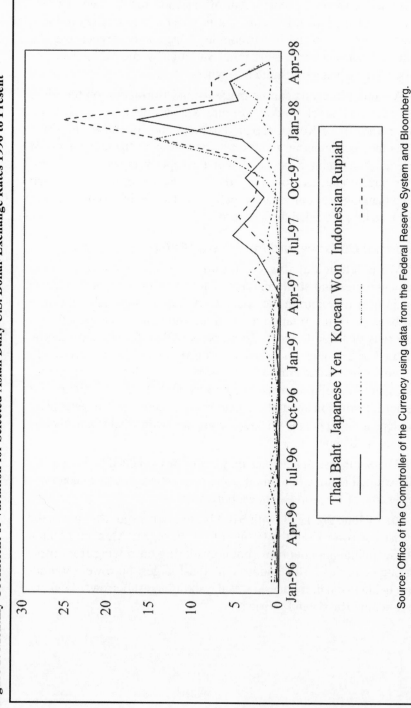

Thai Baht Japanese Yen Korean Won Indonesian Rupiah

Source: Office of the Comptroller of the Currency using data from the Federal Reserve System and Bloomberg.

Figure 3: Daily Stock Indices

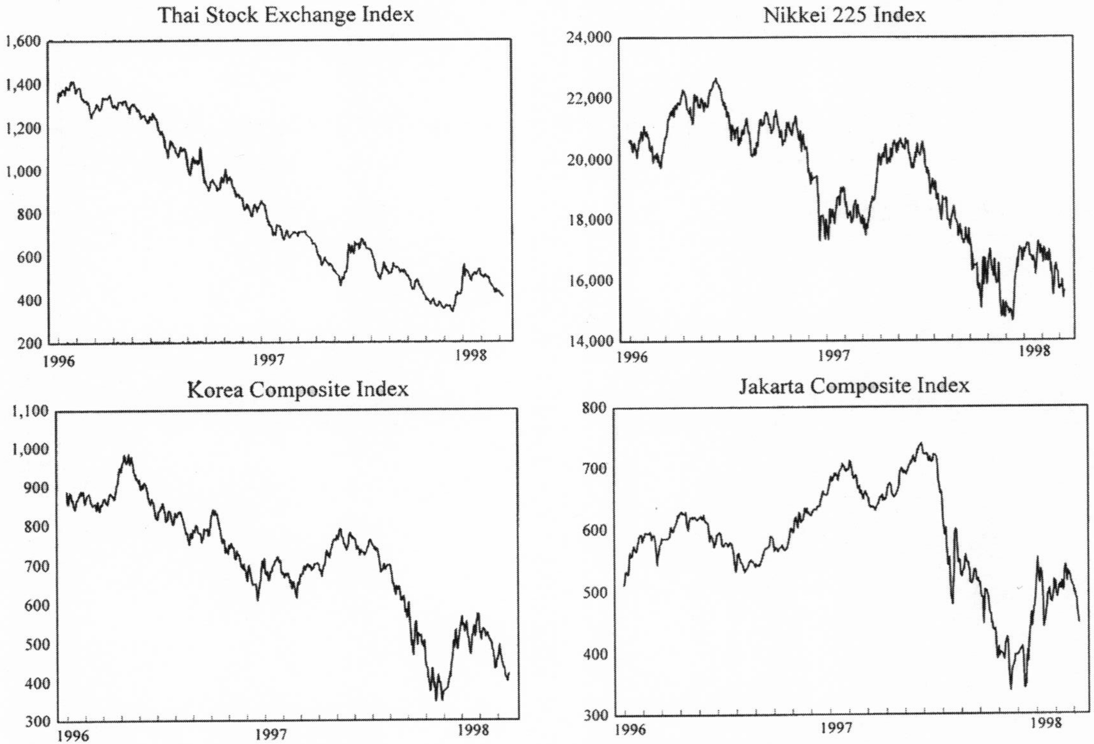

Source: Office of the Comptroller of the Currency using data from Bloomberg.

Figure 4: Monthly Coefficient of Variation for Selected Asian Daily Stock Market Indices 1996 to Present

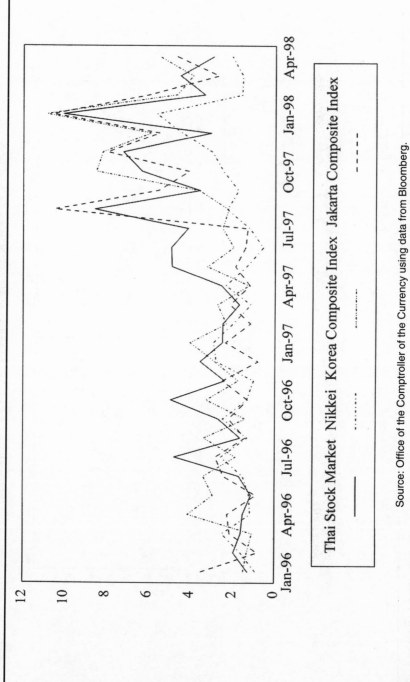

Source: Office of the Comptroller of the Currency using data from Bloomberg.

The major lenders to Thailand and Korea were Japanese financial institutions. Japanese financial institutions also were large lenders to Korea. As can be seen in Figure 5, there is an interesting pattern in this lending to three countries in question. Beginning in 1995, when Japan began to acknowledge problems in its financial sector, lending to Southeast Asia from Japanese institutions leveled. As can be seen in Figure 6, this was true for Japanese bank international lending in general.

One explanation for the Southeast Asian crisis is that it was three speculative bubbles developing in three countries with similar export-based economies. Speculative bubbles require continued increased financing. Although other countries substituted for the reduced loan growth to Korea, Thailand and Indonesia, the change in Japanese financing may be a probable trigger for the collapse of the bubbles.

In that the external financing of each of the three countries is similar, it is possible to conclude that the crises in the three countries were fairly simultaneous events. Rather than a collapse in one leading to a collapse in another or both, the three economies appear to have collapsed together. All bubbles collapse eventually—that is why they are bubbles—and in this case the rapid expansion of lending by Japanese banks appeared to be a factor in the run-up, so the leveling off of lending can be argued to have played a role in the timing of the collapse.

Although problems in Southeast Asia may spill over to Japan and other countries, subsequent revelations about problems in the Japanese financial sector have their roots deeper than the Southeast Asian crisis.

Figure 5: Loans from Banks to Various Asian Countries

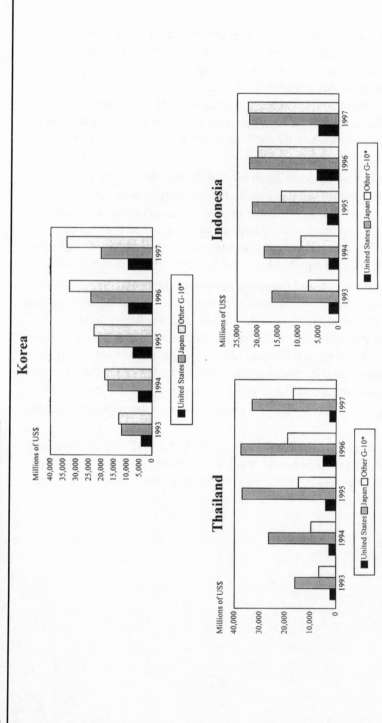

* Not including Switzerland in 1993 through 1997 and not including Canada in 1993.
Source: Office of the Comptroller of the Currency using data from Bank for International Settlements.

Figure 6: International Bank Lending by Japanese Banks to Asian Countries

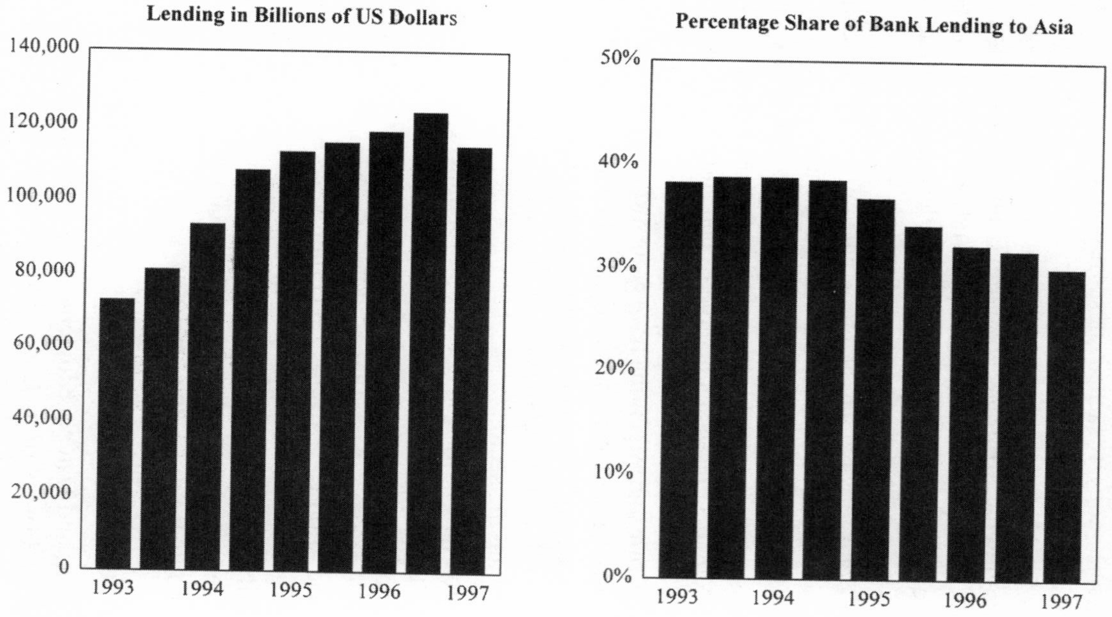

Source: Office of the Comptroller of the Currency using data from Bank for International Settlements.

Conclusions

Though much more is known now about systemic risk than when financial reforms were debated in the late 1980s and early 1990s, economists have not yet reached consensus on many aspects—including its definition. Economic semantics, moreover, are important when the stakes of public policy actions can be so great. Although definitions are somewhat arbitrary, economists need to establish certain conventions in order for the appropriate study of the causes and consequences of and prescriptions for systemic events and financial crises.

It is difficult to conclude, at a time when many are lamenting the spread of crises, that authorities do respond to these events. For example, in the 1980s, the Chilean and Argentine economies experienced banking crises relative to the gross national product that were many times the problems that the United States had and at least as serious as those in East Asia appear to be at this stage. Not surprisingly, authorities in both Chile and Argentina have gone further than many in trying to improve the incentive compatibility of their regulatory systems. It is likely that taxpayers will ensure that similar changes occur in more countries, in effect, raising the cost of the safety net that is being supplied to the banking sector.

The good news, then, is that this development will mean that in the future there likely will be fewer crises originating in the banking sector worldwide than in the last couple of decades. The bad news, however, is that as a result of this regulatory response, nonbank financial intermediation will grow—as it certainly has even in the past two years in Argentina. Given that nonbank finance in many countries is exceptionally lightly regulated, and given the possibility of spillovers from nonbanks to banks, the era of financial crises then may not be ending, but rather just getting underway.

References

Baer, Herbert, and Daniela Klingebiel, "Systemic Risk When Depositors Bear Losses: Five Case Studies," in *Research in Financial Services and Public Policy*, (P. F. Bartholomew and G. G. Kaufman, eds.), Vol., 7, pp. 195-302.

Barth, James R., "Comment on Sources of Risk," in *Research in Financial Services and PublicPolicy*, (P. F. Bartholomew and G. G. Kaufman, eds.), Vol., 7, pp. 171-174.

_____, Gerard Caprio, and Ross Levine, "Financial Regulation and Performance: Cross-Country Evidence," mimeo, The World Bank, 1998, and forthcoming in Caprio and Schmidt-Hebbel, eds. *Banking, Financial Integration, and Macroeconomic Stability*, 1999.

Bartholomew, Philip F., "Banking Consolidation and Systemic Risk," *Brookings-Wharton Papers on Financial Services*, 1998.

Bartholomew, Philip F. and Gary Whalen, "Fundamentals of Systemic Risk," in *Research in Financial Services and Public Policy*, (P. F. Bartholomew and G. G. Kaufman, eds.),Vol., 7, pp. 3-17.

Bartholomew, Philip F., Larry R. Mote, and Gary Whalen, "The Definition of Systemic Risk," presented at the Annual Meetings of the Western Economic Association in San Diego, CA, July 8, 1995.

Caprio, Gerard, Jr., and Daniela Klingebiel, "Bank Insolvency: Bad Luck, Bad Policy, or Bad Banking?," paper presented at the World Bank Annual Bank Conference on Development Economics, Washington, April 25-26, 1996.

Caprio, Gerard, Jr., and Berry Wilson, 1997. "On Not Putting All the Eggs in One Basket: The Role of Diversification in Banking," presented at the World Bank-IMF Annual Meetings Seminar on Building Robust Financial Systems, September.

Davis, E. P., *Financial Fragility, and Systemic Risk*, Oxford; New York; Toronto and Melbourne: Oxford University Press, Clarendon Press, 1992.

Eisenbeis, Robert A., "Bank Deposits and Credit as Sources of Systemic Risk," *Economic Review*, Federal Reserve Bank of Atlanta, Third Quarter, 1997.

Eisenbeis, Robert A., "Systemic Risk: Bank Deposits and Credit," in *Research in Financial Services and Public Policy*, (P. F. Bartholomew and G. G. Kaufman, eds.), Vol., 7, pp. 177-194.

Gilbert, R. Alton, "A Re-Examination of the History of Bank Failures, Contagion, and Banking Panics," *Bank Structure and Competition*, Federal Reserve Bank of Chicago (May 1988).

Goldstein, Morris, "International Aspects of Systemic Risk," in *Research in Financial Services and Public Policy*, (P. F. Bartholomew and G. G. Kaufman, eds.), Vol., 7, pp. 177-194.

Kaufman, George G., "Bank Failures, Systemic Risk, and Bank Regulation, *Cato Journal*, Vol. 16, No. 1, (Spring/Summer 1996).

Kaufman, George G., "Comment on Systemic Risk," in *Research in Financial Services and Public Policy*, (P. F. Bartholomew and G. G. Kaufman, eds.), Vol., 7, 1995, pp. 47-52.

Kaufman, George G., "Bank Contagion: Theory and Evidence," Federal Reserve Bank of Chicago Working Papers Series, June 1992.

Kaufman, George G., "Banking Risk in Historical Perspective," *Bank Structure and Competition*, Federal Reserve Bank of Chicago, 1986.

Lindgren, Carl-Johan, Gillian Garcia, and Matthew I. Saal, *Bank Soundness and Macroeconomic Policy*, Washington, D.C.: International Monetary Fund, 1996.

Mishkin, Frederic S., "Comment on Systemic Risk," in *Research in Financial Services and Public Policy*, (P. F. Bartholomew and G. G. Kaufman, eds.), Vol., 7, pp. 31-45.

Schwartz, Anna J., "Systemic Risk and the Macroeconomy," in *Research in Financial Services and Public Policy*, (P. F. Bartholomew and G. G. Kaufman, eds.), Vol., 7, pp. 19-30.

Section Seven

Flight-to-Quality in Life Insurance Company Investments

George W. Fenn*
Senior Research Associate
The Milken Institute

*The views expressed in this paper are those of the author and not necessarily those of the Milken Institute.

Abstract

Life insurance companies historically have invested heavily in information-intensive corporate-finance markets. This article provides evidence on the flight-to-quality in life insurance industry investments that began in the early 1990s and continues to this day. It also evaluates potential explanations for the flight-to-quality, including major regulatory changes, fundamental shifts in policyholder perceptions of the industry's financial stability, changes in product design, competitive pressures in the financial services industry, and the evolution of capital markets. It concludes that nonregulatory factors are far more important than regulatory factors in explaining both the initial flight-to-quality and its persistence.

Introduction

The life insurance industry is an important, if underexamined industry. With more than $2.5 trillion in assets at year-end 1997, it remains the second-largest financial services industry in the United States. It is about half the size of the commercial banking industry and as large as the thrift, property/casualty insurance, and finance company industries combined. Moreover, the life insurance industry has long specialized in making information-intensive investments in a rich variety of corporate finance markets, including corporate bonds (investment-grade and high-yield), private placements, commercial mortgages and private equity.

Since 1990, however, the industry's investment portfolio has undergone a dramatic and sustained shift from private, relatively illiquid and higher credit-risk investments to public, highly liquid and lower credit-risk investments. In this respect, life insurance companies arguably have become both a less important and less interesting type of financial intermediary. The flight-to-quality in life insurance company investments has gone largely unnoticed and consequently, there is no widespread agreement on its cause.[1] This paper describes the flight-to-quality and explores potential explanations for its occurrence.

---

1. An exception is Prowse (1997), who discusses the credit crunch in the below-investment-grade private placement market.

One possibility, suggested by the experience of banks and thrift institutions in the early 1990s, is that it occurred in response to major regulatory changes, including the adoption of insurance industry risk-based capital requirements. However, a careful examination of these changes suggests that their role in sparking the flight-to-quality were probably minimal. In particular, new regulatory requirements appear to have placed few binding constraints on life insurance company investments, as was certainly the case in the thrift industry and arguably so in the banking industry.

An alternative explanation is that the investment shifts were undertaken in response to the concerns of policyholders. Until 1990, the life insurance industry had an unparalleled reputation for financial stability dating back to the Depression. That year, policyholder perceptions of the industry's financial stability changed dramatically with the announcements of asset-quality problems of several large insurers (Fenn and Cole, 1994). A flight-to-quality by policyholders to safer-appearing insurers may have triggered a flight-to-quality by insurers to safer-appearing (as well as actually safer) investments. There are ample indications that the policyholder flight-to-quality did occur, and in response to slowing sales, insurers would have faced strong incentives to reduce their concentration of higher-risk assets.

The persistence of the shift in life insurance company investments—long after the industry's financial condition has improved and policyholders' immediate concerns have abated—suggests that other factors are also at work. One possibility is an evolution in life insurance product design, away from products in which a significant portion of the return is implicitly linked to investment performance toward products in which most of the return is fully guaranteed. These design shifts have come about because of long-standing policyholder dissatisfaction with the opaqueness of the methods insurers use to allocate returns to policyholders. The shift toward products with more fully guaranteed returns implies that insurers bear a greater portion of their portfolio investment risks; in response they may have chosen to limit the riskiness of their investments.

The remainder of this paper is organized as follows. The second section describes the life insurance industry's investment activities and documents the flight-to-quality that began in 1990 and continued through at least 1996. The third section describes key regulatory developments that could have altered the industry's investment mix, and assesses their probable influence in light of various empirical facts about timing and persistence of investment changes. The fourth section reviews the empirical and theoretical arguments favoring the view that portfolio adjustments were made in response to policy-holder concerns, while the fifth section offers some additional explanations for the flight-to-quality and why it persists. The sixth section concludes with some thoughts on how life insurance companies should structure investment portfolios and capital structures given the attitudes of policyholders toward insolvency risk.

Life Insurance Company Investments

Life insurance companies are unique among financial institutions and other institutional investors as major investors in three distinct corporate finance markets: publicly traded corporate bonds, private placements and commercial mortgage loans. In addition to playing a major role in these more mature markets, they have been among the earliest and largest investors in innovative new markets such as publicly traded, below-investment-grade bonds and private equity.

In the immediate postwar period, life insurance companies held nearly three-quarters of U.S. corporate bonds (Federal Reserve Board, Flow of Funds). Life insurance companies remain the single largest investor group in the public corporate bond market, though their market share has declined with the growth of pension funds and mutual funds. Crabbe and Forrey (1996) report that at year-end 1995, life insurance companies held almost 40 percent of the Merrill Lynch investment-grade index. Within the investment-grade sector, life insurance companies are overweighted toward triple-B and single-A issues, which Crabbe and Forrey interpret as "a compromise between the industry's demand for high yielding bonds and risk-based capital requirements."

In the private placement debt market, life insurance companies remain dominant. Private placements are securities, as defined under the 1933 Act, but are exempt from registration by virtue of their sale to a limited number of qualified institutional buyers (see Carey et al. [1993] for an extensive analysis of the private placement market and Prowse [1997] for a recent update.) In practical terms, private placements more nearly resemble bank loans than publicly issued corporate bonds; the major differences between the two are that private placements are typically longer-term, issued at fixed rather than floating interest rates, and involve fewer and looser covenants. On the other hand, private placements typically involve shorter maturities and more restrictive provisions than public bonds. Market participants estimate that life insurers purchase between 50 percent and 80 percent of private placements.[2]

Until recently, an especially important segment of the private placement market was the below-investment-grade segment. As in the public below-investment-grade market, this market involved loans to smaller, riskier companies. Prior to the development of the public high-yield market, these companies had virtually no alternative to the private placement market for obtaining long-term, fixed-rate financing. Though no precise estimates are available, historical accounts suggest that life insurance companies may have accounted for virtually all of the lending in this market (Shapiro, 1977). As discussed in Prowse (1997), this market has virtually shut down since 1990.

In the commercial mortgage loan market, life insurance companies also have been major investors, though not as dominant as in the corporate bond and private placement markets. At year-end 1990, they held 28 percent of nonresidential, nonfarm mortgages, and 10 percent of multifamily mortgages—or about 23 percent of all commercial mortgages, second to commercial banks. Life insurance companies have traditionally been the largest source of permanent, or long-term financing on new buildings (Jones, 1977); commercial banks, by contrast, provide a large share of the shorter-term construction loans. The industry's market share declined rather sharply in the 1990s as a result of the investment flight-to-quality; in the nonresidential segment, it fell from 28 percent at year-end 1990 to 21 percent at year-end 1996.

---

2.   This figure and the preceding discussion applies to the traditional or non-144A private placement market. The 144A private placement market, by contrast, attracts a much wider range of investors. 144A private placements can be freely traded among institutional investors, and many, especially in the below-investment-grade segment, are issued with registration rights. As a result, their structure is often closer to that of a public bond than a traditional private placement.

Life insurance companies were early investors in the public junk bond and private equity markets. Rasky (1986) estimates that insurance companies held $40 billion of junk bonds at year-end 1986, which at the time was about a third of the market. Their early involvement in the public junk bond market is not surprising given the expertise they acquired from years of below-investment-grade private placement investing. The industry's early involvement in the private equity market also grew out of its private placement activities. Historically, insurance companies financed their riskiest client companies by purchasing debt that had an equity feature, and in the 1970s they provided mezzanine debt to finance some of the earliest leveraged buyouts. With the growth of the private equity market in the 1980s, they began investing in private equity partnerships, in part, to generate additional mezzanine investments (Fenn, Liang, and Prowse, 1997).

Flight-to-Quality in Life Insurance Company Investments

Table 1 describes the composition of the life insurance industry's general account investments at year-ends 1990 and 1996. Using 1989 as the base year would be preferable for documenting the flight-to-quality, because portfolio adjustments began in 1990. However, 1990 is the earliest date for which the comprehensive balance sheet data included in Table 1 are available.

Table 1: General Account Assets of Life Insurance Companies

Assets	General Account Assets, Billions of Dollars		Share of General Account Assets, Percent		Percentage Growth, 1991–96	
	1990	1996	1990	1996	Total	Annual
Public bonds, investment-grade	492.2	915.4	40.0	52.9	86.0	10.9
"Information-intensive" assets	620.0	640.6	50.4	37.0	3.3	0.5
Private placements, investment-grade	165.5	248.6	13.4	14.4	50.2	7.0
Public bonds, below-investment-grade	45.1	37.4	3.7	2.2	-17.1	-3.1
Private placements, below-investment-grade	40.2	27.5	3.3	1.6	-31.6	-6.1
Mortgages, commercial	243.0	186.7	19.7	10.8	-23.2	-4.3
Mortgages, farm and residential	22.7	16.9	1.8	1.0	-25.6	-4.8
Real estate	31.8	37.2	2.6	2.1	17.0	2.6
Limited partnerships	28.7	23.1	2.3	1.3	-19.5	-3.6
Stocks	43.0	63.2	3.5	3.7	47.0	6.6

Table 1: General Account Assets of Life Insurance Companies *(continued)*

Assets	General Account Assets, Billions of Dollars		Share of General Account Assets, Percent		Percentage Growth, 1991–96	
	1990	1996	1990	1996	Total	Annual
Policy loans	62.3	98.1	5.1	5.7	57.5	7.9
Other	56.4	76.5	4.6	4.4	35.6	5.2
Total	1230.9	1730.6	100.0	100.0	40.6	5.8

Source: National Association of Insurance Commissioners

At year-end 1990, publicly traded investment-grade bonds accounted for 40 percent of the life insurance industry's general account assets.[3] These bonds included Treasuries and Agency securities in addition to investment-grade corporate issues. The remainder of the industry's investments—accounting for just over 50 percent of general account assets—consisted of investment-grade private placements, below-investment-grade corporate bonds, below-investment-grade private placements, mortgages, real estate, limited partnerships and stocks. I use the term "information-intensive" to describe these assets because they require significantly more *ex-ante* due diligence and *ex-post* monitoring than investment-grade bonds. Engaging in such costly information production is one of the fundamental roles of financial intermediaries.

Between 1990 and 1996, holdings of publicly traded investment-grade bonds increased 86 percent, or about 11 percent per year, so that by 1996 they accounted for 53 percent of general account assets, a share increase of 13 percentage points. Conversely, holdings of information-intensive assets were virtually unchanged, increasing 3 percent over the period, or about • percent per year. Thus, information-intensive assets as a share of general account assets declined to 37 percent.

To place these changes in perspective, loans and securities of U.S. banks increased at roughly the same rate as insurance company

---

3. The distinction between general account and separate account assets is discussed below. At year-end 1990, general account assets accounted for 89 percent of total industry assets.

investments over this period: 5.4 percent for bank investments and 5.8 percent for life insurance company investments. However, in banking, loans and securities grew at roughly similar rates; consequently, the mix of loans and securities was nearly unchanged.[4]

Life insurance companies pulled back especially sharply from investments in below-investment-grade securities and commercial mortgages. At year-end 1996, neither their holdings of publicly traded junk bonds or below-investment-grade private placements had recovered to their 1990 levels, despite a 38 percent increase in the size of the public junk bond market. Life insurers' commercial mortgage holdings fell 21 percent between 1990 and 1996, while the total size of the market was roughly unchanged.

Persistence and Timing of the Flight-to-Quality

Although the sharpest declines in information-intensive assets as a share of general account assets occurred in the 1991-93 period, declines continued through 1996, the latest period for which balance sheet data are available (see Figure 1). Thus, the flight-to-quality in life insurance investments is readily distinguishable from the normal balance sheet adjustments of financial institutions to downturns in the economy and credit markets. With respect to the onset of these adjustments, investment survey data from the American Council of Life Insurance indicates that a sharp falloff in below-investment-grade private placement investments began in the second quarter of 1990 (see Figure 2), while declines in commercial mortgage commitments became pronounced in early 1991 (see Figure 3).

---

4. Loans increased at a 5 percent annual rate while securities grew at a slightly greater 6.5 percent annual rate; securities increased from 24 percent of invested assets to 26 percent.

Figure 1: "Information-Intensive" Assets as Share of General Account

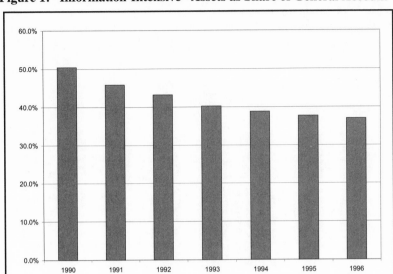

**Figure 2: New Private Placement Investments:
Below-Investment-Grade as Share of Total**

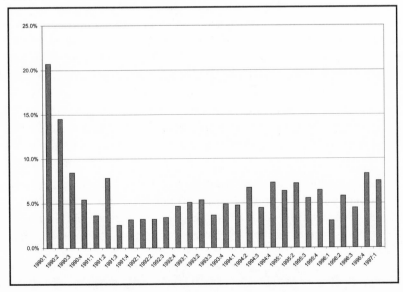

**Figure 3: New Commercial Mortgage Investments
as Share of Total New Investments**

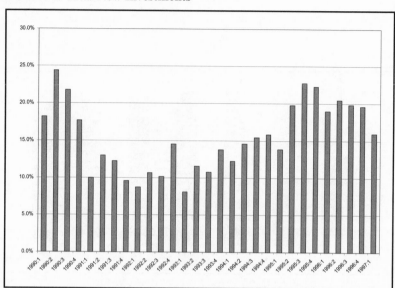

Regulatory Changes in the 1990s

The investment changes described above coincided with some of the most comprehensive insurance regulatory reforms in decades (see Klein [1995] for an extensive discussion of these reforms). Much of this activity was coordinated by the National Association of Insurance Commissioners (NAIC), an association of the chief insurance regulators of each state. Although the NAIC has no statutory authority, the states have long delegated to the NAIC the responsibility for establishing financial reporting requirements. The NAIC's other major responsibility includes developing "model" laws and regulations that state legislatures and regulatory authorities may, but need not, adopt.

Two regulatory developments, in particular, had the potential to significantly alter the industry's investment mix, and were much discussed in the industry trade press: the 1990 revision of the regulatory bond rating system and the 1993 adoption of risk-based capital standards.

Revision of the Regulatory Bond Rating System

For many years, the NAIC through its Securities Valuation Office (SVO) has rated bonds held by insurance companies—both publicly traded bonds and private placements—according to risk. The original purpose of the bond rating system was to enable the calculation of an appropriate Mandatory Securities Valuation Reserve (MSVR).[5] However, the bond rating system served the additional purpose of disclosure, informing policyholders and regulators of the riskiness of insurer portfolios. Since 1986, the below-investment-grade bond holdings of life insurers have been conveniently displayed in Schedule D of the statutory financial statement.

Under the old rating system that was used through 1989, there were four bond-rating categories (Table 2). Only the highest rated bonds, the so-called YES bonds, were considered investment-grade, while the remaining three categories were considered below-investment-grade. However, bonds that were rated below-investment-grade by the major rating services (double-B- and single-B-rated issues) were often rated investment-grade for regulatory purposes. Under the new rating system, adopted in June 1990, the rating system was expanded to six categories, and all bonds rated below-investment-grade by the major rating services were rated below-investment-grade for statutory purposes.

The effect of the new rating system on the reported holdings of below-investment-grade bonds of 41 large insurance companies is described in Table 3. In the aggregate, their below-investment-grade bond holdings increased 54 percent, from $28.9 billion at year-end 1989 to $44.4 billion at year-end 1990, as 39 of the 41 companies reported increases.[6] As a percentage of total bonds, below-investment-grade bonds of these 41 companies increased from 8.6 percent to 12.5 percent, while as a percentage of general account assets, they increased from 4.5 percent to 6.5 percent.

---

5.   Prior to the adoption of risk-based capital, statutory capital requirements were minimal and unrelated to any dimension of an insurance company's risk profile (see below). The MSVR required insurance companies to set aside additional reserves to cushion capital and surplus against bond and stock related investment losses.

6.   Not all of the increase, of course, was the result of the new rating system, as there were a significant number of corporate downgrades in 1990.

Table 2: NAIC Bond Ratings

NAIC Rating Designation	Equivalent Rating Agency Designation	NAIC Definition
Old System		
Yes	AAA, AA, A, BBB, BB, B	Investment-grade
No*	BB, B	Noninvestment-grade–average quality
No**	CCC or lower	Noninvestment-grade–below average quality
No	In or near default	In or near default
New System		
1	AAA, AA, A	Highest quality
2	BBB	High quality
3	BB	Medium quality
4	B	Low quality
5	CCC or lower	Lower quality
6	In or near default	In or near default
Source: Securities Valuation Office of the National Association of Insurance Commissioners		

Table 3: Below-Investment-Grade Bond Holdings of 41 Large Life Insurersᵃ

	1989	1990
Below-investment-grade bonds ($ billions)	28.9	44.3
As share of bonds:		
Total, all firms	8.6%	12.5%
Firm median	5.5%	8.0%
Number of firms greater than 20 percent	1	4
As share of general account assets:		
Total, all firms	4.5%	6.5%
Firm median	2.7%	4.1%
Number of firms greater than 20 percent	1	1
Source: National Association of Insurance Commissioners and Moody's Investors Service		
a. 41 life insurers rated by Moody's Investors Service at year-end 1989.		

New Bond Ratings and Life Insurance Company Investments

The new ratings imposed no significant constraints on insurance company investments in junk bonds. They might have done so had there been regulatory restrictions on junk bond holdings that were triggered under the new ratings. At the time, however, only two states had such limits (Arizona and New York), and they were set at 20 percent of assets. Even under the new rating system, few companies exceeded this limit, and those that did generally did so under the old system as well.

It is possible that the sudden increase in reported holdings under the new system helped focus the attention of policyholders on the composition of insurers' bond holdings, which in turn led insurers to withdraw from the market. But even this interpretation probably assigns too much importance to the new ratings. Fenn and Cole (1994) argue that prior to 1990, policyholders were generally unaware of insurance company junk bond holdings because they did not find it necessary to monitor insurer solvency. Policyholder interest in monitoring insurer solvency in general, and junk bond holdings in particular, was triggered by the publicity surrounding the announcement of large losses at First Executive in early 1990 (see below). Following the First Executive announcement, policyholders and the media likely would have focused on junk bond holdings using any available data, including that available under the old rating system. Smythe (1987) underscores this point when he presciently observes that "the general public is not at all aware that many of the [life insurance] products they buy are funded by BIG bonds. When questioned about this, many answer that they wouldn't buy these products if they knew of this fact."

Moreover, the controversy surrounding insurance company junk bond holdings may have been greater if the rating system had not been revised. Ratings under the old system differed from public ratings primarily because the system had been developed to accommodate private placements (Smythe, 1987). In assigning ratings to private placements, the SVO, as a starting point, attempted to gauge what the rating would be on a comparable public issue. For borderline issues (those that would be rated BB or B) the SVO would often assign investment-grade ratings in recognition of the greater protection of private placements.

As public high-yield bonds gradually became a significant component of insurer's below-investment-grade holdings, regulators faced a quandary over how to rate double-B and single-B issues. On the one hand, publicly traded double-B and single-B bonds did not have the investor protections of private placements. On the other hand, the regulatory definition of below-investment-grade in some respects encompassed lower rated bonds than the public definition. As a compromise, insurance regulators extended the practice of assigning investment-grade ratings to some issues rated BB and B.

Inevitably, controversy began to arise over the arbitrariness by which publicly rated double-B and single-B bonds were assigned regulatory ratings. Dissatisfaction with the rating system was compounded by anecdotal reports that insurance companies were pressuring the SVO to assign investment-grade ratings to bonds they held. Ultimately, the most credible and efficient resolution was for the SVO to simply adopt the use of public ratings.

Risk-Based Capital

The regulatory change that attracted the most attention was the introduction of risk-based capital requirements. The NAIC initially formed a risk-based capital task force in December 1990. The task force's first exposure draft was released in December 1991 and final risk-based capital standards were adopted in December 1992 to take effect at year-end 1993.

Until the adoption of risk-based capital standards, statutory capital requirements in the life insurance industry were minimal. For example, in New York, long regarded as one of the tougher regulatory jurisdictions, the minimum capital required to operate a life insurance company was $6 million, without regard to company size. Recognizing the inadequacy of the existing statutory capital requirements, the NAIC developed a risk-based formula that attempts to establish a prudent level of capital given a company's size and risk (Table 4, panel A). The NAIC also developed a companion set of regulatory guidelines that require stronger degrees of corrective action as a company's risk-based capital ratio falls below 100 percent (Table 4, panel B).

Although the risk-based capital formula identifies four components of risk—asset risk, insurance risk, interest rate and disintermediation risk and miscellaneous event risk—the asset risk component dominates the calculation, and hence received the most attention. Because below-investment-grade bonds, commercial mortgages, real estate and other long-term assets carry much higher risk weights than investment-grade bonds (Table 4, panel C), marginally capitalized companies face strong incentives to substitute investment-grade bonds for other assets.

Table 4: Life Insurance Risk-Based Capital

Panel A: Risk-Based Capital
Risk based capital (RBC) is a dollar measure of the minimum amount of capital that insurers are expected to maintain. The formula used to compute RBC divides life insurance risks into four components: asset risk (C1), insurance risk (C2), interest rate and disintermediation risk (C3), and miscellaneous business risk (C4). The formula is: $$RBC = ((C1 + C3)^2 + C2^2)^{1/2} + C4$$ where C1, C2, C3, and C4 are dollar measures arrived at by summing the product of a set of risk weights and various items from a company's statutory financial statement.

Panel B: Risk-Based Capital Ratios and Corrective Action
The risk-based capital ratio (RBCR) is the ratio of actual capital to RBC. As a company's actual capital falls below its RBC–that is, as the RBCR falls below 100%–successively stronger degrees of regulatory action are triggered:

RBCR Less Than:	Corrective Action
100%	Company must file plan of action with state regulator
75%	Regulators must investigate company and may require corrective action
50%	Regulators authorized to seize company
35%	Regulators must seize company

Panel C: Asset (C1) Risk and Risk Weights
In practice, the C1 component dominates the RBC calculation, especially for larger companies. C1 is the sum of asset risk weights multiplied by corresponding asset values. Select asset risk weights are:

Asset	Risk Weight
Class 1 bond	0.3%
Class 2 bond	1.0%
Class 3 bond	4.0%
Class 4 bond	9.0%
Class 5 bond	20.0%
Class 6 bond	30.0%
Residential mortgage–current	2.0%
Residential mortgage–delinquent	4.0%
Commercial mortgage–current[a]	1.5% - 9%
Commercial mortgage–delinquent[a]	6.0% - 15%
Mortgages in foreclosure	20.0%

Table 4: Life Insurance Risk-Based Capital *(continued)*

Panel C: Asset (C1) Risk and Risk Weights *(continued)*	
Asset	Risk Weight
Real estate–company occupied	10.0%
Real estate–investment	10.0%
Real estate–foreclosed	15.0%
Preferred stock	Bond weights + 2%
Common stock	30.0%
Other long-term assets	20.0%
Source: National Association of Insurance Commissioners	
a. Mortgage weights depend on an individual company's delinquency experience relative to the industry average.	

Risk-Based Capital Results and Effects of Risk-Based Capital on Investment Mix

Results for 1993, the first year that risk-based capital ratios were reported, indicate that industry capital was ample relative to regulatory requirements. Less than 2 percent of all insurers (31 companies) reported risk-based capital ratios under 100 percent, while the industry median was more than 400 percent (Table 5). Although risk-based capital ratios were significantly lower for large companies, each of the 20 largest insurers reported risk-based capital ratios exceeding 100 percent, in most cases by comfortable margins. Moreover, several studies using 1991 and 1992 data found that only a slightly higher fraction of insurers would have failed to meet their risk-based capital requirements in those years.[7] Thus, there is little indication that risk-based capital requirements forced insurers to shift out of higher risk assets simply to meet their capital obligations.

Undoubtedly, concern that risk-based capital ratios would be used by policyholders to rate companies led companies to adopt target-risk-based capital ratios that substantially exceeded the regulatory minimums. This concern simply underscored the role that policyholder attitudes toward insolvency risk were expected to play in the industry. As it turned out, there was remarkably little mention of individual companies' ratios in either the industry trade press or the gen-

---

7.   A Salomon Brothers study estimated that in 1991, only 28 out of 494 insurers (6 percent) would have failed to meet the regulatory minimum. The median ratio for large insurers—those with assets over $10 billion—was 165 percent. Klein (1995) reports similar results for studies conducted by the NAIC.

eral financial press, and companies and their agents were forbidden from using risk-based capital data in their sales practices.

Table 5: Risk-Based Capital Ratios, 1993–95

	1993	1994	1995
All Firms			
1st percentile	79%	81%	76%
5th percentile	142%	140%	145%
25th percentile	242%	251%	261%
Median	411%	433%	462%
Top 20 life insurers			
Min	125%	132%	142%
25th percentile	183%	207%	211%
Median	194%	217%	228%
75th percentile	231%	234%	245%
Max	345%	379%	375%
Source: National Association of Insurance Commissioners			

Policyholder Perceptions of Insolvency Risk

The conviction that policyholder perceptions of financial strength are critical to a company's success now appears remarkably widespread throughout the insurance industry. The importance of reputation to a financial services company may seem unremarkable, but in the life insurance industry it is a rather recent development stemming from the industry's historic record of financial stability. This section briefly summarizes that history, outlines key events that took place in the early 1990s, and summarizes a range of evidence that policyholders became highly sensitized to the issue of financial strength.

The industry's reputation for financial stability extends at least as far back as the Depression. Although there are no comprehensive statistics available on life insurer insolvencies during the 1930s, Buey (1953) indicates that there were no failures of life insurance companies prior to mid-1931. In the following two and a half years, only 15 companies failed, representing 4 percent of companies outstanding and less than 1 percent of the life insurance in force. The industry was generally successful at meeting the demand for policy loans, though by 1932 some members began to consider seeking changes in the law that would permit a temporary moratorium on payment of loans and surrenders. The industry abandoned such efforts fearing that it might cause a stop in premium payments altogether. Policy loans as a share of assets reached a peak in 1932 of 18 percent.

During the banking panic of 1933 a moratorium on both policy loans and surrenders finally became necessary. In March of that year, 21 states adopted emergency legislation and bills were pending in 12 other states. Exceptions were granted for the payment of insurance premiums and in cases of need, and at no time were moratoriums placed on the payments of death benefits. By year-end 1933, most of the restrictions had been lifted.

Overall, the industry appears to have enjoyed continued public confidence throughout the depression decade. Poterba (1997) notes that the sales of annuities grew rapidly in the 1930s as consumers sought more reliable investment vehicles for long-term savings. More recently, the assets of failed life insurance companies were less than 0.14 percent of total industry assets each year between 1976 and 1989, with the exception of 1983 (Figure 4).[8] Again, life insurance companies compared favorably to other financial institutions, such as banks and thrift institutions, which were experiencing large losses, and in the case of thrift institutions, record failures.

In 1990, the industry's reputation for financial stability changed rapidly as the public discovered that asset-quality problems plaguing thrift institutions and commercial banks during the late 1980s—investments in below-investment-grade bonds and commercial real estate—also affected life insurance. Two events highlighted the industry's emerging financial difficulties. In January 1990, First Executive, the sixteenth-largest U.S. life insurance holding company, with more than $18 billion in assets, announced that it was writing down the value of its bond portfolio by $515 million. In October, Travelers, the seventh-largest life insurance company with more than $36 billion in assets, announced that it was reserving $650 million for anticipated losses in its commercial real estate portfolio.

---

8. In 1983 the industry experienced its largest insolvency to date with the seizure of Baldwin-United's insurance subsidiaries. Although Baldwin-United was a large insurer, its difficulties were partly the result of a complex holding company structure where losses were traded among various subsidiaries for tax reasons (Kopcke and Randall, 1991). In this case, one "bad apple" may not have been sufficient to taint an entire industry. A significant part of Baldwin-United's losses were covered by securities brokers that sold its annuities under threat of litigation (Brannon, 1991).

In 1991, six major life insurance companies were seized by regulators over a span of four months, including two First Executive subsidiaries and two First Capital subsidiaries that had invested heavily in below-investment-grade bonds, and Mutual Benefit, the industry's largest-ever failure, which had invested heavily in commercial real estate. The assets of the seized companies totaled $42 billion, more than 3 percent of total industry assets (Figure 4). Over the following three years, companies with more than $9 billion in assets were seized and during 1991-93, the major rating agencies downgraded more than half the companies they covered.

Figure 4: Assets of Impaired Life Insurance Companies

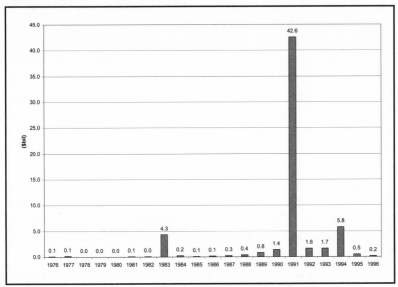

Evidence of a Flight-to-Quality by Policyholders

The announcement of large losses by First Executive and Travelers were defining events for the life insurance industry in light of its prior reputation for financial stability and conservatism. In Fenn and Cole (1994), we document that stock prices of insurance companies with above-average concentrations of junk bonds and commercial mortgages fell sharply on the announcements, especially the stock prices of those companies with more liquid liabilities. The latter finding suggests that the critical factor influencing stock prices was the anticipated response of policyholders. At First Capital, the other California insurer that had invested heavily in junk bonds, new policy sales declined more than 50 percent in 1990 (DeAngelo, DeAngelo, and Gilson, 1996). In Fenn (1995), I report evidence that life insurance companies' asset growth during 1991-92 was extremely sensitive to their below-investment-grade bond holdings; I interpret this finding as evidence that junk bonds had become a stigmatized asset class that policyholders sought to avoid. I also find that financial-strength ratings strongly affected growth.

Another indication of policyholder concerns was the sudden rapid increase in separate accounts. Under a separate account contract, policyholder benefits vary directly with the investment results of the separate account assets. In this respect, the policyholder assumes greater investment risk. However, because separate account policyholders have a preferred claim on separate account assets, which are segregated from an insurer's other assets, they are afforded greater protection if an insurer becomes insolvent.

For many years, separate accounts were a relatively small part of the industry, used primarily to provide policyholders with greater exposure to equities than is permitted in the general account. Beginning in 1991, sales of separate account products increased sharply. Increases in separate account assets accounted for more than one-third of the increase in total industry assets between 1991 and 1994; as a share of industry assets, separate accounts increased from 11 percent at year-end 1990 to 18 percent at year-end 1994 (Figure 5). Unlike the separate account gains posted since 1995, these increases primarily reflected new product sales rather than rising stock prices.

The expanded activities of rating agencies also reflected the concerns of policyholders. Moody's expanded its ratings coverage from 46 life insurance companies at year-end 1989 to 157 at year-end 1996. Standard & Poor's initiated a service that assigns solvency ratings to all insurers. A.M. Best's review process evolved from one that routinely lavished praise and its highest rating on all major insurers to one whose highest rating is now coveted.[9]

Figure 5: Ratio of Separate Account Assets to Total Assets

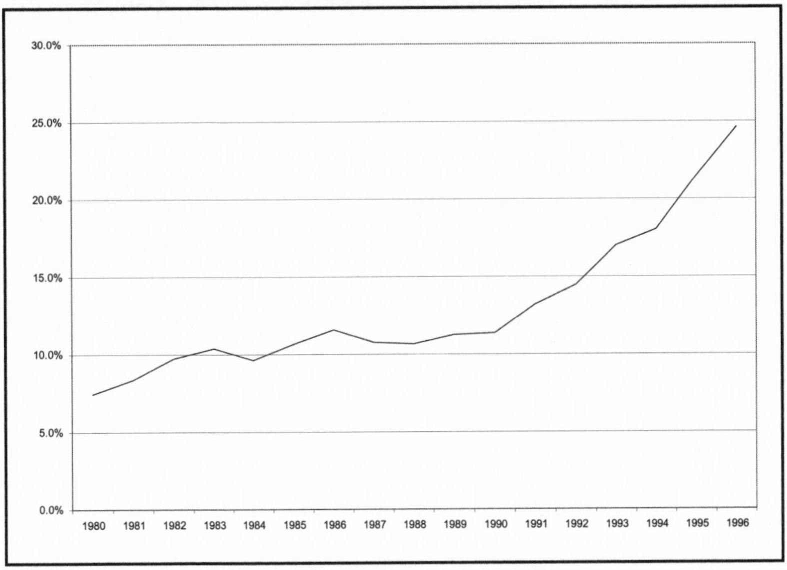

Theoretical Reasons for Flight-to-Quality By Policyholders

In a series of articles, Robert Merton offers a theoretical foundation for the flight-to-quality by policyholders (see Merton, 1993, Merton, 1997). He observes that there is a fundamental distinction between a financial intermediary's customers and ordinary investors, and argues that the two groups view default risk quite differently. Customers, he notes, suffer greater welfare losses if an intermediary defaults because "customers internalize risks that investors can elimi-

---

9.   Along with the expansion in insurance ratings were numerous downgrades. Moody's downgrades were concentrated in 1991 and 1992, when it lowered the ratings of 46 companies while raising the rating of only one company. A.M. Best's downgrades peaked in 1993, when it downgraded over 20 percent of its top rated companies. Even after their downgrades, most major insurers were still highly rated. Moody's assigned only a handful of below-investment-grade ratings and none to the top 20 insurers. A.M Best rated virtually the industry's entire top 100 insurers superior (A++, A+) or excellent (A, A-). What likely concerns policyholders, and hence insurers, are not absolute ratings but relative ratings and the fact that rating agencies differentiate among insurers to a degree that they had not previously.

nate by diversification." Consequently, customers "are identified by their strict preference to have the payoffs on their contracts as insensitive as possible to the fortunes of the intermediary itself."

While Merton has stressed a lack of diversification as the reason that customers are averse to default risk, information costs likely play an important role as well. Life insurance companies are opaque—the risk and return characteristics of both their assets and liabilities are difficult for outsiders to understand—and thus, it is difficult for policyholders to assess and price insolvency risk. It is easier for customers to deal with companies for whom the probability of insolvency is remote. A related concern arises when a company's condition is deteriorating. Sophisticated investors routinely monitor risky assets to determine when and whether it is necessary to sell them. Dynamic credit analysis of this sort is extremely difficult for policyholders to perform; moreover, under many insurance contracts, it is extremely costly or impossible for policyholders to withdraw their funds prior to the contract's scheduled payoff date.

Investment Implications of Policyholder Flight-to-Quality

In the wake of the industry's financial difficulties, life insurance companies, almost overnight, became extremely sensitive about projecting an image of financial strength and prudence. By late 1990, companies had begun to tout their low exposure to junk bonds and commercial real estate (Lublin, 1990). One Top 10 company's advertisement read: "If excitement is investing heavily in junk bonds that end up in default, that's the kind of excitement we can do without." Another company used the slogan: "No junk bonds? No real estate? No kidding!" Companies also routinely began to include their financial-strength ratings in their advertisements.

In this environment, insurers faced strong incentives to reduce concentrations of assets that were worrisome either to policyholders directly (primarily junk bonds) or to rating agencies (primarily commercial real estate). The sharp curtailment of below-investment-grade private placement investments in early 1990 and commercial mortgage investments in early 1991, described above, strongly suggests that reputational concerns and investment decisions were closely linked. Moreover, the timing of these decisions suggests that insurers responded relatively quickly to policyholder concerns.

In an October 1992 survey of life insurance chief investment officers, 80 percent of the respondents reported that credit rating concerns had made their investment strategy more conservative (Bouyoucos and Siegel, 1992). In contrast, only a minority, 38 percent, indicated that they would restructure their portfolios for risk-based capital purposes. When asked to prioritize their concerns, 44 percent indicated that ratings were their top concern, compared with only 12 percent for risk-based capital. Of the respondents, 59 percent indicated that managing credit risk was their top asset/liability management concern.

Role of Insurance Regulators in Runs on and Regulatory Seizure of First Executive and First Capital

As described above, First Executive's difficulties figure prominently in insurance industry developments in the early 1990s. DeAngelo, DeAngelo, and Gilson (1994, 1996) have extensively analyzed the events leading up to the regulatory seizure of First Executive's and First Capital's insurance subsidiaries. In the case of First Executive, they focus primarily on what they argue was a media bias toward First Executive and its junk bond portfolio relative to insurers that experienced commercial real estate problems. They do not attribute the elevated pace of surrenders or loss of sales throughout 1990 to unwarranted regulatory actions. Indeed, they note that it was First Executive's January 1990 announcement that first triggered a massive run; this announcement was at the holding company level and compelled by Securities and Exchange Commission reporting requirements, not regulatory reporting requirements.

Unlike many other insurance companies with smaller junk bond holdings, the vast majority of First Executive's holdings were rated single-B or below; that is, they were not the double-B (NAIC class 3 bonds) that were largely reclassified in 1990. Indeed, Executive Life's reported holdings of junk bonds declined slightly from $6.46 billion at year-end 1989 to $6.37 billion at year-end 1990 (Executive Life of New York's reported holdings increased from $1.59 billion to $2.02 billion).

DeAngelo, DeAngelo, and Gilson (1996) argue that regulators were significantly to blame for the events leading to the seizure of First Capital's insurance subsidiaries. In particular, they argue that its insurance units, seized in May 1991, would have been able to meet the surrender demands of the previous 16 months, but that intemperate remarks by California Commissioner John Garamendi in early May sparked a fatal run that led to its seizure. While First Capital's seizure may have been avoidable, DeAngelo, DeAngelo, and Gilson (1996) point out that new policy sales were drying up, which underscores the impact that events at First Executive were having on the insurance market. In the wake of these events, the marginal contribution of First Capital's actual seizure to policyholder concerns may have been small.

Alternative Explanations for Why Investment Flight-to-Quality Persists

The continued decline in information-intensive investments in the current environment of stable ratings and record capital levels is more difficult to attribute to reputational issues. Of course, even if insurers are not overly concerned about perceptions of financial strength at the present, they may still be extremely reluctant to increase their exposure to assets that could result in higher investment losses in the future in the light of the extremely high reputational costs that such losses impose. This section considers additional explanations for why the flight-to-quality persists.

Evolution of Life Insurance Products

For many years, participating whole life was the cornerstone of the life insurance industry. Like other forms of whole life insurance, participating whole life was a combination insurance and investment product. Although guaranteed returns were generally low, higher rates of return were awarded through policyholder dividends. In principal, policyholder dividends reflected the mortality and investment experience of the insurance company. However, since mortality losses were largely predictable, much of the variation in policy dividends reflected investment performance.

Another key product, beginning with the growth of defined benefit plans in the 1950s, were unallocated group pension products. These are investment vehicles to which plan sponsors contribute funds on behalf of current workers. The accumulated funds are then used to pay retirement benefits directly, or as is more often the case, to purchase an immediate annuity on behalf of the retiree. Traditionally, unallocated group pension products, such as participating whole life, promised low guaranteed returns, but through "experience rating" paid substantially more than guaranteed rates at the discretion of the insurance company.

Among the problems with these products, which ultimately led to their falling from favor, was the fact that the methods by which policyholder returns were determined was completely opaque to the policyholder. In principle they reflected the investment performance of an insurer's assets, but in practice the "sharing rule" among different classes of policyholders and between policyholders and the company were completely unspecified. Thus, these contracts were virtually impossible to evaluate *ex-ante* or monitor *ex-post* (that is, impossible to monitor compliance with the implied sharing rule). Just about all policyholders could do was monitor ex-post returns. Even ex-post returns served as a limited discipline device on insurers, since insurance contracts were often costly for policyholders to walk away from.

Longstanding dissatisfaction with this lack of transparency led to the development of nonparticipating insurance products that paid policyholders a fixed rate of return, or at most, indexed returns to something observable. The fixed rates of return were higher than the low guaranteed minimum rates on participating products; on the other hand, policyholders no longer participated in the investment experience of the insurer's general account (except in the event of insolvency). The major fixed-rate products are single premium deferred annuities (SPDAs) for individuals and guaranteed investment contracts (GICs) for pension plans.

Investment Implications of Guaranteed Fixed-Rate Products

Holding portfolio risk constant, insurers that issue guaranteed fixed-rate products bear more investment risk than those that issue participating products since they are unable to pass through losses to policyholders. Schneider (1991) noted this in connection with commercial real estate losses during the last credit cycle:

> "The ultimate threat to solvency will be determined by their [the insurers'] ability to adjust credited interest rates on the corresponding liabilities. A company

> that holds large amounts of GICs backed by mort-
> gages will be less able to respond appropriately to
> credit problems than will a company that holds an
> identical asset portfolio, but which has used those
> assets to back life insurance products on which the
> credited interest rates may be adjusted as necessary."

From a prudential standpoint, insurers that issue guaranteed fixed
rate products face the incentive to reduce portfolio risk, especially
credit-related risks that are difficult to hedge. The prudential view
predicts that a shift to guaranteed fixed-rate products will result in
less credit risk, lower investment yields and lower (expected) policy
returns.

On the other hand, the sales environment for fixed-rate products
typically is more competitive than for traditional participating products, in part, because policy returns are easier to compare *ex-ante*.
Insurers may therefore face incentives to invest in higher risk assets in
order to profitably offer to pay higher rates of return on their liabilities.

The latter possibility has been frequently described in the literature (see Kopcke 1992, Todd and Wallace, 1992) and undoubtedly
describes the activities of certain rapidly growing insurers in the
1980s, including First Executive's and First Capital's insurance units.
However, the success of this strategy depends on a lack of awareness
of insolvency risk on the part of customers. To the extent that policyholders now better understand those risks, insurance companies will
be less able to compete in this way in the future. Competitive pressures based on policyholder perceptions of financial strength rather
than promised yields may force insurers to adopt the prudential
approach. Alternatively, if insurers wish to invest in higher risk assets
and maintain the confidence of policyholders, they will be required to
put up more capital (see below).

Narrower Credit Spreads

The shift away from information-intensive assets may to some
extent be the result of declining credit spreads in markets for high-
yield bonds, private placements, commercial mortgages and other
higher risk assets. In light of such tightening, the benefits to insurers

of investing in information-intensive assets have declined at the same time that the costs have increased.

Of course, the tightening of spreads owes, in part, to changes in capital markets such as the use of collateralized bond obligations, which has further expanded the market for publicly traded below-investment-grade bonds, the securitization of commercial mortgages and the expansion of the private placement market through Rule 144A. These changes imply that insurance companies' historic investment activities are of marginally less value than they were previously.

Pressure to Reduce Costs

Insurance companies, like other financial institutions, have been under pressure to reduce costs in recent years. Investment departments represent a major expense and many of the industry's largest insurers have cut them aggressively. Once disbanded, they are difficult to reassemble. Investments in investment-grade publicly traded bonds, unlike investments in private placements and commercial mortgages, are easily outsourced.

Strategic Options for Insurers

In this paper I argue that policyholder concerns about financial strength and asset quality have led to a more conservative investment strategy and a shift away from traditional life insurance company investments. Whereas insurers were relatively unrestricted in their investment strategies before 1990, their choices now are more constrained. A key question is the extent to which this departure from historical asset allocations is permanent.

Insurers, I believe, can choose from four combinations of asset, product and capital structures, described in Table 6.

- Under the first scenario, insurers can invest heavily in low-risk, low-yielding assets and offer to pay commensurately low rates on their liabilities. Essentially, insurers will provide insurance and tax-deferral to their policyholders, but no significant asset services to capital markets. This strategy can be executed with conventionally high degrees of leverage.
- Under the second scenario, insurers that maintain the infrastructure and expertise to do so can invest in information-intensive assets, but these investments must be supported by

391

more capital than insurers have been accustomed to holding. The rates paid on their fixed-rate liabilities may be somewhat higher than for insurers that primarily invest in low-risk assets, but not necessarily significantly higher. Nor need they be; if insurers are issuing essentially risk-free liabilities, the promised yield on those liabilities should be near the risk-free rate.

- The third combination—investments in information-intensive assets supported by participating liabilities—most closely parallels the industry's traditional product and asset mix. Only insurers that have established a high degree of credibility in the marketplace for payment of superior levels of participating returns will be able to execute this strategy. Relatively few such companies are in the position to do so today.[10]

- Finally, a growing number of companies will supply separate account products. These products offer policyholders a range of risk and return, but the assets backing these products are generally limited to publicly traded assets. Insurers that offer these products are providing asset management services, but not the kind of information-intensive due diligence and monitoring that characterized their traditional investment activities.

Table 6: Feasible Combinations of Product, Asset, and Capital Structures for Life Insurance Companies

Product Structure	Asset Structure	Capital Structure	Asset Services	Comment
Guaranteed, fixed-rate Low-yields	Public, investment-grade bonds Low risk-return	High leverage	None	Most insurers
Guaranteed, fixed-rate Somewhat higher yields	Some information-intensive investments Feasible risk-return levels depend on capital structure	Less leverage	Due diligence and ex-post monitoring of information-intensive investments	Some insurers Requires expertise to make information-intensive investments

---

10. Northwestern Mutual in the traditional life insurance market and Teachers in the annuity market are examples of companies that have reputations for paying excellent returns. They are also among the companies that have shifted away the least from information-intensive assets.

Table 6: Feasible Combinations of Product, Asset, and Capital Structures for Life Insurance Companies *(continued)*

Product Structure	Asset Structure	Capital Structure	Asset Services	Comment
Participating	Some information-intensive investments Feasible risk-return levels depend on capital structure and degree of risk sharing with policyholders	Less leverage	Due diligence and ex-post monitoring of information-intensive investments	Few insurers Requires expertise to make information-intensive investments Requires credibility for payment of high levels of participating returns
Separate account	Publicly traded assets Wide degree of risk	High leverage	Portfolio management	Many insurers

What almost certainly is no longer an option is the financial strategy that landed insurers in trouble in the 1980s: highly-leveraged balance sheets funded with high fixed-rate liabilities, backed by high yielding but high risk assets. The revealed preference of policyholders suggests that the insolvency risk inherent in this structure outweighs the benefits of higher expected returns.

References

Bouyoucos, Peter J., and Michael Siegel, 1992, "The Goldman Sachs Insurer CIO Survey," Insurance Industry Research Group, October.

Brannon, Gerald M., 1991, "Public Policy and Life Insurance," in *The Financial Condition and Regulation of Insurance Companies*, Proceedings of a Conference Held in June 1991, Federal Reserve Bank of Boston, Richard W. Kopcke and Richard E. Randall eds.

Buey, R. Carlyle, 1953, *American Life Convention*, vol. 2 (New York, NY: Appleton-Century-Croft).

Carey, Mark, Stephen Prowse, John Rea, and Gregory Udell, 1993, "The Economics of Private Placements: A New Look," *Journal of Financial Markets, Institutions, and Instruments,* 2:3, 1-66.

Crabbe, Leland E., and John Forrey, 1996, "An Analysis of Investment-Grade Corporate Portfolios of Life Insurance and P&C

Companies," *Global Fixed Income Research*, Merrill Lynch, June 10.

DeAngelo, Harry, Linda DeAngelo, and Stuart C. Gilson, 1994, "The Collapse of First Executive Corporation: Junk Bonds, Adverse Publicity, and the 'Run on the Bank Phenomenon'," *Journal of Financial Economics*, 36, 287-336.

DeAngelo, Harry, Linda DeAngelo, and Stuart C. Gilson, 1996, "Perceptions and the Politics of Finance: Junk Bonds and the Regulatory Seizure of First Capital Life," *Journal of Financial Economics*, 41, 471-511.

Fenn, George W., 1995, "The Stigma of Junk Bonds in the Life Insurance Industry: How Do Customers of Financial Institutions Assess Default Risk?" unpublished working paper, Federal Reserve Board, Washington D.C.

Fenn, George W. and Rebel A. Cole, 1994, "Announcements of Asset-Quality Problems and Contagion Effects in the Life Insurance Industry," *Journal of Financial Economics*, 35, 181-198.

Fenn, George W., Nellie Liang, and Stephen Prowse, 1997, "The Private Equity Market: An Overview," *Financial Markets, Institutions, and Instruments*, 6:4, 1-105.

Jones, Lawrence D., 1977, "Investments in Income Property Mortgages of Life Insurance Companies," in *Investment Activities of Life Insurance Companies*, ed. J. David Cummins (Homewood, Il: Irwin Press), 59-103.

Klein, Robert W., 1995, "Insurance Regulation in Transition," *Journal of Risk and Insurance*, 62, 363-403.

Kopcke, Richard W., 1992, "The Capitalization and Portfolio Risk of Insurance Companies," *New England Economic Review*, July/August, 43-57.

Kopcke, Richard W. and Richard E. Randall, 1991, "Insurance Companies as Financial Intermediaries: Risk and Return," in *The Financial Condition and Regulation of Insurance Companies*, Proceedings of a Conference Held in June 1991, Federal Reserve Bank of Boston, Richard W. Kopcke and Richard E. Randall eds.

Lublin, Joann S., 1990, "Insurers Tout Low Junk Bond Exposure," *The Wall Street Journal*, December 14, p. B3.

Merton, Robert C., 1993, "Operation and Regulation in Financial Intermediation: A Functional Perspective," in *Operation and Regulation of Financial Markets,* edited by P. Englund. Stockholm: The Economic Council, 1993.

Merton, Robert C., 1997, "A Model of Contract Guarantees for Credit-Sensitive, Opaque Financial Intermediaries," *European Finance Review,* 1, 1-13.

Poterba, James M., 1997, "The History of Annuities in the United States," NBER Working Paper # 6001.

Prowse, Stephen, 1997, "The Economics of Private Placements: Middle-Market Corporate Finance, Life Insurance Companies, and a Credit Crunch," *Economic Review,* Federal Reserve Bank of Dallas, Third Quarter, 12-24.

Rasky, Susan, 1986, "Tracking Junk Bond Owners," *New York Times,* December 7.

Schneider, Robert E., 1991, Discussion in *The Financial Condition and Regulation of Insurance Companies,* Proceedings of a Conference Held in June 1991, Federal Reserve Bank of Boston, Richard W. Kopcke and Richard E. Randall eds.

Shapiro, Eli, 1977, "Developments in the Private Placement Market: The Changing Role of the Life Insurance Industry," in *Investment Activities of Life Insurance Companies,* ed. J. David Cummins (Homewood, Ill: Irwin Press), 37-58.

Smythe, William, 1987, "Insurer Investments in Junk or Below-Investment Grade Bonds: Some Questions and Answers for Regulators," *The Journal of Insurance Regulation,* 6, 4-15.

Todd, Richard and Neil Wallace, 1992, "SPDAs and GICs: Like Money in the Bank?" *Federal Reserve Bank of Minneapolis Quarterly Review,* Summer, 2-17.

Comments on...

Flight-to-Quality in Life Insurance Company Investments

Robert W. Klein
Director
Center for Risk Management and Insurance Research
and
Associate Professor of Risk Management and Insurance
Georgia State University

George W. Fenn offers a thoughtful assessment of dramatic changes in life insurers' investment portfolios since 1990 and the causes of these changes. This is an important topic because of: 1) the significant role of life insurers as financial intermediaries in allocating capital in the economy, and 2) the implications for the evolution of financial services markets, including insurance. The entry of banks and other financial institutions into insurance markets should interest these institutions in this topic.

I substantially agree with Dr. Fenn's analysis of life insurers' investment patterns and the forces that drive them. Hence, my comments will not take issue with his conclusions per se, but rather add some perspective to the causal factors he discusses and the implications for the future direction of the industry and appropriate regulation.

As Dr. Fenn concludes, regulation is only one of many factors affecting insurers' actions and not the principal cause of the flight to quality. Life insurers rely heavily on consumer confidence because of the long-term nature of their contracts, which are intended to reduce policyholders' risk. Consequently, insurers must respond to consumer perceptions and concerns about the quality and stability of their assets. Consumers' confidence in the industry's regulation is also integral to their confidence in insurers' ability to meet their financial obligations.

The Role of Regulation

State insurance regulators' authority is broad, but they tend to use it cautiously, with a few exceptions. Indeed, insurance commissioners are more often criticized for exercising too much rather than too little forbearance (Hall, 1998). Insurance regulation in the United States is rule-based and reactive, and historically less of a constraint on insurers' behavior than is commonly perceived. When legislators and regulators alter the rules governing insurers, they are often following market changes. When an insurer is placed into receivership, it is typically only after all other, nonpublic remedies have failed and the insurer is no longer economically viable.

As Wright (1991) has observed, regulators relaxed their restrictions on life insurers' investments and products after 1950. Hence, regulation did not prevent insurers from investing in large concentrations of higher-yield and riskier assets to support products that would better meet consumer demands and compete with other financial products. Consequently, some insurers experienced significant declines in the market value of their assets when the junk bond and real estate markets tanked. Regulators were forced to seize a relatively small, albeit prominent, group of insurers that suffered the heaviest asset devaluation and were subject to policyholder runs. Many other insurers did not need prodding from regulators to restructure their investment portfolios to restore consumer trust or prevent its erosion.

As Dr. Fenn notes, some analysts argue that California's seizure of Executive Life was precipitous, but most industry observers believe that it was necessary and inevitable.[1] It also should be noted that California did not act unilaterally. It was under substantial pressure from other states in which Executive Life had sold a large number of policies. If California had failed to act when and as it did, it is likely that other states would have forced Executive Life into receivership.

Industry and government officials faced a crisis in public confidence, justified or not, and the call for regulatory reforms was pervasive. The increase in insurer insolvencies and their costs were certainly not an illusion, nor were public fears, as Dr. Fenn indicates. The number of insurer failures and associated guaranty fund costs peaked at 60 and $1.6 billion respectively in 1991, several times higher than their long-run historical averages (Klein, 1995). While the higher insolvency costs still represented a small fraction of industry premiums and assets, it was an ominous trend nonetheless, particularly coming on the heels of the thrift institution crisis and a significant increase in property/casualty insurer insolvencies. Annual

---

1.   There is greater criticism of the way in which California administered the receivership of Executive Life and the relatively low price it obtained in selling its junk bond portfolio.

surveys conducted by the American Council of Life Insurance tracked a dramatic decline in consumer confidence in the industry over this period (ACLI, 1993). Congress conducted an intensive investigation that was highly critical of the states' oversight of insurer solvency.

The states responded by strengthening the financial regulation of insurers. While insurers disagree with some of the specific features of the new regulations, they generally support the concept of enhanced solvency oversight (ACLI, 1990). Recent regulatory initiatives include: risk-based capital requirements; enhanced financial reporting; expanded asset reserve requirements; improved financial analysis, and tighter restrictions on investments (Klein, 1995).

Of these initiatives, investment regulations are the most controversial and the most problematic from the insurers' perspective. Even regulators disagree in this area, prompting the National Association of Insurance Commissioners (NAIC) to adopt alternative prescriptive and prudential model investment laws. What the states will enact remains to be seen. Regulatory policy on investments will likely continue to evolve to avoid placing insurers at a significant competitive disadvantage relative to other financial institutions.

The ultimate effect of recent insurance regulatory changes is also an open question. The greatest impact may have been to enhance the financial transparency of the industry and enable regulators to intervene more quickly against high-risk and troubled insurers. The prescriptive, rule-based approach of U.S. insurance regulation is still inefficient. Regulators are compelled to prevent the rules from binding too many insurers in a substantial way. Fortunately, most insurers have sufficient incentives to maintain their financial risk with reasonable bounds, regardless of where regulatory constraints are set. However, there is still the potential for high-risk and poorly managed insurers to evade regulators under the present system and threaten policyholders' interests. The current structure of state insurance insolvency guaranty funds also exacerbates the moral hazard problem (Hall, 1998).

401

Insurer Reputation and Consumer Choice

Consumers' belief in the ability of life insurers to meet their contract obligations is critical to the industry's viability. Many life insurance and annuity contracts are long term in nature, and policyholders often pay premiums for many years before they receive funds from these contracts. Consequently, consumers must be confident of the financial viability of insurers to be willing to make such long-term financial commitments. As Dr. Fenn argues, consumers' tolerance for default risk on insurance contracts is low. In fact, consumers may have had unrealistic expectations about the risk and return characteristics of insurance contracts that promised both death benefits and a high rate of cash accumulation, expectations that insurers fostered. Hence, the industry's image suffered when consumer expectations were not realized in terms of lower-than-promised rates of return, as well as a higher incidence of defaults.

Consumer choice works through a complex mechanism in life insurance. Most consumers find life insurance purchase decisions confusing and tend to rely on agents with potential incentive conflicts. Agents, however, are not immune from lawsuits or other adverse consumer reactions and, hence, are induced to place buyers with companies with a good reputation and that are believed to be financially sound. Once a buyer receives the agent's assurance of the quality of an insurer and purchases a policy, the typical buyer probably is not aware of changes in the financial condition of the insurer, unless he or she is supplied with information to the contrary. This creates the potential for severe consumer reaction when the industry is subject to adverse publicity and the media play on consumer fears.

It could be argued that consumers' lack of knowledge exacerbates the pendulum swings in their confidence in the industry's solvency. Policyholders became complacent during the 1980s when crediting rates soared at a time when insurer insolvencies remained infrequent. This complacency increased consumers' vulnerability to fears of an industry collapse when several large insurers failed. The media fueled these fears by highlighting individual horror stories resulting from insurer failures.

It is this kind of problem that life insurers seek to avoid. Hence, market forces, not regulation, have played the principal role in the "flight-to-quality" among life insurers. At the very least, life insurers' asset restructuring was a preemptive strike against a potential threat to their reputation and franchise value. The extent to which their flight was compelled by expressed consumer preferences versus the risk of adverse consumer reaction is an interesting question. At any rate, prudence is the better part of valor.

The role of rating agencies also was an important catalyst in the flight to quality. As consumers rely on agents for advice, agents rely on rating agencies to signal the financial quality of insurers. The market for insurer ratings changed from a cozy monopoly to a competitive environment populated by several raters who did not want to be embarrassed by giving high grades to insurers who had incurred increased financial risk. Hence, the rating downgrades cited by Dr. Fenn occurred and insurers' actions preempted more severe downgrading. In hindsight, some might argue that raters overreacted, but at the time there was considerable uncertainty about when and how much insurers' asset values would rebound. On the whole, competition among raters has been a positive development and has enhanced the financial transparency of the industry. Raters have significantly refined their analysis processes in many areas. Rigorous financial rating is indispensable to informed and efficient insurance markets and, in a world of uncertainty, consumers and agents prefer raters to err on the side of conservatism.

The Future

The globalization and integration of the financial services markets will increase competitive pressure on insurers and other sellers of insurance products. Electronic commerce also is likely to widen the scope of the relevant markets and introduce new players. Insurers will have to balance risk, return and reputation in crafting and marketing their products. An insurer's decisions not only will affect its prospects, but also will affect consumers' general perceptions of the industry. The potential for positive as well as negative externalities in influencing consumer confidence raises some interesting questions in terms of insurers' incentives and strategies in an evolving marketplace.

There are two keys to a healthy and successful evolution of the industry. One is better-informed consumers with realistic expectations, assured that they are not being misled or cheated. This is perhaps more challenging with financial products that contain both death benefit (or a life contingency in the case of some annuities) and investment components. Sellers of these products need to help consumers properly value both components in their design and information disclosure.

The industry and regulators share a responsibility in increasing consumer knowledge and sophistication in purchasing insurance. As individuals have become more savvy about investing in stocks, which has had a stabilizing effect on the stock market, individuals must become more savvy about buying insurance. There have been some important initiatives in this area that should be expanded. Consumer information will become more critical as the scope of insurance markets widens to encompass more sellers that are not subject to state regulation.

The second key to a healthy industry is an appropriate and efficient regulatory framework in the United States that will look far different than the one we have today. It will be based on a prudential model, rather than a prescriptive model, which will provide greater discretion and demand more from insurers and regulators. A prudential approach to regulation does not mean deregulation, but rather a more effective targeting of regulatory resources toward insurers who are taking inappropriate risks with policyholders' funds. Some question whether a state-based regulatory framework can meet the challenge of overseeing insurers operating across state and national borders. However, this is not a critical problem if the states can coordinate their regulation of the industry and adopt a more progressive approach, as member countries of the European Union have done.

Industry self-regulation also will likely assume a greater role, given the externalities created by insurers' individual actions. Some initial steps have been taken in this direction, which could evolve into some form of certification or "seal of approval." Also, organizers of electronic insurance marketplaces will have an incentive to screen the insurers they admit.

References

American Council of Life Insurance, 1990 *Report of the ACLI Task Force on Solvency Concerns* (Washington, D.C.).

American Council of Life Insurance, 1993, *Monitoring Attitudes of the Public* (Washington, D.C.).

Hall, Brian, 1998, Risk-Taking Incentives and the Cost of Insurance Company Failures, in Robert W. Klein, ed., *Alternative Approaches to Insurance Regulation* (Kansas City, Missouri: National Association of Insurance Commissioners).

Klein, Robert W., 1995, Insurance Regulation in Transition, *Journal of Risk and Insurance*, 62: 363-404.

Wright, Kenneth M., 1991, The Structure, Conduct and Regulation of the Life Insurance Industry, in Richard W. Kopcke and Richard E. Randall, eds., *The Financial Condition and Regulation of Insurance Companies* (Federal Reserve Bank of Boston): 73-96.

Stanley Zax
Chairman, Chief Executive Officer and President
Zenith National Insurance Corporation

George W. Fenn just talked about the regulatory response, and he described it in what I would call technical terms. I think a broader way of looking at the regulatory response to what he talked about there in the early 1990s would be to focus more on the takeovers by the regulator here in California of three different insurers, based upon their investment practices, and based upon an assessment at a moment in time that three insurers were allegedly insolvent.

Based upon the chart that Michael Milken put up on the board before, talking about mark to market of the banks in the 1980s, even if those three insurers were technically insolvent at the time, the amount that they were insolvent would have been microscopic. So, I would suggest to you that—and I was very much taken, here, by the discussion up until now, with all these different areas—there are tremendous similarities, in terms of the issues, if not some of the conclusions, in all the different fields. Certainly, in the insurance field, where I have operated for the past 20 years, I have dealt with many of the issues that I heard discussed here today.

The one issue, one area that I would call your attention to is what happens when regulation runs amok? What happens when the regulator has no standards and is guided by political judgments?

I would submit to you that what was really involved there in the early 1990s with these three companies was a political response to a phenomenon that an insurance commissioner thought would help him become governor. His judgement was wrong; he did not become governor.

Nevertheless, I was in the same business at the time. I did change my investment practices. Not only did I change my investment practices, I decided to get out of the business. I do not think it is rational for a manager to invest capital in an area where there are no rules and you have no rights to protect yourself against a takeover by a politician acting as a regulator. You know, when it comes to solvency regulation, there is tremendous inherent power afforded to the regulator.

So, it is one thing to look at data; but it is another thing to understand the motivations of managers. I personally did not think it was rational to invest our company's money when there was a political tirade taking place that could expropriate our capital. Even though we have the rule of law, there was no rule of law here in California at that time. You had no rights to protect yourself against a takeover.

You think it is unlikely that there would be a takeover? I want you to know that a member of the Insurance Commissioner's staff testified in a hearing here in the state of California, walked out of the hearing, held a press conference and singled out my company as one of the unsafe companies. I heard about that, I picked up the phone, I called the Insurance Commissioner, I asked him if he was aware of this. He said, "No." I asked him if he agreed that we were an unsafe company. He said, "No." I said, "Well, how do you expect me to run a business if you're causing a run on the capital of my company?"

Running a business under that environment may not be susceptible to analysis retroactively. In reality, we were in a very unusual circumstance at the time. So, we did change our investment practices, and we did eventually decide to exit the business.

With respect to the phenomenon that Dr. Fenn talks about in his paper, which is the increase in the percentage of high-grade assets held by life insurance companies, I submit to you that there's another explanation that maybe would be more rational to explore. It is very simple—if you look at the business of life insurance companies today, it is primarily a business in the sale of annuities.

An annuity is a product that is basically sold to people with an average age of 60. The amount of time that a life insurance company is going to hold those assets is substantially less than the amount of time it would have held assets in the more traditional type of products that they sold. Therefore, even on the face of those type of policies, insurance companies would only need assets that are relatively short. There are not a lot of choices of liquid assets that are relatively short, so they had to change their investment practices.

Annuities do not even stay on the books as long as they planned because of the role played by agents in disintermediating the policies. Agents are finding it very difficult to make a living selling these policies; they can make a living just by switching a policy from

Company A to Company B. So, as they switch the policies, they get a new income source for themselves. The problem is, they cause their customers to incur a penalty.

Going back to the thesis that a flight to quality by policyholders is caused by their concern of insolvency, I would suggest that life insurance policyholders, like investors in mutual funds and pensions, really do not understand exactly what they are doing. In the case of insurance policyholders, they tend to be very reliant on their agents. We have good agents; we have bad agents. We have had agents that spend time trying to understand the needs of the policyholders and match up the product with the right company and the right product for the individual, and we have people that are just trying to make a buck. Given the fact that there isn't a lot of knowledge on the part of the consumer, it is very difficult to reach the conclusion that the policyholders are making a judgment based on insolvency.

Section Eight

Regulating Government-Sponsored Enterprises

John C. Weicher
Senior Fellow
Hudson Institute

Regulation of government-sponsored enterprises (GSEs) has received relatively little serious attention from independent analysts. Regulatory issues have chiefly been discussed as they arise in the political world; much of the relevant literature appears in reports of federal agencies in both the executive and legislative branches, usually as one topic among several. Most analysts have addressed either the role of GSEs in the financial sector—such as whether they should be privatized—or the extent to which they should be required to serve public purposes or social goals by serving specific market segments that policy makers believe deserve special assistance or subsidy. This paper does not discuss either question. Privatization is certainly an interesting subject, especially since two GSEs have been privatized in the last year, but privatization of the two largest GSEs has recently been extensively and ably discussed and debated by several government agencies and private individuals, and I have written about it on several occasions.[1] Social goals are subsidiary to the main purposes of GSEs and are not the most important concerns of regulators, although they can pose significant regulatory issues.

GSEs have been established in three financial sectors: agriculture, education and housing. In this paper I give most attention to the housing GSEs. They are by far the largest; perhaps equally important, I am much more familiar with them. There are, however, interesting parallels between GSEs that operate in different sectors. Moreover, all of them have been the subject of important legislation within the past decade, and the legislation has changed the regulatory framework in each case.

The next section of the paper describes the GSEs and explains their activities and privileges. This leads into consideration of the purposes of regulation and the appropriate regulatory structure. The latter discussion in turn provides a benchmark for evaluating actual GSE regulation.

An Overview of the GSEs

The purpose of GSEs is to conduct financial activities that cannot be profitably conducted by private institutions. The activities may be

---

1. See for example CBO (1996), GAO (1996), and HUD (1996). Reviews of these reports and further analysis have been prepared by Shear (1996), McKinley (1997), and Woodward (1997). My own views appear in Weicher (1987, 1994a, 1994b).

inherently too risky, or private companies may have shown no willingness to undertake them.

GSEs are expected to conduct these activities without losing money. To achieve their purposes at no direct cost to the federal government, they are given special privileges not available to private financial institutions. These special privileges are considered in the financial markets to constitute an implicit federal guarantee of the GSEs' debt, and therefore enable them to borrow at lower rates than private institutions can. The GSEs have no explicit guarantee from the federal government and do not claim to have a guarantee. Still, in the weary words of a Treasury official to the General Counsel of Fannie Mae at a 1990 Senate hearing, "Of course, the Treasury Department doesn't admit there's an implied guarantee and we know you, at Fannie Mae, don't admit there's an implied guarantee. But I think we both know the market feels there is one; they don't believe either one of us."[2]

Seven GSEs have been created. In agriculture, they are the Farm Credit System (FCS) and the Federal Agricultural Mortgage Corporation (Farmer Mac). In education, they are the Student Loan Marketing Association (Sallie Mae) and the College Construction Loan Insurance Association (Connie Lee). In housing, they are the Federal Home Loan Bank System (FHLBS), the Federal National Mortgage Association (FNMA or Fannie Mae), and the Federal Home Loan Mortgage Corporation (FHLMC or Freddie Mac). The ostensibly cute nicknames of most GSEs are imitations of Fannie Mae, which started as a slurring of its initials.

Agriculture

Farm Credit System

The Farm Credit System is the oldest GSE and by far the most complicated.[3] It is a system of cooperatives. As of 1997, it consisted of 206 associations, falling within four categories, that make loans directly to farmers for various agricultural purposes; eight regional

---

2. Remarks of Michael Basham, in U.S. Senate (1990), p. 42.
3. The following discussion is based largely on CBO (1991, Ch. 3) and GAO (1994a, 1994b), with current data from the 1998 federal budget (OMB, 1998, Appendix).

Farm Credit Banks that provide funds to the associations, and two Banks for Cooperatives that make loans to agricultural cooperatives. The member institutions are jointly and severally liable for the consolidated obligations of the FCS. FCS raises funds in the national capital markets, through bond and note sales conducted by the Federal Farm Credit Banks Funding Corporation. System institutions in financial difficulty can receive assistance in the form of federally guaranteed bonds, issued by the Farm Credit System Financial Assistance Corporation; authorization to sell the bonds is given by the Financial Assistance Board. The Federal Credit Leasing Services Corporation provides leasing services to farmers and cooperatives. There is also an insurance fund, managed by the Farm Credit System Insurance Corporation. The FCS provides about 25 percent of the agricultural credit in the United States.

The first institutions were chartered in 1916, with subsequent expansions in 1923, 1933 and 1951. The current structure of the system is the result of major reforms through a series of laws enacted in 1985, 1986 and 1987 in response to the financial problems of many member institutions. Part of the response to the problems took the form of consolidations and mergers. There were 995 retail associations in mid-1974, and 390 at the end of 1987. There were also 13 regional Banks for Cooperatives prior to 1988; all but one merged into a single national institution, and the other now operates nationally. In addition, the Farm Credit Banks, created by the 1987 act, are the result of merging two sets of wholesale lending institutions, one to support real estate loans and the other to support farm production loans.

This system is regulated by the Farm Credit Administration (FCA). Under the 1985 legislation the FCA became an arm's-length regulator with responsibility for the safety and soundness of the FCS. Prior to 1985, it was also the central administrator of the FCS, determining the system's operating policies. The FCA board also serves as the board of the Farm Credit System Insurance Corporation, which was established in 1987.

Farmer Mac

Farmer Mac was chartered in 1987 to guarantee securities that are backed by agricultural mortgages, and to create a secondary market for the securities, including loans guaranteed by the Farmers Home Administration (FmHA). Farmer Mac is part of the FCS, but is financially independent of the other institutions within the system. It is regulated by the FCA.

Education

Sallie Mae

Sallie Mae was chartered by Congress in 1972 as a privately owned corporation to provide funds for loans to college students.[4] Originally, it did so only by buying government-guaranteed loans from financial institutions that originate them (the Loan Purchase Program); since 1980, it has also been allowed to make advances to financial institutions, educational institutions and state agencies, so that these institutions can make student loans (the Warehousing Advances Program). In 1981, Sallie Mae's loan purchase authority was extended to uninsured student loans, and to other activities that would support the credit needs of students. In 1986, it was allowed to finance educational facilities. It holds about 25 percent of all guaranteed student loans.

In 1993 the federal government initiated a program of direct loans to college students, reduced the profitability of guaranteed student loans to private lenders, and imposed a 30-basis-point-fee on all student loans purchased by Sallie Mae after August 10 of that year. These changes sharply cut into Sallie Mae's profitability, and the association concluded that it would fare better as a fully private entity. Privatization was legislated in 1996, at the urging of both the administration and the association. Sallie Mae reorganized as a private, state-chartered holding company in August 1997, with the GSE itself as a wholly owned subsidiary. Under the law, the GSE will wind down and be liquidated by September 30, 2008.

The regulation of Sallie Mae appears to be somewhat of an open question. At a hearing on privatization in May 1995, a Treasury Department official stated that Sallie Mae was regulated by the Treasury under 1992 legislation. The next witness, the president of Connie Lee, included in his testimony a table comparing the GSEs, which

---

4.   The following discussion of Sallie Mae is based on CBO (1985 and 1991, Ch. 6) and Miles (1996).

showed no regulator for Sallie Mae. Nine days later, a Congressional Research Service report was published that stated that oversight was vested in the Department of Education.[5]

Prior to 1992, Sallie Mae was effectively unregulated:

> The Secretary of the Treasury also has statutory authority to examine all financial records of the association. The Secretary is required to report annually to the President and to the Congress on the financial condition of Sallie Mae including: '...assets and liabilities, capital and surplus, or deficit; a statement of surplus or deficit analysis; a statement of income and expense; a statement of sources and applications of funds; and such comments and information as may be deemed necessary to keep the President and the Congress informed of the operations and financial condition of the Association, together with such recommendations with respect thereto as the Secretary may deem advisable...' In the past, the Secretary has fulfilled this requirement by sending copies of Sallie Mae's annual reports to Congress.[6]

Connie Lee

Connie Lee was established in 1986 to support construction and renovation of college facilities by insuring private loans to colleges and hospitals. Connie Lee differs from other GSEs in that it has been a state-chartered corporation; originally it was owned jointly by Sallie Mae (75 percent) and the federal government (25 percent). As of 1996, the federal government owned about 15 percent of Connie Lee's stock. Connie Lee was also privatized under the 1996 legislation when the federal government sold its stock to Connie Lee. Connie Lee subsequently merged and disappeared as an independent business on March 31, 1998. According to its president in 1995, Connie Lee had no federal regulator.[7]

---

5. Bradbury (1995), Sockwell (1995), and Miles (1995), respectively.
6. CBO (1991), p. 259.
7. Sockwell (1995).

Housing

Federal Home Loan Bank System

The Federal Home Loan Bank System consists of 12 regional Federal Home Loan Banks and the Federal Housing Finance Board (FHFB).[8] The regional banks provide funds to financial institutions for residential mortgages in the form of advances collateralized by mortgage loans already issued. The banks are owned entirely by their member financial institutions; to be a member and to borrow from its regional bank, an institution must own stock in that bank.

The system was established in 1932, and considerably modified and expanded in 1933. Prior to 1989, membership was limited to thrift institutions that specialized in home mortgages. The Financial Institutions Reform, Recovery and Enforcement Act of 1989 (FIR-REA) permitted other financial institutions with significant mortgage holdings in their portfolios to become members. These include commercial banks, credit unions and insurance companies. The Home Loan Banks borrow on the national capital markets, through bond and note sales conducted by the Office of Finance within the system.

The 12 regional banks are now regulated by the FHFB. Prior to 1989, they were regulated by the Federal Home Loan Bank Board (FHLBB or the Bank Board), which was also responsible for regulating the thrift institutions that owned the banks. The Bank Board also had some management responsibilities and was an advocate for the interests of the members of the system, including the Home Loan Banks, even as it regulated them.

There are obvious parallels between the Federal Home Loan Bank System and the Farm Credit System, although the latter is certainly more complicated. Both are owned by their members (farmers in one case, thrift institutions in the other), who must buy stock in a system lending institution in order to borrow from it. Both consist of a set of regional banks that provide funds to local lending institutions. Both also have an insurance fund, although there is some irony here: the farm credit fund was not established until 1987, by which time it was clear to any interested observer that the Federal Savings and Loan

---

8. The Federal Home Loan Bank System is described in CBO (1991, Ch. 5) and Weicher (1994a); see also the various congressionally mandated studies (CBO 1993; GAO 1993; HUD 1994).

Insurance Corporation (FSLIC) was inadequate to meet the demands that were being placed on it by the failures of savings and loan institutions. FIRREA reorganized the FSLIC into the Federal Deposit Insurance Corporation (FDIC) just two years after the farm credit fund was created.

The major structural difference is that the primary lenders are themselves part of the GSE in the Farm Credit System, while they are private, independent entities in the housing finance system.

There is also an important similarity in regulation. Both the Farm Credit Administration and the Federal Home Loan Bank Board had multiple, conflicting responsibilities, including regulation, management, and advocacy. "Until the mid-1980s, the FCA was a combination of regulator, consultant and trade representative."[9] The same could have been said of the Bank Board, and often was. Since reform the responsibilities of both are more narrowly regulatory. The Farm Credit Amendments Act of 1985 turned FCA into an arm's-length regulator, and FIRREA in 1989 created the FHFB to serve mainly as regulator in place of the Bank Board, though FHFB retains some supervisory responsibilities.

Fannie Mae

Fannie Mae was created in 1938 to establish a secondary market in home mortgages.[10] It was given a federal charter in 1954; its present form dates from 1968. Fannie Mae buys residential mortgages from lenders and other originators, and issues securities backed by pools of mortgages (mortgage-backed securities or MBS). It was the first GSE to consist of a single entity rather than a system of regional institutions. Originally it was a subsidiary of the Reconstruction Finance Corporation; the 1954 charter divided ownership between the federal government and lending institutions that sold mortgages to Fannie Mae; since 1968 it has been owned by private stockholders. From 1968 to 1992 it was regulated by the U.S. Department of Housing and Urban Development (HUD). It is now regulated partly by the Office of Federal Housing Enterprise Oversight (OFHEO) and partly by HUD.

---

9.   CBO (1991), p. 105.

10.   For an extensive discussion of the historical development of Fannie Mae, see HUD (1986); for more recent discussion, see Weicher (1994a).

Freddie Mac

Freddie Mac was chartered in 1970 as a secondary market institution for savings and loan associations; originally, its primary activity was to issue MBS backed by loans originated by the savings and loan associations. Like the Home Loan Banks, Freddie Mac was owned by the savings and loan associations and was part of the Federal Home Loan Bank System. FIRREA changed it into a privately owned corporation, regulated by HUD; since 1992 it has also been regulated partly by OFHEO and partly by HUD.

Fannie Mae and Freddie Mac now conduct the same activities. Both buy mortgages for their own portfolios and issue MBS. Together they own or have issued securities amounting to over one-third of all home mortgage credit outstanding; since 1990 they have provided about 75 percent of the net increase in mortgage credit.

GSE Financial Activities

From this description of the GSEs it can be seen that their financial activities take five forms. They make loans directly to individuals; they buy loans from primary lenders, to hold in their own portfolio; they securitize loans originated by primary lenders; they make loans (advances) to primary lenders so that the latter can in turn make more loans; and they insure loans made by primary lenders. No single GSE is authorized to conduct all these activities. The FCS, Sallie Mae, Fannie Mae and Freddie Mac all buy loans from primary lenders; Farmer Mac, Fannie Mae and Freddie Mac securitize them. Sallie Mae and the Federal Home Loan Banks make advances. The retail lending institutions of the FCS are the only direct lenders. Connie Lee is the only loan insurer.

Table 1 shows the magnitude of GSE financial activities for various recent years and summarizes them by sector and by type of activity. The housing GSEs are by far the largest and they have grown in relative importance since 1981. They accounted for two-thirds of GSE financial activity in that year; by 1997 they were close to 95 percent, with Fannie Mae and Freddie Mac accounting for more than 90 percent. The table also shows the enormous growth of securitization. In 1981, securitized loans accounted for 10 percent of GSE activity; by 1990, they accounted for almost two-thirds and that proportion has held through the 1990s. In this decade, however, portfolio lending has grown more rapidly, as both Fannie Mae and Freddie Mac have greatly increased their portfolios.

Table 1: GSE Activity, 1981 – 1997 (Dollars in Billions)

GSE Activity	1981	1990	1994	1997
Farm Credit System	$60	$51	$50	$60
Farmer Mac	0	0	1	1
Sallie Mae	5	29	37	41
Loans in Portfolio	2	19	30	44
Advances	3	10	7	7
Connie Lee	0	2	10	0
Federal Home Loan Banks	59	117	103	182
Fannie Mae	60	414	707	1013
Loans in Portfolio	59	114	221	322
Loans Securitized	1	300	486	691
Freddie Mac	25	337	534	627
Loans in Portfolio	5	21	73	157
Loans Securitized	20	316	461	470
Total by Sector				
Agriculture	$60	$51	$51	$61
Education	5	31	47	51
Housing	144	868	1344	1822
Total by Activity				
Loans in Portfolio/Direct Loans	$126	$205	$374	$583
Loans Securitized	21	616	948	1162
Advances	62	127	110	189
Loans Insured	0	2	10	0
TOTAL	$209	$950	$1,442	$1,934

Source: CBO, Controlling the Risks of Government-Sponsored Enterprises; Budget of the United States Government: Appendix, section on "Government Sponsored Enterprises," various years.

GSE Privileges

To conduct their activities profitably and without direct cost to the federal government, the GSEs receive a number of special privileges. Eleven can be identified; one or another of the GSEs may have any or all. Table 2 summarizes these privileges. Most GSEs have the same privileges and most GSEs benefit from most privileges. The exception is Connie Lee, which has received no GSE privileges and

Table 2: GSE Privileges and Ties to Federal Government

Feature	Federal National Mortgage Association	Federal Home Loan Mortgage Corporation	Federal Home Loan Banks	Farm Credit System	Federal Agricultural Mortgage Corporation	Student Loan Marketing Association	College Construction Loan Insurance Association
Chartered by Act of Congress	Yes	Yes	Yes	Yes	Yes	Yes	No
Ownership	Private	Private	Private	Private	Private	Private	Federal & Private
President or presidential appointees appoint some board members	Yes (5/18)	Yes (5/18)	Yes (6/14)	No	Yes (5/15)	Yes (7/21)	Yes (4/11)
Treasury approval of debt issuance	Yes	Yes	Yes	No	No	Yes	No
Subject to GAO audit	Yes	Yes	Yes	No	Yes	No	No
Treasury lending authorized	$2.25B	$2.25B	$4.0B	No	$1.5B	$1.0B	No
Eligible for Fed open market purchases	Yes	Yes	Yes	Yes	n/a	Yes	No
Use of Fed open market purchases	Yes	Yes	Yes	Yes	Yes	Yes	No
Eligible to collateralize public deposits (all US Government; most state & local)	Yes	Yes	Yes	Yes	Yes	Yes	No
Exempt from SEC registration (1933 Act)	Yes	Yes	Yes	Yes	No	Yes	No
Government securities for purposes of the Securities Exchange Act of 1934	Yes	Yes	Yes	Yes	No	Yes	No

Table 2: GSE Privileges and Ties to Federal Government *(continued)*

Feature	Federal National Mortgage Association	Federal Home Loan Mortgage Corporation	Federal Home Loan Banks	Farm Credit System	Federal Agricultural Mortgage Corporation	Student Loan Marketing Association	College Construction Loan Insurance Association
Eligible for unlimited investment by national banks and state bank Federal Reserve members	Yes	Yes	Yes	Yes	Yes	Yes	No
Eligible for unlimited investment by thrifts regulated by FDIC or OTS	Yes	Yes	Yes	Yes	Yes	Yes	No
Exemption of corporate earnings from federal income tax	No	No	Yes	Yes	No	No	No
Exemption of corporate earnings from state and local income tax	Yes	Yes	Yes	Yes	No	Yes	No
Exemption of interest paid from state income tax	No	No	Yes	Yes	No	Yes	No

Source: CBO, Controlling the Risks of Government-Sponsored Enterprises, Table 2; Sockwell, "Statement," Table 1.

has always had a state charter; CBO has therefore not included Connie Lee in its listing of GSEs, although the Office of Management and Budget (OMB) has counted Connie Lee as a GSE in the federal budget.[11]

The other six GSEs all benefit from special status for their debt instruments, and all can use the Federal Reserve as their fiscal agent. All but the newest, Farmer Mac, are exempt from regulation by the Securities and Exchange Commission; their debts are treated as government securities. They also benefit from favorable tax treatment. All but Farmer Mac are exempt from state and local income taxes on their corporate earnings.[12] The Federal Home Loan Banks and the Farm Credit System are exempt from the federal corporate income tax, although in the case of the Home Loan Banks nearly all of their earnings are passed through to the thrift institutions as stock dividends, and are taxable to the institution. Perhaps most significantly, all but the FCS are authorized to borrow from the U.S. Treasury if need be, up to total amounts specified by law for each GSE.

The GSEs have other connections to the federal government which, though they confer no direct benefit, reinforce their status as quasi-governmental corporations in the eyes of the financial markets. The president appoints some of the directors of each GSE except the member institutions of the Farm Credit System, about one-third in each case. (In the case of the Federal Home Loan Bank System, the president appoints the members of the FHFB, which in turn appoints six directors of each regional Home Loan Bank.) The Treasury Department must approve each specific issuance of debt for Fannie Mae, Freddie Mac, the Federal Home Loan Banks, and Sallie Mae because the securities are perceived as being very close substitutes for Treasury securities and the timing of their issuance could therefore interfere with the Treasury's management of the national debt. The Government Accounting Office (GAO) may audit Fannie Mae, Freddie Mac, the Federal Home Loan Banks and Farmer Mac; private cor-

---

11. See for example CBO (1991, p. 2); OMB (1995 Appendix, pp. 1030-1031).

12. For a discussion of the value of this exemption for Fannie Mae and Sallie Mae within the District of Columbia, see Zimmerman (1995). Fannie Mae and Sallie Mae are headquartered in the District. Sallie Mae has been required to locate in the District by its charter; Fannie Mae is now required to be located within the Washington metropolitan area. Prior to 1992 it was required to be located in the District.

porations are not subject to GAO audit, but federal government agencies (including financial agencies) are. In all these respects, the GSEs look like government agencies rather than private companies.

"Implicit Guarantee" and GSE Market Position

These privileges and other ties to the federal government create the financial market perception of an implicit federal guarantee against default. Reinforcing this perception is the fact that most GSEs are perceived as being "too big to fail," even in the absence of their special privileges. The market perceptions were borne out in the mid-1980s, when Congress acted to prevent the collapse of the Farm Credit System.

The GSEs are therefore able to borrow in the financial markets at lower rates than their private competitors can (or would be able to, if they existed). They fulfill the requirement to serve their sector by passing on some of the savings to their borrowers. Fannie Mae and Freddie Mac are able to issue debt at a cost of about 70 basis points less than private competitors (a weighted average of about 105 basis points on callable debt and about 45 basis points on noncallable debt); they also can issue MBS for about 40 basis points lower than the yield that investors require on the highest-rated private MBS.[13] Sallie Mae's cost advantage over competitors was estimated at 20 basis points to 50 basis points during the early 1980s.[14] Not all of the savings are passed on to borrowers. In the case of Fannie Mae and Freddie Mac, there are various estimates of the benefit to borrowers, centering on about 30 basis points.[15] Fannie Mae and Freddie Mac are highly profitable, and until 1993, Sallie Mae was highly profitable also.

There are several useful perspectives for analyzing GSEs. In many respects they operate in the medieval and early modern framework of state capitalism, rather than the system of free markets and open competition that define modern capitalism in English-speaking countries. They have received valuable privileges from the sovereign,

---

13. See CBO (1996, pp. 14-17) and the literature therein cited; see also Seiler (1998) and Ambrose and Warga (1996).
14. See CBO (1985, pp. 32-35). As discussed below, Sallie Mae chose to set a price that permitted other financial institutions to offer student loans. I have not been able to find a more recent estimate of Sallie Mae's cost advantage.
15. See Cotterman and Pearce (1996) and the literature cited therein.

in return for which they are expected to serve the sovereign in various ways. Kings often conferred monopolies to export, import or produce particular goods. Potential competitors were excluded from these activities.[16] The GSEs are not so explicitly protected, but their cost advantages make it difficult if not impossible for private companies without their privileges to compete with them. Thus Fannie Mae and Freddie Mac dominate the conforming loan market for home mortgages, and Sallie Mae dominated the market for guaranteed student loans (GSLs) until the federal government instituted the direct student loan program in 1993. None of these GSEs have bought or securitized all eligible loans. However, Fannie Mae and Freddie Mac set the terms for conforming loans, and lenders try to tailor their loans to be eligible for GSE purchase or securitization. Sallie Mae chose to set the price at which it would buy GSLs, and accept a smaller market share than it could achieve.[17]

The GSEs can also usefully be analyzed as public utilities or "natural monopolies."[18] Natural monopolies benefit from increasing returns to scale throughout the relevant range of output, so they have a cost advantage over any competitor and the efficient market structure is a single company. The most common natural monopolies are the public utilities providing electricity, gas, water, or most recently, cable television within a market area. Enterprises in these lines of business typically achieve their natural monopoly status for technological reasons. It is inefficient to have more than one set of power lines or television cables in a neighborhood or city. They may also benefit from economies of scale in production, as in the case of electricity. Technology may also change in such a way as to eliminate the natural monopoly, as is now occurring in the case of cable television and satellite dishes. Fannie Mae and Freddie Mac appear to enjoy economies of scale because of their implicit government guarantee rather than for technological reasons. Their cost advantages allow them to operate on a large scale, and that scale confers additional benefits on them by reducing the information costs for potential investors.

---

16. See Weicher (1994b) for further discussion. Bindoff (1952) describes the use of monopolies by Queen Elizabeth I of England to control her courtiers and achieve other public purposes.

17. See CBO (1985, especially Ch. II) for a discussion of Sallie Mae's policy.

18. For a more extensive discussion of the housing GSEs as public utilities, see Seiler (1998).

Individually, Fannie Mae and Freddie Mac are not monopolies. Instead, they jointly form a duopoly in the secondary mortgage market. They have almost identical powers under their charters, and they can compete with each other as both portfolio lenders and MBS issuers. They also dominate the market; as previously mentioned, they have bought or securitized about 75 percent of home-mortgage originations annually since 1990. Table 3 shows the rapid growth of their market share, particularly since the early 1980s.

Table 3: Housing GSE Share of Home Mortgage Market, 1975 – 1995

	1975	1980	1985	1990	1995
Panel A: Share of Single-Family Mortgages Originated During Year					
GSE Portfolio	4.7	6.1	29.7	41.8	45.5
GSE Securities	1.2	1.9	21.0	36.6	30.0
Panel B: Share of Outstanding Single-Family Mortgage					
GSE Portfolio	620.00%	5.6	6.5	4.5	5.8
GSE Securities	30.00%	1.4	9.6	21.6	29.9
Source: OFHEO, Annual Report to Congress: 1996; HUD, 1991 Report to Congress on the Federal National Mortgage Corporation.					

Economic theory shows that duopolists do not behave in the same manner as competitive companies. In recent years a number of economists have analyzed Fannie Mae and Freddie Mac as duopolists. They have generally come to the conclusion that the GSEs behave as if they were tacitly colluding duopolists.[19] To quote the most recent study:

> ...although no one piece of empirical evidence may be considered conclusive for our conjecture that Fannie Mae and Freddie Mac are tacitly colluding, the pieces of evidence...taken together support our conjecture. This, combined with the strong theoretical case for tacit collusion, makes us confident that Fannie Mae and Freddie Mac have been engaging in tacit collusion in the conforming market.[20]

As duopolists, Fannie Mae and Freddie Mac are unique among the GSEs. Each of the others has no competition from other GSEs. All of them, however, face potential or actual competition from pri-

---

19. See for example Hermalin and Jaffee (1996) and the literature cited therein; see also Goodman and Passmore (1992) and Seiler (1998). An alternative view is Woodward (1997).

20. Hermalin and Jaffee (1996), p. 253.

vate companies at least on the fringes of their market—among the least risky borrowers whom they serve, for example. (The Federal Home Loan Bank System and Sallie Mae do not face private competition as sources of advances, but they do face private competition as sources of funds for financial institutions.)

The duopoly has developed gradually. The GSEs originally conducted different activities and dealt with different types of home mortgages. Until 1970, Fannie Mae served as a secondary market for government-guaranteed mortgages. When Freddie Mac was created in 1970 to provide a secondary market for conventional mortgages, Fannie Mae was given authority to buy conventional loans as well, but Congress envisioned its role as subordinate to its role in the government-guaranteed market.[21] Fannie Mae did not buy its first conventional loan until 1972. Securitization of government-guaranteed mortgages by the newly created Government National Mortgage Association (GNMA or Ginnie Mae) substantially reduced Fannie Mae's role in that market after 1972, and it began to purchase a substantial volume of conventional mortgages in 1973.[22] From 1977 through 1981, its purchases were split roughly in half between conventional and government-guaranteed mortgages. The GSEs also conducted different activities during the 1970s: Fannie Mae was almost entirely a portfolio lender, while Freddie Mac specialized in MBS issuance, with a small portfolio. Table 1 shows this specialization as of 1981. But in the early 1980s Fannie Mae began to issue MBS in large quantities, and to deal almost exclusively in conventional mortgages; and since the late 1980s Freddie Mac has moved strongly into portfolio lending. Thus, they have become competitors to each other.

Purposes of GSE Regulation

The regulatory issues follow from the fact that GSEs are expected to serve public purposes, and given special privileges to do so, with-

---

21. For a discussion of the legislative history during this period, see HUD (1986, Ch. II, especially pp. 29-36).

22. Ginnie Mae was created when the original Fannie Mae was split in 1968, to provide special assistance to the mortgage market when the federal government considered it necessary, and perform other special functions. It is a government agency within HUD rather than a GSE. For that reason it is excluded from this paper, even though its MBS activities are virtually identical to those of Fannie Mae and Freddie Mac.

out direct cost to the federal government. Because they are supposed to be costless—not to require congressional appropriations—the federal government is concerned with their financial safety and soundness. Because they have special privileges and therefore an advantage over potential competitors, both the federal government and especially those competitors are concerned that they do not extend their activities into markets that are already being served by private companies.

Safety and Soundness

Safety and soundness are relevant to the current activities of a GSE. Is it conducting its business in such a manner as to minimize the threat that it will require financial assistance from the federal government?

GSEs face five types of risk: credit risk; interest-rate risk; management and operations risk; business risk; and program risk.[23] Each poses somewhat different issues for GSE management.

Credit Risk

Credit risk arises from the fact that some loans will default and impose losses on a GSE. No business is able to predict with complete accuracy how many defaults it will incur and what the losses on those defaults will be. Defaults may occur because the GSE exercises bad business judgment in making loans, or because of broader economic changes that affect the borrower's ability to make payments, such as a depression.

A few examples indicate the nature of these problems. During the late 1980s Freddie Mac went beyond its traditional single-family home mortgage business to make loans for multifamily rental housing in a few urban neighborhoods. These projects served moderate-income renters and the loans were intended to support affordable-housing goals. In some cases the buildings needed major repairs and were not well maintained. Freddie Mac incurred substantial losses on these mortgages. In 1990, multifamily loans accounted for 56 percent of Freddie Mac's losses due to foreclosure, although they represented only 3 percent of Freddie Mac's total portfolio.[24] (It should be noted

23. This categorization is based partly on HUD (1991a, 1991b) and partly on CBO (1991).

that multifamily foreclosure losses were less than 1 percent of Freddie Mac's loan portfolio, and Freddie Mac was profitable during that year. The multifamily foreclosure losses reduced net income by about 20 percent.)

Economic change is exemplified by the collapse of oil prices in the mid-1980s and the subsequent regional recession in the Southwest. The housing GSEs, like other mortgage lenders, did not expect the oil price drop and incurred unexpected defaults in that region.

GSEs address credit risk in several ways. To minimize the likelihood of bad business judgment, they can underwrite loans carefully, and also monitor their default experience by loan originator. They can require credit enhancement on risky loans, such as private mortgage insurance, which Fannie Mae and Freddie Mac generally require on mortgages with loan-to-value (LTV) ratios above 80 percent. They can require collateral against advances, as the Federal Home Loan Banks have always done; collateralization was so strong that the banks never incurred a loss during the savings and loan collapse of the late 1980s. Sallie Mae has also required adequate collateral for its advances.

Protection against economic downturns takes other forms. GSEs can minimize the consequences of regional recessions by geographically diversifying their portfolios, as has happened through the merger of the regional Banks for Cooperatives within the FCS. They can plan for the possibility of a major depression by developing econometric models that predict the consequences of such a depression for the GSE under alternative economic scenarios and business strategies. Both Fannie Mae and Freddie Mac have developed these "stress tests." Most important, they can build capital. Stress tests are useful partly to indicate the amount of capital needed to provide protection against a given contingency.

Interest Rate Risk

Interest-rate risk refers to the possible negative consequences of a change in market interest rates. GSEs have often borrowed short and lent long, facing higher interest costs and declining net worth when

---

24. For further discussion, see U.S. Department of Housing and Urban Development (1991a, pp. 17-18).

rates rose. The problem is exacerbated for mortgage lenders because interest-rate changes affect prepayments on fixed-rate mortgages.

This problem was especially acute for Fannie Mae during the early 1980s. Interest rates rose sharply in the late 1970s, during the final stages of the long inflationary period that began in 1965. Fannie Mae was then financing its portfolio of long-term loans with short-term debt. It was forced to refinance the portfolio at much higher rates. As a result, Fannie Mae's net worth was negative from 1978 through 1984. Its net worth became positive again when interest rates fell, and has been positive since then.[25]

Interest-rate changes also hurt the Farm Credit System in the mid-1980s. The FCS traditionally charged its average cost of funds to new borrowers, rather than the current market interest rate. This increased its loan volume during periods of rising rates, including the 1970s. In the late 1970s, it financed its growing portfolio with long-term non-callable debt. When interest rates fell in the 1980s, FCS's lending rates were well above its competitors, and as loans were repaid or refinanced with other lenders, it was left with a large volume of high-rate long term debt and a weak demand for its loans.

Interest-rate risk is a particular problem for portfolio lenders. It can be managed by matching the duration of assets and liabilities as closely as possible. It can also be reduced through interest-rate exchange contracts, or "swaps." Sallie Mae has used swaps to protect itself from interest-rate fluctuations on the relatively few occasions when it financed its variable-rate loan portfolio with fixed-rate debt. Stress tests are also useful to estimate the risk from unexpected interest changes, either rising or falling.

Management and Operations Risk

Management risk relates to "the inherent limitations of even the most efficiently organized management planning and decision-making processes."[26] Poor business judgment is the simplest example. Operations risks refer to inadequacies in both operating practices and internal control systems, including management information systems and audits. Inefficiencies, negligence and fraud may be consequences.

---

25. See HUD (1987, p. 100) for annual net worth estimates from 1978 through 1986.
26. HUD (1991b), p. 48.

To minimize these risks, GSEs have both internal and external auditing procedures and establish appropriate management structures. Fannie Mae and Freddie Mac have separated marketing from credit policy, for example.[27]

A 1992 review by the GAO "uncovered no significant weaknesses in GSE activities" except for Freddie Mac's multifamily program, the problems of which were already well known. The GAO went on to say that its "work was not sufficiently comprehensive to render an opinion on the design or operations of the entire control system of each GSE."[28]

Business Risk

Business risk is associated with changes in the markets within which GSEs operate. Changes can arise from shifts in the demand for the product that the GSEs finance, or changes on the supply side of the GSEs' market, such as competition from alternative sources of funds.

Examples of business risk include the abrupt restructuring of the thrift industry after FIRREA, which sharply reduced the demand for Home Loan Bank advances. Advance volume dropped by one-third between 1988 and 1994. The Farm Credit System's problems in the 1980s resulted in part from the appreciation of the American dollar, which cut into farm exports.

GSEs can address business risk by finding new customers, or by expanding into new lines of business. Home Loan Bank advances have risen above their pre-FIRREA peak as new types of institutions have joined the Home Loan Bank System. Expanding into new lines of business is discussed in the next section.

Program Risk

Program risk can be considered a special form of business risk: the possibility that the federal government will change policy in such a way as to reduce the profitability or even threaten the viability of a GSE. The most obvious example is Sallie Mae's experience in 1993,

---

27. For extensive though perhaps now somewhat out of date discussions of management and operations risks in Fannie Mae and Freddie Mac, see the appendices to HUD (1991a, 1991b). The appendices, describing policies, procedures, and corporate organization, were prepared for HUD by ICF, Incorporated.

28. GAO (1992), p. 2.

already discussed, which led to privatization in short order. Less drastic changes are conceivable in the other sectors. The 1996 farm bill may perhaps affect the market for Farm Credit System loans, for example. In housing, elimination of the home mortgage interest deduction would reduce the demand for home mortgages and perhaps cut into the business volume of the GSEs.

GSEs address program risk by continual, assiduous attention to policy makers and the press, and by closely following political trends.

New Programs

The congressional charters granted to GSEs at their creation identify the lines of business in which they can engage and limit their activities. The charters are occasionally amended to add or delete various activities. The purpose of these charter limitations is to restrict the GSEs to the activities deemed to deserve public support. Without the restrictions, the GSEs could exploit their special privileges and compete on favorable terms with fully private companies in other lines of business.

Despite these restrictions, GSEs often seek to expand into new fields. Their business itself changes from time to time, in response to market forces, and they adapt to it. Certainly the mortgage market today is very different than the mortgage market of 30 years ago, when Freddie Mac was chartered and Fannie Mae was given its present form—to say nothing of the mortgage market of 60 years ago, when Fannie Mae was first chartered and the Home Loan Bank System was established.

There is also competition at the fringes of the GSEs' market. The home mortgage market, for example, includes segments in which the GSEs have not been able to compete effectively (government-guaranteed loans) and segments from which they are barred (the jumbo nonconforming market). It also includes mortgage instruments and securities that did not exist when the GSEs were chartered. In education, Sallie Mae faces competition from colleges and universities that operate their own loan programs, and from commercial banks. In agriculture, the farm credit system competes with commercial lenders, especially small rural banks, for borrowers who could be considered risky or not, as in housing the GSEs can compete with the government guarantee programs for some loans. In the process of competing, the GSEs may find it profitable to develop new programs.

In addition, there are ancillary or related financial services that the GSEs may find complementary to the chartered activities. Both Sallie Mae and the Farm Credit System offer management and operations support to lenders. Fannie Mae and Freddie Mac provide automated underwriting systems, title insurance and a variety of other settlement services to their originating lenders.[29]

New programs are sometimes authorized by Congress. The Farm Credit System started with authority only for farm real estate loans. It expanded into production loans under new statutory authority in 1923, and then into loans to cooperatives in 1933. Sallie Mae started in 1972 with a mission to support the market for government-guaranteed student loans. In 1981 it was given the same authority in the market for uninsured student loans, and in 1986 it received statutory authority to buy, sell, insure, or underwrite loans to colleges and universities for plant and equipment, at the same time that Connie Lee was created. Fannie Mae has a parallel history. As previously mentioned, it started with authority to support the market for government-guaranteed home mortgages. In 1968 it was allowed to issue securities backed by these mortgages. In 1970 its authority was extended to conventional mortgages, at the same time Freddie Mac was created.

Since 1980, new programs have been a recurring issue in Fannie Mae regulation. The 1968 Federal National Mortgage Association Charter Act gave authority to approve new conventional mortgage programs to the Secretary of HUD.[30] In 1981, Fannie Mae received temporary approval to purchase second mortgages. HUD Secretary Samuel R. Pierce Jr. cited the need for liquidity as a key reason for approving the program; mortgage rates were then at unprecedented levels, and many homebuyers were relying on second mortgages to complete the purchase. In 1984, when Fannie Mae sought a second

---

29. For an extensive discussion of automated underwriting systems, see OFHEO (1995, pp. 1-7). For discussion of the GSEs, provision of other ancillary services, see Seiler (1998).

30. The HUD Secretary received similar authority over Freddie Mac in 1989, through amendments to the Federal Home Loan Mortgage Corporation Act of 1970. The amendments were part of FIRREA. Prior to 1989, the Federal Home Loan Bank Board, which was also the board of directors for Freddie Mac, had authority to approve new programs.

extension of this authority, rates were much lower, and Secretary Pierce solicited public comment on the request. Before HUD acted, Congress gave Fannie Mae the authority by statute in 1984 for a three-year period, and then made the authority permanent in 1987.[31] A somewhat similar issue arose in 1990, when Fannie Mae proposed to enter the construction loan market; FIRREA limited the ability of savings and loans to engage in construction financing, and builders sought alternative sources of funds. HUD Secretary Jack F. Kemp granted approval for a pilot program in 1991, and approved a broader program in 1992.[32]

New program approval issues have sometimes arisen because of the dramatic changes in the mortgage market. In 1986, Congress authorized a new type of MBS, the Real Estate Mortgage Investment Conduct (REMIC). Fannie Mae and Freddie Mac were permitted to issue REMICs, subject to the approval of the HUD secretary and the Bank Board, respectively. Freddie Mac quickly received approval. Fannie Mae sought to issue conventional mortgage REMICs; Secretary Pierce claimed jurisdictional authority to approve the program, which Fannie Mae at first contested but then accepted.[33] Secretary Pierce approved the conventional REMIC on a temporary basis in 1987, and gave permanent approval in 1988.

Fannie Mae has also proposed to move beyond mortgage purchase and securitization. In 1985, it announced a program to buy mortgage-backed obligations issued by financing subsidiaries of financial institutions. The leadership of the Senate Banking Committee questioned the legality of this program under the Charter Act, and HUD concluded that it was not authorized. Objections were raised by investment bankers and others in the financing business on the ground that Fannie Mae's agency status would give it a competitive advantage in this market.[34] In 1990, Fannie Mae sought HUD approval for a program to purchase debt obligations secured by conventional mortgages. HUD denied the request for several reasons, concluding that

---

31. For discussion of this issue, see HUD (1987, pp. 49-50, 171-173).
32. For discussions of this issue, see HUD (1991b, p. 57, and 1992b, p. 119).
33. For discussion of this issue see HUD (1987, pp. 175-176). Fannie Mae had charter authority to issue REMICs or other securities backed by government-guaranteed mortgages without the approval of the HUD secretary.
34. For more extensive discussion, see HUD (1987, pp. 47-48, 174).

the requested authority was extremely broad and would allow Fannie Mae "to engage in complex transactions significantly different from the examples given by F.N.M.A. in the documents submitted to HUD and from those engaged in previously," including among other activities the ability to make advances against conventional mortgages, like the Home Loan Banks. HUD also expressed concern that the program would significantly increase the risk incurred by Fannie Mae, by the federal government and the taxpayers.[35]

The 1992 legislation that changed the regulatory structure for Fannie Mae and Freddie Mac also modified the HUD secretary's program approval authority. The secretary can deny a new program if he or she determines that the program is not authorized by law, or is not in the public interest. Since the act was passed, the secretary has approved every new program request by either GSE. In one case, however, Congress took action after the secretary gave new program approval, effectively rescinding it. This concerned Fannie Mae's 1997 request to establish a Mortgage Protection Plan (MPP) that would provide cash-value life insurance and short-term disability and unemployment insurance on first-time homebuyers whose mortgages were financed by Fannie Mae. The profitability of this type of insurance was curtailed in the Balanced Budget Act of 1997, partly because of congressional concern about the MPP. Fannie Mae then decided not to go forward with the program.[36]

On occasion, Congress has acted to limit the authority of a GSE. In 1986, Sallie Mae was forbidden to own or control a bank or similar financial institution. Ownership was allowed under 1981 legislation authorizing any activity that would support the credit needs of students. But such actions are rare. The Farm Credit System did not suffer any diminution of its powers when it ran into major financial difficulties in the mid-1980s.

Implications for Regulation

Several conclusions can be drawn from the foregoing discussion of regulatory purposes. First, although it is analytically convenient to separate safety and soundness from new program approval, in prac-

---

35. For further discussion of this request, see HUD (1991b, pp. 56-57). The quotation is from p. 57.
36. For more extensive discussion of this issue, see Seiler (1998, pp. 28-30).

tice the issues are often joined; the regulator must decide whether a new program is too risky. This issue was confronted by HUD in 1990, for example. Second, once established, a GSE is likely to look for new ways to take advantage of its charter. As it does so, it may invade the markets of established institutions, which in turn may seek statutory or regulatory relief. Third, GSE expansion often occurs in response to immediate but temporary economic problems, such as recession or inflation. The expansion is likely to be permanent. Finally, safety and soundness issues attract more public attention than new programs, but they arise less often. A regulator needs to be able to address both safety and soundness and market structure.

How to Regulate GSEs

The two purposes of regulation raise two issues. To protect the safety and soundness of a GSE, its regulator needs authority to obtain relevant information, ability to analyze it and authority to order and enforce changes in behavior. To address issues of market structure and competition and the appropriate role of a GSE, the regulator needs to be able to weigh the effects of new GSE programs in the relevant markets. Stated simply, "safety and soundness" depends on regulatory powers; "new program approval" depends on regulatory structure.

Regulating for Safety and Soundness

GSEs certainly do not want to incur financial problems, but they happen on occasion. Management can make mistakes, as in any private company; economic conditions can change, sometimes abruptly and decisions that seemed prudent when they were made turn out to be incorrect. Agricultural lenders have the additional problems of environmental changes and weather to contend with. Moreover, the concerns of GSE management are not identical to the concerns of the federal government or the taxpayers. GSEs have their implicit guarantees, and therefore can make decisions and take risks in the expectation that the company will not be allowed to fail. Safety and soundness regulation is therefore desirable.

The GSEs are financial institutions, and need to be regulated as such. In many respects they are. Bank regulators have a range of powers that are also enjoyed by GSE regulators, at least to a substantial extent.[37]

Examination Authority

GSE regulators generally have the ability to require reports from the agencies and to conduct their own examinations in order to verify the accuracy of the information provided by the agency and to assess its exposure to management and operations risk.

Enforcement Authority

Regulators can take a series of steps to forestall or address GSE actions that they think may endanger safety and soundness. These include cease-and-desist orders; authority to remove officers and directors; authority to assess civil money penalties, and in extreme instances, authority to appoint a conservator or receiver.

Authority to Set Capital Standards

Regulators can establish capital requirements, including risk-based standards.

All GSE regulators have these general powers, as do bank and thrift institution regulators. There are variations among the GSE regulators, depending partly on the nature of the GSE and its activities.

The Farm Credit System is the most complicated GSE, and the one most like a banking system. The regulatory powers of the Farm Credit Administration with respect to member institutions are very close to those of bank regulators; the FCA uses the CAMEL rating system to evaluate their safety and soundness. The district banks have general supervisory authority over the institutions in their area, and the FCA has authority over both the district banks and the members. The district banks can refuse to borrow for individual member institutions, certainly a very forceful way of changing institutional behavior.

Before FIRREA, the Federal Home Loan Bank System had a similar structure, regulating member thrift institutions and the regional Home Loan Banks. FHFB now has very broad powers over the regional banks. It approves their budgets in detail. It can determine the compensation of individual bank directors, remove directors

---

37. The following discussion is based on CBO (1991) and the 1992 housing GSE regulatory legislation.

or other employees, and liquidate or reorganize a bank. It lacks the ability to issue cease and desist orders, but in general has the strongest powers of any GSE regulator.

Like the other regulators, OFHEO has examination and enforcement authority, but the GSEs are empowered to contest enforcement actions through hearings and court injunctions, which were not part of the pre-1992 regulatory process. OFHEO also has the authority to set the compensation of senior GSE management. Its ability to appoint a conservator and take some other actions is conditioned on the capital status of the GSE; the 1992 legislation established several degrees of capital adequacy and attached different enforcement powers to the various capital standards.

To exercise these powers effectively, the regulator must be able to develop adequate institutional capacity. This has usually been interpreted to include the ability to determine staffing policies independent of the federal budget. Most regulators can set their own budgets and determine the size of their own staffs. They can pay the staff more than the federal civil service salary schedule. They finance their activities by levying fees on the agencies and institutions they regulate. All of the regulators except OFHEO have this authority. OFHEO's budget is determined by annual federal appropriations, as part of the normal budget process. Its funds come from the GSEs, in proportion to their assets.

Setting Capital Standards

The process of setting capital standards merits special attention. Capital standards are intended to protect the GSE and the federal government from interest rate risk and credit risk. The relative importance of these risks varies from one GSE to another, and varies over time for a given GSE. A variety of approaches have been taken by regulators, other federal agencies, and occasionally even Congress.

The simplest standards set capital/asset ratios, weighted by the riskiness of the different assets held by the GSE. Such standards have been set by the FCA for Farm Credit System institutions, and by Congress for Fannie Mae and Freddie Mac. Capital standards for the Home Loan Banks are set partly by Congress (in the form of statutorily required member purchases of bank stock) and partly by FHFB.

Capital ratios can be thought of as estimates of the amount of capital that might be needed in times of difficulty. "Stress tests" are a more elaborate and sophisticated way to estimate desirable capital levels.[38] They analyze the effect of specified economic changes on the loan experience of a GSE, including changes in cash flow, income and net worth. They produce estimates of the capital needed to survive the economic scenario. Stress tests have been developed and used by Standard and Poor's and by Moody's to analyze the activities of private mortgage insurers, for example.

Stress tests have been used by federal agencies to evaluate the capital position of several GSEs. Obviously, a very large number of scenarios can be created, and it is a matter of professional judgment as to which scenarios are worth considering. In addition, the behavior of the GSE as the scenario unfolds can vary. Thus, different agencies have on occasion reached somewhat different conclusions on the capital adequacy of a particular GSE. For example, the OMB and CBO each performed stress tests on the Farm Credit System in 1990.[39] Both tests were based on a repetition of the difficulties of the mid-1980s. CBO, however, assumed that the downturn began immediately; the OMB allowed for two good years to begin with. There were also differences in the assumed economic changes. Both tests concluded that the system could survive the test with positive capital and could meet the capital standards established by the FCA for most if not all of the period covered. Several district banks, however, could not meet the standard (about five or six in each agency's test).

Stress tests were employed and discussed during the policy debates that led to the 1992 law on regulating the housing GSEs.[40] The two GSEs themselves developed tests, based on different economic scenarios. Fannie Mae's stress test is based on its 1981-1982 experience with Texas mortgages; assumed to occur nationally; it is a national version of a regional recession. Fannie Mae's ability to meet

38. For discussions of stress tests, see HUD (1991c) and CBO (1991).

39. For further discussion of the tests, see CBO (1991, pp. 100-105, especially p. 104).

40. The tests are discussed more fully in various publications: HUD (1990, 1991c) and CBO (1991) for Fannie Mae's own test; HUD (1991c) and CBO (1991) for Freddie Mac's own test and OMB's tests, and HUD (1991c, 1992a, 1992b) for detailed description of HUD's tests, conducted for both GSEs as of the end of 1990 and the end of 1991.

this standard, at least as of 1989, was very sensitive to assumptions about default rates and loan losses. Freddie Mac's stress test is based on a Depression scenario, originally developed by Moody's, projecting the number of years that it could survive.

For the 1992 Federal budget (released in February 1991), the OMB also developed a variant of Moody's test, but with the important assumption that the Depression did not occur for another 10 years, during which time the GSEs reduced their exposure to credit risk.

As the regulator of both Fannie Mae and Freddie Mac from 1989 through 1992, HUD built a stress test based on the Moody's test; it had earlier begun to develop a stress test for Fannie Mae. Results were sensitive to the assumptions about a GSE's response to the Depression, particular how rapidly it recognized that a Depression was in fact under way, and what business strategy it adopted in the face of rising loan defaults. Each GSE could survive 10 years of the scenario if it immediately recognized the Depression and bought no new mortgages during the Depression (a "wind-down" scenario). Neither could survive 10 years if it continued to buy mortgages to maintain its portfolio for more than a year after the start of the Depression (a "zero-growth" scenario).[41] The longer the GSE continued to buy mortgages, the shorter its survival period. Surviving 10 years of Moody's own Depression scenario would meet Moody's requirements to earn the GSE an AAA rating, and therefore 10 years is a significant target.

Freddie Mac's own stress test is based on a wind-down scenario and has results similar to HUD's for that scenario. The OMB used a zero-growth scenario.

In addition to conducting their own stress tests, government agencies have contracted with private rating companies to assess risk. In the aftermath of FIRREA, the Treasury Department employed Standard & Poor's to rate the GSEs, on the assumption that they had no government guarantee, explicit or implicit. On this assumption, in 1991 Standard & Poor's gave an AAA rating to the Federal Home Loan Bank System and to Sallie Mae; A+ to Freddie Mac; A- to Fannie Mae, and BBB to the Farm Credit System. With the implicit guar-

---

41. These results are for the later HUD stress tests, as of 1991, reported in HUD (1992a, 1992b). Very similar, slightly less positive, results were reported for the 1990 tests.

antee, all were actually rated AAA (Labaton, 1991). In 1997 Standard & Poor's rated both GSEs as AA-, absent their government guarantee (Seiler, 1998).

Interest-rate risk became a special concern of policymakers during the early 1980s, when the high rates turned Fannie Mae's net worth negative. Analysts and government officials favored mark-to-market analysis to estimate interest-rate risk. Fannie Mae and Freddie Mac were generally unwilling to report their net worth on a mark-to-market basis until 1990; at that point both had a positive net worth of about $6 billion. Meanwhile, HUD developed a more refined measure of interest-rate risk of the stress test variety, assuming a sudden extreme rise or fall of interest rates and a prolonged period at the new rates.[42] As of 1991, both GSEs were able to survive for 10 years even if interest rates rose to triple their 1990 levels over the course of four years. HUD concluded that neither GSE was likely to be harmed by a return to the high interest rates of the late 1970s and early 1980s. This represented a substantial change for Fannie Mae over the decade of the 1980s, a marked improvement from its negative net worth of the early 1980s after a period of sharp interest rate increases. HUD concluded that credit risk was a more serious concern than interest rate risk for both GSEs in the early 1990s. Congress, however, continued to be much concerned with interest rate risk.

The 1992 GSE legislation established a stress test for determining the capital adequacy of Fannie Mae and Freddie Mac. The mandated test is not based on the Moody's Great Depression scenario. Rather, it is closer to Fannie Mae's regional recession; OFHEO is expected to base the analysis of credit risk on the worst default and loss experience over a two-year period in any contiguous areas containing at least 5 percent of the U.S. population. This region was expected to be Texas in 1981-1982, but subsequent analysis by OFHEO indicates that it is actually four nearby states (Oklahoma, Arkansas, Louisiana and Mississippi) in 1983-1984. The act also specified an interest-rate risk test, with a smaller maximum increase or decrease than HUD's stress test, but occurring more quickly.

OFHEO was required to develop a stress test and establish risk-based capital standards by December 1994 (18 months after the

---

42. These interest rate risk analyses are described in detail in HUD (1992a, 1992b). An earlier analysis appears in HUD (1991c).

appointment of its first director). More than three years after that date, it has not done so. It does not expect to do so for another year or more, and that may prove to be optimistic.[43] There are several reasons for this extraordinary (even for government agencies) delay. One is the time required to set up a new agency from scratch. A second is the complexity of the stress test. It is not easy to write an econometric model into legislation. The most recent stress test of these two very large enterprises is still HUD's 1991 analysis, to my knowledge.

Economic Regulation

Economic regulation raises a different set of concerns. The GSEs' implicit guarantee gives them significant advantages over actual and potential competitors in most markets. The presumption in economic theory and American economic policy is that competition with free entry is the appropriate market structure. A GSE is likely to be in a position to dominate any given market. The regulator therefore needs to be able to weigh the benefits and costs of new GSE programs. It should have knowledge of the relevant financial market sector. It should also have responsibility for regulating other financial market participants, or for operating federal government programs that serve the relevant market. With this knowledge and these responsibilities, the regulator can strike a balance between the GSE and its competitors, who serve the same or related segments of the market.

The appropriate regulators are therefore either Federal Government departments with program responsibility for the financial or real sector served by the GSE, or regulators of financial institutions. In housing, the appropriate federal agency is HUD, with its responsibility for FHA mortgage insurance, which competes with the GSEs at the low-income, risky end of the mortgage market. The appropriate financial regulator is either the Federal Reserve, as bank regulator, or the Office of Thrift Supervision (OTS), as savings and loan regulator; banks and savings and loan associations compete with the GSEs to some extent as portfolio lenders in the conforming loan market, and serve the jumbo market from which the GSEs are excluded.[44] In agriculture, the appropriate federal agency is the Department of Agricul-

---

43. For a discussion of OFHEO's progress and difficulties, see GAO (1997b). GAO also lists several reasons why OFHEO may not be able to meet its latest stated target date (pp. 47-49).

ture, which operates the FmHA lending program, and the appropriate financial regulator is the Federal Reserve Board. In education, the appropriate federal agency was the Department of Education, and the appropriate financial regulator was the Fed.

It is worth noticing that the original regulatory structure for the housing GSEs took this form. Fannie Mae was regulated by HUD, and it supported the market for FHA and VA home mortgages. Freddie Mac and the Federal Home Loan Banks were regulated by the Federal Home Loan Bank Board, and they served the most important conventional lenders, the thrift institutions, which were also regulated by the Bank Board. This distinction of course was lost when Fannie Mae began to deal in conventional mortgages beginning in 1973. The structure was further dismantled by FIRREA, which created separate regulators for the thrift institutions and for the Home Loan Banks that the thrift institutions still owned.

FIRREA, however, established a different regulatory structure revolving around the HUD secretary, who became the regulator of both Fannie Mae and Freddie Mac, and also a member of the board of FHFB, and thus one of five individuals charged with regulating the Home Loan Banks.[45] FIRREA thus created a regulator with responsibility for programs that served the low end of the market, though not for financial institutions that served the high end. As Fannie Mae and Freddie Mac developed new programs to compete with banks and thrift institutions, HUD had some of the expertise necessary to evaluate these programs from its general knowledge of the mortgage market and related financial markets, but not the full responsibility for considering the effect on all market participants.

---

44. There are of course other bank regulators, the Federal Deposit Insurance Corporation (FDIC) and the Office of the Comptroller of the Currency (OCC). I cite the Fed as the largest and most comprehensive bank regulator.

45. Indeed, for a few months in 1989-1990, the HUD secretary was a member of the Freddie Mac board of directors as well as its regulator, and also the only member of the board of FHFB. This situation changed when Freddie Mac stockholders elected a board in February 1990, and when Congress confirmed the four appointed members of the FHFB board, after a dispute over whether their positions were full-time or part-time.

How Not to Regulate

There are two inappropriate structures: a single-purpose regulator and split regulation.

An independent regulator, with no responsibilities beyond regulating a GSE, invites capture by the regulatee. The institutional well being of the regulator is bound up with the well being of the GSE it regulates. As the GSE grows, so can the regulator; if the GSE is threatened by competition, so is the regulator. Regulatory capture began with the Interstate Commerce Commission and the railroads more than a century ago; it was part of the complaint against the Federal Home Loan Bank Board vis-a-vis the savings and loans, and part of the complaint against the Farm Credit Administration vis-a-vis its member institutions. It remains a problem for the FCA despite the reforms of 1985-1987; the FCA is responsible for the safety and soundness of the FCS members, and has no institutional reason to be concerned about the market implications of any new programs.

A sole, single-purpose housing GSE regulator, as has been suggested by the GAO, would have the expertise to regulate safety and soundness of all three GSEs, but again would have no incentive to consider the market implications of any new program by any of the GSEs it regulates, except insofar as the new program affected the interests of one of the other GSEs. Nor is it likely that the single housing GSE regulator would have particular public visibility. Both HUD and the Fed now attract more attention from both policymakers and the press than do either OFHEO or FHFB.[46]

There is some irony in the GAO's position: its July 1997 report advocating a sole single-purpose regulator for the housing GSEs was followed three months later by a report on the problems besetting OFHEO. To be fair, the reports are not inherently contradictory. The GAO argues that the sole regulator would be able to hire better staff, and would create valuable synergies; it could argue that OFHEO would be more effective if it had the additional resources that would come with regulatory authority over the Home Loan Banks. The sole regulator would still have to compete in the labor market with other financial regulators and with accounting and law companies, however, and it could also be argued that a regulator with additional responsi-

---

46. For an opposite point of view, see GAO (1997a).

bilities would be even slower than OFHEO has been. It is also questionable if an independent regulator has the political and institutional strength to meet the GSEs on equal terms, even combining the resources of OFHEO and FHFB. At present, the two regulators have a total staff of about 200 and a budget of $30 million.

A variant of the single-purpose regulator has been suggested by the CBO: an entity with the sole purpose of regulating all GSEs.[47] This raises similar problems. The regulator has no incentive to consider the market implications of any new program by any of the GSEs it regulates, only its possible consequences for the GSE's safety and soundness. If private companies are already providing the services that the GSE proposes to provide, it is likely that the GSE will be able to do so profitably as well, given the advantages of its implicit guarantee. For safety and soundness reasons, also, the regulator must at present acquire expertise in two unrelated financial market sectors.

Split regulation poses other problems. Division of responsibility and authority between two regulators lets a GSE play them off against each other, to the detriment of effective regulation. Split regulation also invites confusion over the boundary lines between the regulators, and conflict is likely to result for that reason as well.

Of course, the current regulation of Fannie Mae and Freddie Mac suffers from both defects. Authority is split between OFHEO (safety and soundness) and HUD (new program approval, and also social goals). This means that nobody has the responsibility for weighing the costs against the benefits of new GSE activities. Each can consider some of the benefits and some of the costs, but not all. OFHEO can disallow new programs on safety and soundness grounds but not consider their public purpose; the HUD secretary can consider the benefits and costs from a market standpoint, but not the risks. The situation is reminiscent of the six blind men and the elephant. Either the regulators have to make a joint decision, or they work at cross-purposes, or one abdicates authority.

In addition, the safety and soundness regulator is an independent, single-purpose entity, and therefore at great risk of regulatory capture, although OFHEO's limited activity to date does not provide much evidence for or against regulatory capture.

---

47. CBO (1991), pp. xxi-xxii.

Conclusion

Usually the public policy issue is what the government should do, not which agency should do it. But in the case of GSE regulation, the opposite is the case. Any regulator can acquire the skills to conduct safety and soundness regulation. The OFHEO experience certainly suggests that it takes time to acquire them, but there are several government agencies, and for that matter private companies, that have been able to hire or train qualified examiners, accountants, lawyers and other professional staff, and OFHEO's problems should not be permanent. Economic regulation is a different matter. Federal agencies have substantive knowledge about the markets in which they are involved. An agency with broad authority over federal policy in a particular sector is best able to consider the appropriate role for a GSE in that sector. GSEs operate in financial markets that serve a particular real sector of the economy, so the appropriate economic regulator could have authority in either the financial market or the real sector, if it does not have authority over both.

Currently most GSEs are regulated by independent, single-purpose regulators. The Home Loan Banks are a partial exception, because the HUD secretary is a member of FHFB; they are the only exception. The independent regulators are in a position to address safety and soundness, but not to consider public purposes and economic implications of GSE activities.

This is especially relevant because most current GSE issues are market issues. The consensus among informed analysts is that all of the GSEs appear to pose no immediate threat to the public treasury, although the FCS and Fannie Mae have posed threats within the last 10 to 20 years, and the Home Loan Banks lost a significant share of their capital when their retained earnings were appropriated in FIRREA as part payment for the costs of the savings and loan resolution. Nor do we know how well Fannie Mae and Freddie Mac are capitalized until OFHEO completes its stress test; they do meet the "minimum capital" ratio established in the 1992 legislation.

Especially in housing, new program issues arise frequently; the GSEs have undertaken more than a dozen since OFHEO was established. In agriculture, there are recurring proposals to expand the role of the FCS. Insofar as the new programs fall within the charters and do not require new legislation, there is no entity in a position to weigh the economic costs and benefits. In this respect, regulation has been moving in the wrong direction.

Finally, of the current regulators, OFHEO has the weakest authority and the biggest job.

References

Ambrose, Brent W., and Arthur Warga. "Implications of Privatization: The Costs to Fannie Mae and Freddie Mac." In U.S. Department of Housing and Urban Development, *Studies on Privatizing Fannie Mae and Freddie Mac*. May 1996. Pp. 169-204.

Bindoff, S.T. Tudor England. London: Penguin Books, 1952.

Bradbury, Darcy. "Statement." U.S. House of Representatives, Committee on Economic and Educational Opportunities, and Committee on Government Reform and Oversight. *Joint Hearing on Privatizing Government Sponsored Enterprises* (GSEs). Serial No. 104-16. May 3, 1995.

Cotterman, Robert F., and James E. Pearce. "The Effects of the Federal National Mortgage Association and the Federal Home Loan Mortgage Corporation on Conventional Fixed-Rate Mortgage Yields." In U.S. Department of Housing and Urban Development, *Studies on Privatizing Fannie Mae and Freddie Mac*. May 1996. Pp. 97-168.

Goodman, John L., Jr., and S. Wayne Passmore. "Market Power and the Pricing of Mortgage Securitization." Federal Reserve Board, Finance and Economics Discussion Series Working Paper No. 187. 1992.

Hermalin, Benjamin E., and Dwight M. Jaffee. "The Privatization of Fannie Mae and Freddie Mac: Implications for Mortgage Industry Structure." In U.S. Department of Housing and Urban Development, *Studies on Privatizing Fannie Mae and Freddie Mac*. May 1996. Pp. 225-302.

Labaton, Stephen. "Bush Plan On Lenders Is Disclosed." *New York Times*. May 1, 1991.

McKinley, Vern. "The Mounting Case for Privatizing Fannie Mae and Freddie Mac." Cato Institute Policy Analysis. December 23, 1997.

Miles, Barbara. "The Student Loan Marketing Association: Charter Rescission ('Privatization')." U.S. Congressional Research Service. May 12, 1995.

Miles, Barbara. "Reorganization and Privatization of Sallie Mae and Connie Lee." U.S. Congressional Research Service. December 18, 1996.

Seiler, Robert S., Jr. "Fannie Mae and Freddie Mac as Investor-Owned Public Utilities." *Journal of Public Budgeting, Accounting and Financial Management.* Forthcoming, 1998.

Shear, William B. "Economic Studies by Four Agencies on the Benefits and Costs of Government Sponsorship of Fannie Mae and Freddie Mac." Unpublished paper, November 1996.

Sockwell, Oliver. "Statement." U.S. House of Representatives, Committee on Economic and Educational Opportunities, and Committee on Government Reform and Oversight. Joint Hearing on Privatizing Government Sponsored Enterprises (GSEs). Serial No. 104-16. May 3, 1995.

U.S. Congressional Budget Office. Government-Sponsored Enterprises and Their Implicit Federal Subsidy: The Case of Sallie Mae. December 1985.

U.S. Congressional Budget Office. *Controlling the Risks of Government-Sponsored Enterprises.* April 1991.

U.S. Congressional Budget Office. *The Federal Home Loan Banks in the Housing Finance System.* July 1993.

U.S. Congressional Budget Office. *Assessing the Public Costs and Benefits of Fannie Mae and Freddie Mac.* May 1996.

U.S. Department of Housing and Urban Development. *1986 Report to Congress on the Federal National Mortgage Association.* June 29, 1987.

U.S. Department of Housing and Urban Development. *1990 Report to Congress on the Federal Home Loan Mortgage Corporation.* July 1991. [1991a]

U.S. Department of Housing and Urban Development. *1990 Report to Congress on the Federal National Mortgage Association.* July 1991. [1991b]

U.S. Department of Housing and Urban Development. *Capitalization Study of the Federal National Mortgage Association and the Federal Home Loan Mortgage Corporation.* December 1991. [1991c]

U.S. Department of Housing and Urban Development. *1991 Report to Congress on the Federal Home Loan Mortgage Corporation.* December 1992. [1992a]

U.S. Department of Housing and Urban Development. *1991 Report to Congress on the Federal National Mortgage Association.* December 1992. [1992b]

U.S. Department of Housing and Urban Development. *Report to Congress on the Federal Home Loan Bank System.* April 1994.

U.S. Department of Housing and Urban Development. *Privatization of Fannie Mae and Freddie Mac: Desirability and Feasibility.* July 1996.

U.S. General Accounting Office. *Government-Sponsored Enterprises: System of Internal Controls at Freddie Mac, Fannie Mae, and Sallie Mae.* GAO/GGD-92-50. March 1992.

U.S. General Accounting Office. *Federal Home Loan Bank System: Reforms Needed to Promote Its Safety, Soundness, and Effectiveness.* GAO/GGD-94-38. December 1993.

U.S. General Accounting Office. *Farm Credit System: Repayment of Federal Assistance and Competitive Positions.* GAO/GGD-94-39. March 1994. [1994a]

U.S. General Accounting Office. *Farm Credit System: Potential Impacts of FCB Mergers on Farmer and Rancher Borrowers.* GAO/GGD-95-19. December 1994. [1994b]

U.S. General Accounting Office. Housing Enterprises: Potential Impacts of Severing Government Sponsorship. GAO/GGD-96-120. May 1996.

U.S. General Accounting Office. *Government-Sponsored Enterprises: Advantages and Disadvantages of Creating a Single Housing GSE Regulator.* GAO/GGD-97-139. July 1997. [1997a]

U.S. General Accounting Office. *Federal Housing Enterprises: OFHEO Faces Challenge In Implementing Comprehensive Oversight Program.* GAO/GGD-98-6. October 1997. [1997b]

U.S. Office of Federal Housing Enterprise Oversight. *Annual Report to Congress*. Various years.

U.S. Office of Management and Budget. *Budget of the United States Government: Appendix*. Various years.

U.S. Senate, Committee on Banking, Housing, and Urban Affairs. *Second Roundtable Hearing on the Safety and Soundness of Fannie Mae and Freddie Mac*. August 2, 1990.

Weicher, John C. "The Future Structure of the Housing Finance System." In William S. Haraf and Rose Marie Kushmeider, editors, *Restructuring Banking and Financial Services in America*. Washington: American Enterprise Institute, 1987. Pp. 296-336.

Weicher, John C. "The New Structure of the Housing Finance System." *Federal Reserve Bank of St. Louis Review*. Vol. 76, No. 4: July/August 1994. Pp. 47-65. [1994a]

Weicher, John C. "Housing Finance Fiefdoms." *The American Enterprise*. Vol. 5, No. 5: September/October 1994. Pp. 62-67. [1994b]

Woodward, Susan E. "Rechartering Fannie Mae and Freddie Mac: The Policy Issues." Unpublished paper. 1997.

Zimmerman, Dennis. "Unfunded Mandates and State Taxation of the Income of Fannie Mae, Freddie Mac, and Sallie Mae: Implications for D.C. Finances." U.S. Congressional Research Service. September 8, 1995.

Comments on...

Regulating Government-Sponsored Enterprises

Marvin Phaup
Deputy Assistant Director, Special Studies
Congressional Budget Office

The usual disclaimers apply, of course. I am speaking only for myself and not for the Congressional Budget Office, nor, certainly for any member of Congress.

John C. Weicher has written a very useful paper about government-sponsored enterprises (GSEs) and their regulation. In discussing his paper, I will return to three questions that he addressed, and in two cases offer slightly different answers. In particular, I will attempt to assess the prospects for restructuring existing regulation by considering: 1) what a GSE is; 2) what is the regulatory problem they present; and 3) who are the de facto regulators of Fannie Mae and Freddie Mac.

The traditional definition of a GSE is a financial intermediary that is privately owned but created by and sponsored by the federal government. A key consequence of federal sponsorship is that this conveys a federal guarantee, which is implied rather than explicit, to the financial obligations of the GSE. An unfortunate weakness of this definition is that it produces such a mixed bag of entities for analysis: the Farm Credit System, the oldest of the GSEs; Farmer Mac, the newest and the smallest; the Federal Home Loan Banks, a vestige of the thrift industry; Sallie Mae, the student loan monolith, and Fannie Mae and Freddie Mac.

We need to pare the list of GSEs to a manageable size based on the magnitude and type of regulatory problem each presents. We can eliminate Sallie Mae from the list because it is in the process of being privatized, an effort worth paying attention to, because this may tell us something useful about the feasibility of privatizing a GSE.

As Dr. Weicher emphasized, the most valuable feature of GSE status to an entity is the implied federal guarantee of their obligations. That the guarantee is implied rather than explicit has advantages to both Congress and to the GSEs. One advantage to the GSE is that it may be more difficult for the government to withdraw an implied guarantee than an explicit one. Inasmuch as the implied guarantee exists despite an explicit statement on GSE obligations that they are not guaranteed by the federal government, it has yet to be demonstrated that the market can be persuaded that an implied guarantee has been withdrawn—short of a default. So the attempt to privatize Sallie Mae and revoke the implied guarantee bears watching.

By also eliminating Farmer Mac from the working list of GSEs on grounds of size and newness, we are left with four: the Farm Credit System and the Federal Home Loan Banks on the one hand, and Fannie and Freddie on the other. These pairs can be distinguished further on the basis of their operating objectives. The Home Loan Banks and the Farm Credit System come out of the cooperative movement, which has left these GSEs a legacy of mutuality and an associated concern with the interest of their borrowers. Fannie and Freddie, and Sallie before the current privatization effort, are really entirely different animals. They are owned by unrelated private investors who, through a variety of means, have managed to align closely the interests of management and shareholders.

Now, ordinarily, this alignment seems desirable from the standpoint of efficiency because investors and managers are both then thought to have an interest in maximizing the value of the company. The trouble with GSEs in general, and Fannie and Freddie in particular, is that maximizing the value of the company is largely accomplished by maximizing the value of the government's implied guarantee. As Randall S. Kroszner mentioned in his presentation, implied guarantees substitute government capital, or government equity, for private equity. It makes sense for the management of a GSE whose interests are aligned with those of the shareholders to try to maximize the value of government equity in the company.

The functions performed by the housing GSEs are straightforward. They essentially engage in two activities: they borrow money in the capital markets and use it to finance a portfolio of mortgages and they guarantee mortgage-backed securities. They accomplish the latter by purchasing mortgages—not for holding in portfolio—but to turn into guaranteed, marketable, mortgage-backed securities. Neither of these functions is highly complex. With current technology, many companies can provide those services efficiently.

What makes these two institutions unique and dominant in their market is that they have been designated "federally sponsored," and awarded this implied guarantee. Management's efforts at maximizing the value of federal equity and thereby leveraging private capital defines the federal regulatory problem of the housing GSEs. That is, having created entities whose function is to maximize the value of the guarantee, government must restrain the size, if not the use, of the on-tap draft and transfer of resources from taxpayers to the GSEs.

As Dr. Weicher points out, the 1992 act established a new regulatory structure for the housing GSEs. Specifically, the Office of Federal Housing Enterprise Oversight (OFHEO) is now the regulator of safety and soundness, and the Department of Housing and Urban Development (HUD), with advice from OFHEO, is the regulator of the permissible range of activities for Fannie Mae and Freddie Mac. However, the record since 1992—as Dr. Weicher chronicles—suggests that neither OFHEO nor HUD have done much to restrain the transfer of federal capital to the housing GSEs. Every proposed expansion of activity has been approved by the HUD secretary, including Fannie Mae's Mortgage Protection Plan (MPP) under which Fannie would have provided life, disability and unemployment insurance to borrowers whose mortgages were purchased by Fannie.

Of course, it is possible that the GSEs have been extraordinarily cautious and have proposed to undertake only such activities as are clearly within the scope of their charters. My observation, however, is consistent with that wag who observed that Fannie and Freddie were early converts to the Washington, D.C., dictum: "Everything that is not nailed down is mine; everything that I can pry loose, is not nailed down." As for OFHEO, the safety and soundness regulator, a risk-based capital standard is not expected to be in place before the year 2000.

If OFHEO and HUD are the de facto regulators of Fannie and Freddie, then there appears to be a mismatch between the fiscal threat and the regulatory defenses put in place by the 1992 Act. In my judgment, however, the active regulators of Fannie and Freddie are not OFHEO and HUD, but rather the Congress in general and the banking committees in particular. The history that Dr. Weicher recounts seems consistent with such direct congressional regulation of Fannie and Freddie, at least since 1992. It was after all, Congress that halted Fannie's planned Mortgage Protection Plan and forced Freddie to abandon its interest-arbitrage investment in Philip Morris bonds. It is just not clear that either HUD or OFHEO have the political clout to restrain the transfer of public resources to the voracious housing GSEs. At best, HUD and OFHEO can assist Congress in monitoring the activities of Fannie and Freddie.

The objective of congressional regulation appears to be to maintain some balance between the value of the implicit guarantee to the GSEs and the value of benefits Congress receives from Fannie Mae and Freddie Mac. Members of Congress do receive significant benefits from the housing GSEs. In addition to assistance in campaign finance, these benefits include:

- Lower mortgage rates for constituents at no explicit budget cost. As GSE lobbyists are fond of saying, "Just look up the conforming-jumbo spread in the newspaper."
- Reliable availability of mortgage funds for home buyers.
- Highly visible district housing initiatives: fairs, hot lines, charitable fund raisers, grants from GSE foundations and the favorable publicity associated with the opening of regional offices.[1]

At the same time, Congress wants assurances that it is not going to have to face the budgetary cost of a financial rescue of a GSE. In fact, congressional interest in the results of various stress tests and the implications for capital standards substantially precedes the 1992 act.

In my judgment, the current regulatory structure of the housing GSEs is close to ideal from the perspective of Congress and Fannie and Freddie. Thus, I would be surprised if Congress were to show much interest in changing this structure now. The current accommodation could be tested in the future, however, as the GSEs attempt to maintain their current rate of earnings growth by expanding into new markets. If this expansion imposes significant political cost on Congress, changes in regulatory structure may appear on the legislative agenda.

---

1. For a more detailed discussion of costs and benefits, see: U.S. Congressional Budget Office, *Assessing the Public Costs and Benefits of Fannie Mae and Freddie Mac,* Washington, D.C., 1996.

Robert Van Order
Chief Economist
Federal Home Loan Mortgage Corporation
(Freddie Mac)

What follows represents opinions of the author and not necessarily those of Federal Home Loan Mortgage Corporation.

Writing on GSEs does not usually bring out the best in people. It is not surprising that this is true for combatants, but it is also true for "impartial" researchers, mainly economists, who often tend to descend into ideology masked by sloppy or nonexistent research. It is pleasing to me, therefore, to read John C. Weicher's paper, which is a serious attempt at describing and understanding the issues surrounding regulating GSEs. It presents a wide range of information on these institutions and a serious discussion of regulation. I do, however, disagree with some important parts of the paper, in particular the conclusions about regulatory structure and the focus on "economic" regulation and I have some suggestions for a better theoretical framework. I shall focus entirely on the housing GSEs, particularly Fannie Mae and Freddie Mac (F&F).

In my view, the central issue with GSEs is embedded options. These options mostly take the form of conjectured guarantees. Depending on your point of view they can be viewed as either subsidies or tools. Of course they are both. I believe that the central focus of GSE regulation should be control of the embedded options.

Analysis of GSEs needs some sort of microfoundation. Mine goes as follows:

1. The relevant industry for F&F is not the secondary market, but rather the mortgage market as a whole. The competitive structure might best be characterized as "dueling charters." That is, there are two charters in the industry, for depositories and for GSEs. Both involve imbedded options, and both have offsetting restrictions on lines of business, different capital regulation and different mission regulation. Both types of charter promote different ways of connecting mortgage markets with the financial markets. The distinction between primary and secondary markets is becoming increasingly

meaningless. What matters is the pluses and minuses of the two charters. Competition is largely about exploiting these charters and the business lines allowed by them.

There is competition. The F&F share of the conventional market was, as Dr. Weicher points out, high in the early 1990s, but it has fallen since. It was more than 60 percent in 1993, but fell to under 30 percent for a while in 1994 and has fluctuated since, with a steady state somewhere around 40 percent. Recent strength by the depositories and innovations such as the Chicago FHLB's plan to act as funding source for thrift institutions are indications that F&F do not always have it their way. In any event the industry cannot be described as a duopoly.

2. Incentives for the companies in the industry are complicated. While a perceived guarantee does produce incentives to take excessive risk, the GSEs also have a franchise, because of the scarcity of their charters, which induces them to be conservative. Indeed the franchise has probably been the most important factor so far in limiting the risk-taking of F&F. Of course both institutions take on some risk. The franchise is worthless if all they do is hold match-funded Treasuries. The major risk of risk-taking is that GSEs have the option to take on more (gamble for resurrection) if they get into trouble, and if the regulators do not catch on fast enough.

3. Welfare effects of GSEs are complicated. They are inevitably "second best" type issues. The central criticism of F&F by economists has been that they artificially distort interest rates and resource allocation by diverting funds toward housing and away from other types of investment. Proponents argue, for instance, that the two produce benefits by stabilizing the market (assuring that it is always open) and promoting home ownership. A major second-best issue is whether any distortions caused by F&F are as great as those caused by deposit insurance for depositories.

Regulatory Choices

Regulation has been suggested for three reasons: 1) safety and soundness; 2) mission; and 3) promoting competition. Dr. Weicher's paper is mainly about the regulatory structure that best promotes these.

GSEs have been created for a number of reasons and often they have survived for reasons quite separate from their creation. I assume that there is some purpose (controversial though it may be). The basic rationale for using GSEs can be summarized as follows:

- Congress wants GSEs because whatever the goal it is that it has in mind it thinks that it can be accomplished better by a profit-oriented institution than by a government bureaucracy.
- The charter acts as a constraint on the lines of business that the GSE can get into. This is meant to ensure that they stick to their purpose.
- There are embedded options. The benefits of a GSE are supposed to come from the efficiency that comes from maximizing profit, e.g., by responding to demand and minimizing costs, rather than by exploiting options. Hence on purely efficiency grounds, safety and soundness regulation is needed.

I do not see much further need for economic regulation. If the central criticism of F&F is that they distort resource allocation and overproduce housing, then more competition further distorts resource allocation. Furthermore, monopoly power, if it exists, provides incentives to take less risk because it increases the value of the franchise. Surely one of the major factors in the thrift institution debacle in the 1980s was the lack of franchise value, which left them with nothing to lose by gambling.

I have focused on efficiency. I see no real equity issue here. It has been argued that F&F's shareholders make too much money. Whether or not they make excess profits is controversial. For instance the subsidy calculation cited by Dr. Weicher is surely too high. Does it make sense to believe that the subsidy is 60 basis points higher for callable debt than for noncallable? Surely this is just a large measurement error, probably from the details of adjusting for different call characteristics. Happily you can phone a dealer and get a good estimate for noncallable, i.e., easy to analyze, debt. Currently the answer is probably less than 30 basis points, although that may be a cyclical low.

The more important point, however, is that any excess profits have already been capitalized into the stock price, and went to past shareholders.

Further, there is no reason to be concerned with equity with respect to competitors. The main competitors are depositories that, if anything, have more valuable embedded options. Indeed, virtually all mortgages for the past 50 years, at least, have benefited from some sort of federal program with some sort of embedded option.

Equity is also not an issue for more recent "private" entrants, because they have largely entered after the GSEs.

The central issue between the two dueling charters should be to keep subsidies about equal and small, and the way to do this is through safety and soundness (or fees) to keep the embedded options in line.

Mission stuff is controversial and should be seen as a kind of user fee.

Given the mission stuff and the charter, the main focus of regulation should be on safety and soundness with an eye on controlling embedded options. Once this is done the regulator should not be involved in, as Dr. Weicher suggests, cost benefit analysis of GSE programs. The market will do that. All that is necessary is to determine if they are legal.

While it is not the only reasonable structure, I like the current dual regulatory setup for F&F. HUD's job is to make sure they stick to the charter and the mission, and OFHEO's is safety and soundness. I think there is a danger in combining the two and especially in having safety and soundness done by an agency with some responsibility for housing. This is because of the temptation to give in on safety and soundness to generate off budget subsidies.

Here are some specific observations:

- Capture may not be all that likely. As Susan E. Woodward suggests in her paper on the SEC, capture is likely to be a function of limited job opportunities (limited to the regulated firms). I don't think that is especially true with OFHEO.

- Implicit collusion has not been studied except in the most superficial way in the papers cited by Dr. Weicher. There is a good deal of competition both between Fannie and Freddie and between them and the depositories. That is not to say that price equals marginal cost, but there is no evidence to suggest differences in comparison with other industries.
- The natural monopoly/public utility model is probably not a very good one. Technology does lead to some scale economies, but scale economies are increasingly unimportant in financial markets.
- It is not clear to me that OFHEO's authority is as weak as the paper suggests. It has powers similar to those of depositories' regulators, and it only has two organizations to oversee.

Biographies

Alexander, Gordon J.

Professor of Finance in the Carlson School of Management at the University of Minnesota. Dr. Alexander received his B.S. (Business Administration) from the State University of New York at Buffalo, and an M.B.A., M.A. (Mathematics), and Ph.D. (Finance) from the University of Michigan. He has been an Academic Economic Fellow at the Securities and Exchange Commission and a Visiting Professor of Finance at the University of California at Los Angeles. He has served as Book Review Editor of the *Journal of Finance*, Associate Editor of the *Journal of Finance and Quantitative Analysis* and Director of the Financial Management Association. In addition to publishing three books, he has published articles in journals such as the *Journal of Finance Economics, Journal of Finance, Journal of Financial and Quantitative Analysis, Journal of Banking and Finance, Financial Management* and *Journal of Portfolio Management*.

Barth, James R.

Lowder Eminent Scholar in Finance at Auburn University and Senior Finance Fellow at the Milken Institute. Until November 1989, Dr. Barth was the Chief Economist of the Office of Thrift Supervision and before that the Chief Economist of the Federal Home Loan Bank Board since August 1987. Dr. Barth received his Ph.D. in economics from Ohio State University with his dissertation supported by a Federal Reserve Bank of Cleveland fellowship. Dr. Barth has also been a Professor of Economics at George Washington University, Visiting Scholar at the United States Congressional Budget Office, Visiting Scholar at the Federal Reserve Bank of Atlanta, Visiting Scholar at the Office of the Comptroller of the Currency, Associate Director of the Economics Program at the National Science Foundation, Shaw Foundation Professor of Banking and Finance at Nanyang Technological University and visiting consultant at the World Bank. Dr. Barth has published more than 100 articles in professional journals and books. He is the author of *The Great Savings And Loan Debacle,* published by the American Enterprise Institute in 1991; coeditor of *The*

Reform of Federal Deposit Insurance: Disciplining The Government and Protecting Taxpayers, published by Harper Business in 1992; coeditor of *Emerging Challenges for the International Financial Services Industry* published by JAI Press in 1992, and coauthor of *The Future of American Banking* published by M.E. Sharpe in 1992. He is a member of the Advisory Council of Georgetown University's Credit Research Center and is associated with Cornerstone Research. He has testified on many occasions before both the House Banking Committee and the Senate Banking Committee on various financial institution and deposit insurance issues. Dr. Barth serves on the editorial boards of the *Journal of Financial Services Research,* the *Review of Pacific Basin Financial Markets and Policies* and the *Financial Services Review.* He also is included in *Who's Who in Economics: A Biographical Dictionary of Major Economists 1700 to 1995.*

Bartholomew, Philip F.

Presently on detail from the Office of the Comptroller of the Currency to the U.S. House of Representatives' Committee on Bank and Financial Services, Democratic Staff, as Chief Economist. Prior to this, Dr. Bartholomew was Director of the Bank Research Division of the Office of the Comptroller of the Currency. In this position, Dr. Bartholomew was responsible for conducting and managing long-term research on a variety of banking issues. Prior to joining the OCC in May 1993, Dr. Bartholomew served as a Principal Analyst at the Congressional Budget Office. At the CBO, he was responsible for making budget projections of the Federal deposit insurance funds as well as writing studies on depository institution issues. In early 1992, he was on loan from the CBO as an Advisor to the Ministry of Finance of Poland to work on Poland's proposed system of national deposit insurance. Before joining the CBO in December 1989, Dr. Bartholomew was a financial economist in the Office of Policy and Economic Research at the Federal Home Loan Bank Board; with the abolishment of the Bank Board in October 1989, he was assigned to the staff of the Federal Housing Finance Board. Prior to joining the Bank Board initially as a Visiting Scholar in 1988, Dr. Bartholomew was an Assistant Professor of Economics (1981-1988) and Coordinator of Canadian studies (1986-1988) at the University of Michigan-Dearborn. Dr. Bartholomew has a B.S. in mathematics from Villanova

University, and an M.A. and Ph.D. in economics from the University of Pittsburgh. In addition to editing books on international banking and Canadian studies, he has published several articles on systemic risk, deposit insurance and thrift institution crisis, the Canadian banking system and the international regulation of depository institutions.

Bozewicz, Jane

Accounting faculty at Babson College. Dr. Bozewicz received her undergraduate degree in East Asian Studies from Vassar College, M.B.A. from the Wharton School, and Ph.D. in accounting from the City University of New York, Baruch College. Previously, Dr. Bozewicz taught at Baruch College, Rutgers University and Manhattan College. Dr. Bozewicz has worked in management as well as public accounting and is a CPA. Her research interests include pensions and financial regulation. She has done consulting on issues relating to regulation of financial institutions.

Brumbaugh, R. Dan, Jr.

Senior Fellow at the Milken Institute. Dr. Brumbaugh's current research interests are focused on the development of global financial markets. Dr. Brumbaugh holds a B.A. from Colgate University and a Ph.D. in economics from the George Washington University. He is coauthor of the forthcoming book, *The Role of Banks in Global Financial Markets* (with James R. Barth and Glenn Yago); author *of The Collapse of Federally Insured Depositories: The Savings and Loans as Precursor* (Garland, 1993), and author of *Thrifts Under Siege*: *Restoring Order to American Banking* (Harper & Row, 1988). He is coeditor (with James R. Barth) of *The Reform of Deposit Insurance: Disciplining the Government and Protecting Taxpayers* (Harper/Collins Business, 1992), and coauthor (with James R. Barth and Robert E. Litan) of *The Future of American Banking* (Columbia University/M.E. Sharpe, Inc. 1992). He is also the author of many professional journal articles on related subjects. Dr. Brumbaugh has spoken and lectured widely on banking crises and the future of financial institutions in an increasingly global market for financial services and products. He has testified frequently before congressional committees on issues concerning financial institutions, and has served as a consultant to financial service companies and industries, to the House of Representatives Subcommittee on Financial Institutions, and to the National Commission on Financial Institutions Reform, Recovery and Enforcement. He was a Visiting Scholar at the Federal Home Loan Bank Board in 1982 and was the Deputy Chief Economist at the Bank Board from 1983 to 1986. In 1986 and 1987, he was President and Chief Executive Officer of Independence Savings and Loan, headquartered in Vallejo, CA. He was a Senior Research Scholar at the Center for Economic Policy Research at Stanford University in 1989-1990 specializing in the economics of financial institutions.

Caprio, Gerard

Head, Financial Sector Research, in the World Bank's Development Research Group. Dr. Caprio received his A.B., Economics at Williams College and his Ph.D. in Economics, University of Michigan. He was formerly Vice President and Head of Global Economics at JP Morgan and has held research and teaching positions at the Federal Reserve Board, the IMF and George Washington University. He has researched and written extensively on financial sector policy, financial reform and monetary policy implementation, including *Reforming Finance: Historical Implications for Policy* and *Financial Reform: Theory and Experience* (Cambridge University Press). His current research is on financial crises.

Cole, Joseph B.

Chief Operating Officer of Hedge Financial Products Inc., a wholly owned subsidiary of the CNA Financial Corporation specializing in the securitization of insurance risks. Dr. Cole's duties include new product development in the emerging markets for insurance derivatives, securitized indemnities and other tradable event-risks. He holds a B.S. from Briar Cliff College, an M.B.A. from the University of South Dakota, and a Ph.D. in Business Administration from the University of Iowa. Before assuming his current duties, he was a Managing Director of Centre Financial Products Limited, the managing agent for Centre Trading Partners L.P., a risk management company specializing in capital market solutions for insurance, environmental and modeling risks. His responsibilities included product and account development and the marketing of structured financial instruments for insurance and environmental trading. Dr. Cole previously served as a Senior Vice President and Special Projects Manager in the Derivative Products Group of Kidder, Peabody & Company. Prior to that he served as Director of Research with Indosuez International Capital Markets and with Indosuez Carr Futures Inc. Previous to that, Dr. Cole served as Director of Research at Drexel Burnham Lambert's Institutional Financial Futures and Options division. There he was responsible for the creation and development of many advanced futures and options, hedging and pricing models, including Modern Option Replication (MOR), Asian or averaging option analytics, arbitrage-free binomial lattice pricing for fixed income options and many other yield enhancement and arbitrage based trading techniques. Dr. Cole also served as an Associate Economist and a Corporate Liaison for the Chase Manhattan Bank and its subsidiary, Interactive Data Corporation. For six years, Dr. Cole served as a speaker and program director of an Executive Seminar series with the Kellogg School of Management at Northwestern University. He has also served as a speaker with the Center for Clean Air, the Berkeley Program in Finance at the University of California, the Banking Institute of the Saudi Arabian Monetary Agency and the World Bank. Dr. Cole was formerly a member of the FERC Committee on National Gas Pipelines Competition, the Board of Advisors of the Illinois Institute of Technology, and the Board of Directors of the Chicago Futures and Options Society. He served as advisor to the Boren-Danforth Senate working group on value-added taxation. Dr. Cole has also served as an expert advisor to the United Nations Commission on Trade and Development on tradable entitlements for carbon dioxide. He has also served as a consultant to several exchanges and financial institutions in the development and analysis of new product, pension fund management and hedge design, as well as bank-holding company asset/liability and futures trading programs.

Craine, Roger

Professor of Economics, University of California at Berkeley. Dr. Craine received his Ph.D. from the University of Maryland. He has served as a senior economist at the Board of Governors of the Federal Reserve System and an economist at the Federal Reserve Bank of San Francisco. He is currently the editor of special projects for the *Review of Economic Dynamics*, and was editor of *Journal of Economic*

Dynamics and Control from 1987-1994. Several of his recent publications focus on risk and incentives in financial contracts: Fairly Priced Deposit Insurance and Bank Charter Policy (1995), *Journal of Finance*, 50, 1735-1747; Debt Guarantees and Inefficient Equilibria (1996) a paper based on the Keynote Address for the 10th Annual Economics Meeting sponsored by the Central Bank of Uruguay; Garantias de Deuda y Equilibrios Ineficientes, *Revista de Economia* (ed. Banco Central de Uruguay), 3:1, Segunda Epoca, 3-24; and Valuing the Futures Market Performance Guarantee (1997), *Journal of Macroeconomic Dynamics*, 1, 701-719.

Culp, Christopher L.

Director of Risk Management Services at CP Risk Management LLC in Chicago, a consulting firm specializing in the management and measurement of financial risk for pension plans, institutional investors, financial intermediaries and other companies. Dr. Culp received his B.A. in economics from Johns Hopkins University and Ph.D. in finance from the University of Chicago. He was formerly president of Risk Management Consulting Services Inc. Before that, he served as senior examiner for the Federal Reserve Bank of Chicago, where he supervised the review of risk measurement models used by Fed-regulated money center commercial banks. He has also held positions at G.T. Management (Asia) Ltd. in Hong Kong, TradeLink LLC in Chicago, and Friedberg Commodity Management in Baltimore. Dr. Culp publishes regularly in the areas of derivatives, corporate finance, risk management and financial regulation, and is a managing editor of *Derivatives Quarterly*. He is Senior Fellow in Financial Regulation with the Competitive Enterprise Institute in Washington, D.C.

Durkin, Thomas A.

Senior Economist, Board of Governors of the Federal Reserve System. Dr. Durkin holds an A.B. degree in History from Georgetown University and a Ph.D. degree in Money and Financial Markets from Columbia University. After nineteen years with various administrative responsibilities, Dr. Durkin returned to full-time research at the beginning of 1998. Before that he had been Regulatory Planning and Review Director at the Board of Governors of the Federal Reserve

System since mid-1988. In that position, he reviewed regulatory changes for consistency with board policies and supervised the Board's ongoing program of regulatory review and improvement. Prior positions at the Board include Senior Economist and Assistant to the Director of the Research Division, and Visiting Professor in the Research Division. He has also been Associate Professor of Finance at Penn State University and Chief Economist and Director of Research at the American Financial Services Association. In that position he frequently testified before congressional committees, spoke to business groups, and appeared on radio and television talk programs.

Esty, Benjamin C.

Assistant Professor of Business Administration at the Harvard Business School, where he teaches corporate finance and valuation analysis in both the M.B.A. and executive education programs. Dr. Esty received his Ph.D. in business economics with a concentration in finance from Harvard University; his M.B.A. with high distinction (Baker Scholar) from Harvard Business School; and a B.A. in Economics with honors and distinction from Stanford University. In 1997, he received the first annual Student Association award for teaching excellence and was named Associate Professor in 1998. His current research focuses on how companies value and finance large-scale capital expenditures with a particular focus on project finance. Previously, he has written on a broad range of topics related to the financial services industry including the use of derivatives to manage interest-rate risk, the incentive effects of leverage, the role of banks in community development, and the relation between interest-rate sensitivity and bank merger activity. His articles have been published in the *Journal of Applied Corporate Finance* and the *Journal of Financial Economics*. In addition, he is the author of more than 20 case studies and notes on acquisition and valuation issues in highly leveraged transactions, emerging markets and Chapter 11 restructurings.

Prior to graduate school, Dr. Esty worked as a consultant at Booz-Allen & Hamilton and Bain and Company, and as the financial manager for the Commercial Mortgage Corporation of America, a start-up financial services company.

Fenn, George W.

Senior research associate at the Milken Institute. Dr. Fenn received his Ph.D. in economics from Stanford in 1989. Prior to joining the Institute, Dr. Fenn spent eight years as an economist at the Federal Reserve Board in Washington, D.C. His research interests include the life insurance industry, risk management, corporate finance and private equity markets. He currently is examining the role of "angel" investors in financing high-tech companies, the rule 144A private placement market, and the ownership and performance of buyout-IPO companies. Previous research has included asset-quality problems in the life insurance industry and its effects on policyholder behavior and the use of interest rate programs. Dr. Fenn coauthored *The Economics of the Private Equity Markets*, a major study that is assigned reading in the entrepreneurial finance courses at leading business schools including Harvard University and the University of Chicago. His articles have appeared in the *Journal of Financial Economics, Journal of Banking and Finance*, and other scholarly journals.

Hunter, William Curt

Senior Vice President and Director of Research at the Federal Reserve Bank of Chicago. Dr. Hunter is a member of the Bank's management committee and also serves as chief economic advisor to the president of the Chicago Fed, Michael H. Moskow, supporting the president's participation in the system's monetary policy group, the Federal Open Market Committee. He is responsible for planning and supervising the Bank's basic and applied research in the areas of monetary policy; financial markets and banking regulation; regional economics; agricultural and international finance; and business economics. Dr. Hunter received a B.S. degree in business and economics from Hampton Institute (now Hampton University) and holds an M.B.A. in finance and a Ph.D. in finance and environment from Northwestern University. Before joining the Chicago Fed he was a vice president and head of the financial markets and banking sections in the research department of the Federal Reserve Bank of Atlanta. Prior to that, Dr. Hunter was an associate professor of finance at Emory University. He has also held faculty positions at Atlanta University, the University of Georgia, Chicago State University, and Northwestern University, and in 1982 was a visiting scholar with the

Board of Governors of the Federal Reserve System in Washington, D.C. He has worked as a consultant to the Small Business Administration, the Chicago Mercantile Exchange, and numerous private corporations. Dr. Hunter has lectured at the NATO Advanced Study Institute, Anacapri, Italy; served as a United States Treasury Advisor to the Bulgarian National Bank and its Bank Consolidation company, and has served as a consultant to the national banks of Hungary and Romania, the Korea Institute of Finance, the Swiss National Bank, and the Federal Agency for Insolvency Cases of the Russian Federation. Dr. Hunter is an associate editor of the *Journal of Financial Services Research* and the *Financial Review*, and a past associate editor of the *Journal of Financial Research*.

Ippolito, Richard (Dick)

Professor at George Mason University School of Law. Dr. Ippolito received his Ph.D. in economics from the University of Chicago in 1974. He was Director of Research and Policy in the Department of Labor's Pension Program from 1979 to 1986. From 1986 to 1999, Dr. Ippolito was Chief Economist at the Pension Benefit Guaranty Corporation. He has published numerous books and articles on the investment, tax, regulatory and labor-market aspect of pensions. Dr. Ippolito's latest book, *Pensions and Employee Performance,* was published by the University of Chicago Press.

Jones, Jonathan D.

Senior Financial Economist in the Risk Management Division at the Office of Thrift Supervision. He received his B.A., M.A. and Ph.D., all in economics, from the University of Colorado. Prior to joining the OTS, he was a Senior Financial Economist in the Office of Economic Analysis at the Securities and Exchange Commission, a Financial Economist in the Office of Tax Analysis at the Treasury Department, and taught at Vassar College and the Catholic University of America. He has published articles in journals such as *Applied Economics, Applied Financial Economics, Managerial Finance, Managerial and Decision Economics,* and the *National Tax Journal.*

Klein, Robert W.

Director of Center for Risk Management and Insurance Research and an Associate Professor of Risk Management and Insurance at Georgia State University in Atlanta. Dr. Klein has a B.A., M.A. and Ph.D. in economics from Michigan State University. He is an expert on the economics of insurance markets and public policy and regulatory issues in insurance. He is leading the Center's Insurance Research and Education Initiative, which is helping key decisionmakers and the general public make informed choices on insurance issues. Dr. Klein has written a number of monographs and articles on various topics in insurance and its regulation, including the structure and performance of insurance markets, price regulation, catastrophe insurance problems, urban insurance issues, workers' compensation, solvency regulation, and international insurance regulation. He also has testified frequently at legislative and regulatory hearings on significant issues affecting insurance consumers and the industry. Prior to joining Georgia State University in September 1996, Dr. Klein was the Director of Research and Chief Economist for the National Association of Insurance Commissioners. He also served as staff economist for the insurance department and state legislature in Michigan. He serves on the Board of Directors for the American Risk and Insurance Association and the editorial boards for the *Journal of Insurance Regulation and Risk Management* and *Insurance Review.*

Kroszner, Randall S.

Associate Professor of Business Economics at the University of Chicago's Graduate School of Business, where he teaches money and banking and international financial institutions and markets. Dr. Kroszner graduated *magna cum laude* from Brown University in 1984 and received a Ph.D. from the economics department of Harvard University in 1990. He has served as an economist on the President's Council of Economic Advisers. He has also been a consultant to the International Monetary Fund, the World Bank, the Inter-American Development Bank, the Securities and Exchange Commission, the Board of Governors of the Federal Reserve System, and the Federal Reserve Banks of Chicago, New York, Kansas City and St. Louis. He has been a visiting professor at the Stockholm School of Economics, the Institute for International Economic Studies at the University of

Stockholm, and the Free University of Berlin. He is an associate editor of *Economics of Governance*. His research interests include the economics and politics of international and domestic banking and financial regulation, organization design, antitrust matters and monetary economics. Dr. Kroszner has written articles for the *American Economic Review, Journal of Political Economy, Journal of Finance, Journal of Monetary Economics*, *The Public Interest* and *Regulation* and the book, *The New Palgrave Dictionary of Money and Finance,* among others. In addition, he coauthored *Explorations in the New Monetary Economics* (Blackwell, 1994) and coedited *The Economic Nature of the Firm: A Reader* (Cambridge University Press, 1996).

Liebold, Arthur W., Jr.

Associated with the law firm of Dechert Price & Rhoads (Philadelphia and Washington) since 1956 (Partner: 1954-1969; 1972-1997). Mr. Leibold is a graduate of Harvard College (A.B.; 1953) and the University of Pennsylvania Law School (J.D.; 1956). From May 1, 1969, until June 30, 1972, he was General Counsel of the Federal Home Loan Bank Board and the Federal Savings and Loan Insurance Corporation. Active in the American Bar Association, he was Treasurer from 1979-1983, and President of the American Bar Endowment from 1995-1997.

Lown, Cara S.

Officer and Senior Economist for the Federal Reserve Bank of New York. Dr. Lown earned her undergraduate degree in mathematics and economics from Bucknell University in 1977, and her Ph.D. in economics from the University of Michigan in 1986. Following graduate school, Dr. Lown worked in the Research Department of the Federal Reserve Bank of Dallas. She joined the Research Department of the Federal Reserve Bank of New York in 1990 and became an officer in 1996. Dr. Lown's research involves understanding the role of the banking sector in the United States economy, as well as understanding the impact of monetary policy on the economy. She has published on these topics in a number of economic journals, as well as in the Dallas and New York Federal Reserve Banks' policy reviews. Dr. Lown spent the 1993-94 academic year teaching at Princeton University.

Marshall, David

Economic advisor and Senior Financial Economist at the Federal Reserve of Chicago since 1994 and an Adjunct Professor of Finance at the University of Chicago. Dr. Marshall received his B.A. in philosophy at Yale University and M.S. and Ph.D. in economics at Carnegie-Mellon University. He was Assistant Professor of Finance at the Kellogg Graduate School of Management at Northwestern University from 1988 to 1993.

Nigro, Peter J.

Senior Financial Economist in the Economics and Evaluation division at the Office of the Comptroller of the Currency. Dr. Nigro received a bachelors degree from the College of the Holy Cross, an M.A. in economics from the University of Southern California and a Ph.D. in economics from Boston College. His research interests include failure prediction and credit scoring models, mutual funds, fair lending issues, and small business economics. He has published articles in *Business Economics, Journal of Business and Economics, Journal of Small Business Finance, Managerial Finance*, and *Managerial and Decision Economics*.

Peristiani, Stavros

Stavros Peristiani is a Research Officer in the Capital Markets Function of the Research and Market Analysis Group at the Federal Reserve Bank of New York. He received his Ph.D. in economics from Columbia University in 1984 and a master's degree in mathematical statistics from Rutgers University in 1980. Dr. Peristiani has worked extensively on various topics in banking and finance. His recent work investigates the effect of household creditworthiness on mortgage refinancings and examines the statistical structure of mortgage-backed securities prepayments. His articles have appeared in the *Journal of Banking and Finance, Journal of Money, Credit and Banking, Quarterly Journal of Economics, Journal of Business*, and *Review of Economics and Statistics*.

Petzel, Todd E.

Executive Vice President and Chief Investment Officer of The Common Fund. Dr. Petzel holds A.B., A.M. and Ph.D. degrees from the University of Chicago. Prior to joining The Common Fund, Dr. Petzel was the Executive Vice President for Business Development of the Chicago Mercantile Exchange. Subsequently, he taught at Macalester College and Stanford University. In 1982, he joined the Coffee, Sugar and Cocoa Exchange in New York as Chief Economist. In 1988, he became Vice President, Financial Research for the Chicago Mercantile Exchange. While in Chicago, he also taught finance classes at the Graduate School of Business at the University of Chicago. Dr. Petzel is the author of the book, *Financial Futures and Options: A Guide to Markets, Applications and Strategies*, and numerous articles and reviews. He serves as referee for a number of journals devoted to economics and finance and as editor of *Derivatives Quarterly*.

Phaup, Marvin

Deputy Assistant Director, Special Studies, United States Congressional Budget Office. Dr. Phaup holds a B.A. from Roanoke College and M.A. and Ph.D. degrees in economics from the University of Virginia. He is the author of numerous articles and CBO reports dealing with the budgetary treatment of complex financial transactions including Federal direct loans and guarantees, deposit insurance, pension insurance, structured loan sales, and government-sponsored enterprises. He was previously a senior economist at the Federal Reserve Bank of Cleveland. In 1995, he received the National Distinguished Service Award from the American Association of Budget and Program Analysis.

Ramesh, Lalita

Research Associate at the Milken Institute. Dr. Ramesh received her Ph.D. in economics from the University of Southern California in 1997, with a specialization in monetary theory and macroeconomics. She is working on the creation of a database of financial and regulatory variables that could influence economic growth via financial markets. Since joining the institute, Dr. Ramesh has worked with data from United States depository institutions (thrift institutions, commercial banks and credit unions) to study the impact of regulation on their performance over time. As part of the Capital Studies Group, she has also helped organize the collection of cross-country data on the size, health and composition of the financial sector as well as indicators of country risk, particularly in relation to the East Asian banking crisis. As an instructor at the University of Southern California, Dr. Ramesh taught classes in macroeconomic analysis. In 1990, she was a research assistant at both the Indian Council for Social Science Research and at the National Institute of Science, Technology and Development Studies in New Delhi, India. As part of her research, she analyzed studies to assess the success of government programs in encouraging the absorption of new technologies in rural areas.

Robinson, Kenneth J.

Senior Economist and Policy Advisor at the Federal Reserve Bank of Dallas, Financial Industry Studies Department. Mr. Robinson joined the Federal Reserve Bank of Dallas in August 1986 as an Economist in the Research Department specializing in macroeconomics and money and banking. He joined the Financial Industry Studies Department in February 1989 and was promoted to Senior Economist in March 1990, and to Senior Economist and Policy Advisor in March of 1993. Mr. Robinson holds a B.S. degree from The University of New Orleans, a M.S. degree from Louisiana State University, and a Ph.D. degree from The Ohio State University. His current research interests lie in the interaction between financial structure, monetary policy, and economic activity, and the functioning of financial markets in the U.S. economy. He has authored articles for *Journal of International Money and Finance, Journal of Financial Services Research, Financial Industry Studies, Journal of Macroeconomics,* and *Economic Review.*

Romano, Roberta

Allen Duffy/Class of 1960 Professor of Law at the Yale Law School. Ms. Romano received her B.A. from the University of Rochester, M.A. from the University of Chicago, and J.D. from Yale. She is the author of *The Genius of American Corporate Law* (AEI Press, 1993), series editor for Oxford University Press's Interdisciplinary Readers in Law Series, and the editor of *Foundations of Corporate Law* (1993) in that series. She is a fellow of the American Academy of Arts and Sciences and Vice President-President Elect of the American Law and Economics Association. She has chaired the sections on Business Associations and on Law and Economics of the Association of American Law Schools. From 1988 to 1992, she was coeditor of the *Journal of Law, Economics,* and *Organization.* She is currently an associate editor of the *Journal of Corporate Finance* and *The Financial Review*; a member of the editorial board of the *Journal of Law, Economics, and Organization* and *The Supreme Court Economic Review,* and a member of the advisory boards of *The New Palgrave Dictionary of Economics and the Law* and *Corporate, Securities and Finance Law Abstracts* on the Legal Scholarship Network. Her research has focused on state competition for corporate charters, the political economy of takeover regulation, shareholder litigation, pension fund activities in corporate governance, and the regulation of derivative securities.

Santos, João A. C.

Economist at the Bank for International Settlements. Dr. Santos received his undergraduate degree from the Department of Economics of the Universidade Nova de Lisboa in 1986 and his master's and doctoral degrees in economics from Boston University in 1995. His research interests include corporate finance, contract theory, banking and banking regulation. Dr. Santos joined the BIS in September 1997. From 1992 to 1994, he was a lecturer in the Department of Economics at Boston University and from October 1994 to August 1997, he was an economist at the Research Department of the Federal Reserve Bank of Cleveland. He has published articles in several journals such as *Cato Journal, Journal of Financial Services Research, Journal of Corporate Finance,* and *Journal of Banking and Finance.*

Scott, Kenneth E.

Senior Research Fellow at the Hoover Institution and the Ralph M. Parsons Professor in Law and Business at the Stanford Law School. Professor Scott earned an A.B. in economics from the College of William and Mary, M.A. in political science from Princeton University and LL.B. from Stanford University Law School. He has been associated with the Hoover Institution since 1978 and has been a member of the Stanford faculty since 1968. His major work has been in the fields of law and regulation of corporations, securities and banking and financial services. Professor Scott spent the first five years after law school in private practice with the firms of Sullivan and Cromwell in New York and Musick, Peeler and Garrett in Los Angeles. In 1961, he became chief deputy savings and loan commissioner and head of the Los Angeles office of the state savings and loan agency. He served 1963 to 1968 as general counsel of the Federal Home Loan Bank Board in Washington. He is a member of the state bar in New York, California and the District of Columbia. The author of two books, *Economics of Corporate Law and Securities Regulations*, with R. Posner and *Retail Banking in the Electronic Age: The Law and Economics of Electronic Funds Transfer*, with W. Baxter and P. Cootner. He is also author of many articles for legal and financial journals.

Staten, Michael E.

Professor of Management and Director of the Credit Research Center at Georgetown University School of Business. Dr. Staten earned a Ph.D. in economics form Purdue University in 1980. He taught at the University of Delaware from 1980 to 1988 and has been Director of the Credit Research Center since 1990. Since its founding at Purdue University in 1974, the Credit Research Center has built a national reputation for its analysis of public policy toward consumer and mortgage credit markets. During the summer of 1997, Dr. Staten supervised the relocation of the Center from Purdue to the Georgetown University School of Business. Dr. Staten has presented expert testimony on credit and insurance issues before committees of the United States House and Senate and various state legislatures. He is coauthor of *Consumer Trends*, the monthly newsletter on consumer financial services published by the International Credit Association. He serves on the Board of Trustees for both the National Foundation for Consumer Credit and the American Financial Services Association's Education Foundation. He also served as Chairman of the Purdue Employees Federal Credit Union from 1995 to 1997.

Van Order, Robert

Chief Economist of the Federal Home Loan Mortgage Corporation (Freddie Mac) since 1987. Dr. Van Order earned his undergraduate degree at Grinnel College, M.A. at the University of Essex in Britain and Ph.D. in Economics at John Hopkins University. His primary responsibility is in research, macroeconomic analysis and forecasting. Dr. Van Order also works with the news media and others to explain developments in the mortgage and other markets, as well as the economy. Prior to joining Freddie Mac, Dr. Van Order served as Director of the Housing Finance Analysis Division at the United States Department of Housing and Urban Development (HUD) and Visiting Professor of Real Estate at the Graduate School of Management, University of California at Los Angeles. He was an economist at HUD from 1976 to 1985. Dr. Van Order has also taught at Purdue University, the University of Southern California, Queen's University in Canada and the American University in Washington, D.C. He was also a Senior Research Associate at the Urban Institute of Washington, D.C., where he conducted international research projects aimed at analyzing mortgage markets in underdeveloped countries.

Villani, Kevin E.

Executive Vice President, Chief Financial Officer and a member of the board of Imperial Credit Industries Inc. Dr. Villani joined the University of Southern California as the Wells Fargo Visiting Professor of Finance in 1990 and remained on the full-time faculty through 1997. From 1985 to 1990, he was the Executive Vice President and Chief Financial Officer for the Imperial Corporation of America, where he was responsible for portfolio management of a $12 billion portfolio as well as asset management of all mortgage and asset-backed securities, high yield bonds, leasing and venture capital. From 1982 to 1985, he served in various capacities at the Federal Home Loan Mortgage Corporation, including Chief Economist and Chief Financial Officer, where his responsibilities included asset and portfolio management. From 1975 to 1982, he served as Financial Economist and Director for the Division of Housing Finance Analysis, Deputy Assistant Secretary for the Office of Economic Affairs and Chief Economist for the Department of Housing and Urban Development. From 1974 to 1975, he was an economist for the Federal

Reserve Bank of Cleveland. From 1990 to 1995 Dr. Villani served as a full-time consulting economist at the World Bank and International Finance Corporation on housing, banking, finance and investment issues in emerging markets. He has published more than 100 books and articles on financial markets and instruments.

Weicher, John C.

Senior Fellow with the Hudson Institute. Dr. Weicher holds an A.B. degree from the University of Michigan and a Ph.D from the University of Chicago. He served as Assistant Secretary for Policy Development and Research at the United States Department of Housing and Urban Development from 1989 to 1993; his responsibilities included support for the Secretary as regulator of key elements of the housing finance system. He previously served as chief economist at the United States Office of Management and Budget and at HUD. Dr. Weicher has held the F.K. Weyerhaueser Chair in Public Policy Research at the American Enterprise Institute. He has been president of the American Real Estate and Urban Economics Association, and has served on the Committee on Urban Policy of the National Academy of Sciences and the Advisory Committee on Population Statistics of the Census Bureau.

Werner, Ingrid M.

Associate Professor at Fisher College of Business at Ohio State University since 1998. From 1990 to 1998, Dr. Werner was Associate Professor in the finance group of the faculty at the Stanford Business School. Dr. Werner has an M.B.A. and an Ekon. Lic. from Stockholm School of Economics, and a Ph.D. from the University of Rochester. Her other affiliations include the National Bureau of Economic Research and the Institute for International Economic Studies. She held a National Fellowship at the Hoover Institution (Stanford University) during the academic year 1995-1996 and a position as Visiting Research Economist at the New York Stock Exchange during 1997. Her research interests range from international finance to market microstructure. She has published more than a dozen papers in academic journals and books. In the market microstructure area, Dr. Werner has studied trading of British cross-listed securities both in London and in the United States, interdealer trading on the London

Stock Exchange, and the trades of New York Stock Exchange floor brokers.

Woodward, Susan E.

Economics professor at the Stanford Law School, a board member of the National Association of Securities Dealers regulatory arm and a consultant to the Security Traders Association. Dr. Woodward received her B.A. and Ph.D. in financial economics from the University of California at Los Angeles. She taught price theory, finance and financial institutions from 1975 to 1985 at UCLA, the Simon School of Business at the University of Rochester and the University of California at Santa Barbara. Between 1985 and 1995, Dr. Woodward worked in Washington, D.C., at first as the senior economist for the Council of Economic Advisors, concentrating on the policy issues for financial markets and institutions. From 1987 to 1991, Dr. Woodward was chief economist and Deputy Assistant Secretary at the United States Department of Housing and Urban Development, working primarily on mortgage market issues. Her most recent Washington assignment was chief economist at the United States Securities and Exchange Commission, concentrating on economic issues in securities law enforcement and policy issues in corporate finance, market regulation and mutual funds. Dr. Woodward has also served as a consultant on various litigation and policy matters in securities, financial institutions and utility regulation. She is preparing a book on mutual funds for individual investors.

Yago, Glenn

Director of Capital Studies for the Milken Institute. Dr. Yago received his B.A. from Tulane University, M.A. from Hebrew University of Jerusalem, and Ph.D. from the University of Wisconsin. He formerly served as Director of the Center for Capital Studies at the City University of New York, which he founded in 1992. Dr. Yago was on the faculty of the Ph.D. program in economics at the City University of New York Graduate Center and a Senior Research Associate at the Center for the Study of Business and Government at Baruch College, City University of New York. He is also the former director of the Economic Research Bureau at the State University of New York at Stony Brook and was an Associate Professor of Management at SUNY for eight years. He has extensively analyzed public policy and its relation to high yield markets, initial public offerings, industrial and transportation concerns, and public and private sector employment. He was previously the chairman of the New York State Network for Economic Research and a Faculty Fellow of the Rockefeller Institute. He has served as an adviser and consultant to the White House Conference on Small Business, Small Business Administration, Competitiveness Policy Council, and Department of Commerce. In addition, he has served as a consultant to Bolivia (President's Council of Economic Advisors), Hungary (State Property Agency), Israel (Capital Markets Conference, Ministry of Finance and Prime Minister's Office) and New York State (Governor's Office and Development of Economic Development), as well as to corporations, law firms, accounting firms and trade associations. Dr. Yago is the author of three books, numerous academic articles and articles in the financial press. He has written several reports on mergers and acquisitions, leveraged buyouts, high-yield securities and IPOs for the Securities Industry Association, the National Association of Securities Dealers, and various investment banks, as well as similar reports for a variety of state agencies and private economic research foundations.

Zax, Stanley R.

Chairman, President and Chief Executive Officer of the Zenith National Insurance Corporation. Mr. Zax began his career in 1961 as an associate, then a partner, with Friedman Mulligan, Dillon & Uris. From 1966 to 1972, he served as Vice President, Secretary and General Counsel for Hilton Hotels and, from 1973 to 1976, as President and Chief Executive Officer of the Great American Insurance Company. In 1977, he became Chairman of Zenith and the following year was named President and Chief Executive Officer. Mr. Zax also served as Chairman and President of the CalFarm Insurance Company and Cal-Farm Life Insurance Company. He is active in several associations, including the Executive Committee and Board of the Center for Strategic and International Studies, Washington, D.C., the Little Hoover Commission, and has served on Governor Wilson's Task Force to Review Juvenile Crime and Juvenile Justice Response. From 1987 to 1989, Mr. Zax served as Chairman of the Insurance Industry Coalition relating to Proposition 103 and No-Fault Auto Insurance.